AN INTRODUCTION
TO FAMILY SOCIAL WORK

AN INTRODUCTION TO FAMILY SOCIAL WORK

SECOND EDITION

Donald Collins
University of Calgary

Catheleen Jordan
University of Texas at Arlington

Heather Coleman
University of Calgary

THOMSON
BROOKS/COLE

Australia • Brazil • Canada • Mexico • Singapore • Spain
United Kingdom • United States

THOMSON

BROOKS/COLE

An Introduction to Family Social Work, Second Edition
Donald Collins, Catheleen Jordan, and Heather Coleman

Acquisitions Editor: Dan Alpert
Assistant Editor: Alma Dea Michelena
Marketing Manager: Meghan McCullough
Senior Marketing Communications Manager:
   Tami Strang
Project Manager, Editorial Production:
   Christine Sosa
Creative Director: Rob Hugel
Art Director: Vernon Boes
Print Buyer: Nora Massuda

Permissions Editor: Bob Kauser
Production Service: Aaron Downey, Matrix
   Productions, Inc.
Copy Editor: Sherri Dietrich
Illustrator: Interactive Composition Corporation
Cover Designer: Lisa Henry
Cover Image: Matt Brasier/Masterfile
Cover Printer: Courier Corporation/Westford
Compositor: Interactive Composition Corporation
Printer: Courier Corporation/Westford

Printed in the United States of America
1 2 3 4 5 6 7 10 09 08 07 06

Library of Congress Control Number:
2006922565

ISBN 0-495-09224-X

For more information about our products,
contact us at:
**Thomson Learning Academic Resource
Center—1-800-423-0563**
For permission to use material from this
text or product, submit a request online at
http://www.thomsonrights.com.
Any additional questions about permissions
can be submitted by e-mail to
thomsonrights@thomson.com.

Thomson Higher Education
10 Davis Drive
Belmont, CA 94002-3098
USA

*To our mothers, Merlie Collins, Mary Jordan,
and Audrey Coleman. Thanks for all the love
and guidance offered selflessly to our families.*

About the Authors

Donald Collins is a Professor of Social Work at the University of Calgary. He is also a part-time family therapist at the Calgary Family Therapy Centre and was a volunteer therapist and supervisor at the Westside Family Counselling Clinic in Calgary from 1995 to 2004. His research includes social work education and his areas of interest include social work practice with individuals of all ages, practice with couples, practice with families, child abuse, family violence, teaching and learning issues, program and case level evaluation, and case management. He has authored and co-authored numerous articles and texts.

Catheleen Jordan is a Professor of Social Work at the University of Texas at Arlington, where she has taught since 1985. She has an MSSW from the University of Texas at Arlington and a Ph.D. in Social Welfare from the University of California-Berkeley. Her areas of expertise are family assessment and treatment, clinical research, and program evaluation. She has served as a clinical director and supervisor in the UTA-SSW Community Service Clinic, and currently is involved in clinical research with homeless dually diagnosed individuals and their families. Her other recent Brooks/Cole publications include *Family Treatment: Evidence-Based Practice with Populations at Risk*, 4th edition (2006, with Janzen, Harris, & Franklin) and *Child Welfare Policy and Practice in the 21st Century: An Evidence-Based Approach* (forthcoming, with Rycraft & Woody).

Heather Coleman is a Professor of Social Work at the University of Calgary. She has also worked in clinical social work practice for over 15 years. She serves as a Member at large, Board of Directors for the Canadian Association of Schools of Social Work. Her research areas include social work education, and child and family social work. Her areas of interest include family violence, family preservation, gender issues, First Nations and addictions, human sexuality, and clinical practice. She has authored and co-authored numerous articles and texts.

CONTENTS

CHAPTER SIX
Quantitative Assessment   156

CHAPTER TWELVE
Interventions with Couples and Gender Sensitive Intervention   329

CHAPTER THIRTEEN
The Termination Phase   350

PREFACE

We offer the second edition of *An Introduction to Family Social Work* to a social work profession that, after a century, is still consolidating its knowledge and experience in working with families. Many current family textbooks emphasize family therapy, a specialized activity that is usually practiced at the graduate social work level. Additionally, these family therapy books are not, for the most part, written by social workers. This is despite the fact that the family has been a focus of social work practice since the beginnings of the profession. Social work pioneers such as Mary Richmond argued for a family focus five decades before the modern family therapy movement, yet social work often has been humble in acknowledging its contributions to families. This book aims to help the profession reclaim its heritage.

At the time of publishing our first edition, nearly 400 accredited baccalaureate social work programs in the United States and Canada educated students to work with families. Yet few courses and textbooks specifically target the role in assisting families that BSWs will play after graduation. The numbers of accredited baccalaureate programs has grown considerably since 1999, making the importance of a social work–focused book on families even more imperative. Thus, the primary goal of this book is to provide undergraduate social work students with sufficient beginning knowledge and skills to work with families in a variety of settings outside the traditional office environment.

Undergraduate social workers often are employed in agencies that do not provide office-based family therapy, and few BSW student field placements are offered in traditional family therapy (office-based) settings. Rather, many beginning social workers are employed by agencies that provide support, teaching, and concrete services to families with a variety of needs and problems. Settings for family intervention include child welfare, family support, mental health, women's shelters, schools, and correctional facilities, to name a few. Similarly, many families experience multiple problems within the family as well as within the community. In fact, social work students and new graduates may be overwhelmed by the number and types of problems experienced by the families they encounter. Difficulties for many overburdened families come from many directions—for example, from unemployment, lack of housing, and/or mental or physical illness. Thus, problems are not exclusively in the domain of relationship dysfunction or disrupted homeostasis, which are the focal points of traditional family therapy approaches. In this book, we honor our social work heritage by placing families within an ecological niche. In this book, we recognize that families require a wide range of services to deal with different types of problems.

New social workers may find it difficult to anticipate what it will be like to see an overburdened family for the first time. They may have basic questions about what they need to know to prepare to see a family for the first, second, and even the third time. In addition, they may wonder how to engage families, earn their trust, and encourage meaningful and lasting changes. Social workers need access to practical information and skills to help families deal with a particular issue or set of issues. This book is intended for undergraduate social work students and new social work graduates who are (or soon will be) working with families for the first time. In it, we provide a framework for thinking about "family," as well as practical suggestions to guide family social work practice.

Most social work programs offer interviewing courses that focus on one-to-one interviews, often with adult clients. Family social work courses often rely on theoretical texts explicating family therapy models. This focus is an important aspect of social work education, but it is often too abstract and office-specific to help students learn about the basics of family social work. The instructor is challenged to be comprehensive enough to equip students with sufficient knowledge and skills to work with families and also to be specific enough to address concrete situations that students may encounter.

In this book, we attempt to present in a clear, succinct manner the knowledge and practical skills needed to engage in family social work. This book can be used in a beginning interview course or a family course as an introductory text on basic family social work theory and practice. It can also be used as a preparatory text before exposing students to the range of theoretical models offered in family therapy texts.

We have restructured and updated the material in the second edition based on the useful reviews of our first edition that we received. The family remains a forum over which political debate wages. We hold true to our social work value base of social justice and anti-oppressive practice by entering the debate and advocating for an open-minded approach to the family. Family diversity is infused throughout the book rather than being discussed in a single chapter. We believe that making diversity part of the core of the book rather than standing out as something "different" helps make it a natural part of family social work. Cultural diversity, gender issues, and different family forms are infused naturally throughout the book. Family systems theory is introduced early and forms the theoretical basis of the book, and this theoretical basis infiltrates the entire book. We have enhanced chapters on family assessment to include both qualitative and quantitative assessment. In addition, we have added a new chapter on family strengths and resilience. The focus on strengths and resilience will help family workers wear a different lens to appreciate the many possibilities that "differentness" can offer the family and the family social worker in times of difficulty. We have kept the balance between theoretical and practical aspects of family social work to assist new family social workers understand and balance the two and to provide a framework with which to integrate theory and practice.

The structure of the book orients the reader to the step-by-step process of family social work (FSW). Chapters 1 and 2 provide a philosophical perspective on family social work and an understanding of family functioning from a systems perspective. Students in family social work need to have a context in which to place their practice and framework for action. In Chapter 3 we describe the practical aspects of family social work, such as how to prepare for a home visit. Chapter 4 introduces the beginning phase of family social work, including basic interviewing skills. Chapters 5 and 6 introduce assessment skills and techniques; Chapter 5 focuses on qualitative methods such as genograms and ecomaps, and Chapter 6 discusses the use of quantitative methods, including standardized measures. These are important for today's managed care environment.

Chapters 7 through 9 provide information helpful during the initial phases of FSW. Chapter 7 describes family life cycle and development issues, and Chapter 8 helps the student to focus on family strengths and resilience. Chapter 9 puts it all together with a discussion of performing assessment with the entire family. Chapter 10 introduces the skills necessary for the intervention phase. Chapters 11 and 12 focus on parent–child and couple intervention skills, respectively. Additionally, Chapter 12 addresses gender sensitive practice. Finally, Chapter 13 provides information and skills related to the termination phase of FSW.

This book is designed to assist students and other new family social workers to understand the general dynamics and principles of family social work. It can be used in a family social work course with each chapter providing the structure for a weekly class. Throughout each chapter a number of exercises are suggested to give students an opportunity to apply the concepts presented in the chapter. Finally, this text can serve as a primer to a family therapy text.

We would like to point out that although the order of authorship was decided a long time ago, the authors actually contributed equally to the writing of this book. The authors are indebted to the support given us by Lisa Gebo and Alma Dea Michelena at Brooks-Cole. They make working fun. We appreciate the hard work of the production staff, especially Aaron Downey at Matrix Productions, and also the reviewers of the draft of the manuscript, including Laura Boisen, Augsburg College; Denice Goodrich Liley, Boise State University; Denise Longoria, Texas A & M; Cynthia F. Reibenstein, University of Houston; Bibhuti K. Sar, University of Louisville; and Stephen J. Yanca, Saginaw Valley State University. Finally, we are ever grateful to our children and to our families, who have provided us with the experiential learning aspects of family work!

THE FIELD OF FAMILY SOCIAL WORK

CHAPTER **I**

Q's about Family beliefs
Principles
Family Diversity

CHAPTER CONTENTS

Bidirectional Relationship between Family & Society

When social work students first begin to work in family social work, they often have many questions that they need answered before they have their first interview:

- What is the purpose of family social work?
- How does family social work differ from family therapy?
- What is my role as a family social worker?
- Will I be able to work effectively with families that are different from my own?
- How do I know what has caused the family's difficulties?
- How can I work with an entire family, all at the same time?
- How will I know what questions to ask family members?
- How can I encourage family members to participate if they are resistant?
- What should I do if family members get angry at me or another family member?
- How should I prioritize a family's problems?
- What do I need to know when making a home visit?
- How can I protect my own safety when making home visits in dangerous neighborhoods?
- Do I know enough to help families?
- What do I need to keep in mind when interviewing children?
- How can I help a family deal with a crisis?
- Is family social work different with families of diverse ethnic or racial backgrounds?

In this book we address these and other questions about family social work. Our goal is to help you be as effective as possible in assisting families and to give you a grounding in family theory and practice. We help you sort out how to assess families, set up a relationship and rapport with them, learn about basic intervention theory and skills, evaluate your practice, and finally to terminate productively with the families that you see.

WHAT IS FAMILY SOCIAL WORK?

Family social work is an umbrella approach to working with at-risk families. It can embrace many different types of programs such as intensive family preservation services, in-home family support, and teaching family models. The overarching purpose is to help families learn to function more competently in meeting the developmental and emotional needs of *all* members. "Disorganized families from the low socioeconomic population require adaptations of traditional family therapy and therapeutic style that take into account their specific characteristics of communication, cognition, and ways of experiencing affect" (Minuchin & Montalvo, 1971). At times, families fall short of their task when one member's needs are sacrificed for other members. Family social work is not the same as family therapy, which uses office-based intervention to help families make systemic changes.

By comparison, family social work targets the following objectives:

1. Reinforce family strengths to get families ready for change (or intervention);
2. Provide additional support following family therapy so families will maintain effective family functioning;
3. Create concrete changes in family functioning to sustain effective and satisfying daily routines on their own.

Family social work is often both home-based and community-based, transpiring within the daily routine and natural social environment of family life. Although the family social worker (FSW) may sometimes interview a family in an office, much of the work is conducted in the family's home. Home-based intervention allows the FSW to become familiar with daily features of family functioning. This approach is particularly helpful during family crises. The FSW might concentrate on concrete needs and daily routines and interactions of client families as targets for change, a focus matching the needs and expectations of many high-risk families (Wood & Geismar, 1986).

There are many ways in which a family social worker can provide on-the-spot, concrete assistance. For example, when a teenager and a parent become entangled in a conflict, the FSW has an opportunity to identify the problem and intervene in a "teachable moment." A FSW can help the parent and child to discover what led up to the argument and identify problematic and repetitive interactions as ongoing patterns that keep arguments going. Once these tasks have been achieved, the FSW can work with the parent and teenager to help them replace problem behavior with more rewarding interactions. When a young child throws a temper tantrum, the FSW can teach the parent more effective methods of dealing with the child on the spot. Additionally, a FSW may be present when a family member threatens suicide, thereby intervening at a moment of crisis. When a parent loses a job or the lease is not renewed, the family worker shares this experience with the family. While office-based family therapy deals with family scenarios after they have happened, many daily family events are not easily reproduced in the office. Ultimately, the FSW supports and encourages successful family dynamics when and where problems appear.

The home is where problems typically arise, making it an opportune place to find and implement solutions. Because the family social worker operates primarily within the family home or community, he or she can make an *immediate* difference in the lives of troubled families within their natural *environment*.

Although family social work addresses a range of individual and family problems in the home, including challenges facing the frail elderly and adult psychiatric patients, the focus of this book is on family social work involving children. We approach family work from a child-valuing perspective, and our guiding philosophy is to promote the well-being of children in their families. We believe that children have the right to live in healthy, supportive, and growth-promoting environments. We also believe that parents have the right to receive assistance to raise children. Consequently, the foundation of family social work rests on the principle that "children are helped when their families function well." Parenting is difficult and requires a range of skills together with a strong social support system. Parenting skills are neither instinctual nor intuitive; these skills must be learned and nurtured. In a nutshell, "The problem with being a parent is that by the time you're experienced, you're unemployed" (Efron & Rowe, 1987). A FSW can accelerate the learning process for parents so that they can enjoy their children and family life.

Historically, society has assumed that parenting comes naturally, contributing to the myth that parents should operate free from outside intervention. In other words, society expects every parent to raise children with the least amount of assistance from the state or other external agencies. This unfortunate assumption contributes to the belief that support is necessary only for "bad," "failing," or "incompetent" parents.

Ironically, while failing to ensure that parents receive necessary support, society holds high expectations for them. When parents struggle, social institutions are often punitive or intrusive. For example, child welfare systems may remove at-risk children from their homes, rather than provide adequate resources in the home to resolve family difficulties and keep families together (Fraser, Pecora, & Haapala, 1991). Instead, social institutions wait until parents fail, rather than providing timely assistance to them. Punitive interventions fail to resolve parent or child problems. Thus, the function of many agencies is to monitor, correct, or evaluate families *after* a problem has been identified. At worst, agencies may remove a child from a home without first providing support and aid proactively to *prevent* the child's removal. Rather than "lend a hand," the motto often seems to have been "point a finger."

Family social work, as a professional practice, is built on the value that parents, children, and the family as a unit deserve support to avoid later (and often more severe) "correction." All families need support from peers, neighbors, communities, and agencies at one time or another. They have a right to receive aid from family agencies that provide a family-centered approach. In keeping with a holistic philosophy, family social work differs from traditional approaches that counsel family members individually, disjointed from the family unit and isolated from their social context.

Based on these philosophical underpinnings, a family-centered approach in family social work is both necessary and practical. Family social workers may work with families who have encountered longstanding problems and multiple interventions from diverse helping systems. Because of previous experiences, vulnerable families frequently have become either "treatment shy" or "treatment sophisticated." They may be hesitant to discuss family problems with a professional who, in their view, operates from within the detached environment of an office, removed from the family's daily and natural life experiences.

FIELD OF FAMILY SOCIAL WORK

Social work's involvement with the family predates the family therapy approaches that exist today. The long tradition of family social work started with early efforts to alleviate human suffering—efforts that removed social problems from the exclusive domain of individual responsibility and placed them into a *context* where they were perceived to originate from a wider family and community context. Early social workers recognized that the family was integral both to human behavior and social organization. Social work's attention to context is perhaps one of its most outstanding contributions and is a benchmark of the profession, distinguishing it from other helping disciplines. This longstanding focus places social workers in a unique and cutting edge position—a position that is now increasingly being adopted by other professions.

The Person-in-Environment perspective has been with social workers since the beginning of the profession and is evident in beliefs about the importance of family and in attention to the features of the social environment such as culture, oppression, and relationships as they play a central role in the quality of life of our clients. The P-I-E perspective is a particularly useful way of understanding and working with multiproblem families. An ecological approach points the services in a direction that makes them more relevant to families and places the emphasis on doing rather than just talking. Studies show that when social workers convey a willingness to help, be with the family, provide support and encouragement and attentive listening, and be willing to provide concrete services, families fare better (Ribner & Knei-Paz, 2002).

Many authors (e.g., Pinsof, 2002) argue that marriage as a focus of science and therapy has existed for only five decades. We disagree. In fact, Mary Richmond, one of the first family social work pioneers, argued for a family perspective in order to understand human problems over half a century before Pinsof made his observations (see, for example, *Social Diagnosis*, 1917). She transformed the art of helping people from religious, moral, and psychoanalytic perspectives into a contextually and scientifically based practice, arguing that the family is an essential crucible in which to understand individual and social problems. Her formulations of family were based on an empirical analysis of case records. Nichols and Schwartz (2004) suggest that the role of social workers in the field of family work might have been overlooked because social workers were in the trenches delivering services rather than writing. In addition, early social workers were mostly women. Beels (2002) describes Richmond as one of the first social systems thinkers, a perspective that took hold much later in family systems thinking. Her vision also propelled social workers to think beyond the family by understanding that families are also located within larger community and social systems. As the result of Richmond's work, social workers have often considered the family as the "case" of focus, rather than the individual.

We admire Richmond's vision and courage in departing from viewpoints that were commonly accepted in her day—that problems were due exclusively to psychodynamic or moral shortcomings of the individual. (However, we also acknowledge her psychoanalytic leanings.) We also admire her tenacity to study problems through scientific investigation, considered rigorous for the day. Richmond's visionary thinking argued for a collaborative stance with families, an open mind, and viewing the family in interaction with the community and larger society, in order to arrive at a comprehensive assessment of problems (Beels, 2002). Social workers who followed, including Satir, Anderson, Papp, Carter, McGoldrick, White, and Epston, for example, reinforced the importance of the family through their own unique way of understanding family functioning. By the mid-twentieth century, other disciplines began to affirm the value of the family perspective.

In this book, we capitalize on the early social traditions by extending Richmond's thinking to include more recent theories of family functioning. We also synthesize the contributions of other disciplines and place them within a social work context. Together, the theory we present involves the social work tradition blended into an eclectic framework for today's families. We blend the concepts through a family systems foundation (discussed in more detail in Chapter 2).

Social work involvement with families has continued for over a century, taking different forms. More recently, the "discovery" of child abuse, the war on poverty in the 1970s, and the growing awareness that too many children are being placed in out-of-home care without due attention to families, have renewed and enhanced efforts in working with families.

FAMILY SOCIAL WORK AND FAMILY THERAPY

Modern family social work is rooted in the early "friendly visitor" movement and work with multiproblem families (Wood & Geismar, 1986). Today, educated professionals "visit" families, offering concrete support and education. Sometimes social work starts when a family first enters the helping network, and social work interventions may eventually lead to family therapy. In other situations, families become plugged into family social work during or after family therapy.

While family therapy does not fall within the domain of a single profession, as mentioned, family social work has been around for over a century. Family social work differs from family therapy in several ways. The broad focus of family social work emphasizes the complex interrelationships of individuals and the many layers of social systems. Family social work also focuses upon clearly defined, concrete events and interactions in the daily routine of a family. By comparison, family therapy is more formal, usually conducted in an office setting, and is often concerned with abstract patterns and structures of relationships and family functioning.

The family therapist restructures family roles and relationships, believing that that newly learned roles and relationships will culminate in more effective family functioning and eventually the elimination of presenting problems. Family therapists believe that individual problems often develop because of the dysfunction of an entire family unit. For family therapists, the family unit becomes the target of change, seldom focusing on individual family members. By comparison, FSWs are free to concentrate on specific problematic issues such as parent–child conflicts or school-related problems that appear as a subset of family dynamics. Thus, the FSW can respond to a wide range of family member needs and relationships. Often responses involve concrete problem solving, providing support, and teaching skills and competencies to individuals, dyads, or the entire family. The FSW also helps the family access concrete services and resources available within the community, such as job training or substance abuse programs.

Family therapy and family social work fulfill roles that are both important and distinct. Therefore, it is critical that the roles of the family social worker and the family therapist be clearly understood to avoid role confusion and working at cross-purposes. Clarity of roles is especially important when a family therapist and a family social worker are involved simultaneously with the same family. In such instances, family therapists and FSWs must work together to provide focused and mutually reinforcing interventions for the family.

REALITIES OF FAMILY SOCIAL WORK PRACTICE

Family social work differs from the traditional family therapy approach of the fifty-minute, once-a-week interview with the family in a therapist's office. By contrast, FSWs often work in the home, learning the intricacies of the daily fabric of the family's life and rhythms. Work occurs with the family when the need for help is most acute and when the family is most receptive to intervention and change. The family may have experienced a recent crisis that has put them into distress. In other instances, the family may need concrete aid and work may entail working alone or in conjunction with a wide range of other services.

This means that the FSW becomes directly involved in the home beyond the once-a-week session that a family therapist traditionally provides. Some FSWs are available to families (around the clock) during crises. Meeting these time demands can be stressful for the family social worker. Working in a client's home instead of an office can challenge workers' beliefs about therapy as well as models of a professional relationship (Snyder & McCollum, 1999). For example, workers may find the level of intimacy different than an office visit as they are exposed to intimate family routines such as people dropping by or telephoning, children playing, or televisions turned on to favorite programs.

FSWs become intimately familiar with daily life experiences of families through directly and immediately witnessing the impact of family events. The FSW provides support, knowledge, and skills in the "here-and-now" and "on-the-spot." Because FSWs are familiar with daily family events and functioning, families do not have to wait for a weekly appointment to work on family issues. Workers become more familiar with home-based clients than they do with office-based clients (Snyder & McCollum, 1999). When FSWs are not in the home, they might be a phone call away, enabling them to be present during critical family incidents. Thus, family social work is "hands-on," practical, and action-oriented.

Not surprisingly, families often see family social work as more informal and less intimidating than family therapy, in part because of the emphasis on developing a worker–family coalition. Relationships might have more of a social quality rather than a "professional" quality (Snyder & McCollum,

1999), challenging family workers to stay on task and make a demand for work. FSWs use engagement and relationship skills to create a problem-solving, growth-oriented partnership with families. Workers must also be finely attuned to working in another's turf where they may feel less in charge of the sessions and the work. Physical and emotional boundary issues may also arise because the relationship might be more "friendly" and less "professional." While workers have at their disposal a wider range of information about the family, they need to develop skills to incorporate this into their family work. Since the family social worker joins with the family and participates in daily events for several hours at a time, rich opportunities for developing this partnership with the family are available. Yet, the partnership between worker and family extends beyond engagement. One of the strengths of family social work lies in the fact that FSWs encourage family members to try new or different problem-solving skills and develop alternative daily living skills that can be called upon during and after the helping process.

Thus, a worker can provide emotional support to an isolated and overwhelmed mother; teach a misunderstood or acting out ten-year-old to express his needs and feelings more appropriately; or help a disorganized family structure meal times, homework, and bedtime routines so it can operate more harmoniously, replacing routines that produce stress and conflict. At the agency and community level, family social workers can advocate for families in accessing other helping systems in the community. The overarching purpose of family social work within the community is to develop fulfilling environments for family members while concurrently meeting the expectations and standards of communities.

During work with the family, the family social worker must be prepared to address concrete issues related to family problem areas. Families, especially those that are poor and overburdened, are most concerned about meeting concrete needs and respond well to an honest and straightforward approach (Wood & Geismar, 1986). Essentially, family social workers help construct the building blocks of a family system, one block at a time. Underlying family social work is the assumption that if enough areas of dysfunction can be altered, the family's future ability to meet the needs of members will be strengthened. This emphasis produces stronger families and healthier individuals. This strengthened competence enhances the immediate environment of the family, equipping children to learn to be more effective parents later. Ideally, family social work can have a multigenerational impact.

THE FAMILY AS A SPECIAL GROUP FORM

The family is the primary "group." That is, every child is born into a family group and grows up in that group, even for a short time. Unlike most other groups, we do not choose the family group into which we are born. Nevertheless, the family exerts tremendous influence over its members in terms of behaviors, beliefs, communication styles, cultural transmission, social skills, and efforts to meet basic human needs. From birth on, every human being is a member of a primary group. As the child grows and develops, the number of groups he or she is a member of expands. Yet, the family remains the first group, a group that is organized to meet the daily demands for food, clothing, and shelter. This group provides members with attachment and socializes children to interact in other group settings outside the family unit. Clearly, all families are organized in unique ways, with different capabilities, and different levels of success in meeting its members' needs.

"The family is a "natural group" in that it forms spontaneously on the basis of naturally occurring events, interpersonal attraction, or the mutually perceived needs of members (Toseland & Rivas, 1984). Unlike many other groups, family groups are formed independently of the FSW and are typically formed well before FSW involvement. They incorporate new members only by birth, adoption, commitment, or marriage. Members can only leave by death (Carter & McGoldrick, 1999). In many ways, family members are also irreplaceable. Therefore, family groupings have a long history, relationships are well established, and are created independently of a professional helper or leader. Nonetheless, there are both similarities and differences between the natural family group and groups formed based on specific professional or recreational objectives and tasks. In addition, some concepts and tasks apply to the different forms of groups.

Nichols and Schwartz (2004) also note the parallels between group and family dynamics. Drawing from the insights of Lewin, they note similarities. First, they suggest that group dynamics are a complex blend of individuals and personalities and superordinate properties of the group. Second, the group is more than the sum of its parts. Third, group discussions, and hence family discussions, are more effective than separate meetings with individuals. They also cite Bion, who sees that patterns of fight–flight, dependency, and pairing are also group patterns applicable to families. They draw parallels between Bennis' stages of group development and the family life cycle. Finally, role theory has been adapted to apply to family work.

WHAT IS A FAMILY?

From a psychological perspective, it is hard to imagine the value of defining any major social group that is not physically or emotionally harming itself or others as deviant or undesirable.

—Pinsof, 2002

One of the most perplexing issues in learning about families derives from the deceptively simple question: "What is a family?" In part, the confusion stems from the changing nature of modern relationships. While the family is a group, it is a special type of group that cannot be easily captured in a single definition. However, attempts to define *family* meet with difficulties similar to defining femininity, fatherhood, or love. Everyone seems to have a personal definition of each, but a generally agreed-upon definition is difficult, if not impossible, to arrive at. Despite this difficulty, social workers must be able to understand what constitutes a family if they are to decide upon eligibility for services from a particular agency and service perspective. How family membership is defined can help family social workers determine who should be included in a family intervention (Hartman & Laird, 1983). On a broader scale, a clear definition of *family* determines who will receive services and resources from agencies, based on the agencies' particular policy definition, and who is eligible to receive benefits such as maternity leave, day care subsidies, public assistance, or health care. It will also help the FSW make a decision about the particular unit they will include in FSW services.

Bowen, among others, views the family as a system. "The family *is* a number of different kinds of systems. It can accurately be designated as a social system, a cultural system, a games system, a communication system, a biological system . . . I think of the family as a combination of emotional and relationship systems" (1971, p. 169). The ideas of how emotions and relationships play out are discussed later in this book.

While little agreement exists on a single definition of *family,* family social workers must develop a clear picture of family that encompasses a range of family structures, roles, and functions. For many beginning family social workers, their only real experience with family functioning has been in their own family of origin (Munson, 1993). Yet, the FSW must move beyond individual experience because singular and deeply personal perspectives can hinder family workers' awareness of the diversity of family types and styles. It will also create biases about what "health" and "dysfunction" actually entail.

On a political level, the definition of family is being fought on a much larger and more contentious scale. We hear about "family values" every day, and those family forms that fail to adhere to family values are criticized. Few people actually know what the term "family values" means, but they are willing to fight to the end to defend them. In the process, women who work outside the home are denigrated, poor families are marginalized, families from other cultures are made to feel inferior or deformed, and single parents are made to believe that they have experienced an amputation and are less than whole or complete. We suggest that strict adherence to "family values" would make us akin to the characters in *Pleasantville:* monotone, boring, and cardboard. The argument has been made that if families were to abide by "family values," social problems would not exist, that it is the so-called disintegration of the traditional family that has caused numerous social problems. The following quotation illustrates how "family values" play out in families.

> *What we often take to be family values—the work ethic, honesty, clean living, marital fidelity, and individual responsibility—are in fact social, religious or cultural values. To be sure, these values are transmitted by parents to their children and are familial in that sense. They do not, however, originate within the family. It is the value of close relationships with other family members, and the importance of these bonds relative to other needs . . .*

—David Elkind (www.Bartleby.com)

In this book we argue that the lack of a supportive social environment contributes to family disintegration. We celebrate family diversity. We believe that diversity, rather than being a threat to families, actually honors families. For example, the demands by gays and lesbians to have legal recognition of their relationships support the importance of families. Rather than being a deficit, diversity provides families with depth, character, and richness. We argue that it is not diversity that creates family difficulties; we believe that hostile social environments create difficulties for families. Families encounter difficulties for many reasons, not the least of which is a *one size fits all* mentality wherein everyone must adhere to the same color scheme. When social attitudes create an oppressive environment for those who do not fit into the mainstream, difficulties are bound to arise. Thus, we need to expand our definition of family.

PURPOSES OF FAMILIES

Families exist both for the well-being of their members and for the well-being of society. They offer predictability, structure, and (ideally) safety in the social lives of members. It is within families that members get basic human needs met. When families fail to meet the basic needs of *every* member, they need help. One of the first things a FSW needs to understand is whose needs are being met and whose needs are not. With few exceptions, children grow up in families. It is within families that children learn and develop skills that prepare them for life outside the family, first in school and later in the workforce. When families do well, the rest of society also does well.

Satir (1967) identifies seven functions of families, which we summarize in the following list. (Discuss in class which of these functions are now outdated.)

1. To provide heterosexual experience for mates
2. To contribute to the continuity of the race by producing and nurturing children
3. To cooperate economically by dividing labors between the adults according to sex, convenience and precedents
4. To maintain a boundary (incest taboo) so that tasks can be performed smoothly and stable relationships maintained
5. To transmit culture to the children through teaching communication, expression of emotions, coping with inanimate environment, and roles
6. To recognize when one of its members reaches adulthood
7. To provide for the eventual care of parents by their children (pp. 26–27).

Families also pass down cultural traditions from one generation to another. Language, beliefs, religion, knowledge, and so on, flow from one generation to another. Yet, such traditions are always in a state of flux, and while some people are nostalgic because society is changing so rapidly, others welcome these new changes. The mass media and cross-fertilization of global ideas are having a strong influence on beliefs and practices.

On an economic level, families produce workers and consumers. One of the authors was interviewed by a conservative magazine about the meaning and implications of the dwindling birth rate. The author asked the interviewer why this was a problem, to which the interviewer responded, "To fill the empty houses of course." The author's response to this was that the interviewer had it backwards. People should not have babies in order to fill houses—instead, houses should be built to accommodate babies. The interview was never published (not surprisingly), but it was evident that the interviewer's assumption was that a growing consumer population is needed to support the efforts of workers, and so on. Families do produce children who become both workers and consumers. Many industrialized countries are opening up immigration because there are not enough workers and consumers to keep the economy moving at a fast enough past. The economy is based on growth. From this discussion, the extent of interdependence between families and the larger society should be clear.

What kind of grouping qualifies as a family, as compared to friends or roommates? Where do extended family members fit in? What about common-law relationships? How do gay and lesbian families fit into definitions of family? Similarly, how do communal relationships or polygamous relationships fit into the category of family? Finally, how do cross-cultural variations of family structure and form fit into your conceptualization of family? Are alternative family forms the "enemy of marriage," as some claim?

Defining the family is not easy, yet a working definition of family is a crucial preliminary task for family social workers. Family social workers also need to be critical of how policy makers have directed family behaviors and structures based on favored political and moral agendas (Pinsof, 2002). Policy makers do have options to support alternative family forms, including cohabitation not sanctioned by the state.

Without a clear definition and conceptualization of family, social workers would have to rely on personal assumptions, beliefs, and stereotypes. They must be able to define the client group in order to devise appropriate interventions. One of our first tasks in this chapter, then, is to examine common biases and beliefs about families.

In colonial times, wealthier settlers established independent households by exploiting the services of poor immigrant workers and slaves. African Americans were denied the legal protection of marriage and parenthood and consequently developed extensive kinship networks (Coontz, 1996). Because of their labors, middle-class, white women were able to enjoy the luxury of domesticity because working-class women liberated them from household tasks that formerly fell to them. Carter and McGoldrick (1999a) remind us that "the traditional stable multigenerational extended family of yore was supported by sexism, classism, and racism" (p. 3).

Throughout history, death, desertion, divorce, and separation made single-parent and blended families a regular feature of family life, contrary to current proselytizing about the erosion of society because of family breakdown. In a blended family, divorced or widowed parents remarry, bringing with them children from the previous marriage. Contrary to popular lore, blended families were quite common in the past because of high mortality rates of women during childbirth and illness. Historically, disease and wars claimed many lives, leaving some adults single several times over adulthood. Remarriages were therefore common. Moreover, poor women and their children worked outside the home even before the Industrial Revolution, again challenging the myth that feminism is responsible for the breakdown of the family. (One wonders whose interests are served by claims that women today are going against the grain by working outside the home.) Given this snippet of family history, we see that the traditional nuclear family primarily existed in middle and upper classes of European lineage and that the current family "ideal" probably serves the patriarchal and capitalist power interests of the day.

Those who blame social problems on changing family structures and other family changes are placing the "cart before the horse." Another way to look at social problems such as economic inequity and the ravages of race, gender, and class discrimination is to consider how such problems *contribute* to the breakdown of the family. As proposed by Coontz:

> These inequities are *not* driven by changes in family forms, contrary to ideologues that persist in confusing correlation with causes; but they certainly exacerbate such changes, and they tend to bring out the worst in *all* families. The result has been an accumulation of stresses on families, alongside some important expansions of personal options. Working couples with children try to balance three full-time jobs, as employers and schools cling to policies that assume every employee has a "wife" at home to take care of family matters. Divorce and remarriage have allowed many adults and children to escape from toxic family environments, yet our lack of social support networks and failure to forge new values for sustaining intergenerational obligations have let many children fall through the cracks in the process (1996, p. 47).

Nearly fifty years ago, Nathan Ackerman (1958) pointed out the disharmony between social needs and individual needs:

> Whatever the term, all are agreed on the trend toward a sense of lostness, aloneness, confusion of personal identity, and a driven search for acceptance through conformity. One effect of this trend toward disorientation is to throw each person back on his (sic) family group for the restoration of a sense of security, belongingness, dignity and worth. The family is called upon to make up to its individual members in affection and closeness for the anxiety and distress which is the result of failure to find a safe place in the wider world (cited in Satir, 1967)

Both Coontz and Ackerman are critical of the failure of society to lighten the load of families, and to help foster nurturing environments for society's citizens. Both see that the difficulties of living in what is often a hostile and alienating social world create added burdens upon the family to meet its members' needs *and* buffer family members from the stress of the environment. Perhaps families are doing more for society than society is doing for its members. What do you think?

DIVERSITY AND FAMILIES

If history has a lesson for us, it is that no one family form has ever been able to satisfy the human need for love, comfort, and security.

—Gillis, 1996, cited in Carter & McGoldrick, 1999a

A historical overview of the family in Western society reveals a variety of family structures that diverge from the traditional notion of the family as a single, monolithic form. Pinsof (2002), in a historical review of marriage, points out that marriages seldom lasted for 15 years, with death being the primary reason for the end of a marriage. It was not until the middle to end of the twenty-first century that divorce overtook death as the primary reason for marital dissolution. The divorce rate has now leveled off. Looking beyond structure will help you develop an accurate understanding of unique family experiences and the common needs of all family units within society. A childless couple; a couple with two (or ten) biological, adopted, or foster children; a single mother with children; or a gay couple with children are all examples of different family structures, but are families nonetheless. So are families that embrace extended kin and families from different cultures that assume forms that differ from the "traditional" family. It is interesting that many definitions consider a unit to be a family only if children are present in a relationship, showing a subtle social bias for children.

Family structure in the United States and Canada is especially diverse. Families differ in many arenas, including lifestyle, cultural heritage, gender role expressions, and sexual orientation, just to name a few. Immigrants come to North America with unique cultural and religious beliefs and heritages that affect family structure and family functioning. Culture plays an instrumental role in how families proceed through the family life cycle (Carter & McGoldrick, 1999). All families are also affected by the socio-historical era in which they live. Gender relations within the family also vary greatly, and we are still a long way from total gender equality. Nevertheless, gender is a major organizing factor in families. Gender influences behavior in families and how problems are constructed (Rampage, 2002).

Families exist within a social environment, and many are disadvantaged in terms of access to social resources and the willingness of social institutions to support them. Some will be from an ethnic minority group. In many ways, the traditional nuclear family has captured a Eurocentric perspective and in doing so has laid the groundwork for a subtle racism that has pervaded family literature. As such, individuals and groups that fall outside the mainstream definition of family often encounter discrimination and lack of service because the dominant group fails to acknowledge or respect their unique experiences and practices. This contributes to marginalization and distancing from social resources. At the same time, they are blamed for their victimization and told to "pull themselves up by their bootstraps." Typically, those doing the blaming have little compassion for powerlessness and discrimination and fail to understand the obstacles that others face. Children in some of these families feel stigmatized and ostracized by the larger community as families struggle to get their basic human needs met with dignity.

Family social workers need to develop both an awareness and a sensitivity to difference that looks at differences from both a structural and an ethnic point of view. *Awareness* means the ability to recognize that differences exist and how it shapes reality in inequitable and unjust ways (Laszloffy & Hardy, 2000). Those who are sensitive to differences are not only aware of issues pertaining to these differences, they are also able to act upon such differences. For example, they may take their sensitivity to a political level and challenge institutional racism or oppressive family policy practices. We recommend that every family assessment include an analysis of oppression and the potential impact of racism on each family.

Children should not feel like they are growing up in a war zone (Garbarino, 1992)! In Canada and in the United States, for example, indigenous or native peoples remain an underserved and marginalized group. Later in this book, we refer to Maslow's Hierarchy of Needs (Maslow, 1968). The premise of this book is that children and families have a *right* to the necessities of life: food, shelter, clothing, safety at home and in communities, education, health care, and so on. Family social work requires a wide-angle lens with which workers understand the social impingements on a family's ability to survive and thrive. According to Sims (2002), and we agree, one of the consequences of living on a low income is that families cannot afford a healthy diet. When nutritional needs are not met, children from poor families experience multiple disadvantages; their growing bodies are starved for nutrition and they perform more poorly in school and play. The playing field is tilted from the very beginning. Moreover, in families where parents are under stress, the parents have a more difficult time nurturing positive relationships. Their energies are placed elsewhere. Two of the authors of this book live in a country where access to health care is a basic human right. They are quite surprised to hear the arguments against universal health care in the United States. When children and families do not have their needs met appropriately, they face an increased risk of experiencing unfavorable outcomes (Sims, 2002).

Family social workers must recognize, accept, and respect a wide range of family expressions. Unfortunately, beliefs about the ideal or "real" family have led many to believe that they grew up in abnormal or dysfunctional families because their families of origin did not conform to the rigid mold. Others, particularly those who buy into the beliefs about what constitutes a "real" family, might be critical of family forms that diverge from the "ideal." This is particularly true for families who are not middle-class, white, or based upon heterosexual unions. For example, many people of non-American descent believe in selfless loyalty to their families. Members of another culture, however, may consider such loyalty as over-involvement or enmeshment (Nichols & Schwartz, 2004).

In learning about family diversity and alternative expressions of family, it is necessary for FSWs to examine their biases and assumptions about what "family" means to them and then challenge them as the "real truth." While social mobility is quite common today, it is also very common for people still to reside in the general area in which they grew up. Local realities and lack of exposure to alternative ways of thinking can impede the FSW from developing an open mind and new ways of understanding the world. Exposure to different ways of thinking and being is the first step in understanding the world.

Many people, children in particular, feel stigmatized or ashamed because they consider their family different from the mainstream—or abnormal. Definitions of family contribute to how we practice, and if a family social worker rigidly adheres to beliefs about an ideal family type, those who do not resemble the ideal become quickly marginalized (Hartman & Laird, 1983). However, it is important to remember that the notion of what is normal is vague and grounded in value judgments. Once armed with the awareness and acceptance that many forms of family exist and are widespread, the family social worker can break down barriers and attitudes so that people who were raised in households that do not conform to the stereotype feel neither abnormal nor dysfunctional. Social work is about relationships with people from different backgrounds and experiences. We can learn much from diversity—about ourselves, about other people, and about the world.

Several parameters determine what "normal" is. The term has been defined by different dimensions:

- Historical
- Religious
- Cross-cultural
- Biological
- Medical
- Psychiatric
- Scientific
- Based on the animal kingdom
- Cultural
- Political
- Personal values

Each dimension of how to define *normal* produces a different angle on the family. For example, conservative groups might define the family in very traditional ways (e.g., two parents, mother stays at home, two children, one dog named Spot, etc.). This definition is both a political and religious one, based on the values of a certain group. It is also an historical artifact. Definitions differ based on various religious, political, cultural, or personal perspectives. This leads us to the question of who has a right to impose his or her definition of what is normal on anyone else. The imposition of values and beliefs is a common practice that benefits only those who have social power and control. Subscribing to the dominant view inherently disadvantages and steals power from those who hold other beliefs.

FAMILY DIVERSITY NOW AND BEYOND

Your basic extended family today includes your ex-husband or -wife, your ex's new mates, your new mate, possibly your new mate's ex and any new mates that your new mate's ex has acquired.

—Delia Ephron

Families are undergoing change worldwide. In North America, less than 10 percent of today's families actually conform to the traditional nuclear family. In fact, over 60 percent of all children will have spent at least part of their childhood in a single-parent household by the age of eighteen, and the majority of these single parents are mothers (Gavin & Bramble, 1996). Of all current families with children, one-fourth are single-parent households, with many parents employed outside the home. However, single-parent families face a greater risk of living in poverty. Today's families have fewer children than in the past, women are bearing children later in life, and people are also marrying later. The average household size is shrinking, and more couples are choosing to remain childless. The divorce rate hovers around 50 percent, and about 70 percent of divorced individuals eventually remarry. Second marriages have an even higher risk of divorce. Serial relationships and serial marriages are now quite common. While some things have changed rapidly, other things have changed more slowly. Women still make less than men. Men are still spending less time in childcare and household tasks.

Cultural diversity in society is also growing rapidly, and whites are slowly becoming a minority of the population (McGoldrick, Giordano, & Pearce, 1996). Minority family values may differ from the dominant culture and may at times bear little resemblance to beliefs and assumptions that guide mainstream family work. Sims (2002) sees culture as social capital, which involves strong relationships to provide a foundation upon which to build community connections. A cultural connection is important and the extent to which people are connected to their particular culture is a form of strength and can be linked to parenting competence. Conversely, disconnecting people from their culture can undermine parenting competence. Socially rich neighborhoods are those settings where people are an asset to the community and give back to others. Hence, the need for a perspective that goes beyond the family.

Family social workers must strive to shed ethnocentrism *and* develop sensitivity and competence in working with different cultures. Of utmost importance is learning that the dominant values and beliefs about families can be oppressive and inapplicable to families from other cultures. Nichols and Schwartz (2004) remind us to not assume that just because a family is different it is sick (p. 321). Unfortunately, in past practices, we have done just that. Respect for diversity also includes acknowledging the impact of sexism, racism, and heterosexism on how we work with families and the models from which we draw. In this book, we take the approach that memorizing a laundry list of characteristics is not helpful. There are far too many cultures and differences within cultures to suggest that a certain culture embraces a specific cluster of characteristics and beliefs. Also, overemphasizing culture can exaggerate the differences between the worker and the family (Nichols & Schwartz, 2004).

Regardless of cultural group or socioeconomic status, families include a range of structures. The most common family structures that include children are presented in the following sections. The same family can fit into two or more categories.

> *Children live in a variety of family forms; they develop normally with single parents, with unmarried parents, with multiple caretakers in a communal setting, and with tradition two-parent families. What children require is loving and attentive adults, not a particular family type.*

—Sandra Scarr (www.Bartleby.com)

FAMILY OF ORIENTATION/FAMILY OF ORIGIN

Most individuals belong to at least two family systems over a lifetime. All have belonged to families of orientation, commonly referred to as the family of origin. This is the family in which a person is born or raised. It is possible for some people to come from two or more families of orientation. For example, a child who is adopted during infancy was, at least briefly, part of a family of orientation with the birth mother. To the child, however, the family of orientation is more likely to be that of the adoptive parents. One definition of the family of origin is "the living unit in which a person has his or her beginnings physiologically, physically, and emotionally" (Hovestadt, Anderson, Piercy, Cochran, & Fine, 1985, cited in Rovers, DesRoches, Hunter, & Taylor, 2000).

FAMILY OF PROCREATION

A family of procreation consists of a couple, whether through self or state sanction, that has developed a relationship and has children. The couple in a family of procreation may be of opposite sexes or the same sex, and procreation may occur through heterosexual intercourse or through one of the assisted reproductive technologies such as artificial insemination or surrogate parenthood.

EXTENDED FAMILY

An extended family includes two or more family units. For example, an extended family may consist of a household in which a grandmother lives with her married son, daughter-in-law, and grandchildren. While grandparents are the most common extension, an extended family may also include aunts, uncles, or cousins. For members of some ethnic groups, the extended family plays an especially important role (Lum, 1992). Grandparenting is discussed in more detail in Chapters 2 and 6.

BLENDED FAMILY

A blended family, or stepfamily, consists of two people living with at least one child from a previous relationship. The parents may also have biological children together.

ADOPTIVE FAMILY

Adoption involves a legal commitment to raise children who have been born to others. Adoption has become more complicated in recent years, with fewer children available to be adopted. Prospective parents can now adopt through an open process, informally, internationally, and interracially. Families may be formed by more than one way of adopting. Moreover, single parents can now adopt and in some states, gay and lesbian parents are also free to adopt (Carter, 1999).

FOSTER FAMILY

In a foster family, parents temporarily nurture children born to others. The length of time in which a foster child is in the home can vary from several days to most of childhood. Although most foster families have a formal arrangement with child welfare authorities, other fostering arrangements can be made informally with friends or relatives. In the United States, nearly half a million children are in foster care. Two-thirds are African American or mixed race, most are between the ages of 5 and 11, and many have behavioral or emotional problems (Carter, 1999). Carter also notes that for-profit businesses in the field of foster care are emerging.

SINGLE-PARENT FAMILY

A single-parent family consists of one parent and one or more children. The parent can be either male or female and can be single as a result of the death of a partner, divorce, separation, desertion, or never having been married. A growing number of single parents are single by choice (Okun, 1996). Over one-quarter of the Caucasian babies and over two-thirds of African children in the United States are born to unmarried women (Pinsof, 2002). This compares to nearly half of the children born in Scandinavia.

DIVERSE FAMILY STRUCTURES

Consider the following families that have been assigned to your caseload at your FSW field placement. How is each family like or not like your own family of origin? What are your biases about these families? What unique challenges, if any, will you face in working with each family?

- The Sims family was referred to you by the high school due to the children's poor attendance and grades. Jeanne Sims is forty-two years old, Caucasian, and a housewife. Jeanne's husband, Dick, is forty-three years old, Native American, and works as a mechanic at a gas station. During your initial interview with Jeanne and her teenage daughter, Lisa, Lisa tells you that many of the family's problems stem from her father's drinking, bad temper, and physical abuse of his wife. Jeanne says she stays with her husband because of her religious beliefs, which require that wives submit to their husbands.

- The Thompson family was referred to you by the local mental health clinic at which the mother, Diane Thompson, receives medication for schizophrenia. Diane is an African American single female in her twenties, who lives with her parents, Jim and Stella. Jim and Stella are concerned because Diane takes her medication sporadically and disappears for weeks at a time when off her medications. The Thompsons have been informed that Diane has been living on the streets during these periods. They are afraid for Diane's safety.

- Liz Frank, a twenty-three-year-old Caucasian female, and her four-year-old daughter Tina were referred to you by Child Protective Services. Tina's day care teacher reported the family to CPS when Liz recently divorced Tina's father and moved herself and Tina in with her new partner Sylvia. The teacher reports that Tina frequently appears at school hungry, unbathed, and dressed in clothes that appear "slept in."

- John Bells and Craig Boyd are a gay couple raising their seven-year-old son. Recently they have had arguments over different parenting approaches and are seeking your help in parenting skills training.

- Joy Jimenez, a thirty-nine-year-old Hispanic female, referred herself and her family to your agency. Joy is the recently divorced mother of six children: sixteen-year-old Alicia, thirteen-year-old Joe, eleven-year-old Maria, seven-year-old twins Carlos and Juan, and four-year-old Dora. Joy, her boyfriend Tom, and the children moved in with Joy's mother and stepfather last week. Joy's parents have volunteered to help out with the children, as Joy's job takes her away from home for many hours each day.

A DEFINITION OF FAMILY

Eichler's (1988) definition of family provides a foundation on which to build:

A family is a social group that may or may not include one or more children (e.g., childless couples), who may or may not have been born in their wedlock (e.g., adopted children, or children by one adult partner of a previous union). The relationship of the adults may or may not have its origin in marriage (e.g., common-law couples); they may or may not occupy the same residence (e.g., commuting couples). The adults may or may not cohabit sexually, and the relationship may or may not involve such socially patterned feelings as love, attraction, piety, and awe (p. 4).

Compare Eicher's definition of family with an early one given by Virginia Satir (1967):

> When Mary and Joe added the parental role to their individual and marital roles, they then qualified, sociologically speaking, as a family . . . [Sociologists]: (1) Generally seem to agree that the nuclear family (made up of parents and children) is found in all societies. (2) They define a family as a group composed of adults of both sexes, two of whom (the mates) live under the same roof and maintain a socially accepted sexual relationship. (3) Families also include children created or adopted by these mates (p. 26).

Finally, Carter's and McGoldrick's definition of family offers yet another perspective:

> Families comprise people who have a shared history and a shared future. They encompass the entire emotional system of at least three, and frequently now four or even five generations held together by blood, legal, and/or historical ties (p. 1).

Cultures differ in how they define "family" and in who is included in the group. The definition of the dominant culture focuses on the nuclear family, whereas African American families include an expanded kin network, Chinese focus on ancestors, and Italians look at several generations of extended kin (McGoldrick, Giordano, & Pearce, 1996). Some Native families consider the entire community in their web of family affiliations (Coleman, Unrau, & Manyfingers, 2001). In minority families, relationships with extended family and kin networks are based on principles of interdependence, group orientation, and reliance on others (Lum, 1992). Cultural values about family practices that someone from another culture may label as "strange" or "unhealthy" also guide people. Family activities may diverge dramatically from mainstream culture. For example, some Puerto Ricans believe so strongly in family obligation that they find it acceptable to use public office to benefit family members (Lum, 1992).

Finally, minority families might be structured according to a "vertical hierarchy of authority" (Lum, 1992); authority in these families often is assumed by males or elders as heads of households. Cultural clashes can occur when children or females from a minority family encounter differences in the dominant culture. Culturally sensitive practice is discussed in more detail throughout the book.

Lack of awareness can lead family social workers to be less objective about families whose backgrounds are either very different from or very much like their own families. In either case, social workers may work less intensely, understand parents poorly, or be unable to overcome communication and cultural barriers, such as language, religious differences, or divergent styles of parenting. Another risk is that social workers may construct inaccurate assessments about parental strengths and weaknesses. Thus, FSWs must be honest with themselves about their own motivations, prejudices, and blind spots. Only then will they be able to work empathetically with parents from different backgrounds.

Contemporary family lifestyles and structures are fluid and evolving. Therefore, the FSW needs a broad definition of family. Despite the difficulty of developing a clear and simple definition of family, most people can construct an unambiguous description to fit their own particular family, and working definitions of the family can be established for most situations. The family, in its most basic conceptualization, is what a person in a family says it is. The experienced "family" reality, rather than strict adherence to a monolithic, static, and rigid definition, is crucial to family social work and lays the groundwork for the work conducted with a family. Social judgments about family structures play an important role in determining what resources and barriers a family will encounter in getting their needs met.

MYTHS ABOUT THE FAMILY

Throughout history and across different cultures, the family has assumed diverse forms; nevertheless all people come from a nuclear family. The nuclear family is any kinship group of more than one person residing in the same household and related by marriage, blood, societal or self-sanction. This definition is so broad that one could easily ask, "What grouping does not qualify as a family?" The definition is broad enough to include all who have been or are currently members of a nuclear family. Indeed, being a member of more than one nuclear family in a lifetime is both possible and likely.

Generally people think of the "traditional family" when referring to the nuclear family. Rigid definitions of the family are limited to members related by blood (i.e., biological parents and children) or legally sanctioned marriages. Clearly, such a rigid view of family could exclude more people than it includes. The idea of a traditional family conjures an image of the mother at home, father at work, and 2.2 children. Distress about the current state of the family has been accompanied by the belief that the best way to resolve serious social problems is to return to this "traditional" form.

In reality, the traditional nuclear family existed more in fiction than fact. North American family structures have always been diverse. The family with a male breadwinner and female full-time homemaker existed as a dominant family form only for a brief period, most commonly in white, middle-class households (Coontz, 1996). During the 1920s, a small majority of children grew up in a family where the male was the breadwinner and the female was the homemaker. Today, this type of family comprises only 7 percent of all households (Gavin & Bramble, 1996). The current idealized "traditional nuclear family" espoused by conservative politicians existed primarily in the 1950s (Coontz, 1996).

BELIEFS ABOUT FAMILIES

Family work starts with an examination of our fundamental beliefs about families and family life. Beliefs and attitudes guide what we see and where we go with families. Indeed, Karl Marx was well aware of this tendency when he commented, "It is not the consciousness of man that determines our social existence. Rather, it is our social existence that determines our consciousness."

Many social attitudes are not helpful to families. Unproductive attitudes blame parents, fail to respect or embrace diversity, impose singular or restrictive views, and erect barriers that prevent an open understanding and acceptance of the struggles of family life and its members. These negative attitudes about families interfere with the partnership that workers must develop in family work.

By comparison, positive attitudes form a necessary base for constructive family work. Family workers must trust that people want to do the best with what they have. They must also develop an optimistic belief that family problems can change and that the family can be healthy and supportive to its members. Viewpoints that are sensitive to realities of family life will guide ethical and humane practice with families and create a road map for productive worker–family relationships. The following beliefs guide family social work.

BELIEF I: FAMILIES WANT TO BE HEALTHY

Typically, people who are committed to an intimate relationship intend to remain together. When people have children they expect to be competent parents. Unfortunately, marriages terminate and children grow up in less than optimal environments. This does not mean that the family did not want to resolve its difficulties. Rather, it may mean that the family considered its problems to be insurmountable or that they did not have the knowledge, skills, or beliefs to make the situation better. Effective family social workers believe that early and timely intervention can create a potent opportunity for change.

BELIEF II: FAMILIES WANT TO STAY TOGETHER AND OVERCOME THEIR DIFFERENCES

Contrary to stereotypical and negative social notions, most people prefer to remain in committed relationships rather than be alone. Most are also motivated to remain together to work out their differences so long as they have hope and a belief that their lives can improve. People do not suddenly decide to break up, but instead attempt to use available resources in the form of knowledge and skills to resolve differences and overcome pain. However, many families do not know how to handle their difficulties and require outside assistance to resolve them in constructive and mutually satisfying ways. For some, the first stage of asking for help is to turn to friends and family for guidance. When close supports fail to provide the needed assistance, the family might turn to family social workers, who can provide practical, supportive, concrete assistance without the biases that many friends and family members might have. Early intervention is important to help the family deal with difficulties in a way that promotes enduring change. When children are removed from the home and placed into care, family social work can intervene to help children return home (Lewandowski & Pierce, 2004).

BELIEF III: PARENTS NEED UNDERSTANDING AND SUPPORT FOR THE CHALLENGES INVOLVED IN KEEPING RELATIONSHIPS SATISFYING AND FOR RAISING CHILDREN

Few people receive training or education on how to be effective partners and parents. Many people base their patterns of relationships and child rearing practices upon what they learned during their own childhoods. Being an intimate partner and raising children demands that people have knowledge, patience, consistency, and unselfishness. People who are struggling with these issues need understanding and support, rather than condemnation and criticism. Often, individuals are blamed when a marriage fails or when parents are inconsistent or ineffective; observers may be quick to judge results without appreciating a family's struggle and pain when a relationship deteriorates. Blaming creates defensiveness and anger. Understanding and support, on the other hand, can open up opportunities for new learning, constructive change, and possible reunification of families.

BELIEF IV: PARENTS CAN LEARN POSITIVE, EFFECTIVE WAYS OF RESPONDING TO THEIR CHILDREN IF THEY HAVE OPPORTUNITIES FOR SUPPORT, KNOWLEDGE, AND SKILLS

All parents can benefit from the support of friends, relatives, and the community. This belief flies in the face of a common social myth that only those who are truly independent are healthy and functional. In fact, supports are necessary for adequate social functioning. However, some parents have had little access to effective parenting role models and knowledge. Helping parents acquire appropriate knowledge and skills benefits everyone. This assumption underlies the belief that all people want to be their best and can improve their skills when they learn more effective and positive parenting techniques.

BELIEF V: PARENTS' BASIC NEEDS MUST BE MET BEFORE THEY CAN RESPOND EFFECTIVELY AND POSITIVELY TO THE NEEDS OF THEIR CHILDREN

Unemployed parents, parents distressed about housing or food, or those who are experiencing other forms of distress often find it difficult to meet the needs of others, despite how much they care. Thus, even when the goal of family social work is to help parents develop more effective ways of enhancing their children's development, attention also must be directed toward helping parents meet their own needs. We are reminded of the airplane metaphor where passengers are advised to put on their own oxygen mask first before helping their children. Helping parents to eliminate stress can free them to manage their children in more positive ways.

BELIEF VI: EVERY FAMILY MEMBER NEEDS NURTURING

People need to feel loved and connected to other people. Sometimes becoming angry and blaming others seems easier than sharing love and caring. Every family needs to be a sanctuary in which each member can experience nurturing and love. If only one person is getting his or her needs met at the expense of others, then the family is not functioning properly.

BELIEF VII: FAMILY MEMBERS, REGARDLESS OF GENDER OR AGE, DESERVE RESPECT FROM EACH OTHER

Within the context of different cultural groups, the family social worker should examine existing power structures in a family rather than assuming that one person is "head" of a household. This means respecting differences and unique contributions to the marriage, parenting, and family. Children should be respected and accorded due rights as people. Gender differences also should be respected. Equal opportunities for growth and participation must therefore be guaranteed to all family members, regardless of age or gender. At the same time, social workers should understand that roles related to gender and age may vary in different cultures.

BELIEF VIII: A CHILD'S EMOTIONAL AND BEHAVIORAL DIFFICULTIES SHOULD BE VIEWED WITHIN THE CONTEXT OF THE FAMILY AND THE LARGER SOCIAL ENVIRONMENT

To understand children, one needs to understand families. Further, to work effectively with children, one must work effectively with their families. Problems experienced by families generally do not reside either within the parents or within the child, but instead are an intimate part of the daily pattern of family interactions.

BELIEF IX: ALL PEOPLE NEED A FAMILY

All children (and indeed most people) need to feel connected with someone who cares for them. This unconditional positive regard and acceptance from another person is critical for a young person's development.

BELIEF X: MOST FAMILY DIFFICULTIES DO NOT APPEAR OVERNIGHT BUT HAVE DEVELOPED GRADUALLY OVER THE YEARS

Although a situational crisis frequently is the catalyst for families to seek help, most problems in families develop over a protracted period. Consequently, change is unlikely to occur overnight. Families need to have an understanding of the need for long-term support during the process of change.

BELIEF XI: A DIFFERENCE EXISTS BETWEEN THOUGHTS AND ACTIONS IN PARENTING

At times, parents may feel overwhelming levels of frustration when managing children; they may even consider leaving their children or escaping from the family. These escape fantasies may lead the family social worker to believe that the parent is unloving or uncaring, but this is probably not the reality. Saying something or thinking something is different from doing it.

BELIEF XII: A DIFFERENCE EXISTS BETWEEN BEING A "PERFECT" PARENT AND A "GOOD ENOUGH" PARENT

No parent, even the most exemplary ones, consistently does the right thing at the right time. Parents may yell at their children, or they may sometimes fail to meet their children's needs. These actions will seldom destroy a child. Rather than being a perfect parent, the goal is to meet *enough*, rather than *all*, of the needs of the young person. The definition of "enough" will be modified over time, paralleling the child's evolving developmental needs.

BELIEF XIII: FAMILIES REQUIRE FAIR AND EQUAL TREATMENT FROM ENVIRONMENTAL SYSTEMS

Many minority families have not been treated justly or respectfully by society and its institutions. Historically, members of different groups have not had equal access to the same resources, opportunities, and systems of helping. We describe certain populations as "underserved." Social workers seek to equalize the imbalance between groups and to promote social justice for all families. Similarly, single-parent families or families who do not conform to the prescribed norms suffer when resources and support fall short of their needs, and the value base of the profession requires that social workers take a political stance to advocate for oppressed populations.

PRINCIPLES THAT GUIDE FAMILY SOCIAL WORK

The following principles equip social workers to emphasize family strengths and positive options in family work. They ensure that the foundation of the work conveys a belief in the family's capacity to evoke positive change.

PRINCIPLE I: THE BEST PLACE TO HELP FAMILIES IS IN THEIR HOME

The home is the natural lived environment for the family. Through in-home observation of family interactions, the family social worker is best able to assess the family. Interventions based on accurate knowledge of the family in their social context provide optimal opportunities for success. Family needs may require the FSW to be in the home for many hours a week, focusing on the family's daily issues and interactions. The FSW in the home can provide immediate feedback regarding alternative methods of interaction and problem solving.

PRINCIPLE II: FAMILY SOCIAL WORK EMPOWERS FAMILIES TO SOLVE THEIR OWN PROBLEMS

One goal of family social work is to help families become more competent. Providing immediate solutions may alleviate current stresses, but imposed solutions will not leave the family better equipped to deal with future issues. Families change by learning and practicing new skills. It is critical for the family social worker to be aware that a major goal of intervention is to promote family participation in change in a way that facilitates increased self-reliance and independence.

Families vary in their ability to cope with stress. Some families have strong coping and problem-solving skills but require extra assistance during a particularly stressful time, while other families require continuing assistance, perhaps from more than one agency. All families have unique strengths and weaknesses, and no family is completely lacking in abilities or strengths. An accurate assessment of the specific capacities of families should precede the design of the intervention.

PRINCIPLE III: INTERVENTION SHOULD BE INDIVIDUALIZED AND BASED UPON AN ASSESSMENT OF THE SOCIAL, PSYCHOLOGICAL, CULTURAL, EDUCATIONAL, ECONOMIC, AND PHYSICAL CHARACTERISTICS OF THE PARTICULAR FAMILY

Family social work begins "where the particular family is." This principle is true whether it is the social worker's first or twenty-first visit. Family strengths and issues must be continually assessed and evaluated to ensure appropriate and timely intervention. What is effective for one family may not work for another family with similar problems.

Interventions based on predetermined formulas do not permit modifications tailored to the special needs of a particular family. One of the advantages of family social work is its capacity to plan interventions that reflect the uniqueness of families. In fact, in the 1980s family workers were challenged to become more culturally sensitive because characteristics of ethnic families such as extended kin networks had been considered dysfunctional by conventional family therapy standards (Nichols & Schwartz, 2004).

PRINCIPLE IV: FAMILY SOCIAL WORKERS MUST RESPOND FIRST TO THE IMMEDIATE NEEDS OF FAMILIES AND THEN TO THEIR LONG-TERM GOALS

Hungry children need food; they cannot grow and develop on promises of future food while their parents learn a trade or seek employment. The family social worker must assess a family's immediate needs and see that these needs are met.

Maslow's hierarchy of needs is a useful road map for assessing and meeting the needs of children and families. Maslow (1968) outlined a hierarchy of needs, starting with basic physical needs such as the need for food and shelter. The second level of needs involves safety. Satisfying these needs involves protection from physical harm, including living in a safe neighborhood. The third level includes needs related to belonging. Belonging needs are met when one is accepted and valued by a group, the family being the first social grouping. The next level involves esteem needs, and the final level is the need for self-actualization. The family social worker first ensures that family members' basic physical and safety needs are met, and then works with the family on its other needs.

ASSUMPTIONS OF FAMILY SOCIAL WORK

Fundamental assumptions form the foundation of family social work. These assumptions include appreciating the value of *family-centered* and *home-based* practice coupled with recognizing the utility of *crisis intervention*. Another strong emphasis is on *teaching* families and children skills that promote new behaviors and create more effective methods of managing family relationships. Finally, family social work recognizes that families are embedded in a set of nested social systems that create both risks and opportunities to families, alternatively known as the *ecological* approach. We briefly present these assumptions of family social work in the following sections, and in more detail throughout the text.

HOME-BASED SUPPORT FOR FAMILIES

Mary Richmond advocated for seeing families in their own homes. Half a century later, Ackerman (1958) also pointed out the merits of home visits, suggesting that they provide a window on the emotional climate of the home, allowing the family worker to see firsthand the psychosocial identity of the family and its specific expressions in a defined environment (p. 129). Ackerman was particularly interested in family mealtime as a useful diagnostic tool.

Interest in home-based family work has reemerged over the last twenty years, particularly in the field of child protection. Conducting family work in the home provides some unique advantages. For example, home-based assessments of family functioning might produce more accurate evaluations of families than office-based assessments (Ledbetter, Hancock, & Pelton, 1989). In the home, family social workers can obtain immediate and direct information about family functioning and assess the relationships between family members as they interact within a familiar environment. Parents like the home-based focus of intervention. In one program, a parent stated, for example, "I liked the home-based services so my child could be observed in a normal atmosphere" (Coleman & Collins, 1997).

Advantages of family social work in the home do not stop with assessment. Office-based therapy operates under the assumption that changes made by clients during an office interview easily generalize to settings and events outside the office in the home and community. Yet, we now know that changes do not consistently or easily transfer from office settings to the home (Sanders & James, 1983). Some studies show that abusive parents do not transfer skills easily from classroom to home (Isaacs, 1982). When compared with an office-based setting, mothers and adolescents reported more home improvement in a group who had received home-based services (Foster, Prinz, & O'Leary, 1983). These studies are among a cluster of studies suggesting that interventions done in settings where problems spontaneously appear are more effective. Office-to-home generalization is facilitated when family work occurs in client homes.

Home-based services also overcome treatment obstacles such as lack of transportation and other causes of missed appointments. Offering services in the home has several additional advantages: (1) service becomes accessible to a wider range of clients, particularly those who are disadvantaged or disabled; (2) dropouts from counseling and appointment no-shows are reduced; (3) *all* family members are more readily engaged; and (4) the home is a natural setting in which interventions take hold (Fraser, Pecora, & Haapala, 1991; Kinney, Haapala, & Booth, 1991). However, caution should be exercised in assuming that *all* family members are more easily engaged through home-based services since others might consider them intrusive and an invasion of privacy.

Home and family are "training grounds" for children's later social adjustment difficulties (Patterson, DeBaryshe, & Ramsey, 1989). Providing family social work in the home, using a flexible service schedule, engages reticent family members more readily in treatment, a pivotal issue for family social workers. Additionally, entrance into clients' worlds where problems naturally emerge produces opportunities to capitalize on teachable moments and allows the FSW to respond immediately to client problems (Kinney, Haapala, & Booth, 1991). Families also value receiving services in the home. In some programs, for example, parents rate the importance of therapists coming to the home highly, highlighting client receptiveness to home-based services (Fraser, Pecora, & Haapala, 1991).

With the FSW working in the home, face-to-face contact with all family members is strengthened, an especially important consideration when involvement of all family members, including both parents, is critical to success. Total family unit participation does not always occur when families must travel to appointments at locations that are often inconvenient. Home-based family social work is also particularly effective in maintaining contact with isolated or impoverished families and families who are resistant to professional intervention or otherwise suspicious of service. Although home-based family work increases the opportunities to meet with all family members, it still may happen that a family member will avoid meeting with family workers by not being present when a social worker visits the home. In a later chapter, we discuss practical strategies for involving family members in the helping process.

Unfortunately, the issue of portability and transferability of changes is a "double-edged sword," since behavioral changes made at home face similar obstacles when applied in settings outside the home, such as school (Forehand, Sturgis, McMahon, Aguar, Green, Wells, & Breiner, 1979). High placement rates for adolescents with problem behavior attest to the complexity of generalization to different settings. Delinquent adolescents, in particular, are often influenced by peers and settings outside the family and become insulated from family and therapeutic influence as they grow older and develop greater independence. Thus, family social workers must also focus on settings where family members work and play, such as schools and recreational organizations. Additionally, early intervention when problems are less entrenched could thwart the development of more severe problems later.

FAMILY-CENTERED PHILOSOPHY

A central belief of family social work is that the family is the springboard from which treatment originates. In this sense, the family is pivotal to children's well-being. Family social work rests on the belief that every child has the right to grow up in a nurturing and protective environment. Further, family-centered work stresses the importance of understanding people's behavior within its natural context.

Considering the family as the focal point of treatment offers many benefits. Parents may experience problems with several children in the same family or have concerns about other children once a targeted child receives treatment. A family-based intervention can address wider problems beyond those presented by the target child. Through work with the entire family, parents learn to use what they have learned with the target child and not repeat the same mistakes with other children, thus giving family social work a preventative edge. Many families value the family-centered philosophy of family social work, as exemplified by the following comments from parents: "Worker put the whole family on a contract," and "[Worker] directed attention to the entire family. It was useful to keep the whole family perspective and value the family as a unit" (Coleman & Collins, 1997).

Changes beyond the target child are an important feature of family work. "Sibling generalization" involves bringing about changes in the behavior of siblings who are not the specific focus of family work. Given that teaching parents about child management techniques is a core feature of family social work, it is reasonable to expect that siblings will be affected by these changes. Logically, skills learned by parents can be used with all children in the family. Teaching parents to manage child behavior problems more effectively has the potential to produce changes in the entire family unit, making it less likely that problems will reappear. For example, one program found that when mothers decreased punishment for inappropriate child behaviors, fathers stepped into the disciplinary role (Patterson & Fleischman, 1979). This suggests that family structure adapts to incorporate new behaviors learned at home.

Working with the entire family unit has been useful in interventions with delinquents. Programs have shown that parents can use what they learned with socially aggressive boys for other children in the family (Arnold, Levine, & Patterson, 1975; Baum & Forehand, 1981; Klein, Alexander, & Parsons, 1977). Family interventions are premised on the belief that parents are effective and preferred therapists for their children and that a change in the family system can also affect the behavior of other children in the family. Such programs have witnessed a decrease in behavior problems of siblings by more than two-thirds, compared with behavior before treatment. Research also suggests that positive changes can continue for several years after services end. Declines in problematic child behavior beyond target child improvement also testify to the importance of family-based social work.

CRISIS INTERVENTION

Because of their immediate on-the-spot presence, family social workers provide crisis intervention during stressful family events. This is particularly important when interventions are triggered by the endangerment of a family member, such as by abuse or suicidal threats. Accordingly, the prompt and on-site presence of the FSW can reduce risk to vulnerable family members, at least until healthy family functioning and individual safety have been restored. During a crisis, the worker's intervention with the family focuses on problem solving and decision making, with the goal of resolving the crisis and helping the family to develop adaptive coping skills. Through crisis intervention, family social work helps members move beyond their collective pain to a point of renewed growth and better coping. To achieve these results, interventions can target concrete and practical problems experienced by the family.

Crisis intervention is effective in working with families that have a variety of problems, and under some circumstances it can be as effective as traditional long-term therapies (Powers, 1990). The dual aims of crisis intervention include immediate resolution of problems and adaptation to abrupt life events, and long-term skill building to reduce failure and maximize adaptation to future crises. Often changes made during crisis intervention remain intact long after services end. Family crisis intervention has been effective in preventing hospitalization for some children and contributing to shorter psychiatric hospital stays for others (Langsley, Pittman, Machotka, & Flomenhaft, 1968).

Unfortunately, social workers often believe that "more is better" in terms of hours devoted to a particular problem. This is not always the case, as some interventions have a "threshold effect." For example, spending fewer hours on a problem does not consistently result in less success. What matters to results is the clarity of assessment and intervention. This means that family social workers must not be overwhelmed by the totality of a family's difficulties. Instead, they must learn to partialize problems and deal with each of them on a prioritized basis. Each targeted problem will have a specific intervention. The family social worker not only deals with family crises but also looks at what led up to a particular crisis in addition to the long-term impact of a crisis on family functioning.

"TEACHABILITY" OF FAMILIES   Strengths

Family social workers often work with family members to increase skills that promote family harmony. Parenting and child management techniques are necessary skills that family social workers can help parents develop. These skills may involve a variety of methods, including (1) reinforcing effective behaviors; (2) helping family members deal with anger; (3) teaching parents how to track children's behavior; (4) using time-outs when family conflict or child behaviors become unmanageable or too stressful; (5) practicing positive behaviors by using techniques such as role-playing; (6) developing social skills for parents and children; (7) teaching relaxation techniques to help parents cope with stress and learn to self-nurture more effectively; and, finally, (8) developing parenting skills and child management techniques.

Studies support the effectiveness of teaching parenting skills to eliminate abuse and change children's behaviors in a positive way (Baum & Forehand, 1981; Foster, Prinz, & O'Leary, 1983; Wolfe, Sandler, & Kaufman, 1981). Abuse and behavior problems are two primary reasons for family social work involvement with families. Behavioral training for parents has also been effective in teaching self-control techniques (Isaacs, 1982) and changing behaviors of delinquent children (Webster-Stratton & Hammond, 1990).

Parent training to eliminate abuse and child behavior problems is built on observations of family interactions on a moment-by-moment basis. Family social workers need to pay close attention to patterns of parent–child interaction and help the family to change these patterns in tangible ways. It is noteworthy that families with abuse and conduct-disordered children show similar types of minute-by-minute interactions. Observations of parent–child interaction reveal ongoing interaction patterns within families, particularly repetitive behavior patterns between parent and child. In these patterns, abusive parents and parents of children with behavior problems communicate less frequently than other parents and use more negative and aversive parenting styles, ignoring prosocial child behavior (Patterson, DeBaryshe, & Ramsey, 1989). One component of parent skills training involves changing dysfunctional "molecular patterns" by teaching parents to respond positively to children's prosocial behavior, first within short time frames, and later extending into longer periods.

ECOLOGICAL APPROACH

Social workers and other professionals have begun to recognize the importance of understanding behavior within a social context. The ecological approach is especially relevant when working with families who are marginalized or disadvantaged. A family's social context promises both risk and opportunity. For example, living in a high-crime area where families do not know one another represents an ecological risk. In such neighborhoods, neighbors cannot watch out for one another and offer support during stressful times. By contrast, ecological opportunity is present in a close-knit neighborhood. When neighbors know and support one another, they are more likely to help a family in need. To develop a comprehensive understanding of families, social workers need to be able to identify potential sources of ecological risk and opportunity. They also need to be aware that the roles performed by family members within the family tend to parallel the roles they play outside the family (Geismar & Ayres, 1959).

A common error of social workers is to focus solely on the internal functioning of a family or its social environment, a split that oversimplifies a complex problem (Wood & Geismar, 1986). In fact, some work with families has met with limited success because all of the family's problems are attributed to patterns of family interaction. This leads to the limiting idea that only family interaction needs to be changed. Conversely, effective family social work involves identifying strengths and resources within both the family and the social environment, as well as assessing the match between the two. Family social work accounts for factors beyond family boundaries and focuses on multiple dimensions of family functioning that go beyond relationships and communication. For example, parental effectiveness is closely linked with the quality of the social environment in which parents raise their children (Garbarino, 1992).

Families live in relationship with their larger environment. Sometimes forces in the larger environment challenge survival. Social barriers sometime impede families from reaching their potential. Family social workers work with families in neighborhoods and communities to expand the material and social supports for families. It is a mistake to see families as single and isolated—all families are intricately connected with their environment. Every family is embedded within layers of overlapping systems and is affected by each of these layers. Family social environments are complex and dynamic. Recognizing the complexity of the interactions between families and their social contexts offers social workers a new set of conceptual lenses to use as they describe, analyze, and intervene. Family social workers must be comfortable with assessing and interviewing in the social environment of each family member. This assessment balances the strengths and resources of the family with the strengths and resources of the environment, examining mismatches between the two. The family social worker assesses family coping and recognizes the ways in which the environment impinges upon family functioning.

Even healthy families, living in oppressive or unsupportive environments, will eventually show symptoms of strain, despite their abilities and strengths. The need for intervention to span home, school, and the community and to promote give-and-take between systems is fundamental to the family social work approach. Building bridges between families and appropriate social support systems in the environment is therefore an essential ingredient of family social work.

Many resources are available within the social environment. These resources can include material or monetary supports as well as social resources. The social environment can be understood by looking at the availability of social support. Social support has mistakenly been identified as a source of dependence. An absence of social support might imply independence to some, although it usually reflects vulnerability and isolation. Family privacy and geographical mobility in our society have isolated families from sources of valuable social s support.

Significant people in the family's environment can provide support and feedback to family members and to the family as a whole. When social resources are adequate, crises can be averted (Berry, 1997), and when resources such as social support are inadequate, family members are more apt to display emotional distress or physical illness. For example, women with little social support are more likely to experience complications during pregnancy than are women who receive a wider range of support, and women who receive sufficient emotional and physical support during pregnancy are likely to give birth to a healthier baby. Thus, social support benefits not only women but also their unborn children. Helping a family nurture new support networks will not only optimize competencies but also help the family avoid becoming dependent upon the worker. By the time the social worker terminates with a particular family, the family members should have established skills and resources from which to draw later.

To prepare for work with families, we need to think about how families function within their social environments or communities. To complete this exercise, think about your own family and other families you know. List four social

TABLE 1.1 | EXAMPLE OF ASSESSING FAMILY ROLES AND
RESPONSIBILITIES IN THE SOCIAL ENVIRONMENT

Social Environment	Roles of Family Members	Responsibilities
Neighborhood	Parents:	
	• Adult	To look out for the safety and well-being of neighborhood children
	• Coach	To coach baseball team of 9- and 10-year-old children
	• Neighbor	To reach out to neighbors and provide support if necessary
	Children:	
	• Family member	To let parents know who their playmate friends are and where they are going
	• Team member	To follow the rules and help teammates

environments in which family members live, work, and play. Next, write down the roles and responsibilities of family members that might be associated with each of these social environments. See Table 1.1 for an example to help you get started.

Considering the environment of the family has direct practice implications for family social workers. Traditionally, family services consisted of interventions restricted to externally predefined needs of children and families. Outside authorities, such as public health, school, or child protection officials, decided what the family was missing and implemented remedial interventions to "fix the problem." These interventions frequently resulted in failure because workers did not consider the context within which problems were occurring.

Working within a comprehensive framework permits a thorough response to the needs of everyone. Families receiving services are often families under stress. Responding to stressors requires resources (Berry, 1997). An effective partnership between a social worker and a family addresses the family's concerns when identifying needs, priorities, and options for service. Developing individualized services tailored to the unique situation of each family replaces standardized interventions to which the family must conform. This approach respects the self-responsibility that family members should assume to obtain the services they need. Conversely, dictating a course of action does not encourage self-sufficiency, nor does prescribing a standard package of services for all families. *One size does not fit all.*

Although the trend is toward providing more comprehensive services, the family's right to negotiate services and to individualize interventions implies that not all families will desire or require a broad-based approach. Often, the FSW and the family negotiate a contract, specifying services to be provided. Social workers should be aware that some families might want help only with one specific issue (such as remedial educational assistance with a learning disadvantaged young person) rather than broader interventions. Broader services are not better services if they do not fit the unique needs and expectations of the family. The importance of formulating a mutually acceptable contract with specific goals cannot be overemphasized. The process of negotiating a contract is a key aspect of family social work and will be discussed in more detail in Chapter 9.

There is growing interest in providing early interventions for problems, before concerns become full-blown or unmanageable, instead of intervening only after the situation has become explosive or destructive. Prevention is preferable to picking up pieces later. Helping people learn parenting skills is more effective if done before, rather than after, an adult has abused a child. Interest in prevention is also reflected in the increased attention to early childhood stimulation programs as opposed to later remedial programs for school-aged children. Early intervention assumes two forms: intervention early in the life cycle and early intervention in the problem cycle. Family social workers do both types of intervention.

Another changing direction in family social work is the belief in building family strengths rather than responding only to deficits and problems. For example, programs for children with special needs are focusing not only on the medical needs of the child but also on helping families include members with social and developmental disabilities in the family's ongoing activities. These principles promote growth and recognize the need to consider the family as part of a larger community of extended resources.

The broad focus of the family social worker does not make decisions easier when he or she must set priorities for services or address conflicting demands within the family. Instead, a wide focus forces the FSW to consider the needs of all family members, not just the child whose problems may provoke the initiation of services. Based on these considerations, the family social worker must identify the needs of family members, decide how to best address specific problems, and locate available internal and external resources. Whenever possible, these considerations should be made in collaboration with the family.

CHAPTER SUMMARY

Families are social groupings that grow and contract depending on constantly changing membership. No family remains static. Family dynamics are shaped by how members define them rather than by a rigid, predetermined formula. Genograms and ecomaps assist the family social worker to understand fluid family dynamics and provide a visual overview of family membership, relationships, and environmental connection.

Effective family social work is contingent upon the application of a set of core beliefs, assumptions, and positive valuing of families and family social work. These beliefs assist the worker to develop competency-based, respectful interventions designed to promote collaborative relationships with the family. Through such teamwork, family social workers can help families capitalize on their own particular strengths and attributes. Finally, family social work is home based, family centered, ecologically focused, and believes that families are teachable.

EXERCISES

1.1   BELIEFS AND PROBLEMS

List some of your beliefs about families, parents, and family social work that will facilitate your work with families. Then, list some of your beliefs that might be problematic.

1.2   FAMILY SOCIAL WORK ROLES

List some roles in specific situations that the family social worker might perform. Alongside the worker list, make a list of some roles that you might expect the family to perform.

1.3   BELIEFS ABOUT FAMILIES AND FAMILY LIFE

List five personal beliefs (values, biases) about families and family life that may have a negative impact on your work with a family.

List five positive beliefs. Propose a solution for what you can do to adjust your biases.

1.4   FAMILY PURPOSES

What purpose (benefits) do families serve? List five purposes for its members and five purposes for society.

1.5   VALUE BELIEFS ABOUT FAMILIES

What values do you hold about families? List five.

1.6   SOCIAL MYTHS AND BELIEFS ABOUT FAMILIES

What myths and biases about families exist in our society? List four myths and four biases.

1.7   YOUR FAMILY DEFINED

Develop a definition of a family based on your particular family. How has the definition of family changed over the years and at what times has your family fit into the standard social definitions?

1.8   BELIEFS ABOUT HUMAN GROWTH

List five beliefs you have that support human growth in your work with families. List five beliefs you have that block growth.

1.9   Family Social Workers' Beliefs

Give examples of how beliefs of family social workers influence the development of interventions with families.

1.10   Family Status

How did ethnicity and social status affect your family? What particular family traits based on gender and social status were depicted in how your parents raised you?

1.11   Social Workers over Time

Make a list of the social workers who have promoted the family over the past century, providing dates, the name of the theory, and the specific concepts. Determine the unique contributions each has made to family social work. Next, make a list of professionals from other disciplines who have contributed to family theory, noting dates, names of the theory, and the unique concepts. What social work contributions have they used to enhance their theory?

1.12   Family Social Work and Family Therapy

Distinguishing between family therapy and family social work is an important first step in defining your role as a FSW and developing a focus. Both play equally important but different roles in helping families. List four of the goals and workers' roles of each approach.

1.13   Different Groups

Make a list of the different groups an individual might be expected to be a member of throughout his or her lifetime. List the similarities and differences of each group from that of the family group.

1.14   Family in Historical Novel

Recall a family from an historical novel. What does the novel tell you about the specific family form described in the book? Discuss in class.

1.15   Family Member Needs

Make a list of the types of needs that a family member might have and, beside each one, determine how meeting these needs might conflict with meeting the needs of other members and of the family as a whole.

1.16   Negative Attitudes

Make a list of six unproductive or negative attitudes that are not helpful to families. How do these attitudes hurt families?

1.17   CHANGING PURPOSE OF FAMILIES

Examine the purposes of families posed by Satir. What purposes seem outdated? What purposes are still relevant? Replace the outdated purposes with purposes that seem more relevant to the current era.

1.18   FAMILY OF ORIENTATION DEFINITION

Develop a definition of a family, based on your own family of orientation. How has your family changed over the years, and when, if ever, has your family fit the description of a traditional nuclear family?

1.19   WHO BENEFITS FROM THE TRADITIONAL DEFINITION OF FAMILY

Who benefits from the traditional definition of family? What power structures are maintained by the traditional definition? How does the traditional definition of family support these power structures?

Hint: A look at religious teaching might be a place to start. How do religions support the sociopolitical structures in society?

1.20   FAMILY TRADITIONS

List five family traditions that you believe should not change and five family traditions that you believe should change. Debate with your class.

1.21   CONSERVATIVE DEFINITION OF FAMILY

Conservatives claim that anything but their favored family form is detrimental to society. What is their argument about how alternative family forms hurt society and "legitimate" family structures? Counter their argument.

1.22   NOT A FAMILY GROUP

Give one example of a group that you do not consider a family. Give reasons to support your answer. Discuss in class.

1.23   SOCIAL POLICY AND FAMILY

Select one specific social policy. Does this policy support or hurt families? Who benefits from the policy and who is disadvantaged?

1.24   ADDRESSING DIFFERENCES

Break into small groups and answer the following questions:

1. How do I define myself racially and from a family perspective?
2. When did I first become aware of race/ethnicity/color in general? When did I first become aware of different family forms?

3. What messages did I learn about race/ethnicity based on that first experience? What messages did I learn about different family forms based on that first experience?
4. What direct and indirect messages did I receive about race/ethnicity from my family and friends throughout my childhood? Adulthood? What direct and indirect messages did I receive about different family forms from my family and friends throughout my childhood? Adulthood?
5. How did the messages I received about race/ethnicity affect how I thought and felt about myself? Others? How did the messages I received about family structure affect how I thought and felt about myself? Others?
6. How did I benefit from my race/ethnicity? How did I benefit as a result of my family structure?
7. How was I at a disadvantage because of my race/ethnicity? How was I disadvantaged because of my family structure?
8. How many friends from a different race or ethnicity do I have? How many friends from a different family structure do I have? (adapted from Laszloffy & Hardy, 2000)

1.25   HEALTH CARE ACCESS

Is access to health care a basic human right? How might life be different for people who do not have adequate access to health care?

1.26   THE IDEAL FAMILY

Describe the concept of the ideal family that is perpetuated by the larger society. When you were growing up, what did you think a family was? What contributed to these beliefs? Make a list of five families that you know currently and discuss how they support or deviate from the traditional definition. Which families fare better? Why?

1.27   FAMILY THEMES

Reflect on the area(s) where you grew up. What were the prevailing themes about the family in your community of origin? How do these family themes support or not support the "traditional nuclear family" structure we refer to in this book? Now reflect on one place to which you have visited or traveled. How does the concept of family from this other place compare with what you have grown up believing? What makes your concept of family the best one? What are the benefits of the alternative family concept to the local reality of that community?

1.28   A FAMILY BIAS

Identify one bias that you have about the "family." Reflect on this bias. What does this bias *tell about you?* Share your answer with the rest of the class.

1.29   THE "NORMAL" FAMILY

Describe a "normal" family.

1.30   WHAT IS "NORMAL"

Take each parameter defining "normal" and discuss in class how each might affect the belief about what is a "normal" family.

1.31   A SINGLE-PARENT FAMILY

Describe a single-parent family that you know. How did the single parenthood come about? What is the impact of single parenthood on the family (i.e., economic, social status, family identity, social perception, etc.).

1.32   CULTURAL DIVERSITY AMONG FAMILIES

Become aware of the cultural diversity among families around you. Compare and contrast different beliefs about the family as well as who is included in the family unit. Make a class list of your observations.

Changing a family changes the lives of its members.
—Nichols and Schwartz, 2004

FAMILY SYSTEMS

Family systems theory is the starting point for most existing models of family work. It is also the foundation upon which most other family approaches rest. Adapted from biology, it now offers a standard assessment and intervention framework with which to understand the functioning of families. Systems concepts have gained prominence in family social work over the past several decades. Systems theory helps workers understand the intricacies of family functions, how families relate to their environment, and guides intervention direction. As Satir notes, "Numerous studies have shown that the family behaves as if it were a unit" (1967). Watzlawick, Beavin, and Jackson take this concept further when they note that families are systems "in which *objects* are the components or parts of the system, *attributes* are the properties of the objects, and *relationships* tie the system together" (1967, p. 120).

Three main ideas form the bedrock of systemic family work:

1. Problems occur as the result of ongoing patterns of communication within the family;
2. Crises encountered by the family create both instability and opportunities for change; and,
3. Families function according to established rules that must be altered before problems can be effectively and permanently resolved.

While family systems theory provides a useful framework with which to understand family dynamics, it has limitations in how it explains serious problems where power differences exist, such as domestic violence and sexual or physical abuse. As such, feminists have criticized family systems theory for its inherent gender bias and how it discounts the importance of power within the family system. (These issues are addressed later in this chapter.) Others have also criticized rigid adherence to family systems concepts. For example, early theorists blamed family systems dynamics on the appearance of schizophrenia and autism. Often mothers have been singled out for their children's difficulties. "Schizophregenic mother" is but one example of the pejorative and blaming concepts put forward by family systems theorists. Moreover, others have criticized systems theory as being too mechanical, through the attempt to apply universal principles such as rules, homeostasis, and circular causality to every family. Nevertheless, we still see much benefit in understanding family systems as both a *metaphor* and a *framework*.

The family is a very powerful environment in which an individual grows and develops. Families are extremely complex entities, and without an organizing framework it is easy to become overwhelmed and confused with the information and behaviors that families present. Perhaps the most important thing that family systems theory has to offer is that it teaches us that families are organized in specific ways for a reason. It also teaches us that every family is organized based on predictable patterns. However, we encourage students to use any theory with a critical lens and avoid applying every theoretical concept rigidly or insensitively to every situation or case.

WHAT IS A FAMILY SYSTEM?

According to family systems theory, all families are social systems, and it is this belief that guides understanding and work with families. Because family members are interdependent, behaviors therefore do not exist in a vacuum. As such, family systems theory helps us see how problems originate from family relationships and transactions. Work is done with the overall network of relationships within the family. Thus, one of the key beliefs of family systems theory is that problems that arise in families cannot usually be attributed to individual dysfunction or pathology. Rather, understanding family dynamics will help uncover the family processes that seem to foster and maintain the presenting problem. Therefore, problems such as parent–child conflict, behavior problems, mental health issues, and so on develop within the family context.

When FSWs provide services to families, they must see beyond individual behaviors and understand the family context, which serves as the catalyst for the creation and maintenance of ongoing communication patterns, rules, and family relationships, and ultimately problems within the family. Thus, family systems theory provides a conceptual framework for assessing family relationships and understanding problems within the context of family functioning.

This central organizing belief is perhaps the hardest for families (and sometimes workers) to understand. We have found in our practice that many parents bring their children into counseling to be "fixed." They would like nothing better than to drop off their child at the agency and pick up that child later "all better." This does not work for several reasons. First, few problems develop or are maintained in isolation. When people live in close relationships with one another, they are affected by and affect one another. How people affect one another becomes entrenched in predictable *patterns* over time. Because these patterns become habitual, they usually escape conscious awareness of the key players. It is quite natural to act unthinkingly in our daily lives. It simply would take too much energy to be aware of every single response we have to those around us. While we expect FSWs to be aware of everything that goes on in a family session, we also realize that in their personal lives people often respond habitually. Wouldn't it be nice if everything people did on a daily basis were *intentional*? Carter and McGoldrick (1999) suggest that when predictable interactional flows are altered, "other family members will be jarred out of their own unthinking responses and, in the automatic move toward homeostasis that is inherent in all systems (discussed below), will react by trying to get the disrupter back into place again" (pp. 437–438).

Second, even if problems develop at the individual level, how people *respond* to the behaviors seems to keep the behaviors going. We also know that when problems occur, doing more of the same thing does not make them better. Families need help to get out of their entrenched ways of responding and make changes so that solutions to problems become more effective. Unfortunately, many people within a family have a hard time accepting that they are contributing to the problem. They have spent much time and effort being angry or concerned about the problematic family member and become defensive when the FSW suggests that they are playing a role in the creation and development of the problem.

In keeping with this belief, the FSW sees a family social system as a complex set of elements in mutual and constant interaction. When a family worker views a family as a system, the FSW conceptualizes a set of interconnected units. The focus of intervention is on how family members and subsets of family members influence one another, rather than on each individual's behavior. In other words, the behavior of one family member is intricately connected with the behaviors and reactions of other family members.

The key to working with families as systems is to understand that family interactions and relationships are reciprocal, patterned, and repetitive. Relationships are reciprocal in that family members affect one another. They are also patterned because over time, responses to one another become solidified and predictable. Finally, behaviors are repetitive because they occur over and over again in the same way. Through these reciprocal, patterned, and repetitive responses, family relationships and interactions become interwoven to create a complex but patterned family quilt. In the process, family social workers must understand how family life creates the backdrop for individual behavior, particularly how each member interacts with others in the family in reciprocal, patterned, and repetitive ways. The focus on family interactions means that the FSW looks first for *what* is happening, rather than *why*.

Michael Crichton wrote the following passage from *The Lost World*, which can help us understand the family as a system.

> It did not take long before the scientists began to notice that complex systems showed certain common behaviors. They started to think of these behaviors as characteristic of all complex systems. They realized that these behaviors could not be explained by analyzing single components of the systems. The time-honored scientific approach of reductionism—taking the watch apart to see how it worked—didn't get you anywhere with complex systems, because the interesting behavior seemed to arise from the spontaneous interaction of the components. The behavior wasn't planned or directed; it just happened. Such behavior was therefore called "self-organizing" (1995, p. 2).

Crichton's observations highlight the shortcomings of observing one family member apart from the others. Like the proverbial watch, the movement of the dial cannot be understood without understanding the various cogs contained in the watch. Similarly, behavior within families is interdependent, and one person cannot be understood by looking at his or her behavior alone and in isolation. The thoughts, feelings, and actions of each family member influence the thoughts, feelings, and actions of each other member.

KEY ASSUMPTIONS ABOUT FAMILY SYSTEMS

It is important to understand the six central ingredients of family systems concepts. Just as one person's behavior cannot be understood by looking at his or her behavior alone, family workers should also be aware that these six central ingredients overlap with each other. These six ingredients include:

1. The family as a whole is more than the sum of its parts.
2. Families try to balance change and stability.
3. A change in one family member affects all of the family members.
4. Family members' behaviors are best explained by circular causality.
5. A family belongs to a larger social system and encompasses many subsystems.
6. A family operates according to established rules.

The Family As a Whole Is More Than the Sum of Its Parts

Family systems theory, as a general framework, can help family workers understand the family as a social system that is more than the sum of the individual characteristics or behaviors of each family member. Von Bertalanffy, the biologist who first formulated general systems theory, suggested that when the component parts of a system become organized into a pattern, the outcome of that organization is an entity greater than the individual parts. No matter how well we know individuals in the family, we can understand a person's behavior only by observing him or her within the context of interactions with others. Families have a tremendous influence on how people develop, their identities, roles, and beliefs, and how they behave.

When the focus of family work is on children, FSWs can best understand them by observing the interactions within the family—how parents and siblings respond to them and how they respond to the responses of others in the family. Through this emphasis, the FSW develops a deeper appreciation of the patterns of family relationships. Thus, the child who is noncompliant with parental and family rules is not understood as a "bad" child. The child is acting out because of the patterns of family members' interactions both before and after the noncompliant episode. Getting the rest of the family to understand the child's behavior can be quite challenging.

Family assessment entails identifying both a family's strengths and problems. Assessment also involves understanding how the interactions of individual family members detract from or contribute to effective family functioning in general and the presenting problem in particular. Many kinds of individual problems either originate or are expressed through family interaction. Consequently, the challenge and goal of family work is to transform dysfunction into mutually supportive and growth-enhancing family relationships. Changed family interaction is both an end in itself and a vehicle with which to understand and address individual difficulties. The overarching goal of family intervention is to improve family functioning by promoting better interpersonal relationships and interactions.

What are the parts of a family system? Consider for example, a family where there are five children—four boys (David, Paul, Peter, and Steve) and a girl (Maggie)—plus a mother and father. The most obvious answer is that the parts are merely the sum total of David plus Paul, plus Peter, plus Steve, plus Maggie, plus mother, plus father. A simple answer is that there are seven parts or subsystems in this particular family. Yet, there are many other subsystems (parts) in this family beyond the initial observation. Subsystems might be identified by family role (parent and child), gender (father and sons, mother and daughter), possible triangles (father, mother, and David), etc.

Another way to understand how a system can be more than the sum of its parts is to think of how musical notes are organized in such a way as to make a tune. Separately, the notes mean nothing, but together, the notes are organized to create a melody. The combination of single notes creates a sound that has characteristics completely different from the individual notes in isolation or from a different combination of notes. Despite how much the FSW knows about individual family members, ultimately, their behavior is best understood through observations of family interaction—the family melody. In conclusion, the interaction of family members creates an entity that is more than the sum of the individual personalities.

FAMILIES TRY TO BALANCE CHANGE AND STABILITY

To survive and fulfill its functions and also to grow and develop, a family system requires stability, order, and consistency. The struggle to remain the same and retain the status quo is known as *homeostasis,* wherein the family acts to achieve balance in relationships (Satir, 1967; Satir & Baldwin, 1983). Maintaining homeostasis is a demanding and energy-draining process, although on the surface it might appear that the family is stable. However, under the surface the family is paddling like the proverbial duck (calm on the surface but paddling frantically underneath) to keep the family on track. Satir suggests that members help maintain this balance overtly and covertly (p. 2). Family rules help to keep homeostasis in check by determining which behaviors are acceptable or forbidden. Just as a thermostat in a house keeps the furnace or air conditioner operating to maintain a stable temperature, homeostasis works to keep a constant balance in the family. In families, the "thermostat" represents family rules (discussed below) through which families strive to function consistently and predictably. Some believe that families are self-correcting systems, although change typically occurs through feedback.

The concept of homeostasis was first identified by Jackson (Watzlawick, Beavin, & Jackson, 1967) who discovered that families of psychiatric patients deteriorated after the patient improved. He suggested that family behaviors, and hence the psychiatric illness, were "homeostatic mechanisms" operating to bring the disturbed system back into its delicate balance (p. 134). In addition, Ackerman (1958) viewed family homeostasis as vital to the family in maintaining effective, coordinated functioning under constantly changing conditions (p. 69).

Families struggle to maintain the status quo to preserve energy and keep things the same. At the same time, they encounter continuous pressure to change and develop in response to a changing external environment and the evolving needs of family members. Children, in different developmental stages, require different things from their parents. Behaviors that were once appropriate for a toddler are inappropriate for teenagers. When families have difficulty responding to developmental demands of children, they are said to be stuck. In the process of responding to such pressures, families must also locate a balance between conflicting demands for consistency and change. Family social workers should not assume that stability and health are interchangeable. Stability merely releases family members from constantly needing to respond to unpredictable demands, giving members the energy to function adequately in daily routines. As families progress through the different stages of the family life cycle, tasks differ according to the activities that are demanded to maintain stability and the activities that are conducive to development.

Homeostasis is a necessary state for families. Stability and predictability make daily life predictable and energy efficient. However, at times, homeostasis can hurt a family. Family crises, for example, upset the homeostasis of a family but after a while, the family will adjust rules, behaviors, interactions, and patterns as it adapts to the new situation. The arrival of a new child is one example of a family crisis. New behaviors are demanded of every family member to adapt. Eventually these new patterns become entrenched in the family and the family system adapts and settles down. Imagine a family that did not adapt to a new baby. What would be the consequences? What if a family did not adapt to death, unemployment, or other threatening family event? For some crises it is impossible not to adapt.

Because of the progression through the family life cycle and because individual family members are also moving through their own developmental stages, it is paradoxical that families must constantly adapt and change to remain stable. Nevertheless, families eventually develop a rhythm that enables stability and change over the life cycle of the family. Destabilizing crises inherent in each of these stages disrupt family patterns, making life both unpredictable and stressful. For example, each stage of the family life cycle contains a potentially destabilizing experience. Arguably, one of the most destabilizing experiences in a family is the birth of the first child.

Moreover, in certain crises or change inducing situations, family functioning seems more or less set. Yet, many crises are unpredictable or unavoidable. After a crisis, the tendency is for the family to revert to they way they functioned before the crisis. For example, if a parent becomes temporarily unemployed and remains at home, the initial stage of adjustment might be marked by crisis while family members adapt to living with an unemployed parent (who may also be depressed). However, after this temporary disruption, the family develops new responses and functioning in the form of routines and patterns based on the new set of circumstances. When the parent returns to work, the family may slowly revert to previous patterns of functioning. That is, the family returns to its "normal" state.

A family's typical reaction is to deny and resist impending change imposed by a crisis. Homeostasis is an important concept as it relates to the particular problem the family is experiencing since homeostasis built around a problem can remain stable for a long time (Satir, 1967; p. 49). However, it is important to remember that resistance is based on the desire to maintain balance and stability. Family resistance to change can be quite intense, as social workers who have attempted to challenge rigidly maintained behavior can attest. This is one reason why family work can be so taxing. The family worker not only has to deal with individual family member resistance; the worker must also address the resistance of the entire unit as well as that of the different family subsystems. Changes in family functioning may be difficult to maintain unless intervention builds in ways to ensure that the family will incorporate the changes permanently. Because of this, we know that families can experience distress or discomfort with new behaviors even when changes are positive, as when an alcoholic member stops drinking.

Resistance involves opposing or avoiding something that is painful. Because the need for stability is so strong, resistance to change by families is normal and should be anticipated. People may seek relief from anxiety, guilt, and shame through resistance. We have found for example, that many families resist the shift from identifying one person as the "problem" to framing the presenting problem as a "family problem."

In addition, the actions of the family social worker might contribute to family resistance. One important skill for addressing resistance is to know the right amount of pressure to use to avoid pushing family members too hard, and yet be challenging enough to move the family past its "stuckness" and problems. The family social worker must develop skills to enter the family's world unobtrusively and join with them in a mutual endeavor designed to address their presenting concerns. The task becomes even more complex when you consider that individual family members might see the "problem" in different ways. One view is to consider the individual with the presenting problem as the sole "owner" of the problem and hold this person to blame for the family distress. Another way to view the problem might be to see a particular subsystem as the problem, such as an overly harsh parent scapegoating a child. Nevertheless, it is a natural tendency of family members to view the problem as belonging to someone else.

Countering resistance requires skills to disarm and neutralize behavior as well as mutual willingness to discuss what is happening in the family work. Even an appropriate intervention may incite resistance because the social worker has asked the family to do something that either makes no sense to them or that they do not wish to do at that particular point. Resistance can be lessened when the family becomes more comfortable with the social worker, when trust has developed, when individual family members feel validated and supported, and when the relationship with the worker is empathic, honest, and genuine.

When a specific change is targeted, the family social worker's goal is to help the family determine how to achieve a new point of homeostasis. Talking to the family about change and stability might be the first task. A shift in family homeostasis demands that the family reorganize and devise new patterns of behavior and communication. For example, when a child is placed into foster care, the family will probably reorganize to deal with this loss. Remaining family members might step up to assume the various roles and functions of the child. For example, if a child is parentified (taking on the adult roles of one of the parents), another child might assume the role of caretaker for the younger children and even for the parents. In fact, reorganization is necessary since failure to achieve a new balance means that some, if not all, of the family members might not get their needs met, perhaps leading to family chaos, disintegration, or the generation of new problems to replace the old. Once a family reorganizes and locates a new state of homeostasis that is organized around the absence of the child (as when a child is placed into foster care), reintegration of the child back into the home might become difficult. If the family does revert to more familiar patterns, the reasons for the child's removal in the first place may not be addressed. The urge to reestablish stability and equilibrium ("normal family functioning") during periods of change is a powerful force that should be considered very carefully by social workers who are trying to create long-lasting change that continues after the social worker is no longer seeing the family.

The family social worker might assume an educational stance and, together with the family, talk about homeostasis and stability and how they play out in this particular family in a way that the family can understand. Connecting what you know with what is happening in the family could lead to an "aha" experience. However, it is important not to force families to agree with you if they see the issue from another perspective. The example provided in the preceding paragraph speaks to the necessity of ongoing work with families whose children have been removed but who authorities determine that the goal is to eventually return that child to the home.

Although it appears that families prefer equilibrium, in fact families are never static. According to Michael Crichton (1995), complex systems seem to strike a balance between the need for order and the imperative for change: "Complex systems tend to locate themselves at a place we call 'the edge of chaos'" (p. 2). The survival of a social system necessitates that it remain on the edge of chaos where there is sufficient vibrancy to keep the system alive. On the other hand, the system needs sufficient stability to keep it from falling into chaos. Boredom and chronic crises are equally threatening to a family, only in different ways.

In the same way, families are always changing. They may be unbalanced and stable at the same time. When families face pressure to change or adapt through an extended crisis, a new pattern of family functioning evolves, creating an altered state of family balance. This is a very important point for family social workers to keep in mind, as much family work is started because of a family crisis. The hope is that the longer parents adopt a new parenting strategy, the better is the chance that they will incorporate these strategies into their "natural" and "normal" parenting style after the social worker leaves. Similarly, it is hoped that new child behavior will remain intact over time. The threat is that if one side of the equation reverts to old patterns, the entire system will shift to the previous levels of functioning that brought the family to seek assistance in the first place.

The coexistence of change and stability is one of the most difficult concepts of systems theory to understand in terms of family social work practice. Often, social workers will view families either as stuck or as being in total disequilibrium (i.e., chaotic). Experienced family social workers appreciate the complexity of families, without being overwhelmed by it. They recognize that when families seem stuck or appear to be moving from one crisis to another, they may be maintaining either rigid equilibrium or chaotic change. Eventually, the family will need to adopt solutions that include a balance between stability and change.

Some family theorists suggest that presenting problems (often child-related problems) are primarily an attempt for the family to maintain homeostasis. However, caution should be exercised in seeing the homeostatic mechanism in families in this way, since it has been used to rationalize and justify a range of problem behaviors in the family such as sexual abuse and domestic violence. This thinking has served as an excuse for not placing responsibility for the abuse on the perpetrator. It has also led some to suggest that victims of abuse play a role in the initiation of abuse and that the perpetrator might even be a victim (see for example, Coleman & Collins, 1990).

Family homeostasis has implications for crisis intervention. Family social workers often encounter families that have experienced a destabilizing crisis such as a report of child abuse. Often the crisis brings the family to the attention of official agencies in the family's community, such as child welfare, schools, or the criminal justice system. Being aware of the usual tendency to fall back to "normal" (maybe even habitual) functioning after a crisis can teach the family social worker to capitalize on destabilizing periods by helping a family create second-order, long-lasting changes. The task of FSWs then, is to challenge families to move to a new state of balance by reorganizing patterns of interaction and creating new rules to regulate these patterns (Goldenberg & Goldenberg, 2000). In this way, the family will abandon past preferred states of balance in favor of new ones.

A CHANGE IN ONE FAMILY MEMBER AFFECTS ALL OF THE FAMILY MEMBERS

To understand families as social systems, we need to realize that a change in one family member affects every other family member (Bowen, 1971). Recognizing this tendency can explain a family's response to a member's attempts at change, as well as the response to the FSW's attempts to stimulate change. Satir (1967) observed that when early workers tried to change one family member's way of operating, they were actually changing the entire family's way of operating (p. 4). However, focusing on just one person in the family, usually the one with symptoms, places a burden on the one with the presenting problems. If one family member begins to behave differently, other members may resist this change in an effort to keep the family in balance. Some authors have suggested, for example, that when one family member's symptoms improve, another individual in the family might then develop symptoms. They call the person with the symptom, the "symptom bearer." Further, if the member changes successfully, the family will be unable to revert to previous patterns because of the changes. In other words, change in one part of the system forces change in other parts of the system. "In a family, if any person changes, his or her emotional input and reactions also change, interrupting the predictable flow" (Carter & McGoldrick, 1999, p. 437).

For example, if a parent yells at the children to complete their homework but eventually does the work for them, children may learn to rely on the parent's help every evening. However, if the parent stops doing the children's homework, the children must learn to finish their own homework, either by getting someone else to do it, doing the homework themselves, or suffering the consequences of not doing it at all. We see, then, that the family system adapts in response to one member's altered behavior.

We recall one humorous incident related to us by a friend who observed that when she and her partner were driving in the car together, she would always sit in the passenger side of the car while her husband drove. She decided to see what would happen if she took over the driver's side seat. She took the driver's seat and reached her right arm over the back of the seat as she casually drove down the road. She did not tell him what she was doing. Her husband's response was quite amusing. At first, he rode in the passenger seat without saying a word. Then he asked her what the matter was. A couple days later, he attempted to reclaim his rightful spot as the driver. This change was obviously too much for the man and he worked hard to revert to the original state of homeostasis! Her husband had no choice but to change in response to his wife's new behaviors. This example also shows, in a very simplistic way, how when one family member changes behavior, others have no choice but to change theirs.

While this example is seemingly trivial, it does highlight how difficult even the smallest piece of change can be for a family. It also demonstrates that when one person changes a particular behavior, others have to concomitantly change their behavior in response. It also illustrates the importance of first-order and second-order change (discussed in the section on family rules).

Family Members' Behaviors Are Best Explained by Circular Causality

As mentioned, families usually function in predictable and patterned ways. For example, it is usually the same person who feeds the dog every day or does the laundry. Patterns of communication in the family can also be predictable. We can accurately guess which child will do homework without coaxing or threats and which child will start to argue when asked to do something by a parent. We can also predict, with a fair degree of certainty, how a particular parent will respond to a child who is throwing a temper tantrum or refusing to comply with a demand. Many of these patterns fall out of the awareness of those performing them. In some ways, these patterns are habits that maintain family stability and homeostasis. They help make daily family routines and interactions predictable. While patterns are unavoidable in families, and even desirable, when they become hurtful or dysfunctional to individuals or to the whole family, they must be altered.

Bateson and Jackson (1974) describe the circularity of interactions as follows:

> ... where A is stimulated to do more of this because B has done this same thing; and where B does more of this because A did some of it; and A does more of it because B did some, and so on. This is the sort of symmetry characteristic of keeping up with the Joneses, some armaments races, and so forth (p. 200).

At the same time, communication patterns in a family are reciprocal and mutually reinforcing. That is, each pattern of communication, in the form of a transactional sequence, cycles back and forth between the two people involved. The responses of one person will influence the responses of the other. Eventually the responses solidify into a fairly predictable and patterned sequence of exchanges between two people. Thus, one of the first tasks of the family social worker is to look for and identify the *repetitive patterns* of communication within the family. These patterns are known as "circular causality." (See Chapter 9 for assessment and intervention with circular patterns.)

Most people think in terms of causation. Another term for causation is "linear causality." Linear causality describes the process whereby one event is believed to directly *cause* another event. For example, when a parent tells a child to do his or her homework, the child either does the homework as requested or refuses to do the homework. In the first example, the child is said to be obedient. In the second example, the child is described as "bad." The parent is doing what parents should do, but whether the child does the homework or not depends solely on the child. Looking at behavior in this way takes behavior out of context and falls short of putting the parent in the equation. How did the parent make the demand of the child? What can the child expect in terms of a parental response if he or she refuses to do the homework? How does the child make meaning of the parental request? What is the relationship like between the parent and the child? These and other questions can be understood once the sequence of exchanges is taken out of a linear context and placed within the context of circular causality.

Similar to the preceding example, temper tantrums often are viewed as linear events. Parents observe that when they say "no" to the child's demands, the child protests. This conceptualization of tantrums allows parents to call the child "bad" or "spoiled." Beliefs about linear causality allow other family members to disown or detach from the role they play in the development and continuation of the temper tantrums. Lineal explanations for behavior problems exclude an understanding of relationships, history, and ongoing communication patterns that start, reinforce, or support the particular behavior that is causing a problem. Ultimately, lineal explanations of individual problems attribute the problem to personality factors. Blaming personality factors relieves others of the role they play in the problem and also relieves them of the responsibility to change. Early on, Watzlawick, Beavin, and Jackson (1967) cautioned against taking a linear perspective, in part because the *punctuation* of the sequence places it in an individual context. "What is typical about the sequence and makes it a problem of punctuation is that the individual concerned conceives of himself only as reacting to, but not as provoking, those attitudes" (p. 99).

Conversely, circular causality places ongoing interaction patterns within a *context* of patterned family relationships. In working with a family, the social worker should look for circular patterns of interaction between family members. Circular causality accounts for how the behaviors are perceived and how members feel about the interaction. It also sets behavior as a response to the behavior of another person. Circular causality challenges the notion that events simply move in one direction, with each event being caused by a single previous event.

Circular causality, then, describes a situation in which event B influences event A, which in turn contributes to event B, and so on. For example, a parent shows interest in her child's homework, and the child then explains the assignment to the parent. This is likely to result in an ongoing circular and reciprocal pattern of interaction. The parent continues to take an interest and offer support regarding the child's homework, the child feels supported and rewarded and may make an extra effort when doing homework, asking the parent for help, thus reinforcing the pattern. The circular pattern is characteristic of ongoing family relationships. Rather than one event causing another, events become entangled in a series of causal chains. The success of circular interactions depends, to a large degree, on the skill and sensitivity with which both parties can understand and respond to one another. In problematic circular interactions, one or both members of the dyad has difficulty understanding and responding to the other person.

Family social workers will often need to become involved in altering maladaptive circular patterns within the family. Consider another homework example. A parent yells at a child to do her homework. The child interprets the yelling as a message that she is bad and a failure, leading her to feel anxious, creating difficulty concentrating, and ultimately leading to poor work on the homework. The parent, observing that the child is not concentrating or doing the work, interprets the child's behavior as laziness and defiance. In response, the parent scolds the child about her poor attitude and performance and the circular maladaptive pattern becomes entrenched after several repetitions of the cycle.

Several authors (e.g., Caffrey & Erdman, 2000; Koslowska & Hanney, 2002) also use systems theory and circular causality to examine attachment relationships within the family, particularly relationships involving the parent and child. In part, early attachment styles can determine the nature and quality of future adult relationships. As such, in the parent–child relationship, the behaviors of each member are both a stimulus and a response to the other person. Attachment behaviors can run in circular and behavioral and affective sequences. For example, a crying child typically brings out nurturing or caregiving responses from the parent. A child who continues to cry draws out further responses from the caregiver. Moreover, factors outside the parent–child relationship will also affect the nature of the parent–child attachment loop, such as stress or violence in the parental relationship. If parents in the family are unable to provide a secure environment for one another, it is quite possible that children's needs will not be met. Instead, the parents will be preoccupied with meeting their own needs. Caregivers can respond to child distress in a number of ways: they might respond to distress with behaviors that comfort, escalate the distress, or respond unpredictably. Parental responses help children structure and organize their behaviors and relationship patterns. In discussing attachment, we would like to remind you that both the expression and interpretation of attachment behaviors are partially determined by culture (Neckoway, Brownlee, Jourdain, & Miller, 2003), such that not all cultural groups assign the same meaning to an infant's cry nor do they share the same beliefs on what to do in response. Moreover, attachment theory has historically considered the mother as the primary caretaker, thus implicating her in a host of attachment disorders of children. For example, in the Native American culture, the child belongs to the family group, making attachment not just dyadic.

Over time, patterns of interaction among family members become repetitive and predictable. In conceptualizing circular causality, however, we must be careful to incorporate power into the analysis. Until recently, power was considered too linear to be applied to patterns of family interactions. However, just as certain components of a mobile are heavier than others, different family members exert more influence over others. As feminists have argued, power imbalances must be taken into account in understanding family relationships.

Figure 2.1 demonstrates how interaction unfolds in a family in patterned and regular ways. The circular patterns account for thoughts, feelings, and behaviors of two people that become engrained over time. Sometimes the interaction is between parents and other times the interaction occurs between parent and child. Some interactions are adaptive and positive. For example, when a person is hurting, another person might give support and affection. Positive interactions are healthy for family members and should be encouraged to continue. It is when interactions are negative and hurtful that family social workers should intervene. Pattern E demonstrates a problematic circular exchange between a parent and a child. Let us use the example of a teenager who is acting out. The teen and the parent are in conflict, and there is a lot of anger and resentment between the two. The teen might be coming home late and violating his or her curfew. This occurs on a regular basis. In response, the parent might be thinking that s/he is a poor parent and feel like a failure. The parent becomes depressed and angry (the two feelings often go together). Affectively (on a feeling level), the parent is feeling inadequate, like a failure, and might even feel rejected, hopeless, and powerless. In response, the parent's behavior shows irritability with the adolescent and yells at the child and has very little tolerance for the teen's behaviors, including the breaking of the curfew and anything else the young person does at the home. The parent might also ignore the teen. The teen, in response to the parent's behavior, feels anxious and unwanted, because there is little positive interaction between the two. The child wonders if s/he was wanted and does not think that s/he can please the parent. The affective response to these feelings is guilt, anger, and hurt. What does the child do when s/he feels guilt, anger, and hurt? Like many teens, the young person turns to friends who can meet his or her needs for acceptance and caring. S/he enjoys the company of friends so much and forgets to watch for the time, only to arrive home late and upset his or her mother. The parent, in response, feels angry and upset, thinks s/he is a failure as a parent, and feels inadequate, powerless, hopeless, and rejected. When the parent experiences these thoughts and feelings, the response to the child is to show irritability, yell, or ignore the child. The child views the parent's behavior and. . . . "What is typical about the sequence and makes it a problem of punctuation is that the individual concerned conceives of himself only as reacting to, but not as provoking these attitudes" (Watzlawick, Beavin, & Jackson, 1967, p. 99)!

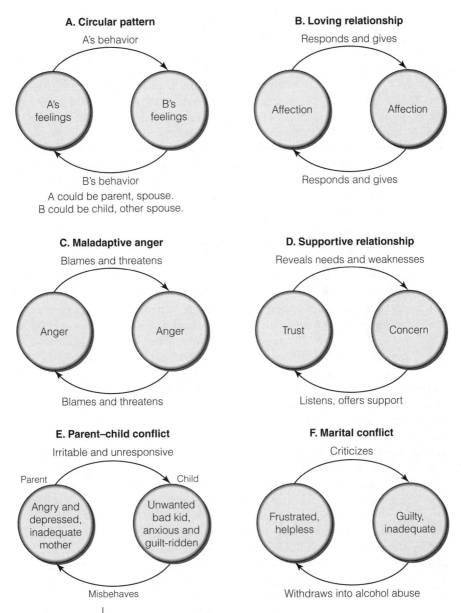

A. Circular pattern

A's behavior

A's feelings

B's feelings

B's behavior

A could be parent, spouse.
B could be child, other spouse.

B. Loving relationship

Responds and gives

Affection

Affection

Responds and gives

C. Maladaptive anger

Blames and threatens

Anger

Anger

Blames and threatens

D. Supportive relationship

Reveals needs and weaknesses

Trust

Concern

Listens, offers support

E. Parent–child conflict

Irritable and unresponsive

Parent   Child

Angry and depressed, inadequate mother

Unwanted bad kid, anxious and guilt-ridden

Misbehaves

F. Marital conflict

Criticizes

Frustrated, helpless

Guilty, inadequate

Withdraws into alcohol abuse

FIGURE 2.1 | EXAMPLES OF CIRCULAR CAUSALITY

A FAMILY BELONGS TO A LARGER SOCIAL SYSTEM AND ENCOMPASSES MANY SUBSYSTEMS

An important systems characteristic concerns the relationship between systems, subsystems, and larger-scale systems (suprasystems). The family system forms multileveled structures of systems within systems. Each subsystem forms a whole and at the same time is part of a larger whole (Kozlowska & Hanney, 2002). All living systems are composed of subsystems in relationship with other subsystems. Subsystems can consist of two or more relationships with unique ways of operating. The family is a group of individuals within a wider family system. The marital subsystem, parental subsystem, and child subsystem are all examples of family subsystems. Subsystems also can be identified within individuals—for example, physical, cognitive, and emotional subsystems. Family subsystems are often organized around gender, age, and power, to name a few. Commonly, the marital subsystem (the parents) is considered the "architect of the family" because it is (or should be) the most influential subsystem with the family (Satir, 1967). Therefore the success of the family is largely dependent upon the parental subsystem, whether it is a single-parent unit or two parents.

Larger systems to which families may belong include the extended family, the city, the neighborhood, recreational organizations, the church, and so on. These in turn are part of even larger systems, such as nations or groups of nations. The FSW will focus on the family, its subsystems, and the larger systems to which the family belongs. We call this the ecological perspective. Cultural blueprints from the wider society have a definite impact on families. For example, in families that are part of a larger patriarchal system, women and children typically have less power in families than men. The person-in-environment (P-I-E) perspective is a benchmark of good social work practice.

Environmental support is necessary for family and individual well-being (Garbarino, 1992). Informal support from friends and family is particularly important. Yet, formal sources of support dominate their support network of many families, and unfortunately, many have a pattern of negative interactions with the social service system (Kaplan, 1986). Too much involvement of formal agencies can lead to chaotic family functioning. (Ecological assessment is discussed in more detail in Chapter 5.)

On the other hand, a rich and diverse network of social relationships is a sign of maturation and health. For example, young children start out in a relationship with one significant person (often the mother), gradually relating to other children and adults in the family. Eventually, children incorporate other children and adults outside the family circle into their support networks. This occurs through school and exposure to others through family activities. Children, and indeed the entire family, are disadvantaged when their parents have a limited support network.

Individuals who consider themselves part of a family do so within the context of family boundaries. Boundaries are symbolic lines demarcating who fits within a particular system or subsystem. Boundaries should exist between generations—as in the parent–child subsystems. A *boundary* determines who is included in the family or subsystem and who is not. Family rules define who is and who is not included in a particular system or subsystem as well as how they are included (Minuchin, 1974). Ideally, there should be clear but flexible boundaries between the parental subsystem and the child subsystem. Boundaries around the parental subsystem are extremely important for the functioning of the family as a whole. Boundaries that are too porous around the parental sub-system allow information and behaviors to spill over into the child subsystem. For example, failure to create clear boundaries might contribute to larger problems in the family such as sexual abuse or the parentification of a child. The nature of family boundaries varies according to definitions based on culture and lifestyle. In Native American communities, for example, the extended family plays a central role in raising children (Pimento, 1985) and in-laws are considered part of the primary family unit (Sutton & Broken Nose, 1996). A boundary related to lifestyle could include a family where both parents have demanding jobs and have hired a live-in nanny. Live-in nannies are often considered members of a family.

Boundaries also determine who belongs to subsystems within the family. Some families have very definite boundaries, whereas in others the boundary between the family and the outside world is unclear. When boundaries between the family and outside world are loose, children might be exposed to sexual abuse by someone outside the family. This is because people are free to come and go and the children might be exposed to high-risk adults. The FSW needs to identify family boundaries in order to decide who belongs within the family system and who interacts with whom. Services most often target individuals within family boundaries.

Healthy families have clear, flexible boundaries that are open enough to assimilate new thoughts, ideas, and resources when needed, but sufficiently closed that the family maintains a sense of identity and purpose. Boundaries must be firm enough to protect family members from harmful people who exist outside the family. Ideally, closeness is neither overbearing nor intrusive to family members. Family environment boundaries should ideally be permeable and allow information and resources to enter and leave the family freely. In rigid families, these boundaries are closed, and no information enters or leaves the family.

Families with boundaries that are too closed or too open expose members to greater risk than do families with more balanced boundaries. As mentioned, families with incest perpetrators often have limited involvement with the outside world, allowing offenders to control family members, while communicating to the victim that disclosure is a betrayal of family loyalty. Friendships, particularly for the victim, are tightly controlled. At the same time, incest is a profound breach of intergenerational and personal boundaries.

Conversely, children in loose-knit, disengaged families may be at risk of sexual abuse by perpetrators external to the family because these offenders are able to move in and out of the family freely, and children may lack adequate supervision. Gender also has an influence on whether the abuse will be intrafamilial or extrafamilial. Male children usually have more independence in Western culture, making it more likely that they will encounter sexual abuse from people outside the family.

Boundaries governing relationships in a family fall along a continuum of rigidity or diffusion, known as disengagement and enmeshment. When family members are cut off from one another emotionally, they are described as *disengaged,* or not very involved with one another (Minuchin, 1974; Kaplan, 1986). In disengaged families, members share few activities and are not well connected emotionally. They may be overly independent and autonomous and disconnected from other family members, having little influence on one another. Neglect can be a sign of disengagement (Kaplan, 1986). Conversely, interpersonal boundaries that are too open and diffused are called *enmeshed,* and they weaken individual integrity and prevent family members from acting autonomously. Enmeshed relationships occur when family members are locked into tight relationships with one another, undermining individual autonomy. They may be extremely devoted to the family, sacrificing their autonomy for the family. Both disengaged and enmeshed relationships are signs of poor functioning in families. This is particularly problematic as children get older, because adolescents strive to be independent of their families. However, it is important to factor in culture and gender when looking at boundaries. When a male worldview is superimposed on family relationships, female relationships may appear to be enmeshed. Similarly, in some cultures family members might be quite close, and it is important not to label the family as enmeshed. North American cultures emphasize individualism and independence, which are often manifested in family relationships.

Boundaries between subsystems and individuals serve similar functions. Boundaries between generations are particularly important in family work. Boundaries between parental and sibling subsystems should be clear and allow for role differentiation based on appropriate development and socially sanctioned functions.

Most theories about families suggest that families should not only have flexible, clear boundaries with the outside world, but they must also have well-established intergenerational boundaries. In other words, the parents should be partners in parenting the children. A dysfunctional intergenerational boundary can exist when one or more children form a coalition or alliance with one parent against the other. This is common in divorcing or conflicted families. Similarly, families experience intergenerational boundary problems when a parent abandons his or her role and a child assumes the parental role. These children are described as *parentified* because the child assumes an adult role and the parent assumes the role of a child. For example, in families with an alcoholic parent, often one child steps into a parental role. If a child becomes primarily responsible for household chores, childcare, or for meeting the emotional needs of family members, intergenerational boundaries are breached.

Families with rigid or overly closed external boundaries restrict involvement of members with the outside world, creating difficulty in accessing external resources. To the detriment of families, Western culture values autonomy and devalues interdependence (Garbarino, 1992). "Self-sufficient" families may come close to imploding before being able to ask for and accept external assistance. In addition, social isolation can hide abuse within the family, protecting perpetrators from detection, placing victims at risk of ongoing abuse. Alternatively, families with loose boundaries fail to regulate involvement with the outside world. Individuals may slip in and out of the family indiscriminately, based not on family needs but on individual needs, regardless of the consequences to family members. Garbarino (1992) has noted that a positive orientation toward relationships beyond the family and even beyond the larger kinship group is important to complement or counteract the idiosyncrasies of individual family patterns.

Consider the following example illustrating a family's problems with boundaries:

> Gloria and Robert Hatfield, a Caucasian couple in their mid-thirties, were referred to you by Family Court Mediation Services. The couple was seeing the court mediator as required during their divorce proceedings for the purpose of establishing child custody, visitation, and support payments for their only child, Elliott, aged three. The mediator noted that Elliott seemed to be having difficulties adjusting to his parents' divorce, showing aggression toward his classmates and his parents. The boy had been expelled from two day care centers for hitting and biting the other children. The parents reported that Elliott's behavior ranged from angry rages to clinging when making transitions between his parents' separate homes.
>
> Mr. Hatfield initiated the divorce proceedings against his wife's wishes, though both report marital problems during most of their fifteen-year marriage. Mr. Hatfield reported that the relationship had been tolerable until the birth of their son. Prior to Elliott's arrival, Mr. Hatfield described the marriage as "two people going our separate ways." He said he and his wife had little in common, few mutual friends, and different life goals. After Elliott was born, his wife became very attached to the baby, and Mr. Hatfield reported having felt excluded by his wife. She wouldn't let him hold or care for the baby unless he insisted. Also, she breastfed Elliott until he was two years old, against her husband's wishes. Mr. Hatfield now believes his ex-wife to be angry about the divorce and especially upset that he initiated it. He describes her as "unable to move on with her life" and to be using Elliott to "get revenge" on him and "trying to turn Elliott against him." He reported that his ex-wife is overinvolved and overprotective of Elliott and that consequently Elliott is a "Mommy's boy, afraid of his own shadow."
>
> Gloria Hatfield denies her ex-husband's allegations, though she does report that they "could have tried harder" to stay together. She reports that they went to marital counseling for a few months, but that Mr. Hatfield felt it was not helping and dropped out. She said that this kind of behavior was typical of her ex-husband; that he withdraws emotionally at any sign of conflict and that he was "unable to establish a truly intimate relationship." She believes that now she is teaching Elliott how to have a close relationship. She is fearful that Mr. Hatfield cannot provide an appropriate male role model for her son. In sum, Gloria Hatfield feels her son's problems stem from her ex-husband's inability to establish an intimate relationship, while Robert Hatfield feels the problems originate from the mother's overinvolvement with Elliott.

A FAMILY OPERATES ACCORDING TO ESTABLISHED RULES

Family rules determine what is allowed and what is forbidden in the family. Rules also regulate family members' behavior toward one another (Goldenberg & Goldenberg, 2000). Most family rules are unwritten, and understanding patterns of interaction within a family allows observers to understand implicit (unspoken) family rules. Family rules typically guide what is permitted in the family, determining patterns of behavior that are acceptable or unacceptable. For example, all families have a power hierarchy and rules govern the nature of this hierarchy (Minuchin, 1974). In many families, both mainstream and minority, the male has the most authority in the family. Some families experience difficulties because children become more powerful than their parents. Families vary both by the nature of the rules they have and by the quantity of rules that govern them. A family with few rules might be chaotic while a family possessing many rules may be static and rigid.

Satir (1971) suggests that, to function as an open system, the family needs rules to allow it to meet changes head-on. The family will inevitably encounter three kinds of changes:

1. Changes within family members that occur between death and maturity in the use of perception of authority, independence, sexuality, and productivity.
2. Changes between family members such as between a child and parent, and husband and wife.
3. Changes that are demanded by the social environment such as a new job, school or neighborhood and so on (p. 129).

As mentioned, family rules act as a family "thermostat," keeping the family environment comfortable and stable. Because they regulate behavior, rules can become entrenched but unexamined aspects of family life. Rules also contribute to predictable patterns of behaviors and interactions within the family. It is through this predictability and the establishment of patterns that homeostasis solidifies within the family. For example, family members know who will make supper one night, who will put the children to bed, and how parents will react if a child breaches a family's rules about speaking out of turn. Without at least an implicit (unspoken) understanding of the rules, families would be consumed by chaos, not knowing who is supposed to behave in a particular way and how others are to respond.

Families often inherit rules based on adult members' experiences with their own families while growing up. Conflict might occur throughout the family's life about which rules will come into play in this new family. In addition, when two people get together, they might also blend rules based on their experiences together. Roles, for example, become established based on family rules, such as how children will be cared for, who does the laundry, who works outside the home, and how the money is spent. Because rules are value-based, understanding them will tell workers much about what the family believes. Division of family labor evolves over time, and children might assume distinct roles. Gendered rules governing males and females in the family, for example, will tell you a lot about beliefs concerning men and women. Understanding family rules allows workers to see how family members view their relationships with one another.

Family rules are established through diverse mechanisms related to gender, age, culturally linked expectations, personal experience, and so on. It is possible to change the rules once they become clear and explicit. A family social worker might say, for example, "It appears that in this family, females are responsible for all the housework." However, family social workers should also be aware that there are *rules about rules* that dictate how members interpret rules as well as how they change them. For example, in some families, talking about a parent's substance abuse might not be allowed. A family social worker might ask, "What rules does this family have concerning speaking about the father's drinking?"

Two types of change can occur within a family: *first-order* and *second-order* change (Watzlawick, Beavin, & Jackson, 1967). First-order change occurs when the behavior of one family member changes, but *rules* that govern the family remain the same. In second-order change, the rules are altered. Consequently, first-order change is likely to result in families reverting to their "normal" pre-crisis patterns. Second-order change, on the other hand, is likely to create more enduring family changes. For example, a family worker might encounter a family where the father makes the decision about where the family will go on vacation. Having other members make the decision will create first-order change. In this case, the behaviors of family members might change but the rules about decision making are not examined at all. However, if the family worker opened discussion in the family about how this particular family makes decisions, it would not be surprising to learn that the rule governing decision making is "the male is the boss."

First- and second-order change revolve around rules (Watzlawick, Weakland, & Fisch, 1974). First-order change involves merely changing the superficial aspects of behaviors and interactions within a family. It might involve something as simple as parents making a conscious decision to stop yelling at their children and their children, in response, making a conscious decision to comply with their parents' requests (so long as the parents do not yell). First-order change might mean that people do less or more of something, and this type of change is less enduring and less meaningful than second-order change. The structure of the family does not change in first-order change.

In second-order change, people develop new ways of understanding their family life. Second-order change has many dimensions to it and involves changing attitudes, behaviors, relationships, and rules about interactions with one another. This type of change essentially involves changing the structure of the family and, in the process, family functioning also changes. Once the rules governing behaviors and interactions within the family are altered, change is more likely to endure and be meaningful within the family.

FAMILY SUBSYSTEMS

As mentioned, family systems are comprised of many different subsystems. Perhaps the simplest family structure is the single-parent family with one child. This family does not consist of subsystems made up of other family systems, but does consist of subsystems based on age, role, and gender. The more components (individuals) included in the family unit, the more subsystems that exist. Every family member is part of a number of different subsystems. The basic subsystems include the parental and sibling subsystems.

SPOUSAL AND PARENTAL SUBSYSTEMS

The emotional health of children in a family is affected by the emotional relationship between the parents.

—Froma Walsh (1998)

Early family therapists recognized the centrality of parents in family functioning and child behavior (Minuchin, 1974; Satir, 1967; 1983). The parents perform critical roles that are crucial to family functioning. As a couple, they must learn to negotiate their roles and support one another. Many times the roles are complementary.

Given the importance of parents in the formation of the family, it is important to understand the circumstances under which parents got together. Satir, for example, suggests that when people get together because of low self-esteem, problems ensue. It is important to involve the child in the parental subsystem and at the same time ensure that the child not be included in matters that pertain to the spouses as a couple. Doing so requires a delicate balancing act.

TRIANGULATION

Triangles are an important family systems concept and thus need to be looked for by the FSW in the assessment phase. Triangulation constitutes circular patterns with a third person involved. Triangles appear when a dyad (two people) relationship is under stress and a third party, often a child, is drawn into the relationship to stabilize the situation. Triangles are not a preferred family subsystem because they do not allow the two people opportunity to deal with their issues (Carter & McGoldrick, 1999). They usually appear when something negative is going on and are often harmful to the well-being of the third party. All intimate relationships have the seeds of instability, and sometimes require a third party to maintain stability. According to Bowen (1978), triangulation occurs when people are insufficiently differentiated and when they are oversensitive to other important people.

Once children are introduced into the family, it is the parents who play the largest role in the behaviors, values, interactions, and so on within the family. The quality of the parental relationship has an enormous influence on the relationship among subsystems in the family. When the parental relationship encounters difficulty, many problems reverberate throughout the entire family. One of the biggest difficulties in families occurs when one child is pulled into the parental relationship. The child becomes triangulated. Triangulation often happens when tension or conflict appears in the relationship between two individuals. A third person (often a child) is then sucked into the relationship to diffuse the tension. The triangle is the foundation of the emotional subsystem.

It is based on the fact that the relationship between two people is unstable and, in order to stabilize, needs to draw in a third party (Kozlowska & Hanney, 2002).

The "original triangle" is the mother-father-baby triangle. The formation of this triangle lessens the emotional intensity of the couple dyad as the parents strive to meet the needs of the newborn. This basic triangle is necessary and functional. When it is functional, the parents acknowledge and support the child to have a healthy relationship with the other parent. Young babies require intense and selfless caretaking and this caretaking omits the other parent. The other parent is not threatened by that parent–child relationship.

However, at other times, such triangles become dysfunctional and problematic, particularly when the third person is used to allow the couple to avoid facing their dyadic issues. In this instance, a triangle develops into a "two-against-one" scenario where the third person is "sucked in" to reduce anxiety and stabilize the relationship. The third person is hurt in some way through this triangulation. Nichols and Schwartz (2004) suggest that triangulation prevents personal and open one-on-one relationships from developing. Problematic triangles occur when the difficulties of a dyadic relationship, usually the parental one, draw in a third party (Brendel & Nelson, 1999). Pulling in a third party helps create stability when there is conflict. Although they might create stability for the family, they also create problems for the family unit. In a problematic triangle, trouble emerges when each parent comes up against the other mate's wishes, trapping the child in the middle. "Each parent now sees the child as a potential: (1) Ally against the other mate; (2) Messenger through whom he can communicate with the other mate, and; (3) Pacifier of the other mate" (Satir, 1967, p. 37).

One classical triangle occurs when two parents are locked in conflict for an extended time. One child might develop behaviors or symptoms that draw the parents' attention away from their troubled relationship. One example is when the parents argue and the child jumps in and draws attention to him or her. As the tension between the parents diminishes, the behaviors of the child become more intense and entrenched, contributing to stability within the family. All of these behaviors happen unconsciously. Yet, the pattern must be interrupted since the child is sacrificed for the marriage through the development of problems. When parents expect the child to choose sides, the child suffers. In one program, for example, workers found that parents redirected their attention toward the distress, anxiety, and attachment needs of their children rather than direct hostility toward one another (Kozwlowska & Hanney, 2002). Thus, unresolved or masked parental conflict can disrupt and even damage parent–child attachments. For example, some research suggests that preoccupied adults are likely to have children with ambivalent attachment (Rothbaum, Rosen, Ujiie, & Uchida, 2002). Acceptable attachment behaviors in one culture can be inappropriate in other cultures.

Marital conflict has a detrimental affect on children. Perhaps the most important awareness to develop about triangulation is that a negative marital relationship is associated with a poor parent–child relationship. On one hand, the child might become the scapegoat, diverting parental anger onto him- or herself. Alternatively, the child might elicit other feelings such as concern and worry such that one or both parents satisfy their needs for closeness through the children. Some children are so drawn into the relationship that they comfort, defend, or distract parents during conflict. An extreme form of this might be when children develop severe problems to keep their parents' attention away from each other and focused on the child. We recall that in one family we saw, the family was so child-centered that the children all slept in a "family bed" with their parents. Once the children started demanding their own beds (a unique twist for sure), the marriage broke up.

Another common family triangle occurs when two siblings are fighting and one or both tries to draw in a parent. "Katy just hit me," is one example of siblings triangulating parents. Therefore one of the first tasks of a family social worker is to understand the presence of triangles, assess how they operate within the family, and make plans to help the family *detriangulate* when problems exist. Sometimes triangles can include previous generations, "whereby patterns of relating and functioning are transmitted over generations in a family" (Carter & McGoldrick, 1999, p. 438). McGoldrick (1999a) gives a fascinating account of the role of triangles in Freud's life.

Which child is selected to be the third leg of a problematic triangle depends on several factors, most of which are unique to this particular family. It may be based on a special characteristic of the child, such as a disability or a child that reminds one parent about another person. Other possible factors might include birth order, sex of the child, or age. Alternatively, the child might be a step-child, adopted child, or a child with special needs such as ADHD. It is important for the family worker to explore all possibilities on how this child came to fill this particular role in this particular family.

Family workers should also be aware that they can easily be triangulated into the family system. They may experience a pull to support either the parental subsystem or the autonomy and well-being of the child. Sometimes, workers might take sides with one member of the family. For example, if in the worker's opinion, a parent is too harsh with an adolescent, the worker might develop loyalty with the teen, colluding against the parent. Should this behavior become a pattern, we would not be surprised to see the parent refuse to participate in family work any more. To prevent worker blind spots from interfering with family work, family workers should reflect on issues from their own family of origin and anticipate what personal issues might blind them to the real issues in the family. For example, some parents, in discussing their experiences in a family preservation program, reported feeling resentful when social workers allied themselves with some family members at the expense of others. Forming an alliance with a child was often perceived as a sabotage of parental authority (Coleman & Collins, 1997).

Workers also can be triangulated into a family when secrets are shared in the absence of one family member (Brendel & Nelson, 1999). This triangulation is very challenging for the worker, who faces an ethical dilemma about what to do with the secret. On one hand, the worker is bound by confidentiality while on the other hand the worker is acutely aware of the impact of the secret on family functioning. Similarly, not sharing the information breaks a trust with the person who disclosed. Conversely, the worker might be colluding with family dysfunction by keeping the secret. According to the International Association of Marriage and Family Counselors, confidences gained in individual work are not to be shared without permission. At the same time, if these confidences interfere with family work, the worker might have to terminate work with the family (cited in Brendel & Nelson, 1999, p. 113). However, there may be circumstances where it is necessary to divulge the secret, such as in cases of sexual abuse disclosure. It is only fair to tell the informer that you have a professional and legal obligation to report this information.

The Sibling Subsystem: Fellow Travelers

In a big family the first child is kind of like the first pancake. If it's not perfect, that's okay, there are a lot more coming along!

—Antonin Scalia (www.Bartleby.com)

As siblings we were inextricably bound, even though our connections were loose and frayed. . . . And each time we met, we discovered to our surprise and dismay how quickly the intensity of childhood feelings reappeared. . . . No matter how old we got or how often we tried to show another face, reality was filtered through yesterday's memories.

—Jane Mersky Leder (www.Bartleby.com)

We think that the sibling subsystem is the most ignored subsystem in family literature. Yet, siblings are the first place where children learn to relate with peers. Siblings teach each other about peer relationships and cooperation. Adler (cited in Prochaska & Norcross, 2003) provided an intriguing analysis of the impact of birth order on child and personality development. For most people, the sibling relationship is lifelong because siblings usually outlive parents. In fact, the death of a child is a major family life cycle disruption that few families are adequately prepared to handle. Because of the centrality of sibling relationships in a person's life, some suggest having a sibling session without parents to gain an understanding of family issues (McGoldrick, Watson, & Benton, 1999).

Sibling relationships can be close or distant and conflicted. Some suggest that sibling conflict is the most common type of conflict within families (Straus, Gelles, & Steinmetz, 1980). Because sibling conflict might be predictive of later antisocial behaviors in adolescents, some suggest that developing interpersonal competence to improve sibling relationships is important (Kramer & Radey, 1997). Doing so will help the child in the development of both peer and sibling relationships.

Early writings about sibling rivalry fail to serve justice to the powerful bonds that siblings might experience throughout a lifetime. The nature of the sibling relationship differs based on a number of factors such as age, gender, physical challenges, and sexual orientation, to name a few (McGoldrick, Watson, & Benton, 1999). For example, children who are close in age share similar family life cycle issues, while children in families with a wide spread in children's ages might have very divergent experiences. In addition, we hear much about the destinies of older versus younger children in the family. For example, older children might be leaders while younger children are more pampered. Moreover, with the declining birth rate, families with single children are becoming more common. Some suggest that only children are more adult oriented and their challenge is to learn to relate to peers (McGoldrick, Watson, & Benton, 1999).

Although some cultures prefer male children over female children, families with female children derive much benefit (McGoldrick, Watson, & Benton, 1999). In large families, older female children are likely to assume caretaking responsibility for younger siblings.

When a problematic triangle involving one of the siblings emerges in the family, it is important to remember that when one child has a "problem," this problem will affect every other member of the family. In many ways, when there is a dysfunctional parent-parent-child triangle, this triangle receives most of the attention from the family worker. At the same time, other children in the family might be ignored. This is a mistake! Other children in the family have special needs when their family is suffering and ignoring them during this time is a problem. It is our experience that when one sibling is in pain, the other children react to that pain. We recall a family where the father was sexually abusing the oldest sister. The worker met individually with the other children in the family and was very touched by the sensitivity and concerns of each of these children about what was happening in their family. Moreover, when the worker asked one child, "What do you worry about?" the child disclosed a litany of worries about his family that kept him awake and crying every night. No one had thought to ask him what he was going through up until that point. He related worries about his sister, his mother, his other siblings, his father, and the family as a whole, and felt very much alone with his heartaches.

FAMILY SYSTEM DISRUPTIONS

It is rare for a family to go through its entire cycle with no disruption. Death, divorce, separation, mental illness, chronic illness, and disability are but six examples of how a family's life course might be unique. With every disruption, it is important to find out how members of the family coped as well as what happened to the marriage at each critical point.

For example, the birth of a disabled child poses many challenges to the family system. Both the nature and severity of the disability determine the impact on the family unit as well as the ability of the family to cope with the challenges. The birth of a disabled child affects both parents and siblings. At the best of times, the birth of a child places the family in a state of disequilibrium. However, the extra emotional, physical, and financial demands of a disabled child create additional burdens on the entire family unit, producing a crisis situation as family members scramble to reestablish homeostasis. The arrival of a disabled child into a family is usually unplanned, and parents experience stress and disruption on many levels. Parents might place additional demands on other children in the family to assist with caretaking, although caretaking expectations vary widely from family to family. "Small families tend to experience more pressure when there is a handicapped child because there are fewer siblings to share the responsibility" (McGoldrick, Watson, & Benton, 1999, p. 148). Age and gender influence the expectations placed on other children in the family. At times, families must struggle with institutionalizing the disabled child. If the child remains at home, parents must then decide what happens during the "launching" phase. Should the child remain with the parents for life? If this is the case, what happens when the parents die? Alternatively, parents might struggle with placing the disabled child in a group home or institution when the child reaches adulthood or even earlier.

Death is another family disruption that leaves "a hole in the fabric of family life . . . and disrupts established patterns of interaction" (Walsh, 1998, p. 187). In the words of Froma Walsh (1998), "the ability to accept loss is at the heart of all skills in healthy family systems" (p. 178). When a family member dies, the system experiences a major upheaval as members maneuver to adapt to the loss. Some loss is expected, as in the death of an elderly parent or grandparent. Other losses, such as the death of a child or a young spouse, are unexpected and might prolong mourning (McGoldrick & Walsh, 1999). When a family member dies, homeostasis is threatened as others attempt to fill the void left by the departed member. McGoldrick and Walsh suggest paying special attention when the birth of a child or a marriage coincides with death, because it may interfere with parenting or assume a replacement function. Family adaptation is also difficult if the deceased member was the breadwinner or filled an otherwise central instrumental or affective role in the family. When the loss is a child, the marital relationship becomes particularly vulnerable (p. 141). Women typically outlive men, making widowhood for many a grim reality.

Death through suicide has long-lasting repercussions within the family. Suicide demands that surviving family members develop individual interpretations of the act. At the same time, they must renegotiate ongoing relationships with surviving family members. One important aspect of family reorganization is the need to recognize and respect differences in grief reactions and coping styles within the family, which can produce a lack of synchronicity in grieving. A challenge for adult survivors is to understand "why." The search for meaning is one element of children's grief, but not the central agonizing and organizing theme for child survivors. Children also worry about losing the surviving parent and may feel personally responsible for the suicide. Family members may find themselves out of step with one another as they seek to regain personal and family balance. In addition, interpersonal tension and marital discord may result from grief incongruence between the surviving adult partners. Funeral rituals vary according to culture, and FSWs should investigate what they are and what death means to a family (Barlow & Coleman, 2004; Barlow & Coleman, 2003).

Alcohol problems also cause disruption in a family system. It is a particularly difficult disruption to deal with because denial is a major issue (Hudak, Krestan, & Bepko, 1999). Alcoholism is a progressive disease that usually ends in either abstinence or death, affecting between 10 and 15 percent of the population (p. 456). It is impacted by gender, race, amount of reinforcement one receives for drinking, and a host of other sociodemographic factors. Hudak and colleagues provide some insight into the presence of addiction in the family, noting that family boundaries may be too rigid or diffuse. There may also be some role reversal wherein a child is parentified by stepping in and assuming the role of the disabled caretaker. When alcoholism is advanced, the family may become socially isolated from extended kin and from the community. The authors suggest asking in assessment the basic question, "How much pain has been caused by drinking?" (p. 459). This pain can be far reaching and include such difficulties as unemployment, illness, marital conflict, domestic violence, depression, sexual, physical, and/or emotional abuse, and so on. Specialized services to treat alcoholism can be useful, and it is important to remember that denial can and usually does affect every family member. Despite the pain and family upheaval caused by the alcoholism, it may be difficult for the addicted member to admit to the problem. We refer the reader to the Stages of Change model developed by Prochaska and DiClemente as a source of understanding the denial on the part of the alcoholic and developing some options about how to handle alcoholics who do not believe they have a problem. Over time, family patterns become set and organized around the addiction. Therefore, intervention is necessary even after the alcoholic member stops drinking so the family can address family dynamics that have become solidified around the problematic drinking. Hudak and colleagues warn that early sobriety may be a difficult time for the entire family.

Immigration is another disruption in family relationships, particularly when immigration occurs in a step fashion, with one adult immigrating and getting established before sending for the other remaining family members. Children in particular can feel the impact of family disruption. Immigrant families are in constant flux as they must constantly reorganize to accommodate the loss and gain of family members. In addition, relationships may be marked by several responses such as grief, guilt, and detachment as the family proceeds through the process.

MULTIGENERATIONAL TRANSMISSION OF PATTERNS

Murray Bowen (1978) formulated ideas to capture how families transmit values, beliefs, and behaviors from one generation to another. He was particularly interested in the historical context of family patterns as they are passed down from one generation to another. In particular, Bowen was concerned with family patterns over several generations such that children grow up and marry partners with similar levels of differentiation to themselves (Piercy & Sprenkle, 1986).

Genograms (discussed in Chapter 5) have the unique capability of capturing these intergenerational patterns. Bowen determined that patterns occur over several generations. He believed that learning in a family over generations plays a role in the development of symptoms. Bowen (1978) believed that multigenerational relationship patterns of reciprocal functioning between spouses and child focus were associated with the same patterns in the nuclear family—and that symptoms were reproduced in the areas of physical, emotional, and social realms. For example, the quality of infants' attachments to their mothers is related to the dynamics observed in the grandmother–mother relationship (Krechmar & Jacobvitch, 2002).

The core of Bowen's theory is differentiation of self. Differentiation of self affects key family relationships. Differentiated people are able to maintain a psychological separation from others, separate the emotions and the intellect, and have independence of self from others. The more one is differentiated, the easier it is to avoid being drawn into the dysfunctional patterns of other family members. In all families, members develop on a continuum based on differentiating the self, and the degree of differentiation is determined, in part, by the relationship patterns in a particular family. People are attracted to partners who have similar levels of differentiation and these levels of differentiation are reproduced over multiple generations. High levels of differentiation are preferable to low levels of differentiation. "The multigenerational transmission concept" is that the roots of the most severe human problems as well as the highest levels of human adaptation are generations deep (Bowen, 1978).

CHAPTER SUMMARY

The family systems approach allows the FSW to assess a family within the context of interactions and relationships. The systems approach complements the developmental approach. The developmental approach considers stages in the family's life cycle. With a systems perspective, relationships at each stage of the family life cycle are the focus of assessment.

From a systems view, the social worker focuses on the family as a whole, rather than on individual family members. The family is seen as trying to achieve a balance between change and stability. Change that affects one member affects the whole family. Causality is "circular" rather than linear. The family system includes many subsystems and also is part of larger suprasystems.

EXERCISES

2.1 FAMILY RULES

As mentioned in this chapter, all families are governed by a set of unspoken rules. Identify the rules of your family as you were growing up. You may want to break down the rules by key components such as age and gender.

2.2   FAMILY HOMEOSTASIS

In reflecting back on your family of origin, try to recall a couple of crisis situations. Describe one situation where the family reverted to homeostasis. Describe another crisis where the family did not revert to homeostasis quickly. Compare the differences between the two.

2.3   FAMILY SUBSYSTEMS

Identify the family subsystems in your family of origin. Describe the nature of the boundaries between these subsystems, such as enmeshed or disengaged.

2.4   UNDERSTANDING FAMILY SYSTEMS

Take time to reflect on your family when you were growing up and try to understand your family of origin as a family system. The following questions will guide your understanding:

List the members of your family system.

Identify family subsystems in your family. How were they divided: generation, gender, interests, and functions?

Describe the family boundaries using an open to closed continuum.

Describe family relationships.

Describe the informal and formal roles assumed by each member of your family. Account for role conflicts and role clarity in this family.

What cultural influences affected the family and how would you described them?

2.5   APPLYING THEORY CORRECTLY

Given the criticisms about family systems, which of the following statements do you most agree with:

1. I should apply the theory to the case.
2. I should apply the case to the theory.

Discuss the difference in class. Give some examples of where you have seen each happen.

2.6   ROLE-PLAY

Break into groups of six. One person will play the role of family social worker to interview a family where a teen-aged child has been charged with possession of drugs (marijuana). The family consists of Katie (mother), Bobbie (father), Phil (14-year-old charged with drug possession), Jackie (16-year-old perfect daughter), and Jimmy (a typical 8-year-old). The court has ordered the family into therapy. All family members are angry with Phil for putting the family through this turmoil. Family members do think that they play a role in the problem.

Role-play this family with the goal of defining the problem as a family issue that each member owns a piece of. Stop when you reach your goal. Share with the rest of the class what happened in your role-play and give the class advice about how you shifted the emphasis from Phil to the entire family unit.

2.7 More Than the Sum of Its Parts?

What are the parts of a family system? Consider for example, a family where there are five children—four boys (David, Paul, Peter, and Steve) and a girl (Maggie)—plus a mother and father. The most obvious answer is that the parts are merely the sum total of David plus Paul, plus Peter, plus Steve, plus Maggie, plus mother, plus father. A simple answer is that there are seven parts or subsystems in this particular family. Yet, there are many other subsystems (parts) in this family beyond the initial observation. Subsystems might be identified by family role (parent and child), gender (father and sons, mother and daughter), possible triangles (father, mother, and David), etc.

Examine the family described in this exercise. Map out all the potential subsystems in this family. How do these various subsystems support the belief that the family is more than the sum of its parts?

2.8 Crises and Stability

Select three possible unpredictable family crises that might threaten the stability in a family. How would each of these crises affect family stability? What might a family do to try to reestablish stability?

2.9 Positive Change and Family Stability

Identify one positive change in a family. Beside this change, speculate on how the positive change might disrupt family stability. Compare your answer in class.

2.10 Family Work with a Missing Member

What are the pros and cons of doing family work with families whose children have been removed from family care? What are the implications of family homeostasis in doing family work with high-risk families such as those with child welfare concerns, mental health issues, or substance abuse?

2.11 Predictable Patterns

Identify a predictable pattern in a social relationship you have. The relationship might be in a classroom, board meeting, or work setting. Without telling the other person(s), do something entirely different. Continue the new behavior for several days, noting the reactions of people around you. Report back to the class. How did other people change in response to what you did? How did they attempt to get the patterns back to the original state?

2.12   PREDICATBLE PATTERN CHANGE

Select one of your intimate relationships, preferably within a family context. The relationship should be one that has been established long enough for predictable patterns to emerge. Identify one of your predictable behaviors and then do the opposite for one day. Select a behavior that is not threatening to the other person, but be as ridiculous as you want. How did other people in your system respond to your new behaviors? What kind of pressure did you experience to revert to your original behavior? How did the others respond when you changed your behavior? Discuss the differences in responses between Exercises 2.11 and 2.12. What difference does closeness and intimacy make in terms of the responses to your behaviors?

2.13   FIRST- AND SECOND-ORDER CHANGE

Given the example in Exercise 2.12, give another example of what first- and second-order change in this family might entail. How would a FSW approach this family to institute second-order change?

2.14   FAMILY RULES

Unspoken rules regulate all families. Identify some rules from the family in which you grew up. Describe how the rules differed according to age and gender of family members. Think of other family rules not related to age or gender. What were these rules? What rules have you brought from your family that are very important to you but that might conflict with the rules that another person might bring into a relationship with you?

2.15   WORKER ISSUES

All family workers have personal issues from their family of origin that they bring to family work. One key to effective family work is to be aware of these issues and stop them from playing out in family work. Issues might include having a parent who was an alcoholic, history of sexual abuse, having turbulent teen years, etc. Reflect on your family of origin and list three or four issues from your past that might interfere with family work. Beside each issue, speculate on how this issue might play out in your work with families and then what you can do about your natural response. This can be a very personal issue, so do not feel compelled to share your responses with the rest of the class. However, if one or two members of the class are willing to share their responses, it might be useful for the rest of the class to hear about and discuss them.

Practical Aspects of Family Social Work

CHAPTER 3

CHAPTER CONTENTS

Pr
First meeting
assessing clients needs

There are many practical considerations involved in family social work. In this chapter we look at some of these "nuts-and-bolts" topics. We discuss the importance of adhering to a regular schedule for family meetings while remaining flexible enough to accommodate unforeseen events. Suggestions are offered for the preparation and care of materials used by FSWs. We discuss how to decide whether to include children in family meetings, and we provide tips for handling disruptions and maintaining contact with families who move frequently. Safety issues are addressed. Within the context of the first family meeting, we introduce the topics of assessing a family's needs and engaging family members in the helping process. Finally, we describe ways to orient clients to family social work and to protect clients' confidentiality.

REFERRAL PROCESS

Families can be referred to family social workers through a number of ways. First, families might refer themselves after hearing about the service and deciding they need assistance. Second, families might be referred by another agency that believes your agency will meet the family's needs more appropriately. Finally, families might be involuntarily mandated by the courts to receive services from your agency.

SCHEDULING FAMILY MEETINGS

Prior to the first home visit with a family, the FSW needs to accomplish the following tasks:

1. Determine the overall purpose of the meeting;
2. Outline specific issues to be addressed during the meeting;
3. Contact a family member to set up the meeting;
4. Locate the family's home;
5. Decide how much time should be allotted for the first meeting.

Adhering to a schedule benefits both the FSW and the family. Changes in the schedule are almost inevitable, but establishing a proposed timetable for visits helps promote steady progress toward the family's goals. Weekly appointments are usually sufficient, but frequency of meetings depends on the goals and needs of individual families. Time for related responsibilities such as meetings with colleagues and supervisors, community liaison and advocacy, documenting, and other related tasks must be worked into the FSW's schedule.

The schedule for family meetings may have to be changed because of unexpected events that are beyond the control of either the family or the social worker. FSWs must develop sufficient psychological flexibility to adapt to changes in plans without excessive distress. A useful tip is to plan carefully but to expect that circumstances may interfere with the execution of these plans. Attention to scheduling is especially important given that FSWs must meet the needs of all the families assigned to them.

Setting Up the First Appointment

In most cases, the social worker's initial contact with the family will be a telephone call to arrange the first meeting. For families who are unreachable by telephone, the FSW will need to write a letter of introduction or drive to the home to make the initial contact.

During the telephone call or visit, both the FSW and the family develop first impressions of one another (Goldenberg & Goldenberg, 2000). The social worker develops an impression of the family's readiness to work and a picture of how family members view the problem. From the family's perspective, first impressions are also important. Clients usually prefer a family social worker who is warm and understanding and who conveys hope and competence. The social worker must be careful not to get caught up in one person's view of the problem (Nichols & Schwartz, 2004).

During the initial contact, the FSW makes an appointment to meet with the family for the first time. For this purpose, many social workers prefer to meet with as many family members as possible. At times, clients may try to exclude family members from this first appointment. They may ask that the social worker see only the child with the problem, or they might try to exclude other family members such as the father or children who do not have a "problem." The general rule is to include as many family members as possible in the first appointment because the number of family members present at the first session affects who will be involved in future sessions (Brock & Barnard, 1992). The social worker can also suggest that the presence of as many family members as possible will help him or her understand the problem more fully and that the presence of the entire family is important because the problem affects everyone.

Allowing for Travel Time

When scheduling home visits, the FSW should be sure to allow enough time to become familiar with the environment and should arrive on time at the family home. If time permits, the FSW may choose to make a trial run to a family's home before the first appointment to determine how much time is needed to arrive at the destination, the fastest routes, and issues related to parking safety. A practice run will ensure a timely arrival for the first family meeting. It will also orient the worker to the family's environment.

Traffic patterns, construction delays, bridge openings and closures, one-way streets, and similar situations that affect travel time should be considered when planning the schedule. A current city or county map is a simple but necessary tool for family social workers.

Within an agency, the distance between families' homes is often the main criterion for assigning cases to social workers. To reduce travel time, supervisors of programs that cover large catchment areas may assign family social workers to cases based on geographic location. This practice may not be as desirable as assigning workers based on the best match with family needs, but it acknowledges the impact of travel time on work load planning. Allowing sufficient time between family meetings ensures that a delay in completing one meeting will not result in subsequent delays for meetings with other families. Mileage sheets can be kept on a clipboard in the social worker's car and filled in immediately after every trip.

Many programs require the social worker to document each meeting before beginning the next one. Thus, time and location for accomplishing this task should be considered when setting the daily schedule. Family social workers, searching for suitable places to complete documentation, often become regulars at coffee shops, libraries, and other convenient locations near the homes of client families.

Accommodating Family Preferences

Timing of home meetings should reflect the mutual needs of the social worker and family members. For example, fluctuating energy levels should be taken into account to ensure a productive visit. The level of difficulty involved in working with various families should also be considered. For example, FSWs may schedule meetings with their most challenging families early in the day or week. Scheduling that allows for personal preferences and needs can help maximize the social worker's effectiveness and promote personal well-being. Managing a demanding caseload according to an inconvenient schedule can contribute to burnout. In addition, an exhausted family social worker cannot provide the level of service that families deserve.

Families have preferences for meeting times. Ultimately their needs should be the most important consideration when scheduling home appointments. Families have varied lifestyles and routines. Some have stable, predictable schedules and home lives that easily adapt to regularly scheduled home meetings. Others have less organized or chaotic lives that make regularly scheduled meetings unacceptable or even impossible. Parents can have varied work schedules, and the family social worker needs to set up meetings to fit within these schedules. Being sensitive to family preferences, habits, and lifestyles will help the social worker to schedule appointments appropriately.

Because family social work meetings often occur within the home, respect for privacy and accommodation to schedules is crucial. Some families, for example, may not want to meet when young children are napping, while others may prefer to meet while younger children are asleep.

Other people may stop in during a family work session. A family member or the FSW should ask them to come back later.

The dedication of some families to certain television programs is another factor worth considering when scheduling home appointments. Family social workers who arrive during these times may be welcomed into the house but might be expected to wait until the end of a program before beginning activities or discussions. Some social workers have found that briefly watching certain television programs with families before engaging in work provides a useful basis for building rapport, particularly with families who find talking difficult.

Scheduling home meetings with parents who work outside the home can be quite complicated. After a day's work, the parents and the FSW may be tired and feel the pressures of impending evening activities. Instead of scheduling every meeting during the evening, the FSW may want to set up an occasional weekend visit. While disruptive to the family social worker's personal routine, meeting at odd hours may be best for some families.

To sum up, the key to scheduling family meetings is flexibility. The FSW needs to aim for a reasonable balance between achieving specific program goals in every meeting and being responsive to the family's immediate needs. Even after the social worker and family have arrived at a mutually agreeable schedule, some meetings may have to be postponed. A family may be unable to benefit from the planned purpose of the meeting on a particular day because of crises such as the threat of eviction, loss of employment, or a child's illness. Under these circumstances, the FSW should attend to the family's immediate concerns and discuss available resources. A crisis may require that the FSW listen to the family's concerns, offer emotional support, encourage active problem solving, or help the family to get help from other agencies. Trying to impose a set agenda upon an unreceptive family can obstruct the helping relationship. As one family social worker phrased it, "Flexibility kept me sane. I had to remind myself that nothing was cast in stone, and that I could really trust my instincts."

PREPARATION AND CARE OF MATERIALS

Another important aspect of planning is preparation and compilation of materials. Materials may be standardized, or they may be created or collected for each meeting. Materials can include activity cards, pamphlets, toys, coloring pencils with paper, books, recording instruments, evaluation measures, or referral forms. Preparing for a family meeting may take as much time as the meeting itself, particularly if materials must be gathered or made. The FSW should bring extra copies of materials that have been left with the family in case they have been misplaced.

Materials should be organized and stored so that they can be located and used easily. This is an important ingredient of planning for the FSW who travels regularly between the agency and family homes. Because different sets of materials for several clients will be needed while traveling from home to home and because other forms or materials might also be kept at the office, an appropriate organizational system is needed. Disorganization can result in loss of time, missed opportunities for effective family interventions, and considerable frustration for both the worker and the family. A family social worker may want to keep a file box in the car for case-by-case storage of recent and current paperwork. The FSW can transfer older materials from the file box to the main office files and add new materials for upcoming meetings.

The FSW must be careful to protect confidential materials from being misplaced, damaged, stolen, or inadvertently combined with other materials that could be distributed during an appointment. A laptop computer makes it easy for the FSW to record data, provide duplicates for office files, and protect clients' confidentiality. If a laptop computer is unavailable, a separate container or secured portable file box should be used for storage of confidential materials both en route to and during home visits. After each family meeting, confidential materials should be filed immediately in the appropriate secure location. Special care must be taken to keep one family file separate from other family files. This will prevent the FSW from mixing files accidentally.

WHAT TO WEAR

Each community and client population has its own standard of dress, and family social workers should be sensitive to these standards. Clothing should be professional, but the degree of formality can vary. In addition, clothing should be appropriate for the planned activities in a meeting. For example, if the meeting requires the FSW to play on the floor with children or be physically active, clothing should be selected with these activities in mind.

INCLUDING CHILDREN IN MEETINGS

The nature of family social work dictates that children will often be the focus of work. Home meetings are often initiated in response to the needs of one child, sometimes called the "target child" or "identified patient." Although only one child may be targeted for intervention, other children in the home may also need help. The FSW should involve the parents in devising a strategy for dealing with children during meetings. The plan might call for the children to play elsewhere, especially when discussion centers on personal adult issues. When the focus is more child-centered, children can and probably should be included in meetings. Obviously the inclusion of children depends on the focus of the session. When no one is available to supervise children excluded from the meeting, special activities may be arranged in another room to occupy their attention. Materials provided by the social worker should include items that can occupy children productively. The FSW should supply materials that will interest the child.

Generally, meetings with parents alone will be easier to manage. As suggested by Satir (1967), "the presence of children might spell anarchy to the therapy process" (p. 136). Nevertheless, the presence of children should be dictated by the purpose of the session, not whether the meeting will be easier without them. Children could be included in the meeting when they are old enough to contribute to family sessions. Satir (1967) also suggests that social workers take an active role in interviews when there are children. For example, the FSW can model ways of communicating with children. Initially, the FSW may want to assess how parents set limits for the children. In one office-based meeting, for example, a parent sat passively while the child ravaged the worker's office, opening desk drawers and otherwise intruding on the worker's privacy. Rather than imposing limits on the child, the social worker asked the parent to intervene.

This incident opened the door to a discussion of limit setting and discipline. The parent in this example believed that limit setting was a form of abuse. She failed to recognize that her child had developed few social skills and was rejected by his peers. Failure of parents to set limits with children during the family meeting provides valuable information about what goes on in the family and how effective parents are in managing their children's behavior. In addition, the social worker can help parents devise limit-setting techniques with children "on-the-spot," providing feedback as the parent practices the new behaviors.

The presence of children in a meeting can provide the social worker with information about family dynamics, parenting skills, and parent–child relationships. For example, when the presenting family problem involves the children, observing the interaction between parent and child will be necessary for understanding the particular problem. Presence of children is also crucial to observe how parents are implementing the changes made during the work.

Approaches to children during home meetings can include negotiating with them to occupy themselves productively, either with their own activities or those brought by the worker, after which they are rewarded with special attention. In difficult situations, another family social worker may be available to be with the children independent of the meeting with the parent. A coworker can also help coordinate a meeting in which the entire family is present. Observing how parents interact with their children during a home visit helps the FSW to assess the parent–child relationship and to design interventions that will promote positive change.

Sometimes, the FSW may need to ask the parent to arrange for the children to be elsewhere during a home meeting; if this is not practical, the meeting can be conducted at another location such as the agency office. This may be necessary when the parent wants to discuss something that children should not hear, such as marital difficulties or intimate personal problems, or when the needs of one or more children require almost constant adult attention. Parents may talk more freely with the social worker when the children are not present.

When assessing the role of the children within a family, the FSW needs to keep in mind that the family is a system in which each member is affected by factors that affect other members. The birth of a physically challenged child, for example, can influence parental interactions with other children and with one another. In addition, the existence of a serious problem such as delinquency or alcoholism will have a strong impact on family needs and interactions. Siblings of target children also need opportunities to talk about their feelings and have their questions answered honestly and directly. Family social workers often mistakenly assume that because a certain child is not the "problem," that child does not need to be included in the session. Asking a child a question such as, "Can you tell me what you are worried about?" may unleash a barrage of concerns. Therefore, family social workers must be sensitive to the dynamics of the whole family and consider all members' needs when conducting meetings.

HANDLING DISRUPTIONS AND MAINTAINING CONTACT

Although most home meetings will run smoothly, the FSW should be prepared for occasions when they do not. Blaring televisions, visits from friends and neighbors, and ringing telephones are all a natural part of the home milieu. The FSW needs to find creative ways of handling such distractions, such as meeting on the front porch or at a restaurant, or having older siblings entertain younger ones. If distractions and chaos continue, the FSW and family need to discuss these obstacles and find a reasonable method for resolving them.

It is important for clients and the FSW to know how to reach each other. Such contact is aided if the client has a telephone; however, if clients do not have a phone another method of reaching the family should be devised. This may involve using a neighbor's telephone or leaving notes at the home. One family worker, after many failed meeting attempts, found that providing the family with addressed, stamped envelopes and stationery to inform her of canceled meetings or unanticipated moves was an effective way to remain in contact. Agency policy may determine whether the FSW provides a home phone number.

Frequent mobility of clients can disrupt schedules. If a family's move is planned and the social worker is aware of it in advance, the appointment schedule can be adjusted. However, some families move without notifying the family social worker, who then has difficulty locating them. At the first meeting, the FSW should request the name and phone number of a person who will always know the whereabouts of the family.

TELEPHONE FOLLOW-UP

Telephone follow-up between sessions is helpful because many parents have additional questions after reflecting on the interview. If the FSW initiates telephone contact, he or she can be more helpful to parents who worry about asking "dumb" questions and are reluctant to bother the family social worker with problems.

When information, instruction-giving, and careful follow-up are insufficient to accomplish the agreed-upon goals, the FSW needs to determine what types of additional intervention may be useful to the parents. The goal is to help parents understand their problems and enable them to change their own behavior in ways that will be acceptable to them. It would be destructive to make recommendations that parents cannot execute. The FSW can judge what can be undertaken immediately, what should be delayed until appropriate preliminary goals have been achieved, and what can be postponed indefinitely.

Consequently, the FSW should be willing to adopt alternative methods based on an assessment of the situation and of parental responses to intervention. Follow-up can help to reinforce new behaviors or help the FSW to decide if further intervention is needed.

SAFETY CONSIDERATIONS

It is impossible for social workers to achieve program goals when their safety is threatened. In some cases, the FSW's safety is threatened by clients who become violent; in others, the risk is created by an unsafe neighborhood. Knowing how to protect one's personal safety is essential in family social work.

Violence against social workers does not appear to be random. Rather, the person committing the violence will often have some complaint against an agency, whether real or imagined (Munson, 1993). For example, an aggressive parent who demands that the FSW bypass waiting lists, help acquire special services, or produce unreasonable results may threaten the family social worker. The FSW must be ready to deal with clients' attempts to manipulate, cross boundaries, or attack. A part of the FSW's usefulness to parents depends on the ability to deflect personal intrusion and impending threat. To protect themselves, social workers must be caring, yet capable of separating involvement on a professional level from involvement on a personal level.

Because families live in all types of environments, from rural areas to inner cities and suburbs, safety issues will vary within and across programs. However, several basic safety guidelines are relevant for all family social workers. To ensure the safest conditions for home meetings, we recommend the following guidelines:

1. Perhaps the most important safety guideline is not to dismiss feelings of danger. When social workers feel vulnerable or unsafe, they should take whatever precautions are necessary for protection. Sometimes FSWs feel awkward about being suspicious of clients' friends or feeling uncomfortable and apprehensive in certain neighborhoods. They might underplay the sense of feeling threatened. Ignoring these anxieties can place the social worker at risk. On the other hand, if FSWs are merely unfamiliar with the client's setting or are meeting in an unfamiliar cultural milieu, the source of apprehension needs to be examined before concluding that conditions are unsafe. Becoming acquainted with diverse cultures and neighborhoods allows FSWs to discern real from imaginary danger.

2. A related guideline for safety in home meetings is to become familiar with neighborhoods where home appointments take place. Learning the layout of the immediate area around clients' homes and the usual types of activities that occur there will provide a baseline from which to assess danger.

3. Make certain that the program supervisor and/or other responsible agency personnel are aware of the FSW's schedule of family meetings. The schedule should include the name and location of the family, the date and scheduled times for the meeting, and the expected time of return. When a home

meeting is scheduled in an unsafe environment, FSWs can develop a monitoring system such as a call-in procedure when the visit is complete. When telephones are not available, we recommend the purchase of a cellular telephone. As cellular phones become more affordable, family social work programs should consider using them. The following scenario demonstrates how a social worker's failure to let the agency know her whereabouts placed her at risk. She related a situation in which she was eight months pregnant and was taken hostage by an angry father. The incident lasted eight hours, but no one from her agency knew that she was being held hostage or even where she was because there were no call-in tracking arrangements at her agency. She managed to leave the situation after keeping a cool head and talking fast, but after that episode she always let several people in her office know her schedule.

4.   Avoid dangerous neighborhoods at night. If this is impossible, arrangements should be made for an escort. For example, one program hired an escort for late afternoon and early evening hours. Social workers in the program then scheduled appointments when the escort could accompany them. Another option is to ask a relative or friend to accompany the social worker into the home and to come back again when the family meeting is over.

5.   Assess the safest route to and from the client's home in advance. If the most direct route does not have well-lit or well-patrolled streets, a safer route should be chosen. Parking in clients' neighborhoods may also present safety problems. The only available parking may be far from clients' homes or in a high-crime area. If safe parking cannot be found, using a paid driver may be worthwhile. One program serving a high-risk urban community hired a full-time driver who escorted FSWs to all of their meetings. If a social worker feels uncomfortable meeting a family in their home, making arrangements to meet in a public place is acceptable. Further, a social worker who feels unsafe during an interview should leave (Kinney, Haapala, & Booth, 1991).

Clients and communities can participate actively in planning for the safety of the FSW, and this can be an important and useful component of an empowerment strategy. Also, safety planning within the family itself is an important aspect of the family social work process. Besides the preceding guidelines, several other safety factors should be considered. Since FSWs usually drive to appointments, they need to maintain their cars in good condition. FSWs who must travel long distances through high-risk neighborhoods should ensure that they have enough gasoline. Further, since confidential program materials may be kept in automobiles, it is imperative that they be secured against theft.

The security of personal possessions should be considered when meeting families in the community. The FSW should avoid carrying more money than necessary. Accessories such as purses and jewelry are generally not appropriate for home meetings. Theft of money or other items from family social workers, while rare, can occur. One home-based worker wore expensive clothing and drove an expensive car to family meetings and was advised by the agency to avoid doing so. Preventing incidents from happening is better than having to deal with them once they have occurred. Worrying about confidential items left in a car may also prevent a social worker from devoting complete attention to a family during an appointment.

FSWs should receive training from their agencies on recognizing signs of potential violence among clients (Munson, 1993). All agencies should have clearly established safety protocols for social workers, in addition to offering training sessions on handling violence when it does occur. If a social worker feels frightened during a visit, he or she needs to assess the severity of the immediate risk and should feel free to leave. Erring on the side of caution is best. Circumstances that might require this response include violence in the home, drug use and drug dealing, the presence of weapons, or the presence of intoxicated or out-of-control individuals. If a social worker encounters any of these situations during family meetings, he or she must discuss the incident with supervisors and explore alternatives for ensuring safety during future appointments. In some circumstances, home appointments may be ended or situated in safer locations.

Another precaution concerns illness in the home. If a family member has an infectious disease, the social worker should use judgment about being exposed to the illness. When confronted with communicable illnesses such as hepatitis or influenza, the worker should consult with medical personnel about the advisability of meeting in the home. Sometimes rescheduling a home visit is the best option. The Head Start home visiting program has clearly defined procedures for social workers to follow when confronted with client illness.

Sometimes family members will offer the social worker refreshments such as coffee or cookies. Normally this will not be a problem. Eventually, however, most social workers will come across unsanitary conditions in some homes and will have to think of a graceful way to decline the offerings without offending the family. Within some cultures, offering food to a visitor is a sign of respect. Families would be insulted if the social worker refused their offer. A brief but direct approach is suggested, such as thanking the family for their offer of food or coffee and explaining that the FSW has just eaten or finished a cup of coffee before arriving for the meeting.

THE AGGRESSIVE PARENT

An aggressive parent who expects unrealistic services and demands that the worker bypass waiting lists, help acquire special services, or produce unreasonable results may threaten the family social worker. Some parents may use threats or alliances to avert negative repercussions against themselves. The FSW must be aware of client attempts to manipulate, attack, or cross boundaries, and guard against such threats. A part of the FSW's usefulness to parents depends upon the ability to deflect personal intrusion and impending threat. To protect themselves, FSWs must be caring, yet capable of separating involvement on a professional level versus involvement on a personal level.

THE FIRST MEETING: ASSESSING CLIENTS' NEEDS

Social workers trained in the skills of individual counseling can become over-whelmed when they begin working with families. They may be uncertain about what to expect or how to proceed. It is important to keep in mind that the purpose of the first meeting is to assess the problem and engage the family in problem solving.

The FSW may offset the apprehension of seeing a family for the first time by obtaining as much information as possible before the meeting. Reading family files, if available, is a good starting point, as is reading literature about the family's specific problem. The supervisor can help the FSW understand how to apply specific theories to the family's problems. The FSW should also examine personal values or biases that may affect his or her performance with a particular family and again consult the supervisor. Gaining understanding of any diversity issues is very important before this first meeting.

Keeping the specific family in mind, the FSW may review the principles and techniques of family interviewing. Topics to be explored include: How should this family be engaged? What particular techniques might be useful in engaging this family? How are goals set in a family meeting, and what specific goals might be set in the first meeting with this family? What are the special cultural issues for this family?

After the FSW has formulated answers to these questions, the supervisor can provide practical feedback and direction. The supervisor and other agency colleagues may be willing to role-play the family so the FSW can practice what to say first, where to sit, whether to accept coffee, and so forth. Role-playing provides the FSW with the opportunity to develop new skills and obtain important feedback before actually meeting the family. It is a form of dress rehearsal. The supervisor may encourage role-playing other tasks, such as engagement and goal setting. Even though the reality will differ from the rehearsal, the FSW will have developed a sense of what to expect during the initial meeting with the family.

Basic patterns to look for at the first meeting involve repetitive verbal and nonverbal communications among family members. The FSW should pay attention to indications of conflict, which individuals get involved in disagreements, where family members sit in relationship to one another, who speaks for family members, and so on.

At the start of the first interview, the FSW should introduce himself or herself and explain the agency's purpose. Description of the agency is especially important if the client is not familiar with the agency. Once this has been done, the FSW should engage the family and begin to assess its problems. Assessment involves understanding what the problem is, what is causing the problem, and what can be done to change the situation (Holman, 1983). Ideally, assessment is a shared responsibility between the worker and family. The worker collects information by encouraging participation by every family member. This involves getting to know names and developing a sense of how each family member understands the problem. It is important to encourage every member to speak. It is common for parents to speak for the children or for one adult to speak for another. This is an example of a repetitive family pattern that the FSW should note and address. Social workers must understand who is speaking for whom in the meeting and begin to get the spokesperson to allow others to speak for themselves. To do so, the FSW may need to challenge family patterns, especially established patterns of family authority. Understanding cultural norms and ways of communicating can also be important.

The process of identifying problems and learning about the family can be complex and must be planned carefully. The worker can gradually engage the family in activities such as drawing a genogram (family map) or an ecomap (diagram of social contacts). These activities will assist in further engagement of family members, facilitate balanced individual participation in the interview, and help the family to define the problem so that family members can accept the plan for future work. To be comprehensive, an assessment needs to be done from an ecological perspective, looking at the interactions between the family and its environment (Holman, 1983). An ecological assessment should be required for all problems.

Social workers should assess the family's living environment. A tour of the home can reveal much about the family, especially differences between public and private areas. Eating areas are another focal point for the family and give information also suggestive of family style and management. A family that dines together every night around a large table presents a different image from the family that eats dinner on TV trays in separate rooms in the house. Going to the "right part of the house" when assessing a family can be of great value in planning future work with the family, especially if the FSW encourages parents and children to discuss perceptions of different spaces and to describe what the spaces mean to each family member.

Maintaining worker–family communication during a home interview includes sitting where everyone can be seen. Eye contact is critical in engaging family members. It is advisable not to begin an interview until all family members are present. Time-consuming social exchanges can be left to the end of the interview. The tone of the interview will help the FSW decide whether refreshments are a distraction or a gift and can be postponed to the end of the session.

Demarcating the physical space in the home interview is useful so everyone can participate. Someone may stomp out of the room in a rage, retreating to a section of the house where he or she can still listen to what is being discussed. If someone goes into the bathroom and locks the door, however, that is a clear indication that they have left the session and the family will have to problem solve about how to deal with the absence. Such events do not curtail work with the family. Instead, they are examples of natural events that can be used to learn more about the family. Additionally, they can provide opportunities for family members to learn new patterns of behavior.

Increasingly, social workers are becoming technique driven, and various interventions and theories compete with one another. The growing interest in demonstrating intervention techniques can make social workers worry that they will be ineffective if they are not using the latest therapy. However, it seems that therapists are more impressed with techniques than are clients

(Miller, Hubble, & Duncan, 1995). For instance, parents report valuing the most fundamental elements of service: support, listening, on-the-spot assistance, and availability of the social worker (Coleman & Collins, 1997).

Basic helping skills of empathy, warmth, and genuineness are crucial to intervention, as is the willingness to ask for clarification when meanings are unclear. Demonstrating these qualities will lay the groundwork for a strong worker–client relationship, often known as the therapeutic alliance (Worden, 1994). Family social workers secure with these basic skills can successfully negotiate both the first and subsequent family meetings with little apprehension. The second interview will be easier and the third interview easier yet. The fourth interview may be more difficult for new FSWs developing critical awareness of their own performance. However, this difficulty and self-consciousness should be welcomed as a positive sign of learning and growth.

BUILDING A RELATIONSHIP WITH CLIENTS

The core of family social work is the relationship between the FSW and the family—a relationship that will make it possible for the FSW to provide help to the family. The relationship is the vehicle that carries interventions and makes them palatable to the family. It contributes as much as 30 percent to the effectiveness of intervention (Miller, Hubble, & Duncan, 1995). The first family meeting marks the beginning of a helpful relationship between the FSW and the family. The relationship may be quite brief or long-term.

It is crucial for FSWs to recognize that when there is family conflict, family members may try to get the social worker to side with them in their particular view of the problem. The FSW should anticipate this maneuver and avoid it by empathizing with individual viewpoints without colluding with them. Family work involves maintaining a delicate balance between neutrality and sensitivity to individual experiences. When neutrality does not occur, certain family members can become alienated from the social worker (Coleman & Collins, 1997). Social workers struggle with issues of alliance with individual family members versus advocating for justice for individual family members, especially those disadvantaged or harmed by family dynamics, as in the case of abuse. Worden (1994) suggests three crucial elements for developing a strong therapeutic alliance with clients:

1. A consensus between the worker and client on the goals of therapy;
2. Worker–client agreement and collaboration on implementation of tasks;
3. A strong, positive, affective bond between the client and worker.

Keeping these three elements in the forefront will assist the family worker to negotiate the complexities of the first family meeting. The therapeutic alliance will be strengthened further by attending to issues involving ethnicity, gender, and stages in the family life cycle (Worden, 1994).

The first family meeting requires special attention, not only because it is the foundation for establishing a positive relationship between the FSW and family, but also because it will affect the quality and course of later work.

Consequently, engaging the family's interest and developing rapport is crucial to the FSW's continued presence in the home. The first family meeting should be time limited, focused, and relaxed.

Another component of the first meeting is instilling a sense of trust to enable family members to express their concerns honestly. Trust is not automatic; it is built gradually as family meetings continue. The FSW can encourage the development of trust by taking a sincere interest in family members' needs, conveying a willingness to help, and sticking all by the family during difficult times. Rapport may be achieved quickly with some families, while other families require patience and persistence. The nature of the family and its problems, the purposes of the family work, the personality of the FSW, and life experiences of family members influence how quickly trust and rapport are achieved. How the family feels about dealing with a problem and their perceptions of the problem influence their receptiveness to family work. Building a relationship with a family takes time.

It is important to foster a supportive atmosphere not only between the family and the FSW but also among family members. A high level of rapport and trust facilitates problem identification and effective working relationships, which in turn contribute to positive solutions. Effective working relationships facilitate behavioral changes that stimulate family satisfaction and self-confidence. One role of the FSW is to help clients clarify personal goals and develop a plan for reaching them. The relationship between social workers and clients is so important to family social work that program objectives cannot be met unless positive interaction is established. The therapeutic alliance is strengthened as family priorities are assessed, information is conveyed, support and encouragement are provided, and self-reliance and effective coping are promoted.

Development of a trusting relationship is not always a steady process. Clients who are disillusioned with helping systems will struggle with issues of trust. Thus, progress made in establishing trust during one meeting may be lost at the next appointment, depending on the family's interpretation of intervening events. These events may or may not involve the FSW per se, but may include incidents from the family's life that create suspicion about others' motives. We know of one situation in which trust was undermined when a family received a visit by a children's protective services caseworker for suspected neglect or abuse of the children. Although the FSW's involvement was not related to the investigation, the family projected its distrust and fear onto the FSW.

In the first meeting, and also in later ones, the FSW should be sensitive to the privacy of the family and avoid being intrusive. Workers must convey respect for the family's territory and show appreciation to the family for allowing the worker onto their turf. In other words, family social workers are guests in family homes (Kinney, Haapala, & Booth, 1991). Questions should focus on information needed to carry out program goals, especially during the first meeting. Some families may be eager to share additional information, but usually this will not be the case. If the family chooses to talk about personal matters, the FSW may listen attentively and respond supportively. The FSW may redirect the conversation to program-related topics if conversation becomes tangential or irrelevant. Probing into the personal life of family members during the early phases may undermine the development of a working relationship with a family. A family member who has shared information freely may later regret having shared so much. The FSW should be supportive and nonprobing early in the work.

ORIENTING CLIENTS TO FAMILY SOCIAL WORK

The intensity of the FSW's involvement with family members and their problems can contribute to feelings of personal closeness, yet the relationship must remain at a professional level. FSWs often work with families who are in severe crisis. Many have endured a lengthy history of family problems plus multiple episodes of prior service or treatment from various agencies. Because the family has probably experienced previous failures, it is important that the FSW establish positive expectations for change and convey hope to the family at the beginning. Support should be provided through use of appropriate opportunities for family change.

Reviewing the purposes of family social work and the nature of the activities to be completed promotes work with families. Focusing on family goals can help make each meeting productive. Time may have passed since the family first agreed to participate in family work, and the FSW will need to help the family remember the specific details originally agreed upon. Reminding the family about these details may also stimulate enthusiasm, interest, and participation.

During the first family meeting, the FSW should explain clearly her or his role, including responsibilities and limitations of involvement. When the limits and structure of the relationship are clarified, the FSW and the family can focus on productive work together. Clarification of roles may need to be repeated and reinforced frequently. Some family programs have narrowly defined roles for FSWs, while others permit and even encourage FSWs' flexibility and independence in establishing work-related boundaries. In either case, clarifying FSW responsibilities and limitations helps prevent the possibility of confusion and disagreement concerning the social worker's role.

The family's role in the change process should also be made explicit. Enlisting the entire family as partners in the process, rather than as recipients of service, establishes the idea that family social work is a mutual responsibility of the family and the social worker. The most obvious contribution of the family is availability for the work. Without access and ongoing participation, the FSW cannot perform the roles involved in the helping process.

The family's perceptions and expectations of family work also should be explored during the first meeting. Sometimes expectations are not realistic. The FSW may discover that clients have misunderstood program objectives or were misinformed. Finding out what the family expects and correcting misperceptions during the first meeting eliminates misunderstanding later. Ultimately the whole family should be encouraged to reach consensus on expectations for family work.

The first home meeting might last between one and two hours, depending on the objectives. It should be ended when planned activities have been completed. If the meeting is proceeding smoothly and the family is becoming engaged, the

CASE 3.1	CONFIDENTIALITY

You receive the Simpson case at a screening and referral. In the first meeting, you inform the Simpsons that you are their new family social worker. They seem a little reluctant to talk, so you encourage them by giving your assurance that anything they say will be held in the strictest confidence. At the time, you believe this implicitly. Later, while you are talking to your secretary, Romalda, you realize that she is typing case notes, including your information obtained about the Simpsons. Still later, in the coffee room of your agency, workers are talking freely about their cases and ask you about your cases. You respond with details of the Simpson case. Later still, you learn that Mr. Simpson has asked for medical assistance and your entry in his file has been shared with various government and medical service agencies. You think with dismay that you might as well have sent the record to the newspaper, only to discover that a sheet of recording has fallen out of your briefcase and been picked up by a neighbor of the Simpsons. You search frantically for the audiotaped interview that you plan to share with your supervisor. Meanwhile, the Simpsons have discovered that what they said to you in strictest confidence is now common knowledge in the social service delivery system. On Friday you meet with your supervisor and give a rundown of your cases. The Simpson case is at the top of your list.

Filled with righteous indignation, the Simpsons complain to your supervisor. Your supervisor gently explains to you the difference between absolute confidentiality, in which nothing your client family says is shared with anyone in any form, and relative confidentiality, in which information is shared with colleagues as required. You realize you will never be able to promise absolute confidentiality as an agency worker and, probably, you will never be able to promise confidentiality at all.

Despite your supervisor's gentleness, you feel that she is convinced of your incompetence. You also feel vaguely resentful; she could have told you about relative confidentiality before.

FSW may extend the meeting accordingly. A successful outcome of the first meeting means leaving the family feeling comfortable and looking forward to the next meeting. The second meeting should be scheduled for a time that will be convenient for all family members.

PROTECTING CLIENTS' CONFIDENTIALITY

Family social work offers professional services to families on a potentially more personal level than other service-delivery systems. Because of the nature of the work, maintaining appropriate confidentiality is critical (Collins, Thomlison, & Grinnell, 1992). Case 3.1 illustrates the high risk of breaching client confidentiality.

GUIDELINES FOR PROTECTING CLIENTS' CONFIDENTIALITY

1. Do not discuss clients outside the interview (i.e., an open-doored office, class, group, restaurant) even with changed names and altered identifying details. Discussing details about clients with family or friends is not

permitted. Family social work is very stressful and social workers sometimes need to "unwind" by talking about their feelings and the stress. The
only time it is appropriate to discuss clients is in a private setting with your
supervisor or colleagues: for example, a case conference. When discussions
involve families, the FSW should be at the office with supervisors and colleagues, not with family and friends who are not bound by the same rules
of confidentiality as the family social worker. Nonprofessionals may listen
with interest to a story about families or agencies, but, in the process, may
lose respect for the social worker, the agency, or the profession. They could
be thinking, "If I have a problem, I will never go to her or any other social
worker; it would get all over town," and it might.

2. If a client is not at home when you call, leave only your first name and say
nothing about the nature of the business. It may be acceptable to leave
your phone number, depending on how recognizable it is.

3. Social workers must not become involved in discussions with colleagues
over lunch or coffee. At a restaurant or other public places, there is an obvious risk for the conversation to be overheard. Even when names are not
mentioned, people might identify the client or think they have. Overhear-
ing personal conversations about work gives others the impression that the
social worker is casual about confidentiality.

4. Arrange for phone calls to be taken by someone else when interviewing a
client at your office. Interruptions lead to a break in rapport and inadvertent breaches of confidentiality. Also, the client may think, "She has more
important things to do than listen to me." When in a family home, if using
a pager, postpone returning the call so that there is no chance for the family to overhear your phone conversation.

5. Ensure that every interview is private and conducted in a private setting
out of the hearing of others.

6. Do not leave case records, phone messages, or rough notes on your desk or
in an unlocked car. Case records often have the name of the client promi-
nently displayed on the file, and they may catch someone's attention.
Secure records and files before leaving your desk, and make sure that client
files are locked up overnight. Clients who observe that the FSW is haphazard in managing files may assume that the FSW will be haphazard in protecting their interests.

7. Clients should not be discussed at parties and social activities. Colleagues
frequently socialize together, and it is tempting to discuss a difficult case or
talk about a case to illustrate a common problem.

8. Even if a client seems unconcerned about confidentiality, it must be respected
anyway. Some clients may want to begin the interview in a waiting room or
initiate or continue a discussion in a public place. In such circumstances, the
discussion should be deferred until a private setting can be arranged.

9. Confidentiality about the internal operation and politics of the agency is
essential.

10. Before linking a family to other community services, the FSW must obtain
permission. When a family gives permission for confidential information

CASE 3.2	PREPARING FOR THE BEGINNING VISIT

Tina and Jim and their six-month-old daughter, Roxie, were referred to the family social worker from Child Protective Services (CPS). The couple has been married for a year and a half and is experiencing marital problems and was reported for the father's violent behavior toward his wife and child. The intake report said that Tina is a stay-at-home wife and mother. Jim has been employed at a pawn shop for five years. Neighbors reported that the couple fight and scream almost nightly, while the baby cries loudly in the background.

To prepare for the beginning visit, the FSW reviewed the intake report and familiarized herself with directions to the couple's home since she had scheduled a home visit at night after Jim's work day was over. She also prepared a folder with recording instruments and measures she believed would be useful, including a family violence index. Since the FSW believed the neighborhood to be unsafe, she asked a colleague to accompany her to the visit. The FSW reviewed guidelines for establishing a positive relationship, establishing rules for confidentiality, and rules for interviewing a family to prepare for her visit.

to be shared with specific agencies or individuals, information should be limited to that which is essential. Most agencies have developed a release of information form to be used in these situations.

11. In most states, confidentiality must be breached if someone (particularly a child) is at risk of harm. Clients need to be informed of this ahead of time. (Items 1-11 reprinted from Collins, Thomlison, & Grinnell, 1992, pp. 186–187.)

CHAPTER SUMMARY

Considering the practical aspects of case planning helps the family social worker demonstrate the skills of a competent professional. Scheduling enough time for meetings, travel time, and locating clients' homes helps instill client confidence. Planning and preparing ahead for requisite materials and for dealing with children in the home also will alleviate stress for the FSW.

Maintaining client contact may be challenging when working with multi-problem families, who are often seen in family social work. The FSW will need to develop ways of dealing with disruptions and locating clients who move frequently.

Ensuring FSW safety is essential, as most family social work is done in clients' homes. The FSW must be aware of the working environment and take steps to avoid danger, such as refraining from wearing expensive clothes or jewelry into a poor neighborhood with a high crime rate.

The first family meeting sets the stage for all other meetings. A clear introduction of self, the agency, and the purposes of family meetings is crucial. Establishing rapport and trust is the cornerstone of family social work. Finally, client confidentiality is essential for a trusting client–worker relationship.

EXERCISES

3.1   USEFUL MATERIALS

Develop a list of potential materials useful for family social work. Break down the materials used for different age groups:

Infant

Toddler

Preschooler

Public school child

Young adolescent

Older adolescent

Parent

Family as a whole

3.2   INTRODUCING YOURSELF

Write a list of opening instructions and/or statements that you can use to introduce yourself and the purpose of family social work.

3.3   DIFFICULT FIRST MEETINGS

Write a list of potential situations from a first interview that would be difficult for you to deal with. For each situation, provide two alternative responses to overcome the difficulty.

3.4   TRUST

Write down one family secret that you have never told anyone in your life. Include reasons why you have not told anyone this secret. Close your eyes, put your pencil down, and spend about five minutes imagining that you must now reveal this secret to a stranger who has just come into your house. What are your feelings about telling this stranger your secret? What must happen (concretely) before you would be prepared to talk to this stranger about your family secret?

3.5   CONFIDENTIALITY

Role-play with another student a discussion of confidentiality with a client.

THE BEGINNING PHASE

CHAPTER CONTENTS

In the preceding chapters we laid a foundation for discussing the phases of family social work practice. First, we looked at the historical underpinnings of family social work and explored changes in family structure. Next, we applied systems theory to family social work. Finally, we explored practical aspects of working with families and offered guidelines for conducting an initial interview. In this chapter we continue our discussion of how to establish an alliance with a family and set the stage for positive change. We begin by describing principles of effective communication, paying special attention to skills needed by the family social worker as he or she begins to work with a family.

Family social work takes place in five phases: beginning, assessment, intervention, evaluation, and termination. Each family meeting includes elements of these phases, and the FSW's overall involvement with a family also spans these five phases. In the following chapters we outline tasks and skills required of the FSW in each phase. The phases of helping are presented one at a time as if they were mutually exclusive, yet in practice they overlap. From the moment of receiving a referral, for example, the FSW begins assessment by reading the referral form or case record. The tasks involved in engaging with a family and assessing its needs continue throughout the FSW's involvement, but they are especially important during the first meetings.

TASKS FOR THE BEGINNING PHASE: ENGAGEMENT AND ASSESSMENT

New social workers often long for a recipe of what to say and do in specific situations. Unfortunately, there are no recipes, just guidelines. It has become cliché to suggest "starting where the client is." A more accurate guideline might be "starting where the social worker is" (Hartman & Laird, 1983), because the FSW influences how assessment and engagement will proceed. The FSW brings to the family an agency mission as well as skills with which to carry out his or her role.

Several conditions must be met before a family is ready to receive assistance. First, the family has to agree *as a family* that a particular problem requires outside intervention. Second, the family must connect with an agency to deal with the problem. Finally, the agency must decide whether the family's problem fits the agency's mandate. Each of these factors will affect the course of family work. In some cases, a family's initial contact with the agency is mandated by the court. Even though the family begins as an involuntary client, often the FSW will be able to help it see the merits of family social work so that it will agree to accept help.

The first two tasks of the FSW in the beginning phase are engaging families in the helping process and assessing the problem with which the family is struggling. Haley (1976) breaks down the tasks of the first interview further:

1. Creating a social stage in which the family is greeted and made comfortable. In this stage, social courtesies are observed without getting into the problem. At this time introductions are made and every family member is personally introduced. Haley suggests using this stage to observe the family, its mood, the family relationships, and their behaviors toward the FSW. The FSW will also want to observe where members sit in relation to one another. The FSW will make initial observations that are subject to change with more information. These opinions and observations will not be shared with the family at this time. This stage will last only a couple of minutes. If it lasts longer, the FSW might have difficulty moving into a discussion of family issues and the topic and relationship might remain superficial.

2. A problem stage in which the conversation revolves around the presenting problem. At this point, the interview ceases to be social and rather moves into a discussion about the problem. The FSW must take control of the process and "get down to business." The FSW can initiate discussion by asking the family why they are here. The FSW will observe how the problem is presented, the emotional quality of this presentation, and the individual responses to the problem description. Family members will usually describe the problem in terms of a person.

3. An interaction stage in which the family members are asked to talk with each other. At this time the role of the FSW shifts to become more of a conductor of the family orchestra. The FSW then takes the time to observe family patterns and interactions as well as family structure, circular patterns, and other issues related to family relationships. At the end of this endeavor, the family and the FSW will have a better idea of what needs to be changed.

4. A goal-setting stage where the family is asked to specify just what changes they seek (p. 15).

Engagement involves forming a therapeutic alliance between the social worker and *all* members of the family. Assessment consists of identifying patterns and issues within the family that relate directly to the problem as well as identifying the connectedness of the family to its social environment. The power of the therapeutic alliance seems to transcend cultural differences (Beutler, Machado, & Allstetter Neufelt, 1994). Rather than looking exclusively at one person's role within the family, the social worker should try to engage all of the family members. This is one reason the entire family should be present at the first meeting with the social worker.

Engagement with the family involves creating a setting where people can safely talk about themselves and about each other (Satir, 1967). The FSW must create an atmosphere that decreases fear and increases confidence of all members. Most important is the development of rapport with the family. Parents may be fearful and lack self-confidence by the time a family social worker enters their home. Most families who have problems feel defensive about it no matter how agreeable they may seem (Haley, 1976, p. 16). They may feel that their need for assistance must be a sign of incompetence. They have probably attempted other remedies to their difficulties before coming to see you. Other parents expect to be blamed for the problems that exist. Very seldom do family members agree on the problem. Parents may feel isolated and dejected after having tried to handle the issue for a long time before formal helpers became involved. Conversely, the child with the presenting problem may have been blamed many times for causing the family distress. The child may worry about being blamed further or being removed from the family altogether. All family members may feel hurt, angry, and incompetent.

Thus, during the initial stage of engagement, the social worker must maintain a neutral stance, not confronting individuals prematurely and not making interpretations before all the information is at hand (Gurman & Kniskern, 1981). Minuchin (1974) refers to this early phase of family work as "joining."

At this stage, the social worker conveys to the family that "I am like you." Joining helps to bridge the social distance between the social worker and family (Hartman & Laird, 1983).

Engagement and assessment are best accomplished in four steps:

MAKE CONTACT WITH EVERY FAMILY MEMBER

The family social worker greets each member of the family, seeking facts that establish his or her distinctiveness. There are no set rules decreeing which person the social worker should turn to first for an introduction, yet gender and cultural issues should be considered. For example, members of some cultures may expect the social worker to speak with the father first. The ordering of introductions should be deliberate. For example, some family social workers avoid turning first to the family member with the identified problem, not wanting to isolate that individual as "the problem." Alternatively, the social worker might validate parental authority by turning to them first. Ideally, the order of introductions should fit the "presenting problem." The FSW makes a personal introduction to the family, including name, agency, how the family came to the agency's attention, and a tentative statement about her or his role.

It is important for the worker to enter into the world of the family, observing family vocabulary and using language that matches the family's style (Goldenberg & Goldenberg, 2000). How members address one another will affect how the social worker addresses them. Regardless of what names are used by the social worker, the names should be selected intentionally. For example, Satir (1967) suggests referring to the parents as "Mom" and "Dad" when discussing parental roles but otherwise using their first names. Additionally, minority families have certain relationship protocols that need to be respected by the worker (Lum, 1992). Special ethnic issues include how to address family members. The social worker's manner of addressing individuals in minority families should adhere to the family's cultural practices. Thus, the social worker needs to learn about the cultural practices of the family's ethnic group and then find out to what degree they adhere to those practices.

DEFINE THE PROBLEM TO INCLUDE PERCEPTIONS OF ALL MEMBERS OF THE FAMILY

In clarifying the presenting problem, the social worker speaks with each family member (except infants) to obtain a description of how he or she sees the problem. The FSW should allow each family member to give his or her perspective on the problem without interference from others. Arguments or interruptions should be dealt with politely but firmly. The person who is speaking should be allowed the floor without interference. The social worker should attempt to understand each member's perspective based on his or her words and behavior. The FSW can also find out what the family members have attempted to do previously about the problem and what ideas they have for the future. If anger and blaming occur, the FSW must ensure that no one is scapegoated for the problem. The social worker should have strong justification for offering assistance to all family members, as some members may resent the social worker's presence (Geismar & Ayers, 1959).

Haley (1976) recommends speaking to the family group as a whole in order to avoid personal involvements and biases. Remember in Chapter 2, we discussed triangles and noted that it is easy for a FSW to become triangulated into the family system. The FSW must be vigilant about this possibility from the very beginning. When deciding whom to speak with first, the worker should be sensitive to issues of blame, gender issues, age, family hierarchy, cultural patterns, and so on. The opportunity to intervene with such variables will come later so long as the worker is sensitive to them and understands, first-hand, how these issues play out in this particular family. For example, starting with the "problem child" might put too much pressure on a child who already bears the brunt of his or her family's anger and blame. Other alternatives are to start with the family member who appears to be removed from the situation, to ensure that person becomes quickly involved. Leaving the question open will elicit the family's usual ways of operating, which is what the FSW wants to accomplish at this stage. At the same time, the FSW does not want to draw premature conclusions.

In cases of suspected child abuse and neglect, assessing whether any child is at risk becomes a critical first task. Risk assessment of abuse can be difficult, because the best information can be obtained when trust is established and the relationship is strong. The social worker may be suspicious because the family was referred specifically for abuse. In other cases, abuse may be suspected as the work develops. In assessing whether a child is being abused, the social worker should first note any physical signs of abuse such as unexplained bruising and cuts. The social worker should also observe the behavior of the child. Behavioral indicators of abuse may include timidity or aggressiveness, although these signs can indicate other, less serious problems. The behavior of the child in front of a parent should be observed. Does the child seem fearful of the parent? Finally, the parent–child relationship should be observed, especially how the parent interacts with the child. Is the parent irritable and impatient with the child? How much does the parent explain things to the child? Is there an affectionate relationship, or is physical contact avoided?

During this first phase, it is important for the worker to "base all his or her behaviors on understanding and showing respect for the family reality, which includes the value system, cultural context, and experiential nature of all family members" (Alexander, Holtzworth-Munroe, & Jameson, 1994, p. 623). Eventually, problems need to be viewed as problems of the entire family. There are several different ways of teaching the family to view problems within a family framework. One common visualization of the family is to present the analogy of a mobile to demonstrate how the behavior of one member affects the other members of the family. Ultimately, the problem should be framed within the context of "what needs to be changed." Describing the problem as something that needs to be changed sets the stage for the work that lies ahead.

During the problem definition stage, the FSW should encourage interaction among family members concerning the problem. Family members should be encouraged to discuss the problem among themselves (Haley, 1976). This stimulation of interaction should only occur after each family member has given her or his own individual opinion. The FSW moves from being the center of the conversation to being an observer and a director of the family conversation.

This will reveal ongoing family patterns that may have contributed to problem development and clarify why the social worker is seeing the family. By the end of the first interview, the FSW should have established a definition of the problem that does not hold one individual exclusively responsible for either its presence or the solution. This is known as "broadening the focus," whereby the problem and the solution are "owned" by all family members (Nichols & Schwartz, 2004). This stage remains one of curiosity on the part of the worker. The FSW will listen to the emotional content of the description as well as family responses when members are describing their individual perceptions. Also important is who is blamed for the problem and who takes responsibility. When one person is speaking, the FSW should observe the reactions of others (Haley, 1967, p. 30). Even though various family members may frame the problem as belonging to one person, the family worker should start to conceptualize (to him- or herself) in terms of a family issue involving every member of the family.

For example, Satir and Haley both suggest that children develop problems when a generational boundary has been violated and a parent becomes overly involved and concerned with that child.

The "problem" then needs to be framed in such a way that it can be changed. One way of doing this is to define the problem in terms of actual behaviors and occurrences. The FSW might be concerned that this discussion places too much emphasis on the "problem" person. One helpful hint is to examine how these difficulties impact family members—and usually the common ground is worry and concern. Every family member wants to feel better about their family, and pointing out how worried and concerned everyone is about the "problem" can aid in locating a common ground upon which every family member can work.

Establish Goals and Clarify an Intervention Process

The social worker and family members must arrive at a common goal related to solving the problem. To agree on a goal, the family and FSW need to cooperate. The social worker will have assessed the level of motivation in the family and understood what the family hopes will happen. Goals should involve the family as a whole, with all members agreeing to work toward the development of behaviors to eliminate the problem. Concrete ideas and plans can be proposed for problem solving, helping the family to feel a renewed sense of optimism that problems can be resolved.

CASE 4.1	FAMILY SOCIAL WORK GOALS

Bob and Anne Smitt, parents of twelve-year-old George, and Cerise Gordon, FSW, mutually agree to work on the following goals.

Focuses of family social work will be (1) parenting skills, (2) husband's unemployment, and (3) child's absence from school.

1. All family members and the FSW agree to meet each Monday in the Smitt home from 6 to 7:30 P.M. for the next six weeks.
2. Ms. Gordon agrees to provide information on parenting classes and job training resources.
3. Mrs. Smitt agrees to attend parenting classes and to work with Ms. Gordon on improving her housekeeping skills.
4. Mr. Smitt agrees to attend parenting classes and to participate in job training seminars.
5. Ms. Gordon agrees to be present when George and his parents meet with George's teacher to develop a plan for him to make up missed work.
6. George agrees to attend school and to participate in the plan to make up his missed work.

CONTRACT WITH THE FAMILY

In this step, the social worker and family reach an agreement on concrete issues such as how often family meetings will be held, who should be present, the length of family meetings, the proposed overall length of intervention, the motivation of each family member, and criteria for judging when goals have been achieved. A definition of the problem should be included in the contract, as well as what everyone can do to address the problem. The social worker and family should reach a consensus on goals and methods (Hartman & Laird, 1983). A written contract lends clarity, formalizes the work that lies ahead, and conveys a sense of seriousness. Contracts should itemize concrete issues such as time and place of meetings and also describe changes in individual and family behaviors that need to be accomplished. An example of a family social work contract is provided in Case 4.1.

COMMON PITFALLS OF NEW FSWS

New FSWs fall into some common traps when seeing families for the first time. These include:

1. Seeing the one with the difficulties as the focus of family social work, making the rest of the family a stressor in that person's life.
2. Overemphasizing history at the expense of what is going on in the here-and-now.
3. Waiting until s/he has amassed a pile of information before intervening.

4. Being overly concerned with destructive underlying feelings and attitudes.
5. Fitting a family to a method.
6. Getting caught up in the struggle of family factions.
7. Overlooking outcomes and goals as important reasons for the family interviews (Haley, 1971, pp. 228–236).

BASIC INTERVIEWING SKILLS NEEDED BY FAMILY SOCIAL WORKERS

Many skills and procedures are essential to be an effective helper. Not only will the skills be useful in accomplishing the tasks outlined in the preceding section, they will also model new behaviors to family members. Basic interviewing skills are necessary for family social work. These skills include:

- Listening carefully to expressed meanings of individuals and the family as a unit;
- Being sensitive to verbal and nonverbal communication about desires and goals from each family member;
- Recognizing family difficulties related to effective problem solving;
- Promoting skills, knowledge, attitudes, and environmental conditions that contribute to effective family coping.

The role of the FSW involves assisting parents to deal with their children more effectively through the development of problem-solving, decision-making, and parenting skills. Unfortunately, few programs provide training to help family social workers to fulfill these objectives.

Interviewing a group is more complex than interviewing an individual. This is because the maze of problems has expanded to include each individual within the family unit as well as the multiple relationships between individuals. Because of the number of people involved in a family interview, the social worker has less control than in an individual interview (Munson, 1993). Social workers often report feeling overwhelmed by information coming from a number of sources, often at the same time. The complexities present in individual therapy are amplified when seeing a family. Especially difficult tasks are trying to understand every family member simultaneously and to avoid aligning with individuals in the family (Shulman, 1992). Issues such as male–female roles, ethnicity, and the number of dyadic (two-person) relationships within the family demand that many factors receive attention in a counseling session (Alexander, Holtzworth-Munroe, & Jameson, 1994). Furthermore, the social worker must acknowledge both the advantages and disadvantages of approaching the family from the perspective of an outsider (Hartman & Laird, 1983).

Before family social workers interview families, they must be able to distinguish between a friendship and a professional relationship and between a social conversation and a task-centered family social work interview. If they are unaware of these distinctions, family social workers are likely to lose focus with a family and fail to initiate problem solving.

GUIDELINES FOR EFFECTIVE INTERVIEWS

The following guidelines can help FSWs develop professional relationships with clients (adapted from Kadushin, 1992):

- An interview is deliberate;
- The content of an interview is related to an explicit purpose;
- The family social worker has the primary responsibility for the content and direction of the interview;
- Relationships are structured and time-limited.

A family interview is *deliberate* and has an established purpose and specific goals that are mutually accepted by all participants. Thus, the focus of the interview is on a cluster of family problems, directed toward a solution. To arrive at a solution, the FSW must overcome the temptation to engage in conversations that detract from the task at hand. For example, *extended* "chit chat" can be a waste of time or a way to avoid painful topics. Small talk may be useful initially to allow the family and social worker to get acquainted with each other (Brock & Barnard, 1991). It may also be useful for engaging a resistant family member. Small talk may be appropriate if the FSW uses it to establish rapport and remembers to return to issues after a resistant member has become involved.

When working with members of a different culture, the FSW should initially engage the family in friendly conversation, rather than immediately focusing on the problem. Rules about relationships differ greatly from culture to culture. The dominant Western culture is often considered direct and even rude and disrespectful by members of less aggressive cultures. Family social workers need to be sensitive to cultural variations in how relationships are established in other cultures. When differences do emerge, discussion of these differences can clear up many misunderstandings.

As soon as rapport is established, the FSW must identify a specific focus for the work. The longer it takes to develop focus, the harder it will become to focus the work on a specific agenda and accomplish later work. Clients may drop out between the first and second meetings if there is a lack of purpose and direction. Establishing a clear direction, focused on family needs and concerns, gets the FSW's relationship with the family off to a positive start.

The *content* of family meetings should flow from an agreed-upon purpose and move in the direction of addressing the identified problems. Spoken words and planned activities must be related directly to the stated purpose. For example, the FSW who initiates a family meeting with a general question such as "How are things going?" will lead the family in a less productive direction than the FSW who begins by saying, "Tell me how the parenting techniques we discussed last week worked out."

In family work, the FSW assumes *primary responsibility* for the content and direction of the interview. Sometimes this responsibility can be challenging for the FSW who may be reluctant to use professional authority and expertise with the family, particularly if the parents are older than the FSW or if the FSW has no children. Parents may ask the family social worker if he or she has any children. They may want to find out if the social worker can understand what they are going through. They may also be doing their own assessment of the social worker's experience. These questions may create insecurity for workers who are new and do not have children of their own. They do not want to appear incapable. The best response to these questions may be to discuss the parents' concerns. For example, the FSW can say, "No, I don't have any children myself. It sounds like you are worried that because I don't have any children, I will not be able to understand your situation or help you. Let's talk about this."

The relationship between the FSW and the family is also *structured* and *time-limited*. This means that activities are intentional and centered around the task at hand, creating an atmosphere in which family members are expected to work on identified problems. It also means that family social work has a beginning and an end. Thus, the FSW must be able to recognize when a family has achieved its task and no longer requires the social worker's assistance. Similarly, each individual session with the family should be time-limited, depending on the nature of the work that needs to be accomplished. As much as family social workers try to achieve a partnership with the family, the relationship is seldom reciprocal. The FSW provides leadership, knowledge, and direction to the family. The interests and needs of the clients are primary, demanding that the needs of the FSW be set aside. For example, families may ask the FSW personal questions. The social worker must decide how much information to share, remembering that the needs of the family and the therapeutic focus come first. Self-disclosure by the social worker to a client must have a definite purpose.

Every action and activity of the FSW must be *intentional,* and words should be selected consciously to have an intended effect. For instance, the FSW may select words based on family interests: if the family is sports-minded, the FSW may refer to the family as a "team." Of course, being deliberate with every word, motive, and action can extract much energy from the social worker.

The FSW–family relationship is guided by clear and firm boundaries ensuring that family needs take precedence over those of the social worker. New family social workers often struggle with the desire to become "friendly" and establish personal relationships with families. This is a natural inclination because family social workers become involved in intimate details of family life and because positive relationships are pivotal to the work. Also, knowing private details about people is associated with intimacy. Family social workers work closely with people in intense and emotionally laden situations. In addition, the FSW may sincerely like clients, and this liking is a crucial ingredient for the work that lies ahead.

Despite temptation, family social workers must retain a professional focus. The helping relationship is different from friendship, because the FSW wields some authority in relation to the family, making a totally equal relationship impossible. Codes of ethics also dictate which behaviors are acceptable and which are breaches of professional conduct. For example, a family social worker arranged to purchase a vehicle from a family, with the family financing the purchase. This was an obvious breach of professional conduct that had to be reported to the agency. Other breaches include sexual involvement with clients (Masson, 1994), taking the family for vacations, or deciding to parent a child from the family in the social worker's home. Social workers should refer to their code of ethics and discuss situations with supervisors when in doubt. A useful guideline is that if the social worker feels the need to keep information from the agency, it needs to be examined for breach of conduct.

Family social workers, thus, must be committed to meeting needs of the family first. The FSW's personal needs are not the focus in this relationship, as attention must be directed to the family's issues. It is natural for social workers to want to do their best and be appreciated, but they should resist comparisons to other social workers, regardless of how families may flatter them by saying, "You are the best social worker we have ever had!" or telling them about the atrocities performed on them by other social workers. The social worker should accept a sincere or spontaneous compliment, but the compliment should not draw in negative comparisons with other workers. Family social work is usually arranged formally concerning time, place, duration, and purpose. Unpleasantness, such as issues requiring confrontation, cannot be avoided and is often necessary to accomplish the tasks contracted for.

PRINCIPLES OF EFFECTIVE COMMUNICATION

The interview is a special type of encounter, and everything said within this encounter conveys a message. All messages should be deliberate. Communication takes place between the social worker and the family, as well as between family members. The process of communication is complex, and experienced FSWs recognize the first axiom of human communication: "*You cannot not communicate*" (Watzlawick, Beavin, & Jackson, 1967). Communication involves more than speaking with words and can include facial expressions, gestures, posture, and tone of voice (Satir, 1967).

Other axioms of communication include:

- Communication conveys both information and imposes behavior. Therefore any time there is communication there is commitment and a relationship. All communication therefore involves content and a message about the relationship—that is, all communication has both a report and command component of it—data about the communication and how the communication is to be taken.
- The nature of a relationship is contingent upon the punctuation of the communicational sequences between the communicants. This punctuation organizes behavioral events. Some relationship conflicts revolve around

disagreements about how to punctuate a series of events. It is interesting that one definition of power is "who gets the final word!"

- Communication is both digital and analogic. Digital communication occurs when a word is used as a symbol of something, such as *cat*, and is tied in with language syntax. Analogic communication, on the other had, is more abstract—something is more "thinglike" and the clarity of what it refers to is more ambiguous. Nonverbal communication is one example. These two forms of communication exist side-by-side
- All communicational interchanges are either symmetrical or complementary, depending on whether they are based on equality or difference (Watzlawick, Beavin, & Jackson, 1967, pp. 48–70).

Tomm also suggests that meaning is conveyed at six levels (1987):

1. Content—what is actually said.
2. Speech—how the message is said.
3. Episode—the social context of the message.
4. Interpersonal relationships—the quality of the relationship between the communicators.
5. Life script—self-image and self-expectations.
6. Cultural pattern—internalized values of one's culture. Effective communication is clear, direct, and honest.

Virginia Satir placed a great deal of emphasis on communication, suggesting that it needs to be clear, direct and honest.

- **Clear** communication is not masked. The communicator says what he or she means.
- **Direct** communication is addressed to the person for whom the message was intended. (Indirect messages avoid conveying personal responsibility and expressing real feelings.)
- **Honest** communication conveys a genuine message.

Simple communication involves sending messages from one person to another as pictured below:

This diagram captures a simple linear communication, such as a parent telling a child, "Pick up your toys." In this message, the linear transmission of the message implies an active sender and passive receiver. However, even in this seemingly straightforward example, additional meaning may be intended or inferred. Imagine that "Pick up your toys" is said by an exasperated parent who believes that the child is thoughtless or careless. The message will then be more than the simple instruction and may contain angry verbal tones and nonverbal behavioral clues revealing the parent's displeasure. The body language of the parent may also seem threatening to the child. Thus, communication involves a circular, interactive process of involvement by participants (Tomm, 1987).

Words contain more than one meaning, and social workers need to realize that the same word can mean different things to different people (Bandler, Grinder, & Satir, 1976). Remember that people seldom select words consciously.

THE COMMUNICATION PROCESS

A transactional explanation of the communication process is given below (Johnson & Johnson, 1994). Note that these transactional patterns break down the sequence of circular interactions discussed in Chapter 2 into five distinct steps:

- Intentions, ideas, and feelings of the sender are formed before sending a message. The sender *encodes* a message by translating ideas, feelings, and intentions into a message appropriate for sending.
- The sender transmits the message to the receiver through a *channel*. Often the channel is provided by words, tone of voice, facial expressions, posture, and body language (Bandler, Grinder, & Satir, 1976).
- The receiver translates the message by *interpreting* its meaning. Meaning is derived from how the message is conveyed as well as the context within which the message is sent. The receiver's interpretation depends on how well he or she understands the content and context of the message and the intentions of the sender. The receiver receives the message through relevant sensory channels such as sight, hearing, and touch.
- The receiver responds internally to this interpretation of the message. Meanings in a message can include the literal content of the message (denotative level) as well as what is inferred from the nature of the relationship between the sender and the receiver (metacommunication). In other words, metacommunication is a *message about a message* (Satir, 1967, p. 76). Additionally, the receiver of the message will connect the message with past experiences that influence how the message is understood (Bandler, Grinder, & Satir, 1976). The life script or internalized self-image of the receiver also influences translation.
- The receiver then responds to the sender's verbal and nonverbal messages.

"Noise" includes anything that interferes with this communication process. Noise for the sender includes attitudes, frames of reference, emotions, and difficulty in choosing appropriate words. For the receiver, noise can include factors such as attitudes, background, and experiences that influence the decoding process. In the communication channel, noise may result from environmental sounds, speech problems such as stammering, or annoying or distracting mannerisms such as mumbling. Successful communication ultimately depends on the degree to which noise is overcome or controlled. From this discussion, the complexity of communication becomes very evident. Actually, it is amazing that people understand each other to the extent that they do.

INFLUENCE OF CULTURAL BACKGROUND

Culture not only affects how people communicate with one another, it also creates unique "noises." For example, ethnicity is often associated with differences in social class. This is because the percentage of non-whites who are poor is larger than that of whites (Davis & Proctor, 1989). Studies in ethnicity have shown that people differ in their experience of emotional pain, how they show it, how they communicate about what is troubling them, their beliefs about the cause of the difficulties, attitudes toward the social worker, and the intervention they expect (McGoldrick & Giordano, 1996). Social workers who follow practices of the dominant culture may not understand when ethnic families communicate in nonstandard ways.

The FSW must carefully consider factors that affect both the verbal and nonverbal behavior of any person. In family social work, we assume that the behavior of an individual occurs within a family context. Similarly, the behavior of a family must be placed within a cultural context. Personal, familial, cultural, and social background affect behavior, and such factors should be considered when interpreting nonverbal or verbal behavior. For one person, lack of eye contact may suggest avoidance; in another, the same behavior may suggest that the person is listening but is from a culture where eye contact is considered impolite. Similarly, talking face to face may be a sign of interest and concern in some cultures but a sign of disrespect in others.

Many are familiar with the different ways individuals greet each other. In some cultures, hugs and kisses are exchanged as a greeting, while in others the same type of greeting would be uncomfortable. Initial FSW impressions of a client's nonverbal behavior should be tentative until the FSW learns more about the personal, social, and cultural background of the client. The best way to become familiar with another culture is to ask questions conveying an interest in learning more about the family's background.

The impact of ethnicity is often overlooked, yet ethnic values and identification are usually retained for several generations after immigration. Ethnic family issues may be filtered by gender, roles, expressiveness, birth order, separation, or individuation. Cultural background may also prescribe norms of communication. For example, an emphasis on keeping things "in the family" or the manner of discussing (or not discussing) certain subjects may be handed down from generation to generation, reflecting individual and cultural influences. Space limitations do not permit detailing beliefs and patterns that every cultural group has about the family. Interested readers are referred to McGoldrick, Giordano, and Pearce (1996), Sue and Sue (1990), and Lum (1992).

Methods of Providing Information

The most commonly used intervention at all professional levels is providing information. The FSW must decide what information to provide to parents and how to evaluate the parents' understanding of this information. If parents have not mastered the material, it is the FSW's job to determine what steps must be taken to assure that the parents either develop the understanding necessary to handle the problem or modify their behavior so that necessary clinical goals are achieved.

The FSW must assess the parents' levels of functioning, including the degree to which they can work as a team. Understanding parents' backgrounds helps the FSW decide how to provide necessary information and direct attention to areas of parental concern. Assessment also gives the FSW an understanding about parental strengths and weaknesses that influence child management. Listening to parents discuss their child and related concerns is the best source of obtaining this understanding, although this may require a new orientation for the FSW who may be more accustomed to imposing strict time limits on interviews with parents.

Even simple instructions to parents must be tailored to fit the parents' unique characteristics. A permissive parent, for example, may be unable to stick to a precise behavioral regime for an acting-out child, while an authoritarian parent may find it impossible to negotiate house rules with his or her child. Between these two extremes are the parents who do well with most instructions if the instructions are clear. The FSW must assess parental styles accurately and modify tactics to provide parents with an individualized approach.

The FSW is charged with continually assessing parents to understand their personalized responses to stresses and also their problem-solving abilities. This process applies even in the seemingly simple task of giving instructions. Thus, FSWs must find clear ways of instructing (teaching) and of determining whether the information is understood.

Complex instructions can be provided in written form to parents at the end of an interview. The FSW may suggest a place for the note, such as the refrigerator door, so that parents may easily refer to the instructions. Parents should be asked to repeat instructions to verify the accuracy of their understanding. This verbal review is one way to assure that instructions are clearly and concisely presented and understood. It also gives parents an opportunity to ask questions. However, the system is not foolproof, and other steps may be necessary as well.

Telephone follow-up is useful, as parents may have additional questions after they have reflected on the interview but be reluctant to ask "dumb" questions or to bother the busy FSW. Another way to assist parents is to encourage them to telephone the FSW freely when needed. However, when speaking with individual members of a family, it is important that the FSW be aware of how he or she can easily get triangulated into family dynamics. Also, reassessment of the situation and discussions with the parents at subsequent visits should be ongoing.

When providing information, giving instructions, and following up are inadequate to accomplish the tasks, the FSW must determine what further assistance is necessary. The goal becomes finding a practical way to help parents understand their problems and change their own behavior if required. The competent FSW can judge what can or must be undertaken, what should be delayed until appropriate intermediate goals have been achieved, and what must be postponed indefinitely. Consequently, the FSW should be willing to adopt alternative procedures based on an assessment of the total situation.

For various reasons, parents may be unable to comprehend even simple directions. In such cases, other forms of help must be found so that supportive and preparatory intervention can take place. In this, as in all aspects of family support social work, the FSW must solicit feedback from parents so they may participate actively in the evaluation process.

ATTENDING BEHAVIORS

Attending behaviors help the FSW to tune in and focus on people in the interview. A common pitfall for new workers is to get trapped into talking about someone outside the room. The FSW knows when this is happening because engaging in such discussions starts to feel like "gossip." These feelings demonstrate that the social worker is paying close attention to what clients are saying and doing. In the process, FSWs must minimize discussion of their personal experiences. Because family meetings are not social situations, the social worker must contain or be in control of self.

Critical to attending is the development of active listening skills. Family social workers must listen carefully to clients and convey an accurate understanding of their messages. Additionally, attending behaviors invite clients into the conversation, because appropriate body language and words to convey interest in what clients are saying. Listening involves hearing, observing, encouraging, remembering, and understanding.

FSWs must use visual attending skills, particularly eye contact and appropriate facial expressions. Maintaining eye contact does not mean staring intensely; instead, it means keeping the client within the range of vision in a continuous, relaxed way. The level of eye contact should respect cultural diversity. In addition to visual attending skills, FSWs use physical attending skills. Ideally, throughout a meeting, the FSW faces family members with a posture that is neither tense nor overly relaxed; a tense posture may convey rigidity, and a very relaxed posture may convey too much informality. Different cultures may have different comfort levels concerning distance, and these should be respected. Leaning forward slightly, especially during vital parts of an interview, motivates clients to speak. Body posture and attending should seem natural, not staged or stilted.

Verbal attending skills involve listening closely to what others are stating verbally (content), para-verbally (voice tone and inflection), and nonverbally (body language). With practice, FSWs can isolate the client's "meta-messages" (hidden messages).

These are suggestions, not hard and fast rules. The FSW must be sensitive to cultural differences that require modification of attending behaviors. For instance, members of some cultures consider direct eye contact disrespectful, and others vary as to preferred distances between speakers. Ultimately, the social worker must learn to use attending skills that are culturally appropriate. Cross-cultural skills are discussed throughout this book.

SELF-AWARENESS

Self-awareness is an important ingredient of family social work. We referred earlier to the influence that values and biases may have on work with families. Every human being has needs, values, feelings, and biases, and FSWs must assess personal biases that could interfere with effective family social work. In achieving self-awareness, the FSW demonstrates honesty and avoids unethical use of clients to fulfill personal psychological needs. All people have unmet needs or quirks that must be examined to ensure that they do not diminish effectiveness. For example, clients who are experiencing problems similar to those of the FSW can cause feelings of confusion or avoidance in the FSW. There are several benefits of self-awareness:

1. Self-awareness strengthens personal competence whereby the FSW does not need to rely on clients to enhance self-esteem. Work with clients can be honest, without false reassurance from an FSW attempting to elicit positive feedback from clients or fearing that clients may drop out of family social work.
2. Self-awareness encourages appropriate use of professional authority. Family social workers have the potential and opportunity to misuse power, which can occur when a social worker is only comfortable when in control or when coercing a client to comply. Power can also be abused through compulsive advice giving or needing to feel superior to clients.
3. Self-awareness enhances managed use of intimacy. FSWs with unmet intimacy needs or a poorly developed capacity for intimacy will have trouble building worker–family relationships. For example, the social worker who lacks self-awareness may show excessive distancing behaviors or become overly involved with the client.

Self-awareness also helps the FSW acknowledge when personal problems, unmet emotional needs, and critical life events interfere with effective work with clients. Transference and countertransference are important concepts related to self-awareness. Transference occurs when clients relate to FSWs as if they were another significant figure (e.g., parent or another authority) in the client's life. Feelings, fears, defenses, and reactions present in another relationship are projected onto the FSW. Countertransference occurs when FSWs transfer their own feelings toward significant others to clients. While such feelings are common within the context of helping, self-awareness allows the FSW to control these experiences rather than vice versa.

Steps can be taken to enhance worker self-awareness. First, workers can undergo personal counseling with the goal of expanding self-awareness. Issues also can be discussed with one's supervisor, and if they interfere with effectiveness or create difficulties in working with particular problems or clients, the caseload can be restricted to clients with whom one can work effectively.

Effective FSWs are in touch with their experiences and feelings and are able to identify and accept a range of feelings and experiences. They are aware of their own values, beliefs, and needs and can develop warm and deep relationships with others. Effective FSWs feel secure enough to reveal who they genuinely are. They accept personal responsibility for their behaviors, receive feedback nondefensively, admit when they are wrong, accept limits placed upon them, and are honest. Effective FSWs set realistic goals with clients, striving for excellence instead of perfection, and are aware of the impact they have on others. Becoming an effective FSW is an ongoing process rather than a one-time endeavor. Thus, FSWs are committed to improving their skills throughout their careers.

CORE QUALITIES NEEDED BY FAMILY SOCIAL WORKERS

Research consistently supports the importance of the social worker's capacity to demonstrate empathy, warmth, and genuineness (Beutler, Machado, & Allstetter Neufelt, 1994). All of these qualities are essential to most helping situations (Lambert & Bergin, 1994), and they are prerequisites for effective social work. Together, they help the social worker to establish a climate of trust and safety in which family members can begin to view their problems in new ways (Lambert & Bergin, 1994).

Family social workers can be reassured by the fact that about 30 percent of change in counseling occurs because of the quality of the worker–client relationship, whereas model and technique contribute only about 15 percent. Strong alliances are formed when families perceive the social worker to be warm, trustworthy, nonjudgmental, and empathetic (Miller, Hubble, & Duncan, 1995). This opinion is supported through interviews of parents who took part in a home-based, family-centered program (Coleman & Collins, 1997). Families valued social workers' basic interviewing skills such as listening, support, and teaching. The researchers concluded that, "families did not remember the fancy techniques. Instead, they recalled the dignity and respect received in treatment."

EMPATHY

The FSW uses empathy to communicate understanding of client experiences, behaviors, and feelings from the client's point of view. Empathy is a core ingredient in establishing and developing relationships with clients. Social workers need to maintain empathy with individuals and respect for the family's way of doing things. Family social work "starts where the client is," even when the client's perspective eventually needs to be challenged. Empathy involves seeing the world through another person's eyes, but differs from sympathy or pity. It must be remembered, however, that some ethnic groups do not focus on feelings directly and the worker must find culturally specific ways of seeing the world through another's eyes.

When it is difficult to understand what a client feels, empathy should never be faked. Admitting to a lack of understanding is acceptable for FSWs, who can then ask for clarification. Poorly executed empathy includes parroting, verbatim repetition, insincerity, and empathy that is inaccurate. In addition, excessive empathy can seem artificial and result in annoying people. One very complex issue for all FSWs to navigate is how to be empathic when another person is being blamed. In these cases, the FSW might say something like, "I can see that you are troubled by Phil's behavior. I can understand how you might be upset and my hunch is that Phil is also troubled. Phil, can you tell us how you feel when you hear Katie saying such-and-such?" The trap of expressing empathy in a family interview is that the worker will empathize with one person and join a coalition against another family member.

Empathy can be expressed at different levels of depth and effectiveness. A five-level scale has been developed by Truax and Carkhuff (1967) to measure empathy.

FIVE LEVELS OF EMPATHETIC RESPONSES

Level 1: At Level 1, the responses of the social worker detract significantly from the verbal and behavioral expressions of the client. The response communicates less than the client expressed, and the social worker shows no awareness of even surface feelings. The social worker may be bored, uninterested, or operating from a preconceived frame of reference that does not recognize the client's individualism.

Level 2: The social worker responds, but not fully, and subtracts from the noticeable affect of the client. The social worker may show some awareness of obvious surface feelings, but depletes from the client's experience.

Level 3: The social worker mirrors client responses. Responses are interchangeable in that they express the same affect and meaning. The social worker responds with an accurate understanding of the client, but may overlook deeper feelings. The response does not add or detract and shows that the social worker is willing to know and understand more.

Level 4: The responses of the social worker enhance the client's expressions, taking client feelings to a deeper level than the client was able or willing to express. The social worker thus takes understanding of what was communicated to a deeper level.

Level 5: The social worker gives accurate responses to all of the client's deeper and surface feelings. The social worker is "tuned in" to the client, making it possible for the two to explore very deeply aspects of the client's existence.

Empathy at levels lower than Level 3 suggests that the social worker has failed to pick up on key client feelings.

The ability to understand the needs of parents is a prerequisite skill to effective work with families. FSWs often identify strongly with children, and at times this identification may be so strong as to appear anti-adult. Such a position can lead to the view of parents as negative influences on the child, often accompanied by a desire to work with the child alone, isolated from the rest of the family.

A unique perspective is required for effective work with families. FSWs must understand parents' needs and empathize with their feelings. Of vital importance is empathy with the struggle that many parents experience in raising children, particularly parents of children with special needs. In addition, the FSW must recognize that parents may feel confused, hurt, and guilty by the time family problems have reached a level where professional help is needed.

To be effective in family social work, FSWs must shift from a child-centered focus to a family-centered one, identifying with both parents and children. In addition, while empathy is an important skill for the FSW to master, family members can also be taught empathy skills to use with one another.

One formula for making empathy statements is:

"You feel_____ (emotion) because_____ (restatement of client's experiences and/or behaviors)."

The following procedure has been developed to help in creating empathy statements:

1. "It seems like you feel . . ."
2. Feeling label.
3. Place the feeling in a context.
4. Make the tense of the feeling *here and now.*
5. Check it out for accuracy.

Other stems for empathetic sentences include the following:

"It sounds like . . ."
"You seem to feel . . ."
"From your point of view . . ."
"It sounds like you are saying . . ."
"Kind of makes you feel . . ."
"I am sensing up that . . ."
"If I am hearing you correctly . . ."
"I am not sure I am with you, but . . ."
"I wonder if you are saying that . . ."
"Is it possible that . . .?"
"Perhaps you're feeling . . ."
"As I understand what you are saying, you felt that..."
"So, as you see the situation . . ."
"From where you stand, it seems . . ."
"It seems to you that . . ."
"Where you're coming from . . ."
"Could it be that . . .?"
"Correct me if I'm wrong . . ."
"You appear to be feeling . . ."
"I get the impression that . . ."

An added step in being empathic in family interviews is to check with other members of the family to locate their feelings about a specified issue.

REFLECTION OF FEELINGS   Reflection of feelings is one way of showing empathy. Since client feelings may be masked or unknown, correct reflection of feelings validates feelings and shows that the social worker is listening. This process is a *mirror* that reflects both feelings and content. Reflection may be difficult when several different feelings coexist, but an accurate reflection may help the client sort out conflicting or unclear feelings. Feelings are expressed both verbally and nonverbally, making it necessary to observe incongruence between verbal and nonverbal expression. For example, a client might verbally express comfort in the meeting with the FSW, but at the same time, the FSW may note nonverbal signs of discomfort such as a scowl or a rigid, closed posture.

While reflections help build rapport and trust, some clients may be uncomfortable talking about feelings; for example, some people use intellectualization as a defense. It is important to vary the sentence stems used and to draw from a diverse range of feelings and words.

EXAMPLES OF FIVE LEVELS OF EMPATHY   Client (describing her husband's reaction to her decision to find a job) "He laughed at me. My own husband just sat there and laughed at me. I felt like such a fool, so put down."

Level 1: What did you say his name was?

Level 2: Uh huh, I see.

Level 3: You sound upset with your husband.

Level 4: You sound be humiliated by his comments.

Level 5: I get a sense that your husband hurt you a lot. It seems to me that you are also feeling angry with him.

ADVANCED EMPATHY   Using advanced empathy, the FSW shares *hunches* about clients in an attempt to understand client feelings and concerns more clearly. The goal is to facilitate client self-awareness, which, in turn, leads to new client goals and behaviors. Examples of advanced empathy through sharing of FSW hunches include the following:

- Hunches that help clients develop a bigger picture, e.g., "The problem doesn't seem to be just your attitude toward your husband anymore. Your resentment seems to have spread to the children as well. Could that be the case?"
- Hunches that help clients articulate what they are expressing indirectly or merely implying, e.g., "I think I also might be hearing you say that you are more than disappointed—perhaps even hurt and angry."
- Hunches that help clients draw logical conclusions from what they are saying, e.g., "From all that you've said about her, it seems to me you also are saying right now that you resent having to be with her. I realize you haven't said that directly, but I'm wondering if you are feeling that way about her."
- Hunches that help clients discuss topics about which they have hinted, e.g., "You've brought up sexual matters a number of times, but you haven't followed up on them. My guess is that sex is a pretty important area for you—but perhaps pretty touchy, too."

- Hunches that help clients identify themes, e.g., "If I'm not mistaken, you've mentioned in two or three different ways that it is sometimes difficult for you to stick up for your own rights. For instance, you let your husband decide that you would not return to college, though this is against your wishes."
- Hunches that help clients completely own their experiences, behaviors, and feelings, e.g., "You sound as if you have already decided to marry him, but I don't hear you saying that directly."

NONPOSSESSIVE WARMTH

An important factor in the relationship between FSW and client is the level of warmth and caring shown to the client. Warmth exists when the social worker communicates with clients in ways that convey acceptance, understanding, and interest in their well-being and make them feel safe regardless of such external factors as the client's problematic behavior, demeanor, or appearance (Sheafor, Horejsi, & Horejsi, 1997). According to Goldstein, "without warmth, some interventions may be technically correct but therapeutically impotent" (Hackney & Cormier, 1996, p. 65). Establishing a relationship based on feelings of warmth and understanding is the foundation for successful client change.

Warmth is more than saying, "I care," although this is nonetheless important. Although it can be conveyed *verbally* by one's choice of words, it is largely displayed *nonverbally*. Examples include (Johnson, 1993, as cited in Hackney & Cormier, 1996, p. 66):

Tone of voice:	soft, soothing
Facial expression:	smiling, interested
Posture:	relaxed, leaning toward the other person
Eye contact:	looking directly into the other person's eyes
Touching:	touching the other person softly and discreetly
Gestures:	open, welcoming
Physical proximity:	close

Warmth or the lack of it can have a strong impact on the client and the worker–client relationship. Without it, "a worker's words will sound hollow and insincere and will have no therapeutic impact" (Sheafor, Horejsi, & Horejsi, 1997, p. 149).

FIVE LEVELS OF NONPOSSESSIVE WARMTH   Five levels of nonpossessive warmth are presented in the following list. Level 3 is the minimal level to be achieved for the effective FSW, while Levels 4 and 5 communicate deep warmth and regard. Levels of warmth that fall below Level 3 fail to convey adequate warmth.

Level 1: The FSW's verbal and behavioral expression communicates lack of respect (negative regard) for the client. The FSW conveys a total lack of respect.

Level 2: The FSW communicates little respect for client's feelings, experiences, and potentials and may respond mechanically or passively.

Level 3: The FSW minimally acknowledges regard for the client's abilities and capacities for improved functioning. The FSW, at the least, communicates that the client matters.

Level 4: The FSW communicates very deep respect and concern for the client. The FSW's responses enable the client to feel free to be himself or herself and to experience feeling valued.

Level 5: The FSW communicates deepest respect for the client's worth as a person and for his or her potential and communicates deep caring and commitment to the client.

EXAMPLES OF FIVE LEVELS OF NONPOSSESSIVE WARMTH   Keep in mind that tone of voice and nonverbal behavior are crucial in conveying warmth.

The client says, "My daughter is a bright girl, but she's been getting bad grades in school. I'm not sure what to do."

Level 1: Uh huh. (No eye contact with the client, bored tone of voice.)

Level 2: That's tough. (Some eye contact, flat vocal tone.)

Level 3: You feel angry that your daughter is not living up to her potential. (Eye contact, leaning toward the client.)

Level 4: It is disappointing for you when your child is not doing well in school, and you are worried about her. (FSW looks into client's eyes. Tone of voice expresses concern.)

Level 5: It must be disappointing for you and your daughter that she is not doing well in school. I can see you are worried about her. Let's look at ways we can help your daughter have a more successful experience in school. (Good eye contact, relaxed and open posture, concerned yet optimistic tone of voice.)

GENUINENESS

The quality of genuineness is perhaps the most difficult to describe. According to Truax and Carkhuff (1967), genuineness refers to a lack of defensiveness or artificiality in the social worker's communications with the client. Barker (1995) defines genuineness as "sincerity and honesty . . . genuineness includes being unpretentious with clients" (p. 150). Like empathy and warmth, genuineness is conveyed at different levels. Level 3 is the minimum for effective social work.

FIVE LEVELS OF GENUINENESS

Level 1: The FSW's verbalizations are slightly unrelated to what he or she is feeling at the moment. Responses may be negative or destructive. The

FSW may convey defensiveness in words and actions and does not use these defensive feelings to explore the helping relationship with the client.

Level 2: The FSW's verbalizations are slightly unrelated to what she or he is feeling. The FSW does not know how to manage negative reactions toward the client, nor how to use them constructively in the interview. The interviewing style may sound mechanical or rehearsed.

Level 3: There is no evidence of incongruence between what the FSW says and feels in the interview. The social worker might take a neutral personal stance. The FSW makes appropriate responses that seem sincere but do not reflect intense personal involvement.

Level 4: The FSW presents cues suggesting genuine responses (both positive and negative) that are nondestructive. Responses are congruent, but the FSW might hesitate to express them fully.

Level 5: The FSW freely expresses self but is nonexploitative. The FSW is spontaneous, open to all experiences, nondefensive, and uses interactions constructively to open further discussion and exploration for both the client and the FSW.

EXAMPLES OF FIVE LEVELS OF GENUINENESS   The client says, "I'm ready to throw my daughter out of the house. She doesn't listen to a word I say, and she does whatever she pleases."

Level 1: You seem to be overreacting.

Level 2: You need to practice tough love.

Level 3: Teenagers are a handful.

Level 4: I know from a personal experience that it can be very challenging to deal with teenagers.

Level 5: I know it can be challenging and difficult to communicate with teenagers. Let's look at how we can help you and your daughter work toward a more satisfying relationship.

DYSFUNCTIONAL BEHAVIORS TO AVOID IN FAMILY SOCIAL WORK

In this chapter we have described a number of beginning skills that are needed in the beginning phase of family social work. In addition to knowing what is helpful in an interview, the social worker should be aware of dysfunctional behaviors that can interfere with effective helping. Accordingly, we provide the following list of behaviors to avoid (Collins, 1989; Gabor & Collins, 1985–86):

• Taking sides with individual family members;
• Giving false reassurance or agreement where inappropriate;
• Ignoring cues about the family's subjective experience of the problem while dealing exclusively with "objective" material;

- Judgmental responding;
- Inappropriate use of humor or other responses that inhibit discussion or undermine trust;
- Premature problem solving;
- Criticizing or belittling family members and behaving in a condescending manner;
- Over-reliance on "chit-chat";
- Overprotecting family members by ignoring clear cues to implicit information.

CHAPTER SUMMARY

Family social work takes place in five phases: beginning, assessment, intervention, evaluation, and termination. Specific skills are required for the family social worker in each of these phases. In this chapter we looked at skills involved in the beginning phase, when the social worker establishes rapport with families. The FSW needs to understand the principles of effective communication and know how to interpret clients' verbal and nonverbal messages. Core qualities required of the FSW include empathy, nonpossessive warmth, and genuineness. The skills and qualities required for effective social work are developed and refined throughout the social worker's career.

EXERCISES

4.1 CHALLENGES FACING THE FSW

Think about types of clients or types of problems you may find difficult to handle. List these, and write what you would do if faced with each.

4.2 SKILL DEVELOPMENT

Think about what skills you need to develop as a family worker. List these skills below, starting with the most important skill.

4.3 REFLECTION OF FEELINGS

List at least twenty-five words that can be used to describe feelings as part of statements to clients.

4.4 CORE CONDITIONS

Provide examples of each of the core conditions: empathy, nonpossessive warmth, and genuineness. Create responses that fit into each of the five levels of response.

Client statement: "I don't know what to do. My husband just left me, my son got picked up for shoplifting, and my daughter just told me she is pregnant.

If that is not enough, my boss told me that I might lose my job because there is not enough business at this time of year."

4.5   THE FIRST FAMILY INTERVIEW

Break into groups of six. One student will be the FSW and another student will be the observer. Formulate a problem and create a family. Role-play performing and interviewing the first family interview. Take ten minutes for each stage outlined above. Report back to the class on how the interview went, including what went right and what the difficulties were in this first interview. At the end of the discussion, brainstorm in the class how to overcome some of the obstacles that were encountered in the role-play.

QUALITATIVE FAMILY ASSESSMENT

CHAPTER CONTENTS

INTRODUCTION TO QUALITATIVE ASSESSMENT

The next five chapters discuss how to conduct a family assessment. The goal of assessment and problem definition is to explore, identify, and define dynamics within and external to the family that contribute to the family's problems and strengths. Assessment is a *process* of collecting enough information about the family to make informed intervention decisions. Careful assessment will lead to the development of realistic and concrete goals because the nature of the assessment will determine what you do as a family worker. For example, if the worker, after assessment, determines that a child's problems are due to triangulation into a conflicted marriage, the worker is likely to work on detriangulation and marital repair (see for example, Chapters 2 and 9). If, on the other hand, the worker determines that a child's difficulties are because the family has not learned the principles of successful behavioral management (see for example, Chapter 11), the intervention will target teaching parents about behavioral principles and child management techniques to help them develop parenting skills that are consistent and appropriate to the child's behavior.

During assessment, the FSW assists the family, ideally with all members participating, to explore issues of concern. This exploration should lead to a deeper, more accurate understanding of the situation faced by the family. Each family member will have his or her own unique perspective of the problem and every individual perspective is important. For example, a problem defined by the family as a child spending time "hanging out with friends" may be a "conforming" issue for the parent, an "independence" issue for the target child, and an "exclusion" issue for siblings. Problems usually span behavioral, affective, cognitive, and experiential domains. In addition, some problems are more likely to arise in particular families at crisis periods in the family life cycle.

Theoretical concepts will shape the assessment and the intervention. The assessment of the family sets the stage for later interventions and is critical to the success of work with the family. There are three approaches inherent in conducting a comprehensive assessment of families (Holman, 1983):

- The interview;
- Observations, and;
- Checklists and instruments.

Two additional kinds of information for assessment include *content* and *process*. Content is the *what*—that is, actual information given to the family social worker. Process refers to *how* family members interact with one another.

In this chapter we describe approaches to qualitative assessment of families. Qualitative techniques help the family worker to understand meaningful events in the family's life using words, observations, pictures, and graphic analyses rather than numbers (quantitative assessment). Typically, family workers will use qualitative approaches to obtain an overview of the family's life and functioning. Qualitative techniques are particularly helpful in this process, as we will see. Our discussion of assessment techniques is informed by *Clinical Assessment for Social Workers: Quantitative and Qualitative Methods,*

| CASE 5.1 | FAMILY ASSESSMENT |

14-year-old Madison and her 49-year-old mother, Jennie, were referred for counseling after Madison started cutting her arms with razor blades and threatened suicide. She moved out of her family home eight months previously for what Jennie's common-law partner, Jack, described as "adolescent rebellion." She lives with her best friend Sarah. Jennie and Jack had been together for ten years. Jennie divorced her first husband, Al, after Madison's older sister Allison disclosed sexual abuse by Al. Allison, 25, lives 2000 miles away from her family and has little contact with them. Al was eventually convicted of sexually abusing Allison. There are two other children in the family: Graham, a 10-year-old boy, and John, who is six.

Jennie has strong support from her sister Judy. Judy has worked hard to hold the family together and has encouraged both Jennie and Madison to be open with each other about their experiences. Several losses have plagued the family in recent years. Judy's daughter died a couple of years ago. In addition, Jennie's mother also died several years ago and her father one year later. The loss of her mother was very difficult for the family, and it did not appear that they had fully grieved the loss.

Madison just recently disclosed that she had been sexually abused by both her biological father and her mother's common-law partner. Jennie believed Madison and immediately ended the relationship with Jack. Apart from dealing with Madison's abuse, Jennie is also experiencing quite severe financial difficulties. The financial problems have worsened since she is now only working one job and since Jack is no longer in the home to add an extra income. Jennie is worried about Madison and recognizes how stressful the disclosure and the abuse are on her. At the same time, Jennie has had a hard time "reading" and understanding her daughter. Because of these difficulties, Jennie was uncertain how to manage her daughter and discipline her. If Madison's problems were merely "adolescent stuff," Jennie would be able to deal with the behaviors as such. On the other hand, if Madison's difficulties stemmed from the sexual abuse, she would handle the behaviors more supportively and in a different way. Jennie needed assistance with understanding her daughter. She worried that once Madison gets older, she would lose whatever leverage she has over her daughter's behavior. At the same time, she wanted to be closer to her daughter.

Where would you start as a FSW?

2nd ed. (Jordan & Franklin, 2003), especially Chapter 5 by Gilbert and Franklin, "Qualitative Assessment Methods" (pp. 139–178). Next, we describe the context of family assessment, and then a number of qualitative techniques are presented.

THE CONTEXT OF FAMILY ASSESSMENT

What is going on with Madison in Case 5.1? Several issues are of concern in this family. The most pressing concern is that Madison is threatening suicide and is harming herself right now through her self-mutilation. Yet, there are many other issues facing this family. What issues should the family worker address? Where should a family worker start in working with this family?

Having appropriate assessment tools will help the FSW and families understand what is going on with the case. As well, conducting an accurate assessment will ensure that the invention is appropriately matched to the problem.

Holman (1983) suggests that a FSW will assess four areas:

1. The problem;
2. The family as a system;
3. The family and its environment; and
4. The family life cycle (p. 21).

Workers struggle with deciding what information to gather in the first and subsequent meetings. While they benefit from knowledge of theoretical concepts related to understanding the family and the presenting problem, different models of family therapy emphasize different things in assessment. Some theories, for example, emphasize dyads and triangles while others look at the entire family unit. Perhaps most important in assessing a family is to treat every family as unique. A clear understanding of the problem is necessary for devising appropriate interventions. FSWs should be prepared to research the literature to see what the experts have hypothesized in terms of contributors to the presenting problem. It will be necessary to understand the duration of the family's presenting problem (often concern or difficulties with a child) and how the family has tried to deal with the issue previously. As well, the FSWs will be interested in identifying the strengths and resources the family has. (Strengths, resources, and resiliency are discussed in more detail in Chapter 8.) The FSWs will be concerned with family roles, communication patterns, skills family members have to carry out required roles, family closeness, and family rules. They will also need to know how the family operates as a system and how various family subsystems such as the parental and child subsystems are functioning.

Several tools are available to workers who are doing family assessment. These include genograms, ecomaps, and family time lines. All these tools represent important family information through visual depiction of data. They are symbols that provide a practical way of pulling an enormous amount of data about a family together on a single page. They put the information collected in a coherent and understandable order, connected with various components of family theory. At the same time, these graphic images can capture process data as families move through their life cycle in interaction with one another and with their environment. In Chapter 2, for example, an image of a circular interaction pattern—circular causality—showed how the repetitive interactions in a dyad are embedded in familiar transactional patterns. This image is both dynamic and capable of capturing complex patterns of interaction in a single graphic image. Similarly, other graphic assessment tools have been developed to capture processes and complex sets of information.

For example, genograms are popular graphic tools that are often used in family work to capture process and content information. In fact, genograms are often a starting point for assessing family functioning. We describe genograms in a section of this chapter. We also look at ecological information that is critical for successful assessment of a family. Ecological information is captured by ecomaps (sometimes known as ecograms). Another useful graphic tool includes the use of a family time line, also discussed later in this chapter.

In the first section of this chapter, we discuss the purposes of family assessment, models of family functioning, and an ecological approach to family assessment.

PURPOSE OF FAMILY ASSESSMENT

Assessing family functioning is complex, and workers often struggle with deciding what information is essential and what can be discarded. Although it is necessary to glean the content of family information from the family, the worker should also observe family interactions. In addition to information gathering through questions and answers and observing interactional patterns within the family in the here-and-now, workers often rely on concrete tools to gather information on which to base their assessment. Aside from focusing on problems, it is also important to understand areas of family strength and resilience. These are discussed in more detail Chapter 8.

Family assessment has several purposes:

1. To assess whether a family will profit from family work, and if so, decide what types of interventions will serve them best;
2. To identify what specific changes in the family should be made;
3. To create short-term and long-term goals of the intervention based on realistic objectives;
4. To identify family strengths and resources as well as environmental and community resources available or needed to move the family toward desired changes;
5. To understand and collect information on baseline family functioning so that the outcome of the intervention may be determined;
6. To identify mutually agreed-upon targets of change so that a termination point can be targeted and so that workers and families will be able to measure achievement of desired outcomes.

ECOLOGICAL ASSESSMENT

We are living in a complex and evolving society. Many of the problems families bring to counseling today lie not so much within families as with societal circumstances.

—May and Larson Church, 1999

As mentioned in Chapter 1, family social work often involves working with families whose basic needs are not getting met, often through no fault of their own. Family social workers seek to understand a family's relationship with its environment. This relationship is reciprocal—that is, families give and take from the community, and the community gives and takes back. Nichols and Schwartz (2004) suggest that ecology is the study of relationships that connect all members of earth's household. The environment plays a role in the development and maintenance of problems that families experience. Helping professionals have fallen into the trap of viewing problems from the perspective of "sickness" or pathology. In contrast, a family ecological assessment contributes an understanding of how a family functions within its environment; strengths and weaknesses are both considered. Each individual family member's behavior has an effect and is affected by the other members. One popular metaphor is to compare a family to a mobile hanging in the wind. Think of each piece of the mobile as a family member. When one piece moves, the others do also; such is the case with family members. One member's behavior produces corresponding changes or responses in all the other members.

Individuals are nested in a set of larger social units, similar to Russian nesting dolls. The first social unit is the family, which is known as the micro system. An ecological assessment identifies the social supports available to the family and the amount of reciprocity between the family and society. Some families rely strongly on environmental supports without returning any resources back to the environment. Others experience severe gaps in environmental supports that prevent the meeting of needs. Generally, when a family has sufficient resources for coping with stress and demands, the overall functioning of family members will be adequate (Rothery, 1993). As children grow older, their ecological niches expand:

> ... the world of the adolescent is now so powerfully defined by systemic forces other than home—peer network, pop culture, school, and neighborhood that working with the family alone is rarely powerful enough to effect change in the life of a troubled teen (Taffel, 1996, cited in May & Larson Church, 1999).

Most children go to school, and it is important for parents to nurture a supportive attitude toward their children's education. Yet, school difficulties can be particularly complex for families and social workers to navigate. Children suffer academically when their home life is too chaotic for them to develop competence in school. Others have difficulty when they are preoccupied with hunger pangs, or when they are bullied or sleep-deprived because of worry. Peer pressure and lack of a structured family routine can take its toll on a child's success. When children bring antisocial behavior to school, everyone suffers. FSWs can provide the necessary linkage between families and schools to help parents and teachers collaborate in addressing the issues that interfere with effective learning. Thus, it is important that the FSW take into account the impact of larger systems upon individuals and families.

A family's support system is also an important component of ecological assessment. Some families have an over-representation in formal networks such as child welfare, the criminal justice system, addictions treatment, and so on. When a family has excessive formal support and a lack of informal supports such as kinships and friendships, their lives may be chaotic as helpers trip over one another and work at cross-purposes. Culture plays a role in the nature of support networks as well, and minority families may have strong kinship ties. In such cases, FSWs must understand the community. Another aspect to examine is the direction of the energy flow—is the community giving to the family exclusively, or does the family return something to the community? Relationships with neighborhoods are also important to assess—how well do people know their neighbors? When given a choice, it is preferable that people rely on informal networks. Formal networks should never replace what a family can do for itself.

An ecological assessment should be multifaceted, and if the worker delves deep enough, the detail will be richly textured and complex. Almeida and colleagues suggest the cultural context model to incorporate the many facets of a family's life.

> Pulling threads from developmental theory, feminist theory, family theory, and cross-cultural studies to weave an integrated web, the cultural context model approaches the family from a multifaceted community-based perspective that addresses gender, ethnic background, and socialization factors (Almeida, Woods, Messineo, & Font, 1998, p. 415).

A comprehensive ecological assessment, using the hierarchy of needs as a guide, involves recognizing concrete realities such as food, clothing, shelter, medical care, employment, and social realities derived from social relationships (Holman, 1983). An example of an assessment protocol built on this approach may be found in several current texts on assessment (e.g., Gambrill, 2006; Jordan & Franklin, 2003). In addition, social networks involve informal or formal supportive persons or formal institutions. Informal supportive persons are an important part of a family's network, and these individuals or groups are known as "natural helpers." For some families, environmental resources are not available, while others may not be aware of them, or alternatively, either not know how to use them or refuse to use them. An ecomap is a useful starting point to obtain information about the family's relationship with its environment. An ecomap can provide important information about how the family gets its needs met, highlighted by Maslow's hierarchy of needs (1968).

Abraham Maslow created a theory placing the hierarchy of needs in five broad layers: physiological, safety and security, love and belonging, esteem, and the need to actualize self (see Figure 5.1). The needs simulate developmental needs as people progress through a lifetime. Physiological needs are mostly apparent and involve physical needs for food, water, and physical sustenance. It is quite disturbing that some people, children in particular, in the wealthiest nations on earth fail to get basic physical needs met. Children go to school hungry and the elderly live on pet food. The second layer of needs, safety and security needs, come after the physical needs have been met. Living in safe neighborhoods, feeling safe from physical and emotional danger, and feeling secure in our jobs are but a few of the safety and security needs that people require. Belonging needs include the need for friendship, love, affection, and a sense of belonging to a community. Esteem needs includes two derivatives: the need to be respected and the need for self-respect. The former is derived from

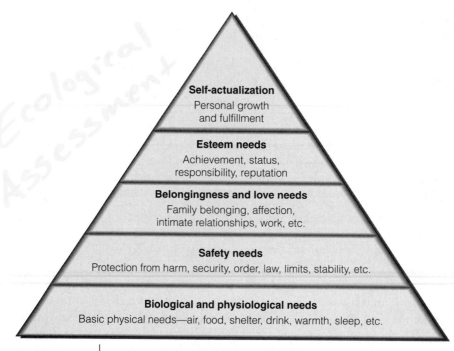

FIGURE 5.1 | MASLOW'S HIERARCHY OF NEEDS

appreciation and dignity, while the latter comes from confidence, competence, achievement, independence and freedom. Maslow saw these four layers of needs as deficit needs—that is, when we do not have these needs met, we have a deficit. However, when these needs are fulfilled, they do not motivate the person. The last level, self-actualization needs, are the needs to grow and be one's best—to transcend. People who are self-actualized possess the qualities of the ideal human being: honest, good, just, playful, unique, and so on. FSWs will not be seeing self-actualizing families in their practice. In fact, Minuchin (1974) pointed out that most low-income families are ensnared in a basic struggle for survival.

Relationships with significant others outside the family constitute an important source of emotional support (Wahler, 1980). Mothers who have little positive daily contact with supportive persons outside the family apparently behave more negatively with their children than those who have more frequent positive interactions outside the family. In assessing the quality of a family's social supports, it is useful to look at *reciprocity, density, complexity, sufficiency, emotional climate,* and, finally, *feedback characteristics* (Rothery, 1993).

- *Reciprocity* involves the extent to which social support is exchanged with others. Many relationships with formal helpers are based on a one-way relationship in which the helper gives and the family takes. A more useful relationship occurs when the family both gives and receives support.
- *Density* involves the number of relationships family members have with others. Ideally, each family member will have multiple relationships outside

the family with supportive individuals. Family members should also be free, depending on their developmental abilities, to form relationships with significant others outside the family.

- *Complexity* refers to the capacity of a social support network to meet a variety of individual and family needs. Social support networks are *sufficient* when social supports are adequate to meet family and individual demands and needs.
- *Emotional climate* refers to the quality of relationships with others outside the family. Relationships that are mostly caring and supportive are preferable to aversive relationships.
- *Feedback characteristics* involve the type of information that is provided by those in the support networks. Ideally, feedback needs to be clear, direct, and honest. It also needs to be corrective or supportive when needed.

The ecomap captures the nature of the relationship between the family and the world around them and how resources and needs match. Ecomaps are discussed in more detail in the Visual Techniques section of this chapter.

QUALITATIVE TECHNIQUES

Qualitative techniques, as mentioned at the beginning of this chapter, aim to describe and understand the meaning behind a family's functioning. The qualitative techniques discussed here include interviewing, observation, and visual techniques, including genograms and ecomaps.

The FSW focuses with the family on a specific topic based on the following guidelines:

- *Severity or urgency:* Is this a topic that needs immediate attention because of the distress it causes, the danger it poses, and/or because of its frequency? Physically or emotionally threatening issues should be dealt with first.
- *Importance:* Is this issue important enough to the client to discuss and act upon? For the family to deal with issues, the problem must have some significance to members.
- *Timing:* Is this a problem that can be managed at this time with available resources?
- *Complexity:* Is this concern a manageable piece of a larger or more complex problem? Can it be divided into parts that are more manageable?
- *Hope of success:* If this issue is the focus, is there a chance that it can be managed successfully? If not, is this the right place to start?
- *Generalization effect:* Is this the kind of problem that, if handled, might lead to improvement in other areas of the family's life?
- *Control:* Is this a problem under client control? To manage more effectively, will the family have to act or influence others to act?
- *Willingness.* Is this a concern or problem that the family is willing to discuss?

During assessment, the family social worker will need to address the following topical areas.

FAMILY HISTORY

AREAS TO EXPLORE

PROBLEM:

1. What factors contributed to the need for the worker's involvement? Why does the family need help now? If the family is involved with an agency involuntarily, how did this happen? How did the family arrive on the doorstep of the agency?
2. What problems are the family currently experiencing, both short-term and long-term? What has the family done about the problem before seeing you?
3. How severe is (are) the problem(s)? What is the urgency with which these problems need to be dealt with? Are any members of the family at risk of harm—physical, emotional, sexual, environmental?
4. Who is in this family? How are they involved with the presenting problem?
5. What is the family structure? Describe boundaries, circular exchanges, roles, communication, relationships, and, coalitions and triangles.
6. What is the family's attitude and motivation concerning the worker involvement? How motivated are individual family members for change compared with the rest of the family? How do family members frame (define) the problem (e.g., shared responsibility versus one member being a problem)? If involvement of the entire family seems warranted, how motivated is each member to being involved in the resolution of the problem? What does the family expect from the worker?
7. What other social systems outside the family are involved with the family? For what issues? What does each family member perceive the problem to be? Are any family members physically or emotionally at risk if they remain in the family during work?

FAMILY INTERNAL FUNCTIONING:

1. What are areas of family competence, especially psychological and social resources used for daily living and meeting crises as they appear?
2. How would family members describe their family as a whole and their relationships with subunits of the family? What is the nature of the relationships within the family? What are the patterns of interaction between family members? What interaction patterns seem to keep the problem going? What are the ongoing patterns and themes in this family?
3. How is the family structured hierarchically? Who has power and how is that power used?
4. What are the strengths and resources of the family unit and of members within the family that can be mobilized to resolve the problem?
5. How does the family communicate? What are the circular patterns of interaction that have become repetitive? Is communication direct, open, and honest?
6. How are family members functioning in their informal and formal roles?
7. What are family boundaries like? How do these boundaries operate—between individuals and subsystems and around the family as a whole?

8. Who is aligned with whom in the family and around which core issues?
9. What are the circular patterns that appear to be causing distress in the family?
10. What are the triangles in the family? Which triangles are hurting family members?
11. How is the parental unit functioning? What is the level of marital satisfaction? Do parents support each other in the discipline and behavioral management of children?
12. What is the nature of relationships within this family?
13. How do parents manage child behavior? Do parents behave consistently with their children?
14. How involved are family members with one another?
15. Whose needs are getting met and whose needs are neglected? What contributes to the differential meeting of these needs?

FAMILY LIFE CYCLE:

1. What is the history of the family? How did the parents meet? What did they bring to their relationship? How did they decide to have children?
2. Where in the family life cycle is this family? How adequately does the family meet the developmental needs of members? What possible developmental issues is the family system facing at this particular point in time? How do these developmental issues fit with the presenting problem and overall family functioning?
3. How well are family members fulfilling their developmental roles and tasks?
4. What are the family's usual means/patterns/mechanisms for resolving developmental crises?

FAMILY ECOLOGICAL ENVIRONMENT:

1. What is the nature of the family's relationship with its environment? Do environmental factors nurture or hinder family functioning?
2. What is the quality of the family's interactions with the social environment, including the breadth and quality of outside relationships and the impact of external factors on the family?
3. How does the family get basic needs met? What is lacking and what are strengths?
4. Who can family members rely on in time of need? What is the nature of contact with support people outside the family in terms of quantity and quality?
5. How dependent or self-sufficient is the family in terms of external resources?
6. How does the family relate to key people, including friends, family, school, work, religious institutions, health care, etc.?
7. What is the family's place in and relationship to their ethno-cultural group?
8. What are the impacts and influences of religious beliefs and values on this family?

9. What is the family's cultural heritage, which can provide strengths and barriers?
10. What are the formal and informal supports for the family?
11. How is this family situated in terms of culture, ethnicity, and religion?
12. What is the extent of oppression and discrimination this family experiences? What is the impact of this oppression and discrimination on family functioning?

Family social workers need to observe the social functioning of the family. Social functioning is best understood by looking at the social roles family members perform. Individual behavior and adjustment reflects how well family members perform their social roles. Geismar and Ayres (1959) proposed four areas of role performance within the family and four outside the family. Internal roles include:

- Family relationships and family unity
- Child care and training
- Health practices
- Household practices

External family roles include:

- Use of community resources
- Social activities
- Economic practices
- Relationship of the family to the social worker

VISUAL TECHNIQUES

Genograms and ecomaps are the preferred assessment tools for most family workers. Events and materials gleaned from genograms and ecomaps are integral to the development and support of the family assessment. They are also useful tools with which to establish rapport with families. From our experience, families are intrigued by these graphic symbols of their lives and are eager to see how their family life is depicted on paper. While the family is engaged in documenting their life history on paper, the focus is off the presenting problem and their difficulties. The tools become a mechanism through which relationship building can start with the family as a system and with individual members. At the same time, both tools depict relationship patterns within and outside the family.

Other assessment devices such as family time lines may be used to supplement genograms and ecomaps. Family assessment devices serve dual purposes. Inasmuch as measurement instruments may be useful for diagnostic information about family functioning, they can also serve as the basis from which family members can examine family functioning themselves, discuss family problems, and set family goals in a focused, structured, and collaborative way.

Because family structures and family problems can be complex, graphic images are useful tools with which to sift through detailed data. Visual recording techniques enable family social workers to select the most appropriate tool for assessment and intervention. Such tools are useful to organize information effectively and help workers develop a coherent plan for intervention. Social workers are relying on graphic tools more often in their work because they are useful to prevent overlooking important details in complex cases. Because of the detail of graphic instruments, many problems and issues stand out. Nevertheless, this does not mean that every problem becomes the target of intervention. Rather, graphics provide a backdrop against which other problems can be understood. These targeted problem areas may then be the focus of intervention. Family social workers will be challenged to select interventions that have the greatest possibility of having an impact. The amount of material included in a single graphic depiction of a family depends on the worker's defined role. Graphics should include enough detail to capture the family's complexity but be simple enough that it can be easily understood.

Genogram

A genogram represents a graphic family tree that can help the family social worker understand who is included in the family and the nature of family relationships. This family diagram can be utilized to depict the structure, the nature of relationships, and the appearance of issues across several generations. As mentioned, family members often find active participation in genogram construction informative as both the family social worker and family members gain insight into family patterns and interactions.

Genograms visually display family information to permit a quick overview or "gestalt" of complex family patterns. They are useful engagement tools for families and provide a detailed picture of significant family events such as births, marriages, separations, and deaths. Genograms can also convey social information such as racial group, social class, and religious status (Holman, 1983). Finally, genograms help the worker conceptualize the past and present family situation to unblock the system, clarify family patterns, and reframe and detoxify family issues (Kaslow & Celano, 1995).

They are appealing to family social workers because they concretely capture a family. Genograms permit family social workers to map family structure clearly and update the family "picture" as it develops. Genograms might change as the family social worker and family members learn new information. As a clinical record, the genogram provides an efficient family summary, allowing those unfamiliar with a family to obtain a vast amount of information about any family rapidly. Family issues also stand out. Patterns of behavior that occur across multiple generations are easily seen with a genogram. Patterns, events, relationships, and behaviors often repeat themselves over multiple generations. For example, in Freud's family, a number of relatives experienced mental illness and suicide (McGoldrick, 1999a). Communication and relationship patterns are particularly important to observe because they reproduce across generations.

Genograms may help prevent the discovery late into family work that a significant person is missing from the intervention. They are especially useful when detailed family information is needed (Hartman & Laird, 1983). Through genograms, family social workers can identify repetitive patterns experienced by a family. They can be used with the family in early family sessions. Although written information may become lost or submerged in the volumes of case files, information on a genogram is highly visible. A single genogram can place pages of narrative information on a single page.

Additionally, genogram construction creates opportunities to establish rapport between the FSW and the family, rapidly engaging the family in the family work process. Working together in genogram construction sets the stage for the worker–family partnership and draws families into a participatory style of problem identification and solving.

How to Draw a Genogram   To start, it is important to note that genograms capture individual perceptions of families and the relationships embedded in them. Before you start doing a genogram, it is important to prepare for the possibility of differences in perception about the nature of relationships. For example, someone in the family might consider his or her relationship with another member extremely close, while the other person might see the relationship as conflicted. Usually such extremes are rare, but the potential is there for hurt feelings. Relationships are affected by the nature of the communication people have with one another. Some relationships may be marked by communication that is marked by anger and/or conflict, while another relationship might be marked by communication that is quite intimate, with the two parties telling each other their innermost secrets.

While no standard method of genogram construction exists—despite the widespread use (see for example, Hartman & Laird, 1983; McGoldrick & Gerson, 1985; Wright & Leahey, 1994)—they all contain the same basic information: who is in the family, when children were born, significant relationships, and deaths. Some genograms are used to document medical ailments across generations. Others depict psychosocial problems such as mental illness, suicide, or alcoholism across generations. Another common use of genograms is to capture the nature of relationship patterns across generations, particularly conflicted, disengaged, or enmeshed patterns. Sometimes workers use color-coding to make intergenerational patterns stand out, although this can take more time than the family worker can allow. However, currently, there is loose consensus about what specific information to include, how to record information, and how to interpret it. Fortunately, the general structure of the genogram follows conventional genetic and genealogical charts. Since it is standard practice to include at least three generations in a genogram (i.e., grandparents, parents, and children), it is important to plan spacing ahead of time. Many symbols are used because the core information of genograms is depicted in shorthand. Figure 5.2 shows examples of the more common symbols contained in a genogram.

Common Symbols in Genograms   The genogram shows family members in relation to each other. It also helps the worker understand who is involved with the presenting family issue and allows the worker to include that person in

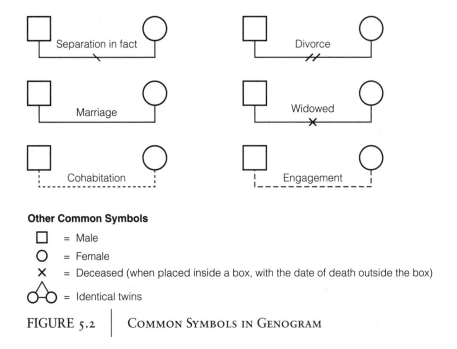

FIGURE 5.2 | COMMON SYMBOLS IN GENOGRAM

treatment planning. Genograms can be quite complex beyond the traditional nuclear family configuration. Divorce, common-law relationships, separations, blended families, affairs, and stepfamilies all should be placed on a genogram. Add stepsiblings, foster children, and adopted children to the mix and you can have a complicated potpourri of relationships.

Individual Symbols

□ = Male

○ = Female

X = deceased (when placed inside a box, with the date of death outside the box)

Every family member is represented either by a box or circle, based on gender. Lines for the individual client (index person, or alternatively the identified patient (IP)) for whom the genogram was constructed are doubled. A pregnancy is a triangle and a miscarriage is represented by a triangle with an X drawn through it. Males are depicted by squares (□), and females are depicted by circles (○). Identical twins start at the same point on the horizontal line above but separate to form a triangle, with either circles or squares placed at the end of each arm. The same is true for fraternal twins, although the arms may have a circle and a square. Foster children are connected to the horizontal line via a dotted vertical line, and adopted children are designated by both a solid and dotted vertical line attached to the line above. Each individual in the family must be represented at a specific, strategic point on the genogram, regardless of

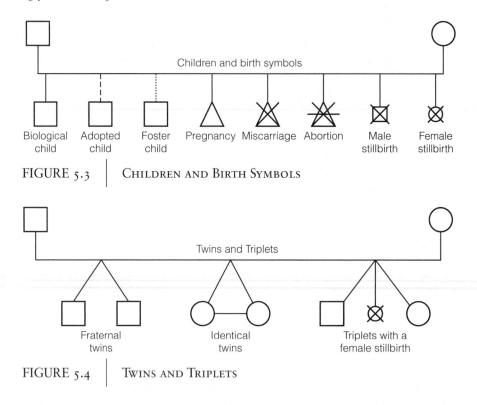

FIGURE 5.3 │ CHILDREN AND BIRTH SYMBOLS

FIGURE 5.4 │ TWINS AND TRIPLETS

whether that individual is currently alive or living in the household at that particular moment. If a person has ever existed, he or she belongs in the genogram. Depending on the number of people and relationships involved, genogram construction can become quite involved. See Figures 5.3 and 5.4.

Relational and Generational Lines A horizontal line connecting people captures adults in a family. Children are placed below the parents' horizontal line, ordered by youngest to oldest from left to right. Family members of the same generation are placed in horizontal rows that signify generational lines. For example, a horizontal line denotes marital or common-law relationships. Divorce is shown by a double slashed line in the horizontal line (///) with the accompanying dates. Separation is captured by a single slash (/). Affairs and common-law relationships are depicted by a dotted line (- - - - - - -) connecting the two people. When remarriage occurs, the ex-partner can be shown with a smaller shape. If there is more than one marriage, they are placed from left to right with the most recent marriage being placed last. Children of a union are placed on a different horizontal line underneath the parents and joined to the line of the parents by a vertical line. Triangular patterns are of particular importance to identify in the family. In addition, FSWs should look for "descriptions" rather than conclusions (Nichols & Schwartz, 2004). This means asking about concrete activities and examples of behaviors rather than getting family members to evaluate relationships. See Figure 5.5.

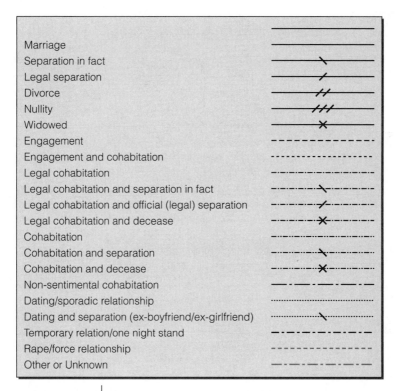

Marriage	
Separation in fact	
Legal separation	
Divorce	
Nullity	
Widowed	
Engagement	
Engagement and cohabitation	
Legal cohabitation	
Legal cohabitation and separation in fact	
Legal cohabitation and official (legal) separation	
Legal cohabitation and decease	
Cohabitation	
Cohabitation and separation	
Cohabitation and decease	
Non-sentimental cohabitation	
Dating/sporadic relationship	
Dating and separation (ex-boyfriend/ex-girlfriend)	
Temporary relation/one night stand	
Rape/force relationship	
Other or Unknown	

FIGURE 5.5 | RELATIONAL AND GENERATIONAL LINES

Additional Detail   Each family member's name and age should be placed inside the square or circle representing that person. The year of birth and date of death are recorded above the gender symbol. Birth dates are displayed horizontally, moving from left to right on the page. Sometimes, if birth dates are past the century mark and cannot be mistaken for another century, the first two numbers in a year can be provided. Outside each symbol, significant data and important events (for example, "travels a lot" or "school dropout") should be recorded. Some events send "emotional shock waves" throughout the family, fostering or shutting down communication (Nichols & Schwartz, 2004). If a family member has died, the year of death, the person's age at death, and the cause of death should be recorded. When the symbol for miscarriage is used, the sex of the child should be identified, if known.

Relationship Lines   Once the important facts about the relationship are recorded, the family worker can move on to describing relationships within the family. Adding lines to show the nature of relationships can make a genogram quite detailed, so it is important to plan ahead and target the most important relationships first. Lines between people on the genogram describe the nature

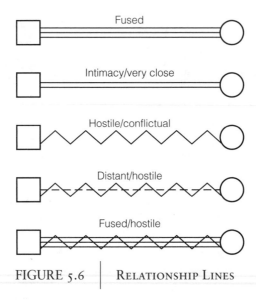

FIGURE 5.6 | RELATIONSHIP LINES

and quality of relationships. Questions such as "What was the nature of your parents' relationship?" or "Who did you feel closest to in your family?" are useful to capture the quality of family relationships. The worker is advised to work with one family of origin at a time. At a later time, the worker can ask the spouses to interpret how their family of origin affects the current family unit—in particular, the marriage. In doing family of origin work, the worker should identify themes and repetitive patterns that may be re-created in the present family. An example of a theme is: "Males have the final say in major decisions affecting the family."

Average relationships between people are depicted with one line, very close relationships with two, and enmeshed relationships with three lines. A dotted line represents a distant relationship between two people and a jagged line shows a very conflicted or hostile relationship between two people. Broken relationships can be shown with a line with two slashes in it. See Figure 5.6.

In Chapter 2 we discussed triangles as being a very important family subsystem. Often a triangle represents the coalition of two people against another. It could be two parents against a child or a parent and child against another parent. Putting triangles in a genogram can be a very important assessment tool.

The website www.genopro.com offers four rules to guide the construction of a genogram[1]:

1. The male is always at the left of the family and the female is always at the right of the family.

---

[1]The diagrams included in this chapter are from www.genopro.com/beta/. The diagrams are free to the public, and the website allows you to download, free of charge, a program that creates genograms. After one month, you must purchase the program if you are going to continue to use it.

2. In the case of ambiguity, assume a male–female relationship, rather than male–male or female–female relationship (when more than two people are represented on the same horizontal line.
3. A spouse must always be closer to his/her first partner, then the second partner (if any), third partner, and so on.
4. The oldest child is always to the left of his/her family, the youngest child is always to the right of his/her family.

Ecomap

While the genogram exposes the internal dynamics of the family, families' external dynamics and relationships can be represented on an ecomap. Some difficulties evolve at the interface between the person and the environment. This map charts family relationships with the outside world (ecosystem) and captures the strength and quality of external connections and areas of conflict with the family. Ecomaps also demonstrate the flow of resources from the environment to the family, in addition to deprivations and unmet needs (Holman, 1983). Ecomaps account for client transactions with the environment that are useful for assessing and conceptualizing families holistically and contextually. Important observations concerning family–community connections can be cataloged through the ecomap.

As with the genogram, the primary function of an ecomap is the visual and conceptual impact of inserting an extensive amount of information on a single page. The map is an easy-to-read depiction of family support systems. Family social work relies heavily on the information portrayed by an ecomap because needs and community resources are central to family work. Creating an ecomap with a family can occur during assessment and planning, concentrating on crucial information about systemic formulations such as boundary issues and the direction, rate, and mutuality of social relationships. It should reduce the amount of narrative needed for case files. However, there may be tradeoffs between the level of detail required and the time it takes to complete an ecomap. Ecomaps can also capture changes over time. They are now a standard part of agency recording, especially in agencies with high staff turnover and clients with many unmet social needs.

As with the genogram, participating in constructing an ecomap can be beneficial to the family, particularly during the early stages of engagement. It is important to note that families of color have experienced societal discrimination and that the effects of this discrimination should be depicted on the ecomap. Ecomaps capture transactions with systems outside the family while genograms identify exchanges within the family. Sometimes the two are used together to develop an integrated picture of a family situation. Both workers and clients find these tools useful. Concrete and diagrammatic depictions of abstract concepts such as genograms and ecomaps produce greater understanding and retention of material. Ecomaps also capitalize on gathering important religious and cultural ties to the community. For minority clients, they can help identify the existence of oppression and financial well-being.

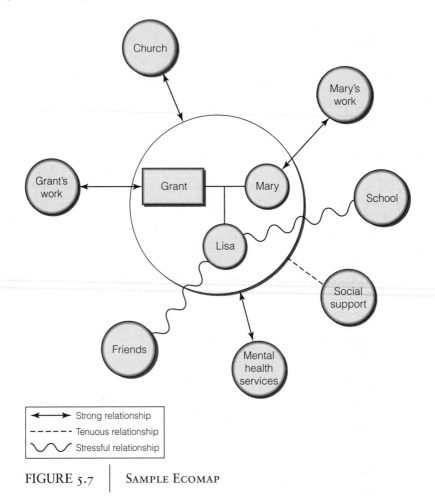

FIGURE 5.7 | SAMPLE ECOMAP

HOW TO DRAW THE ECOMAP   The ecomap is comprised of a series of interconnected circles representing various systems extraneous to the family. The first
step in creating an ecomap is to place the previously constructed genogram in
a center circle labeled as the family or household. Circles placed outside this
center circle represent significant people, agencies, or organizations in the lives
of the members of the family. The size of the circles is not important. Lines
drawn between the inner and outer circles indicate the nature of the existing
connections. Straight lines (---) show strong connections, dotted lines (.......)
denote tenuous connections, and slashed lines (-/-/-/-) represent stressful or
conflictual connections.

Thicker lines represent stronger connections. Arrows drawn alongside the
lines represent the flow of energy and resources. Additional circles can be drawn
as necessary, depending upon the number of significant contacts. The ecomap
may be modified as the family changes or as the family shares further information
with the family social worker. An example of an ecomap is shown in Figure 5.7.

OTHER VISUAL TECHNIQUES

FAMILY DRAWING   Another related technique for depicting family relationships is to request a family to create a family drawing together. Family members can also draw their family separately, and the portraits of individual family members can later be discussed and compared. Another similar technique is to have families arrange a family photograph with family members posing for family pictures. How people are positioned for this photograph will generate information about family relationships. After each exercise, individual family members discuss what they see in the family portrayal.

FAMILY SCULPTURE   Alternatively, family members can be asked to "sculpt" their family (Satir & Baldwin, 1983), that is, have family members physically stand in a room posed in ways to depict a family sculpture of their relationships. Members take turns arranging family members in relationship with one another; body gestures, distance, and physical actions are captured through the sculpture. Each family member takes charge of his or her particular sculpture, instructing family members in the sculpture what position to assume. Essentially, the sculptor treats members as if they were made of clay (Holman, 1983). Sculptures of the same family will differ, depending on the perceptions of the one directing the sculpture. Sculpting is especially useful for nonverbal families to provide a means of expressing and understanding one another (Holman, 1983).

FAMILY TIME LINE   Another interesting assessment tool is the family time line. The family time line is represented on a grid. It is a simple grid designed to capture and rate important family events on the dimension of time. They very rapidly capture significant family events as the family moves across the life cycle—parents meeting, dating, marriages, deaths, births, periods of illness or unemployment, moves, divorces, etc. are all captured on a single time line. A time line can help the FSW quickly pick up enormous detail about a family's history as well as the significance of events in the history. There are two ways to rate the impact of the event. The first way is to place negative events below the line and positive events above the line. The second, and probably easiest way, is to rank the events on a scale of 1 to 10. "1" indicates an extremely upsetting or stressful event, while "10" indicates an event that is extremely positive. Numbers that fall in between indicate important experiences, with "5" being a somewhat neutral response. The points on the line are then connected to reveal highs and lows in the family's development. Events can be analyzed in terms of their impact on the family, starting with the first event, proceeding into the present time. Once the time line is completed, the FSW can initiate discussion with the family to analyze the events in the family's life. More fruitful discussion will ensue if family members disagree about the importance of the events. When this happens, the family worker can help family members understand how different events are perceived differently by every member of the family.

Events that might be important to families include:

- Family moves
- Births of children
- Divorce
- Marriages
- Deaths
- Arrival and/or death of pets
- Family accomplishments
- New jobs
- Personal events of family members (e.g., graduation, getting a promotion, making a new friend)
- Family life cycle events such as when grandparents went into a nursing home, when Mom and Dad went on the Dr. Phil show, etc.

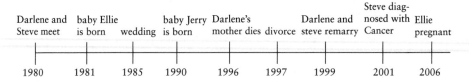

CRITERIA FOR ASSESSING FAMILY FUNCTIONING

Many models are available with which to assess family functioning. Most of these models support one theoretical framework or another. One family assessment tool, for example, the Circumplex Model of family functioning conceives of family functioning as falling on two continua: adaptability and cohesion (FACES III) (Olson, 1986). Another developed by Beavers (1981) looks at family functioning based on competence, structure, and flexibility (Beavers-Timberlawn Family Evaluation Scale) (Beavers, 1981). The Family Assessment Measure, otherwise known as the Family Categories Schema, describes family functioning as involving basic tasks, developmental tasks, and hazardous tasks (McMaster Model) (Epstein, Baldwin, & Bishop, 1983), as well as specific areas of family functioning (problem solving, communication, roles, affective responses, affective involvement, and behavior control) designed to assess the need for counseling (McMaster Clinical Rating Scale) (Epstein, Baldwin, & Bishop, 1983).

Workers can also develop their own checklists for predetermined purposes. Checklists can be constructed to account for physical resources in the home. Conversely, a worker may want to focus on specific areas of role performance of family members. Checklists can also cover physical care of the children or a rating of the emotional climate of the family. The benefit of checklists such as these is that they can be specially tailored to families and their circumstances.

A very useful book for assessing problems, not just with families, but also individuals is *Measures for Clinical Practice* (Corcoran & Fischer, 2000). This text includes many family assessment measures that examine a multitude of areas of family functioning. Some measures are concerned with specific family relationships such as parent–child functioning while others target the functioning of a family unit as a whole. In this book, we present the Family Assessment Measure because it comprehensively covers most areas of family functioning and was developed using a family systems framework. The measure can be used for a quantitative measure of family functioning, or alternatively, the FSW can rely on the conceptual base with which to understand family functioning through interviews and observations.

FAMILY ASSESSMENT MEASURE

A helpful way to understand and assess family functioning is to use the Family Categories Schema based on the work of Epstein, Bishop, and Levin (1978). These authors designed an instrument for FSWs to complete after their initial meetings with families. The quantitative instrument is a sixty-item self-report questionnaire containing eight categories: (1) problem solving, (2) affective responsiveness, (3) affective involvement, (4) communication, (5) role behavior, (6) autonomy, (7) modes of behavioral control, and (8) general functioning. If the FSW decides not to use the specific instrument, s/he can, as mentioned, try to understand family functioning using the categories provided. After describing each category, we will present a sample item from the instrument.

PROBLEM SOLVING

Problem solving is how a family copes with threats to emotional or physical well-being or to the family's survival as a functioning unit. Threats can be either instrumental or affective. *Instrumental* threats involve "mechanical" or concrete aspects of living, such as economic, physical, or health concerns. Thus, parental unemployment or the physical abuse of a child are two examples of instrumental threats to the family. *Affective* threats endanger the emotional well-being of family life—examples include a depressed child, an overwhelmed parent, or a maladaptive circular interaction. Frequently, instrumental and affective problems overlap. A parent feeling depressed because of unemployment is one such example. Walsh (1998), in describing resilient families, suggests that although well-functioning families are not characterized by the absence of problems, what distinguishes resilient families is their ability to manage conflict well. In addition, there are several steps in effective problem-solving processes: first, recognize the problem; second, communicate about it; third, collaborate in brainstorming; and fourth, initiate and carry out action, monitor efforts, and evaluate success (Epstein, 1993, cited in Walsh, 1998).

An example of a self-report statement related to problem solving is, "We resolve most everyday problems around the house." Other questions to ask include: "Give me an example of a family problem that you have had. How did you handle this problem? What are the problems that make life difficult or stressful for the family?"

AFFECTIVE RESPONSIVENESS

Family members should be able to express a variety of emotions within a supportive family environment. The range of emotions can be divided into two major categories: *welfare emotions* such as happiness, joy, tenderness, love, and sympathy, and *emergency emotions* such as rage, fear, anger, and depression.

The FSW should assess the family's ability to respond with the appropriate quality and quantity of feelings to affect-provoking stimuli. Family social workers are concerned with the welfare and emergency emotions expressed in the family, as well as with the pattern of their expression. This involves whether the expression of emotions is clear, direct, open, and honest or indirect, masked, and dishonest. The degree to which individual family members participate in the affective interchange is also important. Walsh (1998) suggests that empathic sharing of emotions, combined with loving tolerance for differences and negative emotions, is an important aspect of resilient family processes.

An example of a statement related to affective responsiveness is, "Some of us just don't respond emotionally" (Corcoran & Fischer, 2000).

AFFECTIVE INVOLVEMENT

To what extent do family members become emotionally involved with one another in activities and interests that go beyond those needed for instrumental family functions? Involvement transcends mere expression of affect and captures the amount and quality of the emotional involvement that family members have with each other. It is one thing to praise a child for doing homework, and it is something else to actually sit down with the child and discuss homework. We strongly endorse the need for parents to support children; thus, parents need to be actively involved in their children's interests and activities.

One example of a statement related to affective involvement is, "It is difficult to talk to each other about tender feelings?" (Corcoran & Fischer, 2000). Questions to ask might include: "What are you involved in or interested in? Who shares your interests? How do they show this interest? Do you feel in your family that family members go their own way and do not care about what you do? How do you relate to the children? How would you describe your relationship with so-and-so?"

COMMUNICATION

Communication can be quite complex. An adage of communication theory is: *You cannot not communicate.* Hence, the verbal and nonverbal communication that occur within a family are both important. Communication serves two functions: to communicate content, and to define the nature of the relationship between the speaker and listener. The second function is called *metacommunication*. Listening carefully to how family members communicate with one another will give the FSW important clues about a family's relationships. A message conveyed out of care will come across differently from a message conveyed out of anger, even if the content of the messages is the same.

Healthy family communication is clear, direct, open, and honest. As with problem solving, communication can be categorized into affective and instrumental areas. *Affective communication* is defined as that in which the communicated message is mostly emotional in nature, whereas *instrumental communication* occurs when the message is primarily "mechanical." An instrumental message is related to the mechanics of "getting things done," and involves the regular, ongoing tasks of family living.

Communication occurs both verbally and nonverbally, through posture, voice tone, gestures, and facial expressions. If a person says, "I'm listening," while making eye contact and smiling, the words are interpreted differently from how they would be perceived if the speaker were hiding behind a newspaper. Ideally, verbal and nonverbal communication should be congruent. Additionally, information that is exchanged should be reciprocal and positive (Brock & Barnard, 1991).

An example of a statement related to communication is, "When someone is upset, the others know why" (Corcoran & Fischer, 2000). Other questions to ask might include: "Do people talk much in this family? Who talks to whom? Who do you speak with in your family when you are feeling upset?" To find out whether communication is masked, you can ask: "How did so-and-so let you know that s/he was upset? How did you get the message? What was so-and-so getting at when s/he said 'It's up to you?' What did so-and-so just say? So-and-so, is that what you just said?"

Walsh (1998) elaborates on communication processes within the family:

CLARITY

- Clear, consistent messages (word and actions)
- Clarification of ambiguous information: Truth seeking/truth speaking

OPEN EMOTIONAL EXPRESSION

- Sharing wide range of feelings (joy and pain; hopes and fears)
- Mutual empathy; tolerance for differences
- Responsibility for own feelings, behavior; avoiding blaming
- Pleasurable interactions; humor

COLLABORATIVE PROBLEM SOLVING

- Identifying problems, stressors, options, and constraints
- Creative brainstorming; resourcefulness
- Shared decision making: Negotiation, fairness, reciprocity
- Conflict resolution

- Focusing on goals; taking concrete steps
- Building on success; learning from failure
- Proactive stance: Preventing problems, averting crises, preparing for future challenges (p. 107).

ROLE BEHAVIOR

Every family faces daily pressures, tasks, and obligations. To cope, each family member plays roles that develop into established and predictable patterns of behavior. *Roles* are repetitive patterns of behavior that serve a function in day-to-day family life (Brock & Barnard, 1991). They can take many forms, such as those that follow traditional role definitions (such as gender roles) and roles that deviate from traditional roles, known as idiosyncratic roles.

Traditional roles involve those of mother, father, husband, wife, son, or daughter, as traditionally defined and accepted by a culture. Roles based on gender are much less clear today than they used to be, as are spousal and parental roles. However, most people still regard children as more the mother's responsibility than the father's (Eichler, 1997). Roles that are not always clearly agreed-upon include the parental role to socialize children and be responsible for their emotional and physical well-being. Idiosyncratic roles fall outside the traditional social prescriptions. For example, a mother may assume the role of primary financial provider (traditionally the male role) while the father cares for the children and takes care of household tasks. Some idiosyncratic roles are related to the family's presenting problem, as when one child takes the role of scapegoat. Other idiosyncratic roles, such as the clown and the hero, are seen in alcoholic families.

Optimal family roles include:

- Clearly differentiated roles of parents and children;
- Flexibility of roles when the situation demands;
- Roles that are performed competently (Brock & Barnard, 1991).

An example of a statement related to role behavior is, "Each of us has particular duties and responsibilities." Other questions to ask are: "How do you decide who does something in the family? Who does a particular role in the family? What if a job doesn't get done?"

AUTONOMY

Autonomy concerns the ability of family members to act independently and to make individual, responsible choices. Autonomy is demonstrated when each member has a sense of identity as a separate person rather than as an extension of others, is able to make choices in selecting or rejecting outside influences, and is willing to take responsibility for making personal choices. Autonomy should be assessed in light of each member's age, developmental abilities, and potential. Also of importance is the degree of individuation that occurs in the sphere of the family unit and in the individual members' life beyond the family unit. *Individuation* refers to the sense of being a unique individual, distinct from others.

An example of a statement related to autonomy is, "Mom is always telling me what clothes I should wear."

MODES OF BEHAVIORAL CONTROL

Behavioral control involves the family's way of dealing with impulses, maintaining standards of behavior, and coping with threatening situations. Four modes of behavioral control are described in the following list.

- *Rigid:* A fixed pattern of familial behavior that is intolerant of individual variation (e.g., children are never allowed to sleep over at a friend's home).
- *Flexible:* A familial pattern of behavior that is firmly and clearly defined but at the same time involves a flexible style allowing for individual variation (e.g., agreed-upon family rules are present but may be bent in the case of special circumstances, i.e., children usually are not allowed to have sleepovers on weeknights, but the rule is bent to celebrate a birthday).
- *Laissez-faire:* No effective or established patterns of behavioral control exist (e.g., the rule might be that no sleepovers are allowed on a school night, but the rule is altered inconsistently, such as when a child pleads).
- *Chaotic:* A pattern of complete inconsistency in modes of behavioral control within the family (e.g., there is no rule about sleepovers during a school night, and on one occasion the child is permitted to sleep over, but on other similar occasions the child is denied a sleepover; thus, the child is not aware what rules regulate sleepovers).

These four modes of behavioral control can be evaluated with regard to whether they are consistent or inconsistent—that is, whether the mode of behavioral control is predictable or unpredictable.

An example of a statement related to behavioral control is, "We have rules about hitting people."

ASSESSING PARENTING SKILLS

Family social workers will need to assess parenting skills, especially if a child's safety is at risk. The following criteria can be used to assess parenting (Steinhauer, 1991):

1. **Level of attachment:** Attachment is necessary for the formation of trust, self-esteem, and the ability to develop future intimate relationships. The child's primary attachment should be with the parents. Parents must recognize their child's needs and respond appropriately. Parents with personal problems such as immaturity or self-absorption are often unable to

accurately understand their children's needs. In addition, parent–child relationships should be neither enmeshed nor disengaged.

2. **Transmission of values:** Parents are responsible for teaching their children to distinguish between right and wrong. Through teaching and modeling, children learn to respect the rights of others and to control their impulses. Morality should be congruent with that of the larger culture while respecting distinct cultural patterns.

3. **Absence of rejection, overt or covert:** Neglect and abuse are examples of overt rejection, whereas covert rejection is more difficult to identify. It may involve subtle or blatant emotional abuse.

4. **Continuity of care:** A continuous relationship between parents and child is crucial, and the care should match the developmental needs of the child.

Sometimes the court or a custody lawyer will ask the FSW to assess the ability of parents to care for their children. At other times, the social worker will have to make a decision about whether children can safely remain within their families or whether they should be placed in foster care, at least temporarily. Making these decisions can be extremely difficult. In assessing parenting ability, the family social worker will need to look at the child's development as well as the history of the parent–child relationship. Sometimes the FSW will need to consult a specialist for expert assessment of child development or diagnosis of psychiatric disabilities in a parent or child. The starting point for assessment, however, should be to determine the quality of the parent–child relationship over time.

Assessment of Child Development

Information on the child's development—including cognitive, emotional, physical, and social abilities—should be included in the assessment. Social workers should have knowledge of normative child development to supplement their observations. According to Steinhauer (1991), child assessment should include information about the following topics:

*   Behavior in the areas of cognitive, behavioral, emotional, or academic functioning;
*   Parental attitudes toward the child;
*   Attachment issues pertinent to parent–child relationships, including a history of separations and parental abuse;
*   History of psychiatric or social disabilities on the part of the parents, including any evidence of substance abuse or antisocial/criminal behavior;
*   History of involvement with social service systems and agencies;
*   Risk assessment of child safety in the areas of abuse (emotional, physical, or sexual) and neglect;
*   Attainment of developmental milestones;

- Medical/physical history;
- Attitude of parents toward the child and indications of current or past parental rejection and/or hostility;
- Corroboration from external sources regarding the above-mentioned areas;
- School and friendship history; and
- The development of the child based on one or more theories of child development: psychosocial, cognitive, psychosexual, etc.

ASSESSMENT OF PARENT–CHILD RELATIONSHIP

The family social worker will need to make a detailed observation of parent–child interactions. Observations should be repetitive and lengthy. The FSW needs to observe how the parent and child relate to one another, noting normative, age-appropriate data. Especially important are the amount and quality of physical and emotional contact that parents and children have with one another. The FSW should also observe the parent's disciplinary style and boundary setting. Children may express opinions indirectly through play. In addition to relationship issues, the social worker should assess how well the child's physical needs are being met (i.e., whether the child receives adequate nourishment, clothing, shelter, and supervision and whether the child receives adequate social and intellectual stimulation). Further, the social worker may refer clients to other professionals for in-patient assessment or psychological tests of the parent or child.

Through experience, the social worker may find that there are three levels of parenting capacity (Steinhauer, 1991). At the highest level are families who are functioning well, child development is proceeding normally, and any help provided will be at the request of the parents. In the second category, child development is impaired as the result of a temporary crisis rather than a long-standing, chronic problem. A child-related crisis may have destabilized the family so much that it temporarily lacks the resources to cope. Parents in this category have no chronic emotional or social disabilities and are cooperative with the assistance offered. Parents accept responsibility for their role in the development of the problem and also show willingness to deal with the problem. In the third group, there may be significant impairment in child development. The family's problems appear to be chronic, and lack of parenting abilities is longstanding. Children display significant disturbance in one or several areas of their lives. Parents are significantly disabled either socially and/or emotionally and have a history of unsuccessful social service involvement. Parents are uncooperative and do not accept personal responsibility for their role in problems.

CONSIDERATIONS FOR ASSESSING MINORITY FAMILIES

Mapping techniques such as genograms, ecomaps, and time lines are particularly helpful because they emphasize assessment of the extended family. The FSW will also observe family interactions during home visits.

ASSESSMENT ISSUES FOR AFRICAN AMERICAN FAMILIES

Socioeconomic status, educational level, cultural identity, family structure, and reactions to racism are important variables in assessing African American families (Sue & Sue in Jordan, Lewellen, & Vandiver, 1994). An ecomap can be used to collect important information about family strengths and community resources, the quality of relationships between family members, and family members' relationships with their neighbors (Ho, 1987).

ASSESSMENT ISSUES FOR HISPANIC AMERICAN FAMILIES

Hispanic American families may experience discrimination, underemployment, and lack of housing or other resources, and these problems should not be overlooked in the assessment (Jordan, Lewellen, & Vandiver, 1994). Level of acculturation, or assimilation into the ways of the dominant culture, is a major issue for Hispanic families. Three levels of acculturation are commonly found among Hispanic American families: immigrant families who have just arrived, immigrant-American families, and immigrant-descent families (Padella et al., and Casas & Keefe in Jordan, Lewellen, & Vandiver, 1994).

The first group, newly arrived immigrant families, have yet to be acculturated into the new country's values and ways. Family members usually speak little or no English. Immigrant-American families, the second group, consists of parents born in the old country and children born in the new country. This may result in a clash between oldsters and youth as children are acculturated more rapidly into the new country. The third group, immigrant-descent families, consists of all generations born in the new country. Members of this group are likely to be fully acculturated into the new country.

ASSESSMENT ISSUES FOR ASIAN AMERICAN FAMILIES

Acculturation to the dominant society is a concern when assessing Asian American families. Barriers to service provision may include unfamiliarity with the health care system in a new country, language difficulties, and cultural traditions and values that conflict with those of the dominant culture (Jordan, Lewellen, & Vandiver, 1994). Vietnamese and Laotian families may have spent time as refugees in resettlement camps, and thus been exposed to great traumas. The family social worker should be sensitive to this possibility and assess the family's need to obtain appropriate services for stress-related illnesses.

ASSESSMENT ISSUES FOR NATIVE AMERICAN FAMILIES

Red Horse (1980) describes three types of Native American families that require different kinds of assistance. The first type is the traditional family governed by tribal customs and beliefs. Older members speak the native language, and the extended family network is influential. The second type is the nontraditional or bicultural family. Though the extended family network is important and the older generation may speak the native tongue, English is primarily spoken. The family interacts freely and comfortably with members of the dominant culture.

The third type is the pan-traditional family. These families are seeking to reconnect with their cultural heritage. Bicultural families are most apt to seek services from mental health professionals. When traditional or pan-traditional families require help, they are likely to consult tribal community helpers or religious leaders.

In addition to considering the family type when assessing Native American families, the family social worker should be aware of their history as victims of discrimination. Historically, Native Americans were coerced into signing unfavorable treaties that stripped them of their land and way of life. In some cases, children were separated from their parents. Consequently, Native Americans have experienced poverty, unemployment, alcoholism, family disruption, and other effects of discrimination.

PSYCHOSOCIAL ADJUSTMENT

The family social worker must be sensitive to ethnic and cultural factors when doing a psychosocial assessment of a child from an ethnic minority family. The social worker must have knowledge of the family's ethnic group, including familiarity with its beliefs, customs, and values. However, the FSW must also recognize that within each ethnic group, much individual variation exists. Therefore, it is important for the social worker to learn as much as possible about each family's beliefs, customs, and patterns of interaction. Areas to be covered in the psychosocial assessment include:

1. *Physical assessment:* Low-income, ethnic minority children may be experiencing physical problems due to malnutrition or lack of proper medical care such as routine checkups and vaccinations. A physical (or eye or dental) exam may be needed.
2. *Emotional assessment:* Feelings of self-esteem, competence, and other aspects influencing children's affect may be a product of the children's ethnic background. The family social worker should verify his or her assumptions to ascertain cultural norms.
3. *Behavioral assessment:* Behavioral factors such as aggression and achievement may be culturally determined and different from the dominant culture. For instance, achievement in sports or music may be valued more highly than academic performance. Guilt or shame may be used by the family to manage aggression.
4. *Coping and defense mechanisms:* The child may learn externalizing behaviors as coping and defense mechanisms to deal with anxiety or fear. Examples are acting-out behaviors such as fighting or talking back.

RELATIONSHIPS WITH FAMILY MEMBERS

The family's view of appropriate child behavior is a critical element for assessment. Areas to look at include:

1. *Parent–child relationship:* Ethnic minority families may differ from the dominant culture with respect to the relationship between parents and

children. Variations range from hierarchical and patriarchal relationships, such as those seen in some Asian American families, to the egalitarian parent–child relationships of some Native American tribes.

2. *Birth order:* Families characterized by hierarchical structures may have rigid role prescriptions for the children. For example, the youngest daughter in an Asian American family may be charged with caring for her elderly parents.

3. *Age:* Sibling relationships may be prescribed by age; for instance, older children in Native American families may provide teaching and role modeling for younger siblings and cousins.

4. *Sex:* Male and female family members may be expected to perform different roles and may hold higher or lower family status.

5. *Family expectations:* Other expectations may be imposed on family members, such as dictates about whom children should marry or who will care for children or elderly relatives.

SCHOOL ADJUSTMENT AND ACHIEVEMENT

School is the environment in which children interact most often with others outside the family. Factors related to school performance provide important indicators of well-being, but assessments must include attention to ethnicity. Four important indicators of school adjustment and achievement are psychological adjustment, behavioral adjustment, academic achievement, and relationships with peers.

1. *Psychological adjustment:* Ethnic minority parents and children may fear school or view it negatively if the values of the dominant culture differ drastically from those of the family.

2. *Behavioral adjustment:* Ethnic minority families may teach their children externalizing behaviors to cope with or to solve problems. Use of these types of acting-out behaviors may get children into trouble in the school setting. It is also important for FSWs to recognize that behavioral problems may reflect underlying health problems, such as attention deficit disorder, fetal alcohol syndrome, or vision problems.

3. *Academic achievement:* If a minority child's grades in school are below average, the child may be having trouble with books and tests that are not culturally sensitive. Parents who are unfamiliar with the school system may not provide appropriate support or modeling of efficient study skills.

4. *Relationships with peers:* Children may fear appearing different from their peers and thus may be excluded (or exclude themselves) from peer group activities. Peer support from children of their own ethnic group may be unavailable.

The example in Case 5.2 illustrates some of the issues faced by children who belong to ethnic minorities:

| CASE 5.2 | ETHNIC MINORITIES |

Sally Redmond, a seven-year-old second grader, came to the family social work agency with her parents because of problems at school. Sally told the FSW that she did not like her school and did not care if she never went back. Her teacher has reported that Sally is quiet and withdrawn at school, has no friends, and does not take part in most activities.

Sally's parents, Lou and Darlene, adopted their daughter when she was two years old. Sally's birth parents were both Korean, and she was placed in a Korean orphanage at birth. The little girl has black hair, black eyes, and dark skin, unlike Lou and Darlene who are fair-skinned blondes.

The family social worker visited with Sally on the school playground, where she also had the opportunity to observe Sally's behavior during recess. The other children ignored Sally for the most part, but when she got in the way of some boys playing football, they called her "dumb." Later, when asked about the boys, Sally said they always talk to her like that and often make fun of the way she looks. She said she feels best when playing with the African American children "because they have skin like mine."

Sally told the FSW that she wished she looked more like her (adoptive) mother and that if she did, she would have more friends. Her teacher mentioned to the FSW that Sally does not do well in school because "She does not give me eye contact when I talk." After talking with Sally, her parents, and her teacher, the FSW began to realize that none of the adults had much knowledge about Korean culture.

PEER RELATIONSHIPS

Assessment of the minority child's peer interactions gives the family social worker an important indicator of the child's level of acculturation into the majority culture.

1. *Peer interactions:* Children's relationships with peers may be an indicator of their well-being. "Fitting in" with others and having a peer support group are important to the child's self-esteem and sense of belonging. Indicators include the child's report of friendships as well as involvement in group activities.
2. *Degree of involvement:* The family social worker can assess the level of involvement by asking questions about the child's hobbies and other activities. Examples include sports or other team memberships, Girl or Boy Scouts, and clubs. Also, does the child have a close friend among his or her schoolmates?
3. *Opposite-sex relationships:* For adolescents who are beginning to think about opposite-sex relationships, assessment considerations include availability of partners. For instance, does the minority adolescent feel accepted by others at school dances and in dating relationships?

ADAPTATION TO THE COMMUNITY

Indicators of community involvement are important to the assessment of the minority child's fit into the broader social environment. The family social

| CASE 5.3 | GENOGRAM |

The FSW received a report to investigate a large family living on the edge of town in a small house. The family was new to the little community and neighbors reported a chaotic situation with multiple generations coming and going at all hours, as well as several small children who seemed unsupervised.

When the FSW arrived at the home, she found that the neighbors were correct about the confusing number of family members living in the home. She decided to interview the family and fill in a genogram to better understand the family composition. She was able to arrive at a time when most family members were present and could participate in the activity. The genogram the FSW put together is shown in Figure 5.8. The FSW found that three generations were living together in the grandparents' (Ellen and Ted) home; their daughter (Bonnie) was living there with her husband (Al), and Bonnie's children were also in the home (Ben, Jake, Sue, Ann).

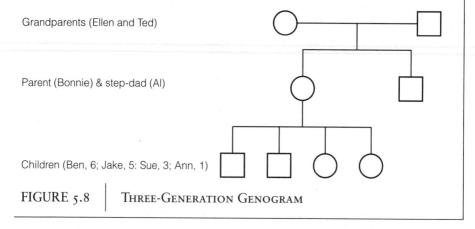

Grandparents (Ellen and Ted)

Parent (Bonnie) & step-dad (Al)

Children (Ben, 6; Jake, 5: Sue, 3; Ann, 1)

| FIGURE 5.8 | THREE-GENERATION GENOGRAM |

worker can assess group and work involvements, as well as family members' reactions to the child's community activities.

1. *Group involvement:* The family social worker may need to assess groups in which the child participates, such as church, recreation centers, and clubs. Also, the level of involvement is an important indicator of the child's successful participation. For instance, how often does the child attend church, does he or she have friends there, and in what church-sponsored activities does the child participate?

2. *Work involvement:* Adolescents may hold jobs in the community that must be assessed for their appropriateness. Concomitantly, adolescents may want jobs but need help in finding appropriate employment.

3. *Family members' reactions to child's community involvement:* Family members' level of acculturation may affect their reactions to the child's group and/or work activities. The family social worker may need to help families accept their children's interactions outside of the family; or they may need to help the family to allow children freedom to explore relationships in the community.

4. *Child's special interests or abilities:* Identifying children's special interests, and especially their special abilities, is important to the development of a successful intervention plan. The family social worker may build on the child's strengths to help promote adjustment to a culture different from that of the family of origin. For instance, some children may excel in sports or music rather than academic endeavors. Successful performance in these areas may mitigate poor school performance and increase the child's self-esteem.

CHAPTER SUMMARY

Chapter 5 presents the area of qualitative assessment—that is, using words, pictures and observations to understand the client family. In contrast, quantitative assessment uses numerical tests and scales to quantify client strengths and weaknesses.

The context of family assessment was first addressed and included the purposes of family assessment, models of family functioning, and the ecological assessment. Then qualitative techniques were discussed. These included ecomaps, communication techniques, and visual techniques such as genograms and ecomaps. The next four chapters further detail family assessment.

EXERCISES

5.1 BRAINSTORM

Break into groups of three. Brainstorm about all the issues faced by the family discussed in Case 5.1. Develop hypotheses for what lies behind each of these difficulties. Then, beside each of these problems, suggest an intervention for each. Please note that each problem should have a unique intervention plan (unless the problems are all related). What further information do you need to collect in order to plan an intervention with this family? Reconvene into the larger class and each group will share their answers with the rest of the class. What similarities and differences of opinion exist in the class? Discuss.

5.2 TARGETING ISSUES

The lists in this chapter of issues to focus on in a family assessment interview cover several of many possibilities. Break the class into groups of three and brainstorm what other issues and questions might be asked. Report back to the main group. Assign a class member to collate the lists given by all the groups. This list can be distributed to the entire class for future reference.

5.3 RULES OF GENOGRAM CONSTRUCTION

Following the four rules of genogram construction provided in the chapter, map out a woman who has been married four times. She had three children in her first relationship, no children with her second partner, two children with her third, and none with her fourth. However, her fourth husband brought two children from a previous relationship. Compare your answers with the rest of the class.

5.4   CREATING A GENOGRAM

Select a movie or television family where there is sufficient detail about the family and multiple generations. Construct a genogram on this family. Share this genogram with the class. Then, break into small groups and analyze the information contained on this genogram. Develop a list of questions to ask this family about their genogram. Compare your answers with the rest of the class.

5.5   A GENOGRAM OF YOUR FAMILY

Create a genogram of your family. Start by planning what information you want to obtain and how far back the generations will go. Part of this will depend upon how much information you have at your disposal. If you would like to go back several generations, but lack the necessary information, you might want to ask your parents (if they are available) some questions before you start. Questions might include important dates, names, and relationships, and useful pieces of information such as occupation, education, and significant medical or mental health difficulties. The easiest way is to draw the genogram by hand, although there are electronic resources available to purchase or download from the Web. Make yourself the "IP" in this genogram and select one of your issues. See if you can trace the history of this "issue" through the generations or, alternatively, from your family of origin.

5.6   ROLE-PLAY CREATING A GENOGRAM

Break the class into groups of three. One person will serve as a coach/observer, one person will be the family social worker, and the third person will be the client. While respecting privacy and boundaries, create a genogram on the client. The client has the right, in this role-play, to refuse to answer specific questions.

5.7   ECOMAP

Continue the above role-play, but this time instead of creating a genogram create the client's ecomap. Discuss with the client what changes he or she would like to see if they could change their social system interactions.

5.8   FAMILY FUNCTIONING

Develop at least two questions from each of the eight areas of family functioning identified in this chapter. Be especially alert to any sexist, ageist, or cultural biases that enter into your questions.

5.9   MEETING FAMILY NEEDS

The following list includes needs that all families have. Give examples of needs for each category. Beside each example indicate possible available ecological resources that can meet these needs. In the examples of ecological resources provide a variety of formal and informal sources of support as well as whether they are developmental or basic.

> Needs
> Physical needs
> Safety needs
> Belonging needs
> Esteem needs
> Self-actualization needs
> Example formal
> Example informal

5.10   HIERARCHY OF NEEDS

Using Maslow's (1967) hierarchy of needs, make a list of examples of these needs for individuals within the family, possible ways of getting these needs met, and how the needs might be threatened.

5.11   ASSESSMENT OF A CHILD

Select one child you know and conduct an assessment of that child using Stenhauer's ten-point child assessment areas.

5.12   FAMILY FUNCTIONING

Compose four questions, each relating to the six areas of family functioning selected by Epstein, Baldwin, and Bishop. Be especially aware of any sexist, ageist, or cultural biases that enter into the questions you have formulated.

6 CHAPTER | QUANTITATIVE ASSESSMENT

We introduced the idea of qualitative assessment in Chapter 5. Qualitative assessment refers to using descriptive methods to attain client information; these include mapping techniques and open-ended interviewing. Chapter 6 introduces the use of quantitative measures to inform assessment. Quantitative assessment includes using measures to arrive at "numerical indicators of a particular aspect of client functioning" (Franklin & Corcoran, 2003, p. 71). This chapter discusses the purposes of quantitative assessment, gives frameworks for incorporating quantitative assessment, describes commonly used measurement instruments, and discusses using measurement to link assessment and intervention.

PURPOSES OF QUANTITIVE MEASUREMENT

Our approach to quantitative assessment and measurement includes the following assumptions about assessment. Assessment must be evidence based—that is, it must make use of the best techniques from a literature search. From this perspective, measures shown to be highly reliable for the population to be assessed should be used. A second assumption is that assessment should be systems oriented. In other words, problems should not be narrowly defined and measured apart from the context in which the problems occur. We consider clients from a systemic perspective, taking into account the multiple contexts within which they live, work, and interact.

A third assumption is that assessment should be based on multiple measures of client strengths and problems. *Triangulation* is a term that has been used to describe this perspective. Triangulation encourages use of a three-prong measurement system for any client problem or strength: (1) client self-report, (2) client behavioral observation, and (3) external report or observation. Using this type of system allows the FSW to obtain a more accurate view of what is going on with the family.

Fourth, the use of a quantitative assessment approach allows for a better grasp of the extent of the family's problems. Additionally, monitoring and evaluation of practice activities are ensured. This quantitative approach is required in today's managed care environment.

Additional benefits of quantitative assessment are the possibilities for improving treatment because of the continual monitoring of practice, for contributing to the clinical research literature, and for receiving feedback allowing the FSW to increase skills, competence, and accountability.

SELECTING A MEASUREMENT INSTRUMENT

When selecting a measurement instrument, it is important that it be both *valid* and *reliable*. These terms are discussed in greater detail in the following sections. In *Measures for Clinical Practice,* Corcoran and Fischer (2000) review the psychometric properties of each of the instruments they include in their book. We provide some examples from their book in the Exercise section. By the end of this discussion, it is hoped that you will understand the concepts of reliability and validity, and use this understanding to select the best instrument to use with your families. Be prepared, the discussion is quite technical!

Empirically based practice is becoming an important component of social work. The growing recognition that the profession needs to be accountable has led to the development of measures to monitor and evaluate clinical practice (Corcoran & Fischer, 2000). Inasmuch as the effectiveness of socio-behavioral science can primarily be determined by its instruments, we need to develop systematic approaches to measurement. This is, however, a development that has occurred over the past several decades (Carmines & Zeller, 1979).

Many of the issues demanding the attention of social scientists are abstract, making measurement a difficult exercise at times. Measurement technology has become a fundamental component in the development of a knowledge base and evaluation of clinical practice. Measurement involves the "process of linking abstract concepts to empirical indicators" (Carmines & Zeller, 1979, p. 10), or the "process of quantifying a variable." By definition, measurement is often an empirical process of linking observable events with concepts that are theoretical but frequently not observable. Usually an instrument consists of a variety of items that can be graded and summed, resulting in a score for each case. The cornerstone of such a process is the establishment of reliability and validity for any measurement being developed. These terms are defined in the following sections.

Finally, instruments should be culturally sensitive. This means that the instruments selected can be safely used with a particular culture and that the concepts being measured take cultural differences into account. Sometimes in the development stage, instruments are tested only with one culture. Applying untested instruments to other cultures is problematic and will affect both the validity and reliability of the instrument. Moreover, the criteria measured in the instrument need to be appropriate to that particular culture.

RELIABILITY

Theory of test construction has evolved primarily from classical test theory, a large part of which is aimed at the elimination of error (Pedhazur & Pedhazur, 1991). The true score model derived from classical test theory is the dominant theory guiding the estimation of reliability, and is simply expressed by the equation $O = T + E$. That is, observed scores consist of the true score plus error. While it is virtually impossible to obtain absolute true scores, the objective of measurement is to eliminate error as much as possible. Measurement error may be either systematic or random or both. Good measurement practices dictate the elimination of both types of error.

Any measurement device contains both random (unsystematic) and nonrandom (systematic) measurement error. A device is reliable when repeated measurements are not influenced by random error. Since random error is unsystematic, the errors are assumed to cancel each other out. Random error includes all those "chance factors" that confound measurement, and it may evolve from several sources such as clerical mistakes, interviewer fatigue, and the respondent's failure to follow instructions. Reliability is inversely related to the amount of random error present in the measurement process.

Nonrandom error systematically biases the results of measurement and is a problem for determination of validity because such error prevents indicators from representing the theoretical concept under study (Carmines & Zeller, 1979). Validity therefore depends on the extent of nonrandom error present in the measurement process.

Classical test score theory is a useful model for assessing random measurement error. True scores are hypothetical, unobservable quantities that cannot be directly measured. Any particular observed score will not be identical to its real score because of "noise," acceptance of which is based on the assumption that the fluctuations are random and cancel each other out with a mean of 0. The reliability of a measure varies between 0 and 1. Thus, reliability can easily be expressed in terms of variances of true score and random scores.

A good instrument is one that produces stable results and minimizes error. Reliability is concerned with the "extent to which an experiment, test, or any measuring procedure yields the same results on repeated trials" (Carmines & Zeller, 1979, p. 11). Thus, the consistency and stability of a measurement over time are the focus in the determination of reliability. The measurement precision and consistency of reliability lend themselves more easily to mathematical formulations than do measures of validity. Although it is virtually impossible to completely eliminate error, the aim of attaining reliable measures is to eliminate as much error as possible. Adequate measures that tend toward consistency from one measure to another indicate high reliability. Reliability of a test score is the freedom of the test from errors of measurement and is essentially a theory of error. A reliable instrument yields small error since reliability is based on the amount of error that is contained in the observed scores. The resultant score is known as the reliability coefficient. If the reliability coefficient is large, the instrument is considered reliable, whereas smaller coefficients are indicative of less reliability.

Some disagreement exists regarding the range of acceptability of a reliability coefficient (Pedhazur & Pedhazur, 1991). However, a reliability coefficient of .60 or greater is generally acceptable for science whereas .80 or greater is advocated for clinical practice (Corcoran & Fischer, 2000). For the purposes of interpretation, a score of .80 indicates that 80 percent of the variance of observed scores is systematic (Pedhazur & Pedhazur, 1991, p. 86) while $(1 - .80)$ refers to the proportion of variance due to random errors. The difference in acceptability levels between science and clinical practice stems from the fact that science can average out errors by using large samples.

Several problems are inherent in determining reliability in measurement. One is that the instrument may somehow change the people to be measured. Repeated measures are affected by practice and recall. Because of this, the reliability of measures in the socio-behavioral sciences is usually estimated by studying the extent to which individuals retain their relative positions to a group. The degree of confidence placed in a score is then based on comparisons among individuals. The four basic methods for estimating reliability of empirical measurement include: (1) test re–test, (2) the alternative form method, (3) the split-halves method, and (4) the internal consistency method.

TEST–RETEST METHOD   In the test–retest method, a group is measured twice using the same instrument and reliability is computed as the correlation between a set of scores obtained by a single scale on two separate occasions (Hudson, 1982). This procedure is based on the assumption that the underlying observable scores are constant (i.e., that there has been no change in scores from time 1 to time 2). The lower the correlation, the greater the random error of measurement. This method attempts to capture the stability of a device over time. Corcoran and Fischer (2000) suggest that a coefficient of .69 is acceptable if the tests are conducted one month apart and a coefficient of .80 is acceptable for shorter periods between testing.

Problems inherent in the test–retest approach of determining reliability include the possibility that actual changes in the theoretical concept may have occurred with the respondents in the time between testing or that respondents may have been affected by the process of measurement at the first testing (reactivity). If the time interval between testing is brief, the respondent may be affected by recall (carry-over effect). If the test is too short, the respondent is more likely to experience test recall. Memory effects lead to inflated reliability estimates (Carmines & Zeller, 1979). Longer tests increase the likelihood of measuring real change, which therefore underestimates the true reliability. Although the test–retest method of determining reliability is common, Pedhazur and Pedhazur (1991) argue that the flaws of this approach mitigate against its use. Hudson (1982) concurs, stating that few efforts to obtain reliability for the clinical measurement package have been attempted. The approach may also be negatively impacted by subject attrition.

EQUIVALENT FORM, ALTERNATE FORM, OR PARALLEL FORM METHOD   This procedure involves the administration of an alternative form of the same test designed to measure the same construct. It reflects reliability to the extent to which the two forms used are a measure of the same attribute. The correlation between the two parallel forms serves as the estimate of reliability of either. It is a direct estimate of the alternate form of reliability that would be attained if an equally good alternative form of a particular scale were available. The two subtypes of alternate form reliability are the *strictly parallel model* and the *parallel model* (Norusis, 1990). The strictly parallel model is based on the assumption that all items have the same variances for the true scores and same error variances over replications. The parallel model is based on a relaxation of these assumptions and is the most commonly used method.

Carmines and Zeller (1979) suggest that this is superior to the test–retest estimate, although its fundamental flaw is that the reliability may be contaminated by true change, which may become indistinguishable from unreliability. This is particularly true if the two measures are taken over wide spans of time. Additionally, the use of parallel forms may be a problem in that it may be difficult to construct or obtain another instrument that measures exactly the same concept.

The range of acceptable coefficients for this approach to validity varies, but Corcoran and Fischer (2000) recommend at least a coefficient of .80.

THE SPLIT-HALVES METHOD   This approach to estimating reliability involves splitting the scale into two parts and examining the correlation between them. The split-halves method is conducted on one occasion, thereby eliminating some of the problems involved in both the parallel and test–retest methods. It is a convenient form of testing for reliability and is based on the fundamental assumptions of classical test theory—that is, that the traits measured are constant and the errors are random. In other words, the errors are equal to 0.

In this method of testing, the total set of items is divided into half and the scores on the halves are correlated to produce an estimate of reliability. Each half of the test correlated with the other rather than with the total score. A statistical correction for length is introduced (Spearman-Brown prophecy formula) to enable the researcher to determine reliability with the total test. A corrected reliability coefficient is necessary because the reliability of a test increases as the number of items increases, provided that the average correlation between items does not change (Norusis, 1990). The formula can also be used to adduce the total number of items required to obtain a predetermined reliability coefficient. It is based on all inter-item correlations (the mean of all split-halves reliabilities). The split-halves method ends up being an estimate of coefficient alpha.

The most common method of splitting a test is to divide the test according to odd and even numbers. In fact, an indeterminate number of ways exist to split a test, including separately scoring the first and second halves of the items and randomly dividing the items into two groups (Carmines & Zeller, 1979). Other methods include the Guttman split-half coefficient, which does not assume that the two parts are equally reliable or have the same variance. The reliability coefficient varies depending upon what splitting method is used.

Difficulties with this procedure derive from the way the items are split to be separately scored. The use of split-halves reliability is based on the assumption that the halves are strictly parallel and that increases in the size of an instrument would increase reliability. However, doubling the length of an instrument does not double its reliability, and increasing the size eventually leads to diminishing returns (Pedhazur & Pedhazur, 1991).

INTERNAL CONSISTENCY   An instrument has internal consistency if the items are consistent with one another and are judged to measure the same variable (Corcoran & Fischer, 1987). Internal consistency is garnered usually from a single test administration, and Cronbach's alpha is a commonly used estimate of reliability. Alpha is based on the internal consistency of a test. The average correlation of an item with all other items in the scales tells us about the extent of commonality. The values of Cronbach's alpha depend on both the length of the test and the correlation of the items in the test. Theoretically, it is possible to have a large reliability coefficient even when the average inter-item correlation is small, provided the number of items in the scale is large enough. Acceptable values for Cronbach's alpha vary, and some suggest that it needs to be .80 or more for widely used scales (Carmines & Zeller, 1979).

For measures with dichotomous rather than ordinal items, Kuder-Richardsons's 20 is the preferred statistic to measure internal consistency. In this method dichotomous items are dummy coded (0 and 1) depending on whether or not the respondent has the characteristic under study. The KR-20 is a special case of alpha that is interpreted the same way as alpha. Ordinal or continuous variables should not be collapsed to dichotomous variables since valuable information is lost in the process.

Validity

Validity reflects the extent to which any measuring instrument measures what it is designed to measure (Corcoran & Fischer, 2000; Carmines & Zeller, 1979). It is a unitary concept in that there are not types of validity. Rather, there are different approaches to ascertaining validity. Thus, the following classification system of validity does not imply a set of mutually exclusive and exhaustive categories, much less different types of validity—the methods are interrelated facets of the same process. *Validation* refers not to the specific measure in question but to inferences made on the basis of scores obtained on it. One therefore validates not the measuring instrument itself but the measuring instrument in relation to the purpose for which it is being used (Carmines & Zeller, 1979). Thus an instrument may be valid for measuring one kind of phenomenon but invalid for assessing another.

Validity is predicated upon two expectations: that it measures the concept in question and that the concept is measured accurately (Bostwick & Kyte, 1988). Approaches to validity are applicable both in the measurement context and the research design context. As with reliability, validity is a matter of magnitude and there are often shades of gray. While reliability is necessary for validity, the converse does not hold. Additionally, validity is determined or limited by its reliability, and we thus need to guard existing validity by protecting reliabilities. The upper limit of the validity of any scale is established as the square root of its reliability (Hudson, 1982). The several approaches to validity include: (1) content, (2) criterion related, (3) construct, and (4) factorial. Approaches to validation are blurred in the literature. This becomes particularly evident when distinguishing between methods of criterion and construct validity.

CONTENT VALIDITY   This approach to validity refers to a "domain" of content, taking into account content relevance inasmuch as the concepts are both adequately covered and relevant. Therefore, the content of the measure must be consistent with the definition of the construct (Pedhazur & Pedhazur, 1979, p. 80) and contain an adequate sample of items that represent the concept.

Since content validity depends on the extent to which an empirical measurement reflects a specific domain of content (Carmines & Zeller, 1979, p. 20), it needs to completely include all the components believed to be representative of the content in a testable way. Items must also reflect the meaning associated with each dimension of the concept under review. Unfortunately, in the social sciences there is often widespread disagreement regarding the domain, and determination of content validity becomes dependent upon subjective judgment and is vulnerable to error. Since it is virtually impossible to create a total population of items to represent different measures of a single construct, a sample of items is therefore used. Ideally, the total domain should be specified, items sampled from the domain, and then put into a testable form. At the outset of item sampling, too many items are preferable to too few in that inadequate items can be eliminated from the instrument at a later date.

Content validity is frequently accomplished through the combination of critical thinking and the consensus of competent judges who possess expertise in the field. Naturally, the researcher strives for high consensus among judges. Ultimately, a measure that is not content valid is unlikely to survive other tests of validity. Because concepts to be measured are abstract, they are subject to disagreement as to what the relevant domain of content is. It also may be difficult, if not impossible in the social sciences, to comprehensively sample the content, and thus the researcher needs to formulate a set of items believed to best reflect the content or domain of the concept.

Two approaches for determining content validity are logical sampling validity and face validity. *Logical validity* involves "the careful definition of the domain of behaviors to be measured by a test and the logical design of items to cover all the important areas of this domain" (Allen & Yen, 1979, p. 96). Logical analysis is predicated on careful consideration about the selection of issues and the manner in which they are scored. A particularly useful procedure is to generate a counterhypothesis derived through critical thinking. Such critical analysis needs to be grounded in a sound knowledge of theories and research findings relevant to the particular construct.

Face validity is considered the weakest approach to determining validity, which becomes a matter of judgment based on the *appearance* of what concept the instrument is designed to measure. An underlying problem in determining face validity is that there is often little consensus about the definition of the concept to be measured. Furthermore, the concept may be a multidimensional one consisting of several subconcepts, for which the measure becomes lengthy and complex. While face validity may be important to the respondents and lack of it may aversely affect responses, it becomes a necessary but not sufficient form of validity.

CRITERION-RELATED VALIDITY   The criterion validity approach involves comparing scores with external criteria that, preferably, have been previously validated and shown to be reliable. It "is at issue when the purpose is to use an instrument to estimate some important form of behavior that is external to the measuring instrument itself, the latter being referred to as the criterion" (Nunnally, 1978, p. 87). This method is empirically based. Thus, the degree of criterion-related validity depends on the extent of correspondence between the test and event or criterion. Validity coefficients are usually much smaller than their theoretical upper limit, and "good" coefficients range from .40 to .60 (Hudson, 1982).

Criterion validity is further subdivided into two categories: predictive and concurrent. Concurrent validity is useful for diagnostic purposes whereas predictive validity is concerned with the prediction of a criterion (Anastasi, 1988). Predictive validity demonstrates the ability of an instrument to measure (predict) a future event. It involves the administration of the instrument to all relevant subjects and then correlating the results with a criterion at some future date to obtain the validity coefficient. It is concerned with the degree of successful prediction, regardless of whether or not it is possible to explain the process leading to the phenomenon that is being predicted (Pedhazur & Pedhazur, 1991, p. 32). The same authors recommend building a regression model to predict the criterion. In the process, a cutting score is determined but is subject to false positives and false negatives. Cutting scores are imperfect indicators due to SEM. For example, some instruments in the CMP have a SEM of about 5, making the cutting score of 30 indeterminate. The model can also be extended to differential prediction, referring to differences in regression equations for the different groups. In this statistical approach, tests for statistical significance can be conducted on beta and the intercepts. Attenuation due to possible range restriction must also be considered. Cutting scores have been clearly described by Hudson (1982), who uses the procedure for the purposes of diagnosis.

Concurrent validity correlates the test scores with the criterion scores at the same time rather than being separated by a time interval. It seeks to distinguish between one group that displays the criterion being measured and another group that does not. Again, this correlation is subject to a range restriction when sampling may be done on those who display the criterion under examination. Concurrent validity is determined by correlating a measure and the criterion at the same point in time (Carmines & Zeller, 1990) and requires independent evidence of the extent to which the measurement of the criterion is valid. Problems arise in social sciences when irrelevant criterion variables exist. This is particularly evident with highly abstract concepts.

According to Hudson (1982), two strategies can be subsumed under concurrent criterion validity: concurrent instrument validity and the known groups method. The former involves correlating the new instrument with one that has previously been accepted as a valid measure of the same construct. In the known groups method, groups are selected and subdivided on the basis of whether they have the same trait, attribute, etc. under consideration. Based on a comparison of the two cumulative frequency distributions, cutting scores are determined that minimize both false negatives and false positives. A valid instrument will detect statistically significant differences between the two groups. Additionally, if the two groups are treated as the independent variable and the score of the scale as the dependent variable, a point biserial correlation between group status and the scale can be used as a coefficient of validity. Hudson (1982) refers to the latter as a coefficient of discriminant validity.

CONSTRUCT VALIDITY   This approach to validity is often considered the strongest validation procedure and the most useful in social sciences. It refers to the degree to which an instrument measures the construct or trait that it was designed to measure (Allen & Yen, 1979). Kerlinger (1979) suggests that construct validity is the central kind of validity. It is "concerned with the extent to which a particular measure relates to other measures consistent with theoretically derived hypotheses concerning the concepts (or constructs) that are being measured" (Carmines & Zeller, 1979, p. 23), and thus involves both the validation of the instrument and of the underlying theory (Bostwick & Kyte, 1988). This is often accomplished by correlating a scale device with another piece of evidence to attain support for the construct.

The process of construct validation is theory driven, involving specification of the theoretical relationship between the concepts, the empirical relationship between concepts and then interpreting the empirical evidence. Osterlind (1983) warns about test item bias, which appears as systematic error in the measurement process, affecting all measurements the same way and negatively impacting construct validity. Construct validation requires a consistent pattern of findings from a variety of researchers employing a variety of theoretical structures. When the process yields negative evidence, the theoretical framework may be flawed and the testing procedure may either lack construct validity or reliability. Multiple indicators should ideally yield results that are consistent, of the same direction, and of similar strengths. Testing hypotheses generated by construct validation can involve either convergent or discriminant validation. Some authors subsume factor validity under construct validity while others view it as a distinct category.

a) If two independent measures of the criterion under study produce similar results, a measure is deemed to possess convergent validity. "Convergent validity is demonstrated by high correlations between scores on a test measuring the same trait by different methods" (Nunnally, 1978, p. 111). For example, if a newly constructed instrument designed to measure depression yielded similar results to previously validated instruments to measure depression, the new instrument could be said to possess convergent validity.

b) If the construct is independent of other unrelated constructs, it is considered to possess discriminant validity. It thus positively correlates with other measures that have been validated but does not correlate with measures the instrument it is not intended to measure. Using the preceding example, the newly constructed instrument to measure depression may be uncorrelated to a measure designed to measure life satisfaction and therefore is said to possess discriminant validity.

FACTORIAL VALIDITY   Factor composition of measures plays a part in the aforementioned approaches to validity. Factor analysis can be used to determine internal consistency and is based on the assumption that the items in the scale are parallel and measure a phenomenon equally. When items measure a single phenomenon unequally or when items measure more than one concept equally or unequally, then factor analysis is a useful tool. Factor loadings are used to determine the extent to which each item is correlated with each factor. Items from other scales can also be factored together to determine if each item measures the construct under examination or another construct. A factorially valid measure will exhibit high correlations with similar measures of the construct and low correlations with unrelated items.

FRAMEWORKS FOR INCORPORATING QUANTITATIVE MEASUREMENT

Two frameworks for incorporating quantitative measurement into the FSW practice are presented here. They are single subject design and goal attainment scaling.

SINGLE SUBJECT DESIGN

Single subject design provides a framework for setting up a quantitative measurement system to ensure accountable practice. The following seven steps are adapted from Bloom, Fischer, and Orme (2005).

Step 1. Measure the problem. During this step, the FSW is concerned with beginning the relationship with the family, gaining entry into the system, establishing rapport, and beginning assessment, including collecting data. At this step, the data collection may be qualitative (see Chapter 5). Qualitative tools such as genograms or ecomaps may help to engage the family while also helping the FSW to view the range of the family's problems and strengths.

Step 2. Perform repeated measures over the course of assessment and treatment. Step 2 moves into the use of quantitative measurement to further capture information about specific client problems and strengths. Specific measurement instruments to measure the targets of the intervention are identified, and these measures will be used over the course of the treatment. For example, if the client is depressed, a Beck Depression Inventory may be used on a weekly basis to monitor the client's progress during the intervention.

Step 3. Decide on the unique design. A typical single subject design is the A/B design, in which A refers to the baseline phase of treatment and B refers to the intervention phase. The baseline phase is the period when quantitative information is collected prior to beginning the intervention. This data can then be compared to the intervention phases data, the data collected during the administration of the intervention. See Figure 6.1 for an example of how the A/B data is graphed.

Step 4. Collect baseline data. Step four involves collecting baseline data during the initial assessment meetings. The data is then graphed as in Figure 6.1. Note that in Figure 6.1 the baseline data (A phase) was collected for three weeks prior to beginning the intervention (B phase). The intervention should be clearly defined so that the FSW can learn what treatments work with specific clients as she builds up her repertoire of graphs from various families. The FSW then continues collecting data after the baseline phase is over and intervention begins.

Step 5. Analyze the data. Simple analysis of the data may be done by "eyeballing" it. For example, what is the trend and slope of the data in both phases? Note that in Figure 6.1 the slope and trend of the baseline data are

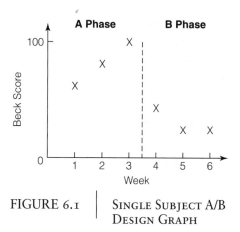

FIGURE 6.1 | SINGLE SUBJECT A/B DESIGN GRAPH

in an upward direction. In the case of the Beck Depression Inventory, which is being used in this example, higher scores indicate more significant levels of depression. Looking at the slope and trend of the intervention phase data, we see that the scores are improving as they move downward to a non-clinically significant level. Later in this chapter, we will we talk about standardized measures, such as the Beck Depression Inventory, and cutting scores and norms will be discussed. These refer to scores that can be used for comparison with our clients' scores. Using these we can look at the specific score obtained on the test and tell whether or not our client is depressed compared with scores from clinical populations. This is one of the advantages of using standardized tests that have such comparison information.

In some cases, such as when using direct behavioral observations, we do not have comparison scores. Statistical procedures are available to compare baseline scores with intervention scores. These include the Shewart Chart, the Celeration Line, and the T-Test. For more information about these, see Bloom, Fischer, and Orme (2005). Additionally, the FSW can compare several families by using other single subject designs or by using standard scores to make results comparable (Bloom, Fischer, & Orme, 2005).

Step 6. Perform follow-up measurement. Follow-up is an important concept to the FSW. Tracking clients to keep up with their whereabouts can be challenging. It is important, however, especially when families are troubled and likely to need continuing services from the FSW and the agency. It is important to continue to monitor the families after discontinuation of the services to ensure continuing positive progress. Tracking is easier when mechanisms for tracking are built in to the assessment from the beginning. Some strategies include getting names, addresses, and phone numbers of extended family members or friends of the family in treatment in the initial meetings. It is important to get the names of those with whom the family will keep in touch in the event that they move away. Another strategy is for the person doing the assessment and treatment to also be the tracker. The assumption is that rapport has been built and the family will likely respond to an FSW with whom they have a warm relationship.

Step 7. Present the results. Finally, we have discussed how the results of single subject data collection are valuable to the client and to the FSW. Others who may be interested in this data are supervisors, community members, and funding sources. The data can be used for the larger purpose of program evaluation and applying for funding

GOAL ATTAINMENT SCALING

Another way of evaluating your practice is to use goal attainment scaling (GAS). In goal attainment scaling the FSW, in collaboration with the family, describes areas of change along with identifying the range of possible outcomes, ranging from the most unfavorable outcome to the most favorable outcome (Jordan, Franklin, & Corcoran, 2005). The advantage of GAS is that areas of focus can be completely individualized for the particular family. The least favorable outcome is rated as −2, while the most favorable outcome is given a score of +2. See Figure 6.2.

MEASUREMENT INSTRUMENTS

The section on single subject design discussed how to set up a framework for using quantitative assessment. Types of quantified measures are presented in this section. These include client self-anchored and rating scales, direct behavioral observation, and standardized measures. Other ways of quantifying client data also are presented. This section is from Franklin and Corcoran (2003).

SELF-ANCHORED AND SELF-MONITORING INSTRUMENTS

Self-anchored and self-monitoring instruments are the most common type of quantitative measure used in practice. These are generally very high in validity because they are designed for the specific client or family and take into account their unique issues. Client and FSW usually design these instruments together. They may be a combination of qualitative and quantitative. Figure 6.3 is an example of this. Note the combination of Anger Diary (qualitative) and Rating Scale (quantitative). In this measure, the client takes it home and fills it out as situations occur. An example of a quantitative question is, "How many arguments this week?" The client provides a discrete number. A qualitative question from the diary is, "Which intervention steps did you use?" The clients are asked to narrate in their own words what happened when they had an argument. Adding this qualitative dimension to quantitative measurement gives the FSW more information to know what went right or what went

Goals: To feel better overall and to not use drugs.

SCALE ATTAINMENT LEVELS	INDICATOR #1: *To decrease thoughts of using drugs.*	INDICATOR #2: *To decrease repetitive thoughts of Ian.*	INDICATOR #3: *Lisa sleeps well at night.*
−2: *Most unfavorable treatment outcome likely*	Lisa thinks about using drugs more than once a day, everyday.	Lisa always thinks about Ian.	Lisa has nightmares every night.
−1: *Less than expected treatment outcome*	Lisa thinks about using drugs once a day everyday.	Lisa thinks about Ian frequently.	Lisa has nightmares more than 5 times a week but less than 7 times.
0: *Expected treatment outcome*	Lisa thinks about using drugs less than 7 times a week but more than 3 times a week.	Lisa thinks about Ian occasionally.	Lisa has nightmares less than 5 times a week but more than 3 times.
+1: *More than expected treatment outcome*	Lisa thinks about using drugs less than 3 times a week.	Lisa thinks about Ian rarely.	Lisa has nightmares less than 3 times a week but still occasionally has nightmares.
+2: *Most favorable treatment outcome*	Lisa does not think about using drugs.	Lisa never thinks about Ian.	Lisa no longer has nightmares.

Modality: Individual therapy was used with Lisa. Specifically, motivational interviewing and cognitive-behavioral therapy were used.

Dates of ratings:

Nov. 19th, 06   Indicator #1: −1   Indicator #2: −1   Indicator #3: −1

Dec. 17th, 06   Indicator #1: 0   Indicator #2: −1   Indicator #3: 0

Jan. 21st, 07   Indicator #1: 0   Indicator #2: −1   Indicator #3: 0

Feb. 18th, 07   Indicator #1: +1   Indicator #2: 0   Indicator #3: 0

Mar. 18th, 07   Indicator #1: +1   Indicator #2: 0   Indicator #3: +1

Apr. 15th, 07   Indicator #1: +1   Indicator #2: 0   Indicator #3: +1

FIGURE 6.2 | GOAL ATTAINMENT SCALE

Name _____ Date _____

How many arguments this week? _____

Rate (1–10) how angry you were? _____

What were your internal signals?

_____

Which of the intervention steps did you use?

_____

What happened afterwards?

_____

FIGURE 6.3 | ANGER DIARY AND RATING SCALE

From: Jordan and Franklin (2003). *Clinical assessment for social workers: Qualitative and quantitative methods.* Chicago: Lyceum.

Instructions: Circle the number that applies every day before 8 A.M.

1   2   3   4   5   6   7

Energetic,   Tired, no energy

feel alive   feel like lying down

and ready to go to work   and never getting up

FIGURE 6.4 | SELF-ANCHORED SCALE FOR DEPRESSION

From: Jordan and Franklin (2003). *Clinical assessment for social workers: Quantitative and qualitative methods.* Chicago: Lyceum.

wrong about the treatment. Further refinements or adjustments then can be made. Note that we can assign several family members to complete an anger diary, thereby giving us the triangulated system we discussed earlier in this chapter.

Figure 6.4 is an example of a self-anchored scale designed by the FSW and the client together. This self-anchored scale measures depression, but almost anything can be measured in this simple way (e.g., client resistance to treatment). Note that the self-anchored scale usually has 7 points and is anchored on both the high and low end of the scale. These anchors are developed from the client's unique responses to depression, in the case of Figure 6.4. Other clients would have different anchors. For another self-anchored scale, see Figure 6.5, which measures conflict avoidance. Note that many client issues or problems might be measured in this simple way. The rater could be the client, a family member, the FSW, or some other participant (e.g., school teacher or other professional).

Inadequate 1   2   3   4   5   6   7   8   9   10 Adequate

Changes the subject,	Stays on topic,
Leaves the room,	Engages in
Refuses to talk about issues	conversation about
	conflictual issues

FIGURE 6.5 | CONFLICT AVOIDANCE SELF-ANCHORED SCALE

From: Jordan and Franklin (2003). *Clinical assessment for social workers: Qualitative and quantitative methods*. Chicago: Lyceum.

COUPLE'S RATING SCALE TO RATE COMMUNICATION ROLE-PLAY

Inadequate 1   2   3   4   5   6   7   8   9   10   Adequate

- Speak for self
- Send I messages
- Use a stop action
- Ask for feedback
- Listen
- Summarize
- Validate
- Ask open questions
- Check out

FIGURE 6.6 | BEHAVIORAL OBSERVATION RATING SCALE

From: Jordan and Franklin (2003). *Clinical assessment for social workers: Qualitative and quantitative methods*. Chicago: Lyceum.

DIRECT BEHAVIORAL OBSERVATION

Figure 6.6 is an example of a chart for recording information obtained from direct behavioral observation. In other words, the FSW set up a communication role-play for a couple, and then observed their communication. The scale in Figure 6.6 lists the elements of good communication that have been the focus of the couples' communication intervention. The FSW observed the couple and rated each of the elements on the scale. These types of rating scales for direct observation are easily made, especially if the elements of the intervention are easily broken down or the goals easily operationalized. Other aspects of clients' behavior may also be observed and documented in this way, for example, child behavior problems. The FSW may observe the child in a classroom

This questionnaire is designed to measure the way you feel about your family as a whole. It is not a test, so there are no right or wrong answers. Answer each item as carefully and as accurately as you can by placing a number beside each one as follows:

1 = none of the time

2 = very rarely

3 = a little of the time

4 = some of the time

5 = a good part of the time

1. ____ The members of my family really care about each other.

2. ____ I think my family is terrific.

3. ____ My family gets on my nerves.

4. ____ I really enjoy my family.

5. ____ I can really depend on my family.

6. ____ I really do not care to be around my family.

7. ____ I wish I was not part of this family.

8. ____ I get along well with my family.

9. ____ Members of my family argue too much.

10. ____ There is no sense of closeness in my family.

11. ____ I feel like a stranger in my family.

12. ____ My family does not understand me.

13. ____ There is too much hatred in my family.

14. ____ Members of my family are really good to one another.

15. ____ My family is well respected by those who know us.

16. ____ There seems to be a lot of friction in my family.

17. ____ There is a lot of love in my family.

18. ____ Members of my family get along well together.

19. ____ Life in my family is generally unpleasant.

20. ____ My family is a great joy to me.

21. ____ I feel proud of my family.

22. ____ Other families seem to get along better than ours.

23. ____ My family is a real source of comfort to me.

24. ____ I feel left out of my family.

25. ____ My family is an unhappy one.

1,2,4,5,8,14,15,17,18,20,21,23

FIGURE 6.7 | STANDARDIZED MEASURE: INDEX OF FAMILY RELATIONS (IFR)

From: W. Hudson in Jordan and Franklin (2003). *Clinical assessment for social workers: Qualitative and quantitative methods.* Chicago: Lyceum.

and count the number of times that the child gets out of seat, talks out of turn, etc. Teachers are sometimes good adjuncts to treatment and can record this information for the FSW.

STANDARDIZED MEASURES

Standardized measures have been prepared and tested by experts in their areas. The testing is most useful when it has been done on similar populations to your clients. Testing establishes the reliability (accuracy) and validity (truth) of a measure—in selecting a measure to use with your clients, this is an important consideration. Also, the types of questions asked are important because there are multiple ways to measure any construct. For instance, one family satisfaction scale may focus on behavioral interactions of family members while a different family satisfaction scale may measure family dynamics. We recommend that the FSW take any measure to become familiar with its questions, scoring, and so forth before getting a family member to take it.

A handbook with multiple measures that may be used by the FSW is a two-volume set called *Measures for Clinical Practice* by Kevin Corcoran and Joel Fischer. Standardized tests "assess a broad spectrum of client behaviors such as personality, intelligence, marital satisfaction, self-esteem, and just about all aspects of human behavior" (Corcoran & Fischer, 2000). As mentioned previously, these measures are particularly useful when they have cutting scores or norms to which we can compare our clients' scores. Figure 6.7 is a partial scale that measures family relations. An example of a quantitative family measurement described in Corcoran and Fischer is the Family Assessment Measure. This measure is described in qualitative terms in Chapter 5.

OTHER QUANTIFIED MEASURES

Other ways of quantifying clients' problems and strengths include behavioral by-products and psychophysiological measures. Behavioral by-products are material symbols of the problem. For example, a client trying to quit smoking might count her cigarette butts in the ashtray. Psychophysiological measures, such as biofeedback equipment, require specialized training. For more information on these and other measures, see *Clinical Assessment for Social Workers: Qualitative and Quantitative Methods* (Jordan & Franklin, 2003).

USING MEASUREMENT TO LINK ASSESSMENT AND INTERVENTION

This section provides guidelines for assessing when clients are ready to move from the assessment phase to intervention. It is taken from Jordan and Franklin (1999).

CLIENT READINESS FOR TREATMENT

It's important **not** to push the client toward intervention if he or she is not ready. This is a surefire way to ensure failure! Following are ways of telling if clients are ready to move forward in the family social work process.

Client indicators: An important question to ask is if the FSW has established rapport with the family. Practitioner ability to influence the client in a positive direction is an important indicator for success of the intervention.

Data collection: It is important that the FSW completely understands the clients problems and strengths. The quantitative and qualitative data collection is key here.

Agency/social workers variables: Another key consideration is whether or not the FSW and/or the agency can provide the intervention that the client requires. If not, referral should be considered.

TREATMENT PLANNING

Treatment planning involves defining measurable goals, objectives, and outcomes, as well as evidence-based treatments known to be effective with specific client problems and populations. Jordan and Franklin (2002) detail five steps involved in the treatment planning process.

Step 1: Problem selection: Problem selection involves understanding the problem from both a qualitative and a quantitative perspective, taking into account the context within which the family lives.

Step 2: Problem definition: Quantitative methods in particular help to define and operationalize problems so that they can be measured and tracked.

Step 3: Goal development: The goal statement is a broadly stated description of what successful outcome is expected. There should be a goal statement for each problem. Goals may be long-term expectations.

Step 4: Objective Construction: Objectives are the measurable steps that must occur for the goals to be met. Each goal should have at least two objectives. Objectives are operationalized in measurable terms. Target dates may be assigned to each objective.

Step 5: Intervention creation: Interventions should be matched with each objective. Interventions are selected based on the clinician's orientation; however, the trend is toward brief, evidence-based methods that have proven efficacy for specific individuals, families, or problems. Also, manualized interventions and treatment planners are recommended. See Jongsma's & Dattilio's *Family Therapy Treatment Planner* (2000), for example. Also, see Figure 6.8 for an example treatment plan.

Problem: Behavior problems

Definitions: Distractibility, inattentiveness, angry outbursts, and occasional aggression

Goals: To improve attentiveness at home and at school

To eliminate angry outbursts

Objectives:	Interventions:
1. Parents and teachers learn how to help Anthony stay on task	1. Teach parents and teachers develop a reward system for A's staying on task.
2. Anthony learns to control anger	1. Teach Anthony anger management

Diagnosis: 314.01 Attention-Deficit/Hyperactivity Disorder, Combined Type

---

FIGURE 6.8 | EXAMPLE TREATMENT PLAN

From: Jordan and Franklin (2003). *Clinical assessment for social workers: Qualitative and quantitative methods.* Chicago: Lyceum.

CASE 6.1 | QUANTITATIVE ASSESSMENT

Sharon, age 14, her mother, Joy, and stepfather, Otto, were reported to Child Protective Services by Sharon's school. According to her teacher, Sharon has been playing hooky at least once a week and her grades have dropped from an A average to a C level this semester. At the home visit, the FSW found that Joy and Otto were at a loss to know what to do with Sharon's behavior. Joy said that Sharon "had never acted this way before." Otto, the stepfather, was a new entry to the family, and Sharon's problems started when Joy and Otto married about 4 months ago, according to Joy. Otto said that he had decided Sharon needed a "firm hand" and that Joy was "too easy" on her. His disciplinary techniques were not working, as the parents reported that Sharon was misbehaving at home in addition to her school problems. They gave an example of Sharon jumping out of a second-story window to stay out all night at a rock concert with friends.

The FSW recommended that the parents make a contract with Sharon where appropriate behavior (staying at school, following parents' rules, maintaining at least a B on school assignments) would be rewarded. These were chosen because they could be easily measured by a checklist. Compliance with at least 90 percent of the list would earn Sharon points that could be traded in for privileges or concert or movie tickets. Conversely, if Sharon's performance fell below the 90 percent expected rate, then she would lose privileges (e.g., telephone privileges, outings).

CHAPTER SUMMARY

This chapter presented the area of quantitative assessment. Its purposes are improving treatment, contributing to clinical research, providing a basis for practice evaluation and accountability and increasing FSW's skills and competence.

Two frameworks for incorporating quantitative measurement in the FSW's practice were presented. Single subject design can help to target client problems and monitor progress throughout the course of the family work. Standardized measures frequently are used to collect the quantified data. Another method, goal attainment scaling, is frequently used in agency settings. Any problem can be quantified using this system.

Types of quantified measures were presented. These included self-anchored and self-monitoring scales, direct behavioral observation, standardized measures, and other measures. Finally, guidelines for using measurement to link assessment and intervention were presented.

EXERCISES

6.1   PURPOSES OF QUANTITATIVE ASSESSMENT

Consider an agency where you have worked or in which you have done a field placement. What purposes of quantitative assessment and measures could serve the particular agency that you have in mind?

6.2   FRAMEWORKS FOR ASSESSMENT

Considering the same agency you used in Exercise 6.1, how would you suggest to the agency director that a single subject framework be employed? Next, describe how a goal attainment scaling framework could be used.

6.3   MEASUREMENT INSTRUMENTS

Think of a client family you have worked with or might work with in the future. Design a self-anchored scale to measure one of its problems. Can the same problem be measured by direct behavioral observation? How would you, for example, record the data of a client role-play?

Do a literature search for standardized measures that might be used to measure the same client problem.

6.4   LINKING ASSESSMENT TO INTERVENTION

Describe some of the client and agency variables that you might use at your agency to select an intervention.

Make up a treatment plan for a client problem that your clients are likely to experience.

6.5   FAMILY ISSUE MEASURE

Select a specific family issue. Then locate a family instrument designed to measure this issue. What are its psychometric properties? How well do you think the instrument measures what you would like to measure?

6.6 SELECTING AN INSTRUMENT

The following are two excerpts from *Measures for Clinical Practice* (Corcoran & Fischer, 2000) describing two separate instruments. Using the information provided at the beginning of this chapter, select the instrument with the best psychometric properties. You might want to work in groups for this exercise.

1) **FACES III** is a 20-item instrument designed to measure two main dimensions of family functioning: cohesion and adaptability. *Reliability:* FACES III has only fair internal consistency, with an overall alpha of .8 for the total instrument, .77 for cohesion, and .62 for adaptability. Test–retest data are not available, but for FACES-II there was a four- to five-week test–retest correlation of .83 for cohesion and .80 for adaptability. *Validity:* FACES-III appears to have good face validity, but data are not available demonstrating other types of validity. On the other hand, a number of studies have shown FACES-II to have fair known-groups validity in being able to discriminate among extreme, mid-range, and unbalanced families in several problem categories. A good deal of research is being conducted on FACES-III, which might generate more information on validity (Corcoran & Fischer, 2000, p. 246).

2) **FAD:** The FAD is a 60-item questionnaire designed to evaluate family functioning according to the McMaster Model . . . it identifies six dimensions of family functioning: problem-solving, communication, roles, affective responsiveness, affective involvement, and behavior control. *Reliability:* the FAD demonstrates fairly good internal consistency, with alphas for the subscales ranging from .72 to .92. No reliability figures are reported for the overall measure; test–retest reliability data are not available. *Validity:* When the general functioning subscale is removed from the analysis, the six other subscales appear to be relatively independent. The FAD demonstrates some degree of concurrent and predictive validity. In a separate study . . . the FAS was moderately correlated with the Lock-Wallace Marital Satisfaction Scale and showed a fair ability to predict scores on the Philadelphia Geriatric Morale Scale. Further, the FAD has good known-groups validity, with all seven subscales significantly distinguishing between individuals from clinical families and those from nonclinical families (Corcoran & Fischer, 2000, pp. 250–251).

Other things may change us, but we start and end with the family.

—Anthony Brandt (www.Bartleby.com)

7 CHAPTER | FAMILY DEVELOPMENT AND THE LIFE CYCLE

UNDERSTANDING A DEVELOPMENTAL PERSPECTIVE

Family social workers must be able to assess how a family is functioning and identify what it needs at particular points in time. In this chapter we build upon family systems theory by discussing family development, an important theoretical framework with which to understand the predictable growth and crises of family life. Most people are familiar with stages of child and adult development, but fewer are aware of family developmental stages. The family life cycle perspective helps us identify which problems might emerge at specific stages (Duvall, 1957; Carter & McGoldrick, 1988; 1999). Understanding a family from a developmental perspective can help the FSW understand whether a family is meeting social expectations for child rearing (Holman,

1983). It can also help workers and families predict issues and tasks that a family faces down the road. Few families move seamlessly from one stage to another, and problems are particularly likely to arise during vulnerable family stages, such as the birth of the first child or adolescence. One now famous study depicted marital satisfaction as a roller coaster, with significant decreases in marital satisfaction beginning early in marriage and continuing a slide until children leave home (Olson, 1983). Nevertheless, individual variations in the family life cycle as well as marital satisfaction do occur.

We begin our discussion by outlining developmental stages that may be typical for middle-class families. This model is merely a template and is based on the assumption that families remain intact from formation to death. However, it fails to account for diverse family forms such as never-married, childless couples, divorced parents, or gay and lesbian couples who are not legally permitted to get married in many jurisdictions. It also assumes that the stages are sequential and linear and that people enter and exit the cycle at the same points. We point out, however, that the sequential and linear model of family development is becoming the exception to the rule. Rather than being a closed group, membership to a modern family grouping is more open-ended than the family life cycle portrays. No single list of stages is sufficient or inclusive, and the breakdown of stages is arbitrary (Carter & McGoldrick, 1999). Families vary in the expression of each stage of development according to personal experiences, socioeconomic circumstances, culture, religion, and sexual orientation. Child bearing now occurs later in life, many people do not remarry after a relationship ends, and others are choosing never to get married. Moreover, forces related to racism, sexism, homophobia, classism, and ageism also create differences in family life cycle patterns (Carter & McGoldrick, 1999, p. xv). Finally, migration to North America creates unique permutations in family life cycle patterns.

We discuss variations of family development under these divergent themes. We would like to point out, however, that groups are not homogeneous. Presenting typical patterns for groups risks pigeonholing them. We do not intend to present stereotypes, and we encourage the reader to recognize that cultures and subcultures have enormous diversity within the groups.

FACTORS AFFECTING FAMILY DIVERSITY OVER THE LIFE CYCLE

CULTURE

Culture has an enormous impact on the family life cycle, starting with how a family defines itself. Some cultures define family as the immediate nuclear family, while others incorporate extended kin, ancestors, and friends. The dominant Anglo definition focuses on the nuclear family, whereas African American families include an expanded kin network. Chinese families focus on ancestors, and Italians look at several generations of extended kin (McGoldrick & Giordano, 1996). In minority families, relationships with extended family and kin networks are based on principles of interdependence, group orientation, and reliance on others (Lum, 1992). Cultural values about family practices that a member from another culture may label as "strange" or "unhealthy" also guide people. Family activities may diverge dramatically from mainstream culture. Puerto Ricans, for example, believe so strongly in family obligation that it is acceptable to them to use public office to benefit family members (Lum, 1992).

A group's history affects the definition of family. For example, African Americans use a more inclusive definition of family, probably stemming from their history of oppression (Hines, Preto, McGoldrick, Almeida, & Weltman, 1999, p. 70). Gender roles and expectations also play out through culture, including how parents relate to their children. Culture also affects how families celebrate transitions such as weddings and deaths. Remember *My Big Fat Greek Wedding*! What other movies can you think of that mark family transitions in culturally unique ways? Culture plays a role in the timing of when children leave their families, how close they remain to their families, how the generations relate, and the level of intimacy within the families. History of a culture is an important determinant of family life cycle norms.

Cultural traditions influence family life cycle stages. Mexican-American families experience shorter adolescence but longer courtship. For other cultures, the involvement of the extended family marks a different relationship and different perspective on such stages as childbirth, launching young adults into the world, and the formation of a new family unit. For example, a daughter in a family from India is expected to live with her parents until she is married, and a grandmother in a Japanese family may take an active role in raising young grandchildren. Poor African American families experience a condensed life cycle in which the generational cycle seems to overlap (Moore Hines et al., 1999). In addition, the percentage of single-parent families has increased in these households (p. 72).

Finally, minority families are often structured by a "vertical hierarchy of authority" (Lum, 1992). Authority in these families often lies in paternal authority and authority assumed by males or elders as heads of households. Cultural clashes can occur when children or females from a minority family encounter differences in the dominant culture.

SOCIAL CLASS

Many families that FSWs see are families that are lacking in economic and social resources, are politically powerless, and are likely to experience unemployment or the throes of job instability. Many also experience oppression by dominant and more fortunate groups, are members of a social minority, and are prone—because of all these aforementioned issues—to experiencing multiple difficulties. Kilman and Madsen (1999) refer to these groups as the working class and the underclass. They live without hope and struggle to get basic needs met, on a daily basis. Social class is affected by factors such as culture, ethnicity, education, and gender. Poverty is a poor buffer against disruptions and crises in the family and might decrease life span, collapse the family stages, lead children to leave home earlier and set up their own families at younger ages, make grandparenting occur earlier, decrease educational opportunity, and contribute to decreased employment opportunity. Today, economic conditions differ from those faced by previous generations, making it more difficult for young adults to purchase their own homes and sometimes even live independently "in the style in which they are accustomed." Moreover, young people who grow up in poor families may also drop out of school early and face an elevated risk of unemployment. Early pregnancy among some teen girls means that they start adulthood on shaky ground.

In more economically advantaged families, children are extending the family life cycle by remaining financially dependent and continuing with their education. Some children leave and return many times, leading to the term "boomerang children."

Issues related to social class are best dealt with ecologically when appropriate. In addition, FSWs need to be aware of their biases, many of which stem from a middle-class value system.

GENDER

The conundrum of responsibility without power has long characterized women's lives.
—McGoldrick, 1999b, p. 107

We discuss gender in more detail in Chapter 12. Social changes affecting women are affecting their roles within the family and their movement through the family life cycle. Women are getting more education and are marrying later in life. They are less likely to endure abuse when they have alternatives, something that education and independence allows them. Available contraception ensures smaller families and less financial dependence upon a partner. Moreover, a growing phenomenon in the family life cycle concerns the "sandwich generation" of women who are taking care of both their children and their parents. While responsibilities for child rearing have changed somewhat, women still assume most of the responsibility. Some women stay out of the paid workforce to raise children, and others work outside the home throughout their lives. Each of these choices brings with it unique challenges. Once they enter old age, men are more likely to die earlier than women, leaving many women isolated and financially destitute.

Similarly, males have unique challenges in the family life cycle. Women are becoming more financially independent, making marriage more dependent on caring rather than on financial dependency. They are also facing threats including the erosion of male prerogative in marriage and increased demands to be more involved with childcare (not just "helping out") and domestic chores.

IMMIGRATION

Globalization is creating unique circumstances for families who immigrate to North America. In the United States, one-fifth of the nation's children are growing up in immigrant homes (Suarez-Orozco, Todorova, & Louie, 2002).

A common way of immigrating involves one family member moving ahead of other family members to get established in the new location. When it is the mother who initiates migration, the children are left in the care of the extended family. All family relationships are affected by the move—both children and spouses may become disengaged in the process. Reunification of the entire family unit might be complicated. If children are left behind, they may become quite attached to their caretakers in their home country.

Because migration can take many years and is impacted by financial issues, it affects the family life cycle in powerful ways. When working with an immigrant family, it is first important that the FSW understands the reasons for immigration. The FSW must also understand who came with the family and who remained behind. The final point for a FSW is to understand the culture from the immigrant's homeland—especially roles of women, attitudes toward minority groups, the political situation, and religion. What were the hopes and expectations of the family? Did the family come to the new land because of positive or negative reasons? It is important to remember that every group in North America except indigenous peoples is or has been immigrants at one time or another. People who flee war-torn homelands come to a new country for very different reason than those looking for economic security.

Migrating to a new land is perhaps one of the most stressful experiences that a family can undergo. Migration alters the family life cycle in rather unique ways. Young adults might adapt to the new culture most easily (Hernandez & McGoldrick, 1999); the older the person, the more difficult the move may be. When people come as a couple, uneven levels of adaptation might cause tension in the home and create dependency (p. 175). When families with children migrate, hierarchies and roles might be disrupted because children tend to acculturate more quickly than their parents (p. 177). Children can also be caught between their parents' culture and the new culture, producing conflict within the family.

SEXUAL ORIENTATION

In this book we emphasize that families come in many sizes, shapes, and forms, making the definition of "family" difficult. Here we look at an emerging and growing family form: gay and lesbian families. Gay and lesbian people face oppression through homophobia and heterosexism (Adams, Jaques, & May, 2004). In addition, gay and lesbian parents encounter multiple oppressions because they are members of a minority group. Because of social work's unique anti-oppressive and person-in-environment perspectives, social workers are well positioned to challenge the status quo and advocate for social justice for all clients, including gay and lesbian families. To do so, they must be informed. They also must be critical and analytical of social messages from their own particular sociocultural subgroups such as their family, a religious group, or their community's value systems. We must understand how our beliefs about gay and lesbian families reflect the political/social climate; the lack of social and institutional support; and personal beliefs, attitudes, and prejudices (Adams,

Jaques, & May, 2004). This means becoming sensitized to heterosexist and antigay language and also advising that policies and practices be inclusive.

The actual number of gay and lesbian families is unknown, in part because they are not granted legal legitimacy in many jurisdictions. As of writing, Spain, Canada, Belgium, The Netherlands, and South Africa are the only nations to legally recognize gay and lesbian intimate relationships. Because of discrimination and stigmatization, when gays and lesbians become parents, they fear that they will lose custody or visitation rights to their children. They therefore are anxious about how and to whom they reveal their sexual orientation. In addition to custody disputes, fear about family-of-origin reaction, negative peer reaction, and decisions about when and whom to tell affect how public the families decide to be (Adams, Jaques, & May, 2004). Patterson (1995) suggests that "the phenomenon of large numbers of openly lesbian and gay parents raising children represents a sociocultural innovation that is unique to the current historical era" (p. 263).

Gay and lesbian people can become parents in a number of ways. New reproductive technologies such as artificial insemination and surrogate parenting are providing gay and lesbian people with a greater number of options for becoming parents. Lesbian women have the option of artificial insemination of one of the partners. Gay men are now able to enter into surrogate parenting relationships with the assistance of artificial insemination. What stands out about these latter two arrangements is that parenting is a *choice* for these people. Pregnancy and parenting is not an accident as it might be in heterosexual relationships. We are touched by friends involved in both types of arrangements and their devotion to their children. Despite the fact that the decision is well thought out, and perhaps even extremely expensive, gay and lesbian parents are often the subject of legal discrimination, based on negative assumptions about the outcomes of gay and lesbian parenting. Unfortunately, these assumptions have been aided and abetted by the social sciences. Early versions of the *Diagnostic and Statistical Manual* originally classified homosexuality as psychopathology, and social biases suggest that gay and lesbian parents are mentally ill or that lesbian mothers are not maternal. However, emergent research is proving otherwise.

Lambert (2005) summarized the research on gay and lesbian parenting. In this discussion, we remind students that much diversity exists in any social grouping and suggest that information that supposedly represents all groupings within a particular social grouping fails to capture the richness and diversity within groups. We encourage students to carefully synthesize the studies contained in Lambert's article. The review of research is summarized in the following list:

1. Divorced lesbian mothers score "at least as high" as divorced heterosexual mothers on measures of psychological functioning.
2. There are no differences in parental sexual role behavior, interest in childrearing, responses to child behavior, or ratings of warmth toward children.
3. Divorced lesbian mothers are more fearful of losing children in custody disputes.

4. Lesbian mothers are more likely to provide children with toys relating to both genders.
5. Divorced lesbian mothers were more likely than heterosexual mothers to be living with a romantic partner.
6. The extent to which mothers are "out" and involved with feminist activism has a positive relationship with children's psychological health.
7. Less information exists on gay custodial fathers. Gay fathers report higher incomes and are more likely to encourage children to play with gender-specific toys than are lesbian mothers.
8. There are no significant differences in sexual orientation, gender identification, or gender role behavior in young adults from lesbian relationships.
9. Children in lesbian relationships are more likely to consider the possibility of having lesbian or gay relationships. This might be due to the "climate of acceptance" in which they lived.
10. Most children of gay or lesbian relationships identify themselves as heterosexual. (The authors wonder how this matters.)
11. Children of gay and lesbian relationships have normal peer relations.
12. Children of gay and lesbian relationships report more teasing and bullying about their parents' sexuality. If parents fear safety (Adams, Jaques, & May, 2004), children also have a legitimate fear.
13. Early studies of lesbian mothers report that their children are more likely to have contact with fathers than are children of heterosexual mothers.
14. Children in gay and lesbian families experience more stress in their daily lives.
15. Gay/lesbian families maintain an egalitarian division of labor.

Because of their imposed marginalization from mainstream society, many gay and lesbian couples have had to make their own mark on the family life cycle. Johnson and Colucci (1999) note that for many gay and lesbian people, their friendship network is considered a family unit, partly in response to the mainstream definition of family as blood or legal ties. However, these authors argue that rather than dismissing the existing family life cycle model, the model can be amended. Challenges during each phase become quite complicated, given that the world is primarily based on heterosexual issues. Unique issues emerge at every juncture of the life cycle, including coming out and disclosing to family, dating, moving onto a job or career, setting up a romantic relationship, and parenting. What typically comes easily for heterosexual counterparts comes at a high cost for gay and lesbian people. Their struggles are exacerbated by homophobia and oppressive or insensitive reactions from the larger society.

DEVELOPMENTAL STAGES

The family is the context within which individuals grow and develop throughout a lifetime. Relationships with parents, siblings, and other family members change as they move along the life cycle (Carter & McGoldrick, 1999, p. 1). It is at times of transition that relationships and the family system experience stressors. Moreover, when stressful family events co-occur and when they are not resolved, they can be the catalyst for problems at a later stage. Similarly, multigenerational issues surrounding particular individuals can pop up down the line.

Because family relationships and behavioral demands in different stages change in relatively predictable ways as the family moves through time, one useful way to understand them is to examine each developmental stage. Though it is difficult to predict how a specific event will unfold within a given family, it is easier to identify the types of crises families may experience over a lifespan. Each family reacts uniquely to life events, yet all families encounter a similar range of developmental crises, such as the death of a member, and must cope with loss at times. Families generally progress through similar developmental processes, marked by an identifiable beginning or transition event such as a wedding, the birth of the first child, or the retirement of parents. Each stage challenges the family with unique developmental issues, tasks, and potential crises to be resolved. Knowledge about the family life cycle can help social workers observe ways in which a family has become "stuck" and identify changes that will help the family to move on. Nevertheless, it would be a mistake to assume that the progression is linear—from one phase to another—or that the lack of movement from one phase to another is deviant. Pinsof (2002) suggests that pair bonding (he challenges the notion of marriage as the only way to go) might begin with cohabitation, and can be followed by the birth of a child, which could then be followed by marriage because each of these three events are independent choices. Cohabitation gives two people the opportunity to "check one another out" (p. 148). Moreover, the pattern varies by ethnicity, class, and sexual orientation.

Family social workers need to understand how a family needs to shift attitudes and modify relationships to adapt to evolving family life stages (Holman, 1983). Family crises can be anticipated, and no family can sidestep them. Life cycle transitions intensify family stress, and family problems that arise at certain points suggest that a family is having difficulty functioning at a particular developmental stage. Every family responds to crises in unique ways. Some families have evolved excellent problem-solving skills and strategies and well-developed support systems. Others have not. Family social workers who are aware of developmental issues facing the family are in a better position to assess the family's issues, the crises that occur as a result, and the coping tools used by families to address these issues. During developmental crises, family social workers can provide much-needed knowledge, skills, strategies, and support to families who are overwhelmed by difficulties associated with developmental crises.

Geismar and Krisberg (1956) suggested a direct relationship between social functioning and the family life cycle. Families with limited economic and social resources become more disorganized as they progress through the family cycle. Family disorganization suggests a bad fit between the family's *need* for services and resources and the *availability* of services and resources, as well as the family's ability to use them. The growing need for economic and social resources strains the family's economic, social, and emotional resources.

Certain tasks accompany each family stage. Transition to a new stage is usually accompanied by some kind of crisis, whether large or small (Petro & Travis, 1985). Moreover, rituals also mark some transitions, such as baptisms, weddings, funerals, puberty, and so on. For example, Latino families preserve life cycle markers and appropriate rituals such as birthdays, religious rituals, holidays, or Sunday picnics, which are usually opportunities for large family gatherings (Falicov, 1999). While transitions between stages are not discrete, each transition point places demands upon the family system to adapt. Roles of family members change as children mature. Additionally, family boundaries need to adapt throughout the family life cycle to fit the changing needs of family members. For example, as children enter adolescence, family boundaries should become more flexible to embrace the changing developmental and social needs of teenagers. If family boundaries are too rigid during adolescence, parent–child conflict may result. If the adolescent complies with overly restrictive boundaries, the teen may have problems developing the social skills and independence needed to survive as an adult. Conversely, if the boundaries are too loose during adolescence, the child may lack adequate monitoring of activities and become prematurely disengaged from the family.

The stages of family development presented in Figure 7.1 are adapted from three models: Carter and McGoldrick (1988; 1999), Becvar and Becvar (1993), and Duvall (1957). The stages of family development include marriage/partnering/coupling/pair bonding, birth of the first child, families with preschool children, families with school-aged children, families with teenagers, and families with young people leaving home. Later family stages are relevant to this text inasmuch as grandparents are an important part of family life for some families. To this list of stages, we add children returning home after they have been launched—colloquially called "boomerang children." In part, we are jesting about this being a significant transition; on the other hand, we believe that children returning home after being out of the home is a significant cultural pattern because it demands a large family adjustment, preventing parents from dealing with issues as a couple. (We are also hoping that our children will read this chapter!)

This model of the stages of family development is helpful, but it has some shortcomings. First, each family is unique, and developmental stages may vary greatly from one family to another. Second, developmental models tend to focus only on the milestones of one individual, usually the eldest child (Becvar & Becvar, 1996). How would we classify a family that included both a newborn child and a teenager who was ready to leave home? Where would a never-married single parent fit into the family developmental life cycle? There are many variations of the family life cycle, some of which are quite complex. Breunlin (1988), for example, depicts family transitions as moving back and forth between stages rather than as a linear progression from one stage to the next.

The number of alternative family forms has been increasing in recent years. Similarly, strict adherence to the stage-to-stage progression through the family life cycle has changed a lot. Some couples have children before

Stage	Family tasks
1. Marriage/coupling/pair-bonding	• Committing to the relationship • Formulating roles and rules • Becoming a couple while separating from families of origin • Making compromises and negotiating around concrete and personal needs
2. Families with young children	• Restabilizing the marital unit with a triangle • Bonding with the child and integrating that child into the family • Realigning relationships with one another, deciding on work or career and domestic chores
3. Families with school-aged children	• Allowing greater independence of children • Opening family boundaries to accommodate new social institutions and new people • Understanding and accepting role changes
4. Families with teenagers	• Dealing with teen demands for independence through appropriate boundary adjustments • Adjusting to a new definition of personal autonomy • Rule changes, limit setting, and role negotiation
5. Families with young people leaving home	• Preparing young person for independent living through schooling and job skills • Accepting and promoting youth's self-sufficiency
6. Boomerang stage*	• Readjusting families to accommodate children returning home as adult children • Dealing with couple issues • Renegotiating personal and physical space • Renegotiating roles responsibilities
7. Middle-aged parents	• Adjusting to new roles and relationships not centered on children
8. Aging family members	• Involvement with grandchildren and partners of the children • Dealing with issues and difficulties of aging • Striving to maintain dignity, meaning, and independence

FIGURE 7.1 | STAGES OF THE FAMILY LIFE CYCLE

Adapted from Becvar & Becvar, 1993; Carter & McGoldrick, 1988; Duvall, 1957.

*The authors would like to thank Randy Krichbaum for his suggestion to make this an official phase of the family life cycle.

marriage, and others do not marry but do have children. Some people are involved in serial relationships. New reproductive technologies are making parenthood available to those who previously had little choice over whether to have children. There are growing numbers of births to unmarried women or gay and lesbian couples. Additionally, many families undergo changes initiated by separation, divorce, and remarriage. Between 38 and 50 percent of children born in the United States during the 1980s will experience the divorce of their parents. Most typically, mothers retain custody and fathers receive visitation status (Curtner-Smith, 1995). In many families both parents work outside the home, and childcare must be arranged. Some couples prefer to remain childless, while others delay having children beyond age 40. Spousal roles are often no longer premised on traditional gender arrangements, and social changes have led to altered family structures that at one point in our history were excluded from the mainstream, such as parenting by gay or lesbian couples. Finally, issues inherent in the changing family life cycle include grandparents' involvement as primary caretakers, parenting later in life, and intergenerational family configurations (Helton & Jackson, 1997). Diversity in family development is discussed later in this chapter.

Families in different ethnic groups show cultural variations not seen in the "typical" family life cycle. For example, the African American family may consist of an extensive kin network, often including more than one household. Several families may live under the same roof, and children may reside in a kinship household different from the one in which they were born. Recent immigrants to North America often show cultural variations in which the previous generation exerts control over the new family, and families function as collective units (Lum, 1992). Lum also suggests that the collective interdependence of the minority family requires that the social worker thoroughly assess intergenerational linkages between parents, children, grandparents, and other members of the extended family since family members often base decisions on how they will affect the complete family unit.

MARRIAGE/PARTNERING/PAIR BONDING/AFFILIATIVE ORIENTATION

Of all dilemmas in the life cycle, the existential dilemma of coupling is probably the greatest.

—McGoldrick, 1999c, p. 231

Boy meets girl. Boy marries girl. Boy and girl angst over which family they visit at Thanksgiving and which one in December and whether or not it's best to serve turkey or goose for the family feast. When first faced with the reality that the family you married into does things differently, the warmth of tradition can take on a chill.

—Marge Kennedy (www.Bartleby.com)

The nature of marriage or coupling has changed enormously over the past generation. We hesitate to use the term "marriage" exclusively to describe the various types of coupling or pair bonding (Pinsof, 2002) that can occur;

CASE 7.1	TRANSITION

The following case example illustrates some of the crises a family may face during a time of transition.

The Lee family consists of Sam and Lark, both in their early forties, and their three daughters, ages seven, nine, and fourteen. Problems with Mary, age fourteen, have brought the couple to the family social work agency.

Sam and Lark were both born in mainland China, and they met while studying at the University of California. The Lees describe enjoying a "traditional Chinese lifestyle." Both Sam and Lark are devoted parents who want their children to know and respect their Chinese background and culture.

The family's problems began when Mary entered junior high school. Although Mary had continued to receive high grades at her new school, her behavior had undergone a radical transition. Their previously compliant daughter had become defiant. She had cut school to be with her friends on several occasions, and she had been absent from several family celebrations against her parents' wishes. When her parents had tried to correct Mary's misbehavior, she had become agitated and started yelling at them.

The event that had brought the family to the agency was Mary's reaction to an argument with her parents during the previous week. She had left home during the night, apparently climbing through an upstairs window. Mary had stayed at the homes of various friends for five days, and her parents had been frantic.

Mary, who has accompanied her parents to the FSW's office, tells the social worker that she needs some freedom from her parents' autocratic parenting. She feels that her parents are old-fashioned and unfair in comparison to her friends' parents. She explains that although she loves her parents very much, she does not share their attachment to traditional Chinese culture. She wants to be like her friends.

The family social worker, assessing the Lee's situation from a developmental perspective, sees a family with intergenerational values conflicts as well as developmental issues that frequently arise when children enter adolescence.

Sanders and Kroll (2000) offer the alternative term "affiliative orientation." McGoldrick (1999b) notes that patriarchal rules of male domination get in the way of realizing the union of two equals (p. 107). In fact, deciding not to enter into a state-sanctioned relationship is now a viable option for many intimate relationships. Some people live together before marriage while others move from one partner to another. Children may or may not enter the relationship. Before a new relationship can occur, young people usually leave their families of origin. Young people seem to be leaving home later and marrying later. People who marry are now marrying between the ages of 25 and 35. The younger the age at marriage, the greater the likelihood for breakup, and according to McGoldrick (1999c), it is better to marry later than earlier. Many people are involved in "serial monogamy," a practice that was highly frowned upon one or two generations previously. At the same time, fewer people consider that they have failed in a life goal if they do not marry. In more than half of marriages, the couple lived together before the formal ceremony (McGoldrick, 1999c). Internet dating, sometimes leading to marriage, is quite common among all age groups, a scenario unheard of two decades previously. The term "marriage" is a culturally and politically laden term that supports the state definition of what is a family.

Political discourse in North America now centers on whether to extend marriage rights to gay and lesbian people. Conservatives argue that doing so erodes the meaning and sanctity of the family. However, others say that denying gay and lesbian people the opportunity to legally marry is discriminatory and is a basic human rights issue. Regardless of the legal right to marry, gay and lesbian coupling is a fact of life. McGoldrick (1999c) suggests that gay and lesbian unions may be freer of traditional gender roles but at the same time face social stigma. Some couples have not come out to members of their family of origin, making contact with them stressful. Not coming out may even alienate young people from their parents.

In North American relationships, it is believed that people marry for romantic love, or at least because they want to (Pinsof, 2002). Nevertheless, the reasons for getting involved in a romantic relationship involve a complex set of factors including personality, social and cultural expectations, family history, and economics, to name a few. The wedding ceremony, if there is one, is a major ritual in the family life cycle. Wedding ceremonies are also big business, and families might feel pressure to put on an expensive and elaborate wedding. Cultures have unique rituals around weddings. Once the ceremony is over, the couple will learn to relate to in-laws and will be guided by different rules and expectations. The Native American culture has no word for "in-law," while in the mainstream culture the mother-in-law is the subject of jokes and derision.

Each new stage in a family's life cycle is a critical transition point requiring an adaptation in roles and tasks. Change creates stresses and conflicts that must be resolved for the family to reach fulfillment and satisfaction. Three major tasks of the newly partnered couple are establishing a mutually satisfying relationship, realigning relationships with extended families (who must accept the new partner), and making decisions about parenthood. People bring to a new relationship ways of living that they learned while growing up. Upon entering a new relationship, they must face different ways of living that may contrast sharply with what is familiar to them in all areas of family life. Most aspects of life will need to be negotiated. Areas of negotiation include (McGoldrick, 1999c, p. 232):

- Economic
- Emotional/intimacy, dependence, etc.
- Power arrangements within the relationship, including physical, decision making, domination, etc.
- Interpersonal boundaries with each other and boundaries around the couple, such as with parents, family, and friends
- Sexuality
- Deciding whether or not to have children
- Domestic responsibilities

Forming a relationship with another person, whether in marriage or by mutual agreement, requires adjustment, compromise, and hard work. Partners also must adjust to the behaviors, feelings, habits, and values of another person. The realities of adjustment to extended family; shared finances; and conflicting wants, desires, and living patterns mean that the couple will experience pressures that must be resolved for the relationship to succeed. A great deal of tension can emerge as the couple is navigating these difficulties, making this stage quite difficult. The difficulty of this stage is overshadowed by the cultural stereotype of the "newlyweds" who are joined as one for eternity in wedded bliss. McGoldrick (1999c) suggests that more than any other life transition, marriage is used as a solution to life's problems (p. 232). On a more realistic level, the FSW must assess the couple's satisfaction with their own relationship, their relationships with extended family, and agreement concerning decisions about parenthood. In assessing the marital relationship, the FSW will find a marital satisfaction scale to be helpful (see Corcoran & Fischer, 2000).

Cultural myths have infiltrated marriage. The first is that marriage is harmful to men and that marriage privileges females, providing security, happiness, and social status. In fact, the opposite is true (McGoldrick, 1999c, p. 233). Marriage improves men's mental, social, and physical health. On the other hand, married women tend to experience greater depression, career interruption, and longer hours spent on domestic chores. The second cultural myth arises because traditional nuclear marriage comes from a Judeo-Christian tradition that can disadvantage other traditions. One must consider different cultural contexts when looking at marriage. For example, slavery undermined both African American marriages and gender roles (Pinderhughes, 2002). African American relationships have also been affected by migration, socioeconomic conditions, and unequal sex ratios, factors that have less influence among white populations.

Issues may arise on several fronts during the first phase of the family life cycle. A partner who has not successfully negotiated independence from his or her family of origin may experience divided loyalties that threaten the fragile, new relationship. Similarly, a partner who wishes to continue the social life of a single person also imposes stress on the relationship. Moreover, if a couple has children early into the marriage, there may be little time to sort out crucial issues within the relationship.

BIRTH OF THE FIRST CHILD AND SO ON

Rearing a family is probably the most difficult job in the world. It resembles two business firms merging their respective resources to make a single product. All the potential headaches of that operation are present when an adult male and an adult female join to steer a child from infancy to adulthood.

—Virginia Satir, *Peoplemaking* (www.Bartleby.com)

Deep inside us, we know what every family therapist knows: the problems between the parent become the problems within the children.

—Roger Gould (www.Bartleby.com)

The sequence of marrying before having children is no longer normative, and many couples are having children before committing to a legal relationship. As mentioned in Chapter 1, one-quarter of Caucasian babies and two-thirds of African American babies are born to unmarried women. This compares with half of all babies born in Scandinavia (Pinsof, 2002). Some couples will eventually marry, but not all will. Others who are blocked from forming a legal relationship, such as gays and lesbians, are committing to a relationship outside the legal system and at the same time are having children. When pregnancy occurs during single adolescence, young people must decide on what to do about the pregnancy. Moreover, should the young single mothers seek employment, they must also concern themselves with childcare, transportation, housing, food, and clothing costs.

Parenthood is a major life change, requiring changes in lifestyle. Whether or not to have children is a puzzle for many parents, and more and more people are deciding not to have children. Some researchers have wondered whether reproductive decisions are decisions at all (Peterson & Jenni, 2003). Satir (1967) suggests that there are many reasons for having children, including fulfilling social expectations, obtaining a feeling of immortality, and addressing issues from the parents' past. Even when having a child is a decision, it may be made with some ambivalence. Moreover, making the decision to have a child is seldom a discrete and definable moment. In fact, for some, the negative consequences of having a child might be more potent than the abstract positive consequences (p. 354). At times, men are thought to be disengaged from reproductive decisions, which is not necessarily the case (p. 353). In addition, some couples that want children of their own have difficulty conceiving. As much as having children can be stressful, not being able to conceive also creates strains for many couples. It can be helpful for the FSW to explore with the parents the reasons and expectations associated with having children.

Having children is romanticized in North American culture, yet it is a stage in family life that can be, and often is, demanding. Previously, childrearing was a family focus for most of parents' lives—now childrearing consumes much less of parents' time (Carter & McGoldrick, 1999a, p. 8). For some people, the birth of the first child is a crisis that initiates a critical (although usually temporary) family adjustment period (LeMasters, 1957). Once people accept responsibility for a child, they are expected to continue to accept that responsibility for many years, maintaining a joint commitment to their child as well as to each other.

The arrival of a child complicates family life and can create upheaval for the couple. For example, some studies show an initial decrease in marital satisfaction after the arrival of the first child (Rampage, 2002; Spanier, Lewis, & Cole, 1975). The first crisis of this stage, then, is preparing for and adapting to the birth of the child and resolving conflicts regarding commitment and fears associated with becoming a parent. Conflict can arise if the couple does not agree about whether or not to have a child. At first, a newborn interacts with only one person at a time, most often the mother. Mothers have traditionally assumed responsibility for childcare and domestic chores while husbands "help out" (Carter, 1999). The birth of a child creates the first triangle in two-parent families. The triangle is created out of necessity since the child's needs must be met for it to survive. The parents' relationship must be reconfigured.

Moreover, they are also charged with the task of consistency in parenting—no easy feat.

Satir (1967) points out the trap of having a child to fulfill one's emotional needs, only to discover that the child's needs are more pressing than one's own. New parents may experience conflict about caretaking roles that may threaten the existence of the marriage. Research indicates that couples who have negotiated a successful relationship adapt more easily to having children (Lewis, 1988).

With the birth of the first child, a range of new roles and responsibilities are demanded. Cultures vary in the extent to which new parents receive support during this phase. For example, in Latino families, the birth of a child draws relatives into the family circle to celebrate (Falicov, 1999). The arrival of children can precipitate or entrench gender differences and gender inequalities in domestic life (Doucet, 2001). Having children can be a difficult adjustment, contributing to grief about lost freedom in lifestyle, recreation, and career options. Before the child was born, parents had the opportunity for self-care, career development, and couple bonding. With the birth of the child, lifestyles change. Suddenly the couple has less time for themselves and each other, less money, and more responsibility. Parenting a newborn child takes time and energy, and it requires new levels of self-sacrifice and self-denial. Needs of children must take precedence over the needs of the parents, and people who have difficulty getting their own needs met have a hard time meeting the needs of others, particularly those of young children. The stress of adjusting to the demands of a newborn can threaten family stability. Of particular importance to the family system is the shift in power between the parents with the arrival of children. The arrival of children creates an environment that makes it easy to revert to traditional gender patterns (Carter, 1999; Rampage, 2002).

A lot of attention has been given to the concept of "bonding" or "attachment." Most hospitals now encourage ongoing contact between parents and the child immediately after birth to encourage parent–child bonding. Hospitals also encourage the father to be present during childbirth. Yet, in the early phases of a child's life, mothers typically assume most of the childcare responsibilities (Carter, 1999; Garbarino, 1992; Mackie, 1991).

Being reasonable, patient, consistent, and cheerful is difficult when night feedings, colic, and diaper changing disrupt sleep patterns. The arrival of the child requires adjustment by both parents, and the strain on the couple's relationship may result in one or both parents feeling neglected or misunderstood by the other. Meeting the needs of one's child and also one's partner requires much effort even when the child is wanted. Parents must make decisions about childcare and work while learning how to get personal and couple needs met. Some work sites are supportive of working parents while others create hurdles for working parents to jump.

Adjusting to parenthood is complicated by the fact that parents are expected to be equipped automatically with knowledge and skills to meet the needs of children without having received any education on parenting skills or child development. Many new parents rely on their own upbringing or parents for advice at a time when they are still trying to redefine that relationship in "adult to adult" terms. More than likely, the grandparents also had little preparation for parenthood. During this stage, parents must develop a mutually satisfactory, reciprocal parent–child relationship. To help the child learn to trust others, they must be dependable in meeting the child's needs. It is necessary for both to feel good about the relationship, but reciprocity is difficult when the newborn does not reward the parents by smiling, laughing, or talking. It is easy for new parents, especially parents who are needy themselves, to become frustrated by the one-sided nature of the early relationship with a child.

Again, our description of this stage in the family life cycle is based on typical situations. Children born with disabilities stress most families, and families may not have adequate resources and skills to care for children with special needs. Families with disabled children should be given an opportunity to share their grief and sadness (Carter, 1999). Alternatively, one of the partners may face infertility, requiring the couple to decide whether to undergo infertility treatments, adopt a child, or remain childless. Other children are unanticipated and even unwanted.

If both parents are working, the couple must decide if one person will remain at home to care for the child. Decisions about childcare can stress low-income families, and some families such as single-parent families or African American and Latino families rely on relatives for childcare (Carter, 1999). Usually, the decision has a greater impact on the woman, regardless of whether or not she returns to work. If she returns to work, she often assumes responsibilities related to the child. If she stays at home, her earning power lessens, career advancement is placed on hold, and interpersonal power in her marriage drops. A child born to an impoverished family or a family with many social problems may exacerbate the stress that the family already experiences.

As the child matures, his or her relationships gradually encompass more people and more complex social situations. A child benefits from a varied family life that includes diversity of relationships. A family with very rigid boundaries is less likely to introduce new people into children's lives and is also more likely to severely restrict contact with others outside the family. The "social riches" of a child's life are augmented when relationships are multifaceted, reciprocal, and lasting (Garbarino, 1992). When families with children are homeless—an unfortunately growing phenomenon—children lack basic provisions, and only about half attend school. Many shelters cannot accommodate two-parent families, thereby contributing to family breakup.

FAMILIES WITH PRESCHOOL CHILDREN

Being in a family is like being in a play. Each birth order position is like a different part in the play, with a distinct and separate characteristic for each part. Therefore, if one sibling has already filled a part, such as the good child, other siblings may feel they have to find other parts to play, such as rebellious child, academic child, athletic child, social child, and so on.

—Jane Nelson (www.Bartleby.com)

The child who was formerly completely dependent soon becomes more active and strives for independence. As motor skills improve, nothing may be too risky for the child to try, including hopping off the stairs or climbing into the toilet. Superman pajamas may transform the youngster into a superhero recklessly jumping off furniture. The child's energy seems inexhaustible. At the same time, the parents' energy may be depleted and their relationship strained by lack of privacy. A young child greets each new experience—the moon, a dog, or another child—with glee. The toddler absorbs the world with wide-open eyes and sees what adults take for granted. New experiences contribute to the growing cognitive abilities of the child. Unfortunately, the exploratory skills of the child are a mismatch with the child's awareness of safety, making parents tense and on guard for disaster. Inadequate parental supervision during this time creates risk for the child. So does the failure of a parent to provide sufficient cognitive stimulation.

Parents should be concerned about the safety of their children during this stage and provide an acceptable amount of stimulation while at the same time ensuring safety. It may be difficult for parents to encourage independence and at the same time protect the child. Parents either allow too much independence, placing the child at risk, or become too protective, thereby discouraging development.

Parental energy levels can also be an issue. Sometimes parents become careless or rigid because they run out of energy. The energy drain on the parents can be compounded if a second child arrives while the first is still a preschooler. We believe that adding a second child to the mix is more than twice the work and adding a third child increases the work and demands exponentially. Changes in family dynamics due to the addition of more children might not be appreciated by older children, and can result in sibling rivalry and increased parental stress and fatigue. The increased cognitive ability of the firstborn can intensify the stress as the first child strives to attract the parents' attention. For example, a three-year-old may try to distract the parents' attention from the newborn by using creative strategies such as filling the kitchen sink to take a bath or urinating on a rug during the infant's feeding. These represent the child's attempts to recapture center stage of the parents' attention.

At this stage of family development, children need to develop increasingly complex social relationships that emphasize work, play, and love (Garbarino, 1992). Optimal development requires that children have access to a variety of significant others, gradually expanding relationships from parents and siblings to a peer group.

FAMILIES WITH SCHOOL-AGED CHILDREN

The school should be the appendage of the family state, and modeled on its primary principle, which is, to train the ignorant and weak by self-sacrificing labor and love, and to bestow the most on the weakest, the most undeveloped.

—Catherine Beecher (www.Bartleby.com)

Family adjustment is stretched again when the oldest child reaches school age, because family members must begin to plan schedules around school and extracurricular activities. The daily process of separating from and reuniting with the parents usually is established by the time the child reaches school age, and most kindergartners are ready to take their first major step away from home. Children and parents might have difficulty separating from the safe family environment. Family tasks in this stage involve supporting the child's adjustment to a formal learning situation in which he or she interacts cooperatively with peers and authority figures other than parents. During this period, children must also learn to adjust to a regulated routine. As mentioned, children in homeless families are disadvantaged because of lack of access to proper schooling.

Children from minority families face social institutions for the first time. They may have been sheltered from discrimination by their parents, and going to school can be difficult for some families. In immigrant families, children might learn more English than their parents, leading to some role reversal. For example, immigrant parents might rely on their children to translate and interpret situations. Competing cultural values place children in between two cultures, upsetting their parents. When children enter the school system knowing their native tongue only, the children experience stress in having to learn a new language on top of having to learn "reading, writing, and arithmetic" (Falicov, 1999).

Some parents believe that having school-aged children resembles running a taxi service. Baseball practices, swimming lessons, school meetings, and numerous other activities are very time-consuming for all of the family members. Skills required to negotiate this phase include organizing, cooperating, and supporting family members. At this stage, differences in family income levels become strikingly apparent, and some children notice that their schoolmates have more possessions than they have and are involved in more activities. Classmates may have more clothes, toys, access to recreational services, and spending money even if they attend the same school. Another difference that has an impact on families is the amount and type of food available to children from different socioeconomic backgrounds. Children who have not had a nourishing breakfast or who do not have enough to eat for lunch are disadvantaged in the classroom. Parents who cannot afford to provide children with the basics, let alone the luxuries, often feel inadequate when their children enter school.

The effort involved in getting children to school makes this endeavor overwhelming for some parents. Just getting children ready for school each morning is a major task that includes organizing lunches and books and choosing clothes. Getting the children out of the door on time can be exhausting. It becomes even more complicated if the parents also are trying to get themselves ready for work, particularly if they must leave before the children do.

When children reach school age, working parents face the need to make arrangements for adequate out-of-school care. Arrangements should include care and supervision before and after school hours and during school vacations, holidays, and other school closures. Meeting this requirement can be difficult. If arrangements are inadequate, the children become vulnerable to potential danger at home and on the street. Low-income parents may find out-of-school care too expensive and may be unable to make safe after-school arrangements because of inadequate income for childcare or no extended family support. Although a responsible adult should be with children when they are not in school, too many children come home to an empty house after school. These young people, often seen wearing a house key on a string around their neck, are called "latchkey children."

The increase in the number of women, and consequently parents, in the workforce is well documented and might even be described as a revolution that has taken place since the end of World War II. More than half of new mothers work, and the number has grown steadily over the past ten years. Younger new mothers are more likely to stay home with their children than are women over the age of thirty. College-educated mothers are more likely to return to work, as are single parents. Finally, African American new mothers are more likely to return to work within the first year of a child's birth than are Hispanic mothers (Hunter College Women's Studies Collective, 1995).

The growing participation of both parents in the workforce has affected family life enormously. Parents face tremendous challenges as they try to juggle work responsibilities, child rearing tasks, and household chores while attempting to meet their own personal needs. The demands are even more difficult for single parents, because they often have fewer economic resources and assume all household and childcare responsibilities alone.

In single-parent or two-career families, children may be left at home unsupervised. Children are more likely to be injured when they are home alone (Peterson, 1989). They may experience increased anxiety and fear. Ideally, young children should not be unsupervised. When this is not possible, children should be given explicit instructions on safety, including rules concerning cooking, answering the telephone and doorbell, and what to do in case of an emergency. The length of time a child can remain unsupervised depends on the age and competence of the child, as well as the risks that the child is likely to encounter. Failure to supervise a child adequately is a familiar complaint to child protective services.

Another task of parenting during this stage is to assist children to acquire necessary skills and attitudes for survival in a school environment. In today's society, school success is equated with life success. To help children succeed in school, parents must adopt an "academic culture" and communicate a positive regard for schooling (Garbarino, 1992). Parents can help children interpret the new world of school, and when children have accomplished something, the parents should reinforce the accomplishment. At other times, they can provide the safe place to which children return to escape the stress of school. Most important, parents can help children learn to assume responsibility for learning. The ability to value knowledge is a gift that parents can give their children. One of the best ways to help a child do well in school is to establish a predictable evening routine during which the child is expected to do homework.

This means turning off the television and setting aside a quiet part of the home to allow concentration.

During this phase of the family cycle, parents should make strong connections with those institutions that work with their children. Parents who value school have a greater chance of encouraging academic success than those who do not (Garbarino, 1982). Again, close involvement with the schools will help a child develop competence and skills in preparation for later life.

FAMILIES WITH TEENAGERS

Adolescence has the reputation of being a time of family turbulence. It is a period of rapid change for the youth as well as the family. The adolescent is moving toward adulthood and seems to want the whole world to know it. The family focus shifts from a crucible in which children are nurtured and sheltered into one in which teens start to venture out on their own in efforts to assume adult responsibilities and commitments (Preto, 1999). This is a difficult transition for parents, who agonize over the changing world and increased threats outside the home. It is during this stage that families encounter increasing demands to change every fiber of family functioning such as relationships, finances, and responsibilities. While letting go of some things is important, so is limit setting. The concurrent demands of letting go and maintaining limits challenges even the most flexible family.

Family structure may change and emotions might run high. Preto (1999) suggests that attempts to resolve conflict may reactivate unresolved conflicts about issues embedded in the previous generation. Despite popular lore's suggestions that the teenage years are stressful, most teenagers endure this period with no more difficulty than they encountered in previous stages of development. Problems, if any, are more likely to be the fruit of family stress and difficulty adjusting rather than an unavoidable consequence of puberty. Teenagers must face issues regarding sexuality, dating, renegotiating relationships with family, making decisions about what direction to head in school or future career, and navigating between social norms and family norms.

Generally, the family's task during this time is to help the young person reach maturity and learn skills that will enable him or her to eventually leave the family as an independent adult. The parents assist the young person to develop habits required for work, including assuming greater responsibility and independence. The young person also is learning about sexual relationships, a process facilitated by the parents' role of "sounding board."

Many adolescent "problems" represent the teenager's misguided attempts at achieving independence and adult autonomy. During this period, adolescents struggle to define themselves and make their own decisions. Parents, however, may not recognize that "problem" behaviors are part of normal development and may focus on inappropriate clothing or makeup, outrageous attitudes, and noncompliance with family rules. An adolescent can display emotional upheaval culminating in unpredictable behavior, one day playing ear-splitting music, the next day being silent, withdrawn, and brooding.

Perhaps most threatening, parents find themselves being challenged and out-reasoned by their formerly manageable child (if they had such a child to begin with). Compliant children may suddenly develop an independent style of logic seemingly contradictory to the facts. Parents may feel uncomfortable or threatened when challenged by children who in the past were obedient, loving, and accepting of parental guidance and direction. Children from minority cultures face an escalation of issues because they are caught between the teachings and practices of their own culture and those of mainstream society.

Despite the strife that often accompanies adolescence, teenagers can also be a joy. The process of growing up may be difficult to understand and stranger to watch, but the results can be quite healthy. Teens require support and encouragement during this time. The difficulty for parents is to support the youngster's struggle for independence and maturity while providing necessary structure.

Adolescence is a time of contradiction. The adolescent reviews and repeats all of the previous developmental stages as he or she struggles toward adulthood. Tasks include learning to trust others, acquiring a stable identity, and addressing the questions of purpose in life. Questions of intimacy, relationships, morality, peer associations, and life goals are important as the young person assumes new roles in an attempt to determine his or her future directions.

A significant developmental issue is sexual maturation, often accompanied by strong and frequently conflicting feelings. All at once, it seems, the adolescent has grown into a different body, and sometimes the changes can be frightening. The task is to develop a new self-image, but this new view of the self can seem distressingly fragile. It is no wonder that many young people think of adolescence as a period of embarrassing self-consciousness and self-reflection.

Teenagers demand more privileges and freedom than they have had previously, but they may still have little sense of responsibility for their actions. At this stage, much behavior is centered on peer standards because the approval of friends is preferable to parental approval. Parents are regarded as naive, embarrassingly out of touch, and ancient. The rapid changes suggest that the role of parents during this stage is different from that of previous stages. Their role is more to provide support when needed and back away when they are not needed. Wise parents do not intrude except in cases of need, painful as this often may be to all concerned.

As adolescents loosen family ties, they establish closer relationships with peers, a difficult transition for some parents. While moving toward greater independence, freedom, and responsibility in preparation for leaving home, they are developing skills while remaining within the shelter of the family unit. Unfortunately, some teens leave families prematurely, before they have had the opportunity to develop skills needed for independence.

Adolescence is marked differently in different cultures. In lower socioeconomic groups there is a narrow age difference between the generations (Petro, 1999). Becoming a grandparent before the age of forty is not unusual. Burton (cited in Petro, 1999) offers an astonishing picture of a family where the great-grandmother was forty-three. Some ethnic groups struggle to keep teenagers at home (p. 281).

FAMILIES WITH YOUNG PEOPLE LEAVING HOME: LAUNCHING

This phase was once called the "empty nest." However, the implication of this label was that women's roles revolved primarily around their children and that they experienced depression and lack of meaning when their children finally left home. This depiction is a myth for many women. We now know that many parents (mothers particularly) celebrate when their children leave home—there is less work, more time, fewer worries, and more money. Television commercials are starting to recognize this delight, such as when the child returns home only to finding the parents using margarine instead of butter. The child packs his bags and leaves home in disgust. The parents pretend to be heartbroken. After the door shuts, the parents start to dance together! Of course, all parents wants their children to leave home "the right way"—that is, to leave home with a solid plan in place and the resources to follow through on this plan. Fulmer (1999) suggests that early theory placed too much on separation and independence, particularly for males, but we believe that an extreme response to the reverse is also not useful, as the boomerang phase suggests.

At this stage of life, members must separate from their parents, develop intimate peer relationships, and become established in work (Holman, 1983). How far behind people leave their parents depends upon culture as well as occupational opportunities. Today, however, young people in middle-class families tend to live with their parents longer because of increased educational demands, lack of employment opportunities, and overall economic difficulties. In other families, young people are leaving prematurely, running away from home, leaving school early, and working in low-paying, unskilled jobs. How individuals leave their families of origin will greatly affect the rest of their lives. Although people can return to school later in life, this becomes more difficult when they are responsible for a family. Thus, there are wide variations in how and when young people leave home and what educational and career skills they bring into relationships. They will also differ in the degree to which they have separated from their families of origin.

When young people leave home (for good!), the size of the family shrinks and parental responsibilities change. Parents, if they are still together, must renegotiate their relationship without the triangulation of others in the household. Young adults may leave the family in a series of slow steps culminating in permanently moving out of the home. This may be a back-and-forth process with the young person leaving and returning a number of times, creating mixed reactions to the transition on the part of the parents. The leaving and returning process is becoming so predictable and patterned that we suggest making it a distinct stage. Parental reactions might range from ecstasy to grief, or a combination of the two, depending on the age of the child, the relationship the child had with the parents, and the process of how the child is leaving. Running away from home at the age of 16 can evoke quite different feelings than the feelings that arise from a 19-year-old child leaving for college. Because of this back-and-forth process, young people are busy doing adult activities such as being involved in serious relationships, working, or attending school, requiring further adaptations in the parent–child relationship. However, an unfortunate (for parents) outcome of these activities is that if young people are working, some do not contribute their income to the family finances, and instead use their money on personal items. If parents wanted to get out of debt at this point, many are disappointed.

How much parents assist the launch depends on several factors, including individual choice, socioeconomic status, and culture. For example, Anglo and Polish children might receive little parental assistance compared with the assistance given in Italian or Brazilian families (Blacker, 1999, p. 289). If children continue schooling, middle- or higher-class families provide more assistance.

Parents face issues of their own as they experience their own aging process and changes in relationship to each other. They can no longer deny that they are getting older since they now have adult children. When parents have focused much of their adult lives on their children, the last child's final departure from home demands a distinct kind of adjustment. Adjusting to the stage requires that parents find an alternative to their traditional focus on their children. Some people pressure their children to produce grandchildren, while others develop new hobbies or employment. Children leaving home can enhance marriages as couples decide to focus on one another. If their preoccupation and responsibilities toward children masked marital discord, children leaving home might provide an opportune time for divorce. Another concern is that men and women can have different priorities as they go through midlife, which usually coincides with launching (Blacker, 1999). They may make plans about their relationship once their children have left. They need to examine their relationship to work as well. Moreover, once people retire the power balance shifts in many homes, with men slowing down at work and developing other interests. On the other hand, women may re-invest in a career once family responsibilities diminish. Another issue is that grandparents may be frail and elderly, demanding more attention from the couple. Women are usually the ones to take care of parents.

During this stage, young people focus on establishing themselves as independent adults, capable of functioning on their own. They will focus on preparing for work and solidifying a few special relationships (Fulmer, 1999). In some cases, they will be struggling with starting their own families. If they left home early, or had children early, this struggle can be difficult. On the other hand, difficulty finding work or getting into postsecondary education means that many young people delay leaving home, which also can be stressful. The move to independence is compromised by a continued dependency on parents. In fact, rumor has it that the experts have added another ten years onto adolescence because of the longer time it takes for children to leave home once and for all.

Gender, ethnicity, social class, and sexual orientation mediate the timing and substance of how young people leave home (Blacker, 1999; Fulmer, 1999). Young men are expected to be independent and, because of this, might separate early. In earlier times, young women often left by getting married, although now some may leave by moving on to college. Nevertheless, females usually remain more connected to family relationships. Gays and lesbians usually come out in stages (e.g., self-definition, self-acceptance, and disclosure), although the process typically starts in young adulthood. Coming out contributes to unique relationship gymnastics with parents and extended kin, particularly if the person has been in a heterosexual relationship previously. Family support and family acceptance will affect the psychological adjustment of GLB people (Elizur & Ziv, 2001). Low income and few work skills may keep members of low socioeconomic groups at home for extended periods. This might be complicated by having children at a young age, criminal activities, and gang membership.

When is a child ready to leave the home? This question is difficult to answer. Many young people are leaving home much later than children were a generation ago. Some young people leave home before they are ready. Some may leave home prematurely to escape difficult family situations such as abuse, poverty, or chemical dependency. On the other hand, for middle-class families, adolescence is extending beyond the teenage years as children remain at home while they continue school or get financially secure. Many middle-class parents can no longer afford to send their children away from home for college education. However, youth in families where postsecondary education is not pursued face difficulty because blue-collar jobs are becoming increasingly scarce in Western, industrialized countries (Garbarino, 1982).

BOOMERANG PHASE

As mentioned, we have taken the liberty to add this phase to the family life cycle. Many young people leave and return home for different reasons. More sons than daughters appear to be moving home (Blacker, 1999). They might return home from college for summer break. They might encounter some relationship difficulties or financial setbacks. They might become ill and need the care of their parents. Some will bring their dogs or cats. Sometimes, particularly when marriages have broken up, adult children move back home and bring their children. Whatever the reason, the leaving-returning-leaving cycle requires a lot of flexibility and active negotiation to allow young people and their parents to keep relationships running smoothly and to allow everyone sufficient personal, physical, and emotional space. The challenge of this phase is for children to assume adult roles and not revert to earlier parent–child days when the parent was the boss. This phase is not the continuation of childhood dependence. While the economy almost demands extended periods of financial dependency on parents, society still expects individual freedom (Fulmer, 1999).

Blacker (1999) suggests that the return of adult children is more likely to occur under three conditions: (1) if the parent–child relationship is positive, (2) if the family agrees to continue to provide support, and (3) if the parents have remained together rather than forming a new stepfamily or being a single-parent household (p. 299).

The challenge for parents is to recognize that their young person is an adult and capable of setting his or her own rules and guidelines without undue interference. On the other hand, young people must also assume responsibilities within the home. These responsibilities include chipping in financially (no matter how well off the parents are), respecting the personal space of others, contributing to domestic chores, and recognizing that at this point in their lives parents are not obligated to take care of their children.

Issues for Older Parents

One's family is the most important thing in life. I look at it this way: One of these days I'll be over in a hospital somewhere with four walls around me. And the only people who'll be with me will be my family.

—Robert C. Byrd (www.Bartleby.com)

Our focus in this book is on social work with families that include children who are living at home. Thus, the other developmental stages of the family will be mentioned only briefly. The next stage describes middle-aged parents who no longer have their children living with them. Their major task is reestablishing themselves as a couple, and they may go through a new courtship stage as the partners find new roles and rules in their relationship. This can be a difficult time for couples who find that they no longer have a reason to stay together without the children at home to bind them together.

The final stage, that of the aging family, lasts until the death of one of the partners. The couple must adjust to becoming older and facing death. Couples might become isolated during this stage as friends die or as they are forced by ill health to move to institutions such as nursing homes or hospitals. This stage is even more difficult if the couple suffers from inadequate financial resources. Another area of potential stress for the couple is the trend of older people moving into the residence of one of their adult children. This role reversal, whereby the adult child may take on a care giving role for his or her parent, can be stressful for everyone.

Middle-aged couples or singles may find themselves caring for their own children as well as their aging parents. With lengthening longevity, many older people wish to remain at home. Many do so, although some will have physical problems and illnesses that require ongoing support and services. Interestingly, if it is the male partner who is infirm, the female partner is likely to keep him at home and take care of him. On the other hand, if the infirm partner is female, she is more likely to be institutionalized. It is at this time that one of the adult children will step in. These adult caretaker children have been dubbed the "sandwich generation." The sandwich role was common in past years when society was less mobile and extended families stayed together. It is more difficult in today's society, in which both partners in a marriage often work full-time. If one parent has deceased, the adult children will be required to step in and provide extra support. When there are cutbacks and limited services to seniors, it is often adult female children who are expected to fill the gap.

We would like to remind you that the developmental stages discussed in this chapter are generalizations about families based on assumptions that all families have children, remain intact over the lifetime of the parents, and so on.

Of course, this is not the case. Divorce rates remain high, and there are growing numbers of single-parent families, blended families, and couples that marry later in life and therefore have fewer years together as a family. The number of couples who remain childless also has increased. Each of these factors creates specific issues for the family that need to be taken into account when working with families. It is important to remember that each family, regardless of its composition, is unique. In the context of uniqueness, however, the vast majority of families are similar in that families get bigger and then get smaller. Not only do children grow up to form their own families, but family size is affected by divorce and death. At each transition, the family experiences stresses and strains as its members attempt to respond to the changes.

VARIATIONS AFFECTING THE FAMILY LIFE CYCLE

As we mentioned earlier, sailing through the family life cycle according to the linear and sequential description in the life cycle model is more the exception than the rule. Even the Brady Bunch was a blended family! Economic trends have influenced how families move through the life cycle. More women are actively involved in the workforce now than in past decades; in fact, married women in the workforce exceed the number of full-time homemakers (Eichler, 1997). Poverty is more prevalent among children and women. Female-led, single-parent families often experience more severe economic disadvantage than do two-parent families or male-led single-parent families. Moreover, approximately half of all marriages end in divorce. Live-in relationships occur frequently. Death and desertion may disrupt the family life cycle. Eichler (1997) has identified major demographic patterns in industrialized countries that have an impact on the family life cycle: the decline in fertility, postponement of marriage, a sharp rise in the incidence of divorce during the 1970s and 1980s, and a growing proportion of people living in small households. The diversity of family styles brings with it differences in family development.

SEPARATION AND DIVORCE

A major challenge that is central to the destigmatization and cultural normalization of divorce is the creation of nontraumatic legal processes that do not become party to and inflame the acrimony and alienation that most families bring to the divorce process.

—Pinsof, 2002, p. 152

When I'm alone, I can sleep crossways in my bed without an argument.

—Zsa Zsa Gabor, on being between marriages (www.Bartleby.com)

Divorce is probably of nearly the same date as marriage. I believe, however, that marriage is some weeks the more ancient.

—Voltaire (www.Bartleby.com)

Divorce is a cultural, financial, legal, parental, emotional, and spiritual issue (Murray, 2002). While some religions are making divorce possible, the degree to which divorced individuals feel supported and accepted will vary. Carter and McGoldrick (1999a) suggest that dissatisfaction with the traditional nuclear family produced the 50 percent divorce rate of the recent past. They also suggest that, statistically, the pattern is now marriage, divorce, remarriage, and redivorce (1999b).

It is now cliché to suggest that marriage should be more difficult to enter into and divorce easier. Divorce and other forms of family dissolution have always been part of the family landscape, with the rate varying depending upon the era and the legal and religious restrictions (Pinsof, 2002). Several factors have affected the divorce rate: increased longevity, changing women's roles, changing cultural values, and changing legal restrictions. Given the different types of coupling configurations, the following statistics represent only one kind of coupling—legal marriages. The statistics exclude relationships formed outside the parameters of legal and religious arrangements, and little is known about the permanency and stability of other types of relationships. In fact, divorce rates apply only to those who marry and for whom the state keeps a record. Moreover, the statistics do not tell the story of people who are happy in relationships and what proportion of families are happy. They merely tell the story of how many remain together. We also need to point out that at the same time that divorce rates have risen, marriage rates are falling. It appears as though marriage is losing its appeal in Western society and is diminishing in importance as a life goal.

While the divorce rate was only 10 percent during the mid-nineteenth century, by the mid-1980s, approximately half of all first marriages and 61 percent of remarriages ended in divorce (Nichols & Schwartz, 2004, p. 138). The divorce rate leveled off after 1980. In fact, one-quarter of all marriages last less than seven years and about half will end before their twentieth year (Pinsof, 2002). The divorce rate depends upon ethnicity, with African Americans having the highest divorce or separation rate (63 percent) in the first marriage, compared with 48 percent for whites and 52 percent for Hispanics. For second marriages, the trend for whites is 39 percent (Pinsof, 2002). Several demographic characteristics increase the risk of divorce: marriage before the age of 20, lower income and education levels (with the exception of well-educated women with good incomes), African American ethnicity, Protestantism, and not living together before marriage (Ahrons, 1999).

Many believe that divorce is a life crisis requiring adjustment by all family members, while others (e.g., Pinsof, 2002) argue that the crisis can be mediated by factors such as co-parenting and a sustained relationship with the noncustodial parent. In addition, trauma can be diminished by redefining divorce as normal, increasing social connectedness and social support, and dealing with shame and stigmatization. Why should someone be forced to remain in a relationship that is chronically deeply troubled or riddled with addiction, abuse, unhappiness, intense conflict, or mental illness? Many family social workers enter families where intense unhappiness or severe conflict exists. They might set as a goal keeping the family intact, feeling that their work is a failure if the parental relationship dissolves. Yet, we encourage family workers to reexamine this position and develop opinions that embrace divorce as a viable and sometimes preferred option for families they are working with.

Regardless of the philosophical debates about whether FSWs should work to keep *all* families together, it is well known that divorce is a major life stressor. Gottman (1999) contends that the dissolution of a marriage is often a bigger stressor than marital unhappiness. Divorce is associated with physical and psychological difficulties.

There are two high-risk critical periods for divorce in the family life cycle (Gottman & Levenson, 2002). Nearly half of all divorces occur in the first seven years of marriage, which is seen as a volatile and emotional phase of marriage. The second high risk time for divorce is midlife—a time when most families have adolescents. This latter risk occurs when marital satisfaction bottoms out. It appears that intense emotions, particularly anger leading to conflict, make it difficult to stay in the relationship. When this affect transforms to indifference, it is easier to stay in the relationship. However, over time the indifference poses another risk in that it causes distance and indifference leading to the demise of the marital relationship.

Despite the frequency of divorce, it is still often viewed as a failure. Though divorce is not necessarily a failure, it is one of the most stressful life events that people face. Divorce punctuates the life cycle of the family in rather unique ways. It frequently lowers the economic status of family members and requires new coping skills. The major tasks during divorce are to end the relationship while cooperatively parenting the children. Issues involved in divorce include making the decision to divorce, planning the dissolution of the relationship, separating, and finally, going through with divorce. During each stage, family members must come to terms with personal issues related to divorce. For example, partners must acknowledge their roles in the failed relationship. If the decision to divorce appears imminent, partners must learn to accept the inevitable. At times one partner is more reluctant to divorce than the other. Additional issues include forging new relationships with extended family members and mourning one's losses. Once the divorce is final, the partners must rebuild their lives as single people or adjust to life with a new partner.

A couple's decision to separate and divorce is not made overnight. Rather, it is a process that occurs over several stages: the decision, the announcement, and dismantling the family (Ahrons, 1999). Murray (2002) broadens the process to seven stages: emotional divorce, legal divorce, economic divorce, coparental divorce and the problems of custody, community divorce, psychic divorce, and religious divorce. It is apparent that some people may be divorced legally while the other stages are left to fester.

It is not *what* couples argue about; rather it is *how* they argue that leads to divorce. Usually one person initiates the divorce. This person has probably been agonizing over the decision for a long time. The person who decides to leave (usually the woman) experiences mounting dissatisfaction coupled with accumulating evidence to justify the decision. Gradually, one person emotionally disengages from the relationship. Sometimes a crisis will mark an announcement, but other times the move is more gradual. The movement toward divorce is often marked by feelings of guilt, anger, and betrayal. Once the announcement is made, separation occurs. Separations can be orderly or disorderly (Ahrons, 1999, p. 389).

Divorce brings with it longstanding issues that affect every member of the family. Few divorces are without distress to its members, regardless of how satisfying couple and family relationships were. Divorce affects families on multiple levels: family life cycle, financial, individual well-being, friendships and support networks, and relationships with extended kin, to name a few. Many authors claim that it takes up to three years to adjust to the issues posed by divorce. Moreover, divorce is not a binary process—it is not true that one day you are a couple and the next day you wake up divorced. The processing of arriving at a divorce can be winding and emotionally draining. Divorce is an emotional process that brings with it many decisions.

Although the impact of divorce on children is a special concern, much of the research on the effects of divorce on children fails to make fair comparisons. For example, Pinsof (2002) suggests that a fairer comparison would be with children from unhappy and deeply troubled marriages. Most children cope emotionally with the separation or divorce of their parents, but for many it still exacts a psychological toll. For a child, divorce and marital separation are comparable to losing a parent through death (Wallerstein, 1983). Wallerstein and Kelly (1980) suggest the major pitfall of divorce for children is the impact on their development. Parents undergoing a divorce often feel psychologically drained because they have to deal with their personal grief and stress, sapping available emotional energy needed to take care of the children's emotional, physical, and social needs. For example, during postdivorce adjustment, custodial parents are less supportive, less nurturing, and more anxious in their relationship with children than they were before the divorce (Bolton & Bolton, 1987; Wallerstein, 1985). Children benefit when the relationship between the parents is supportive of the children maintaining contact with the noncustodial parent. Decisions should be made based on what is the best for children. Unfortunately, children are all too often used as pawns to get at the other parent, and children suffer in the process.

Children between the ages of six and eight often feel responsible for the marital breakup (Thompson, Rudolph, & Henderson, 2003), although guilt is not confined exclusively to this age group. Additionally, children may experience academic difficulties, anger, or other behavioral problems related to the divorce. It is not unusual for children to experience feelings of rejection and anxiety following a divorce, but these emotions are not often acknowledged or dealt with by significant people in the child's life. Divorce is especially hard on young males, for whom it may take up to two years following a divorce to stabilize their lives (Hetherington, Cox, & Cox, 1978). Thus, children are often victims of divorce as they face long-term ramifications of marital dissolution (Wallerstein, 1985).

Family disruption risks depleting psychological resources available to the child (Garbarino, 1992). For example, many separations and divorces are bitter, and the child's loyalty to both parents becomes strained. The custodial parent (usually the mother) assumes much of the childcare and household responsibilities, and her financial resources often become strained. In addition, children who are unsupervised for extended periods of time are twice as likely to belong to single-parent families as to families with two parents (Garbarino, 1982).

Children may experience divided loyalties between the custodial and non-custodial parent, and in bitter breakups a child may be used as a pawn between parents. Custody and access arrangements may be sabotaged, child support payments may be evaded, and allegations of abuse may be made. Some non-custodial parents simply give up the battle and disengage completely from the children.

Thompson, Rudolph, and Henderson (2003) propose several tasks that children of divorce must successfully accomplish in order to move on with their lives:

- *Feelings of anxiety, abandonment, and denial:* Parental support is a critical factor in helping a child overcome negative feelings. A parent must explain to the child what has happened without blaming the other partner.
- *Disengaging from parental conflict and distress, and resuming their regular activities:* Divorce should not be allowed to encroach on the routine activities in which children have been involved.
- *Resolution of loss:* Children must grieve not only the loss of a significant person in their lives, but they may also mourn the loss of other important aspects of their lives such as familiar surroundings and neighborhood friends.
- *Resolving anger and self-blame:* Children may feel responsible for the breakup or blame one parent for the divorce.
- *Accepting the permanence of the divorce:* Children often do not consider divorce final. They may hold on to a reconciliation fantasy long after the divorce. Some children may even scheme to reunite their parents or develop problems aimed at getting parents reunited.
- *Developing realistic hopes regarding relationships:* Children need to recognize that although their parents' relationship failed, positive marital relationships are still possible and that they cannot over-generalize their parents' failure to all relationships.

Because divorce is laden with many potential land mines for all parties, a growing area of intervention has been in divorce mediation. Outcome studies suggest that a successful agreement is reached between 50 percent and 85 percent of the time (Hahn & Kleist, 2000). In some jurisdictions, mediation is mandated. Mediation is most often used to settle disagreements involving the division of property and to help decide custody and visitation rights. Apparently, mediation results more often in joint legal custody than in adversarial processes (Hahn & Kleist, 2000, p. 166).

Wolfe (2001) uncovered a number of difficulties that children from divorced families faced. She found that children from divorced homes experienced more depression than children from non-divorced homes, many of them experiencing a clinical level of depression. These children also had low self-esteem and were observed to be irritable. Many children also had sleep disturbances and somatic complains, typically associated with depression. Many also had problems in school. She also uncovered overwhelming evidence of extreme parental stress among those who divorce, some of whom were so stressed that they were at risk for child abuse. While most parents viewed themselves as competent, many also experienced their parenting responsibilities as a burden, in part perhaps because they were not receiving sufficient emotional and practical support. Wolfe concluded that depression among children of divorce was linked with stressful and undesirable life events. Their parents had little emotional and practical support, and their families were unstable and characterized by emotional problems or drug and alcohol abuse. Families also experienced conflict between husband and wife, and perhaps conflict among the children. In other words, their parents were highly distressed. Wolfe concluded that the problem of depression is so pervasive in divorcing families that workers should make direct enquiries. Parents should also be assessed for stress.

SINGLE PARENTING

More people are living single than at any other time in history. The number of people who never marry, although still a minority, is growing (Berliner, Jacob, & Schwartzberg, 1999), and never marrying is becoming a viable option. People are also delaying the age at which they decide to marry. At the same time, the number of single-parent families rose from 12 percent in 1970 to 26 percent in 1995 (Mannis, 1999). In addition, the proportion of children born to mothers who have not married is also increasing. What do these statistics reveal? We impose our ideological beliefs upon the world around us. For example, religious conservatives might suggest that they are the result of feminism, the decline of religion, the diminished importance of the "father," or the erosion of "family values." Single-parent families in some quarters are depicted as deviant or as undermining male prerogative.

Single parenting can occur for several reasons: death, divorce, desertion, and never having been married through choice. The various pathways to single parenthood suggest that even single-parent-led families have great diversity of form. Regardless of the reason for single-parent status, single parents might share feelings of loneliness, sadness, guilt, and anger (Goldenberg & Goldenberg, 2000). In addition, divorced parents need to decide whether to cooperate with and support contact of the child with the ex-spouse and his or her family (Carter & McGoldrick, 1999b).

It is important to recognize that children can and do grow up in healthy single-parent households and that not all women choose to share a household with a male partner. Nevertheless, raising children single-handedly is difficult for many people. Often, single-parent households are poor, primarily because of the feminization of poverty. In addition, single parents have a hard time getting time for themselves because there are few people who can or will step in when the parent is tired or overloaded. Single parents can experience role overload as they are burdened with tasks that are usually divided between two people. Perhaps the burden is greatest when the children are young and when they need more care and attention. Once the children become adolescents, parental power may dwindle with no one to back up the authority of the parent (Anderson, 1999). Task overload may be reflected in family disorganization, social isolation, and problems in the parent–child relationship. Single parents who have a rich network of kin and friends fare better than single parents who are socially isolated. The temptation might be to become romantically attached with another partner, a solution that works for some but not all.

Nearly half of all children in the United States live in a single-parent home at some point during childhood. Most single-parent homes are mother-led. Children from single-parent households show more problems than children from two-parent homes (Blum, Boyle, & Offord, 1988). They have a greater incidence of behavior problems such as conduct disorders, attention deficit disorder, poor school performance, and emotional problems. This is not to suggest that every child from a single-parent family is destined to experience adjustment problems. Nevertheless, problems of single-parent families are compounded by economic difficulties (Eichler, 1997; Goldenberg & Goldenberg, 2000; Nichols & Schwartz, 2004; Pett, 1982) and fatigue (Okun, 1996). On the positive side of the equation, maternal education ameliorates the negative impact of these stresses (Tuzlak & Hillock, 1991).

Single parents experience role strain while they balance household tasks, care of the children, employment, and personal lives (Burden, 1986). Mothers who have sole responsibility for their children are more likely to behave punitively toward them (Smith, 1984). Isolation is associated with depression, and depression has been associated with child abuse (Zurvain & Grief, 1989). However, social support may buffer the effect of role strain and poverty for single-parent families (Gladow & Ray, 1986). Both mothers and children in joint custody arrangements fare better than mothers with sole support (Hanson, 1986). Courts need to recognize and support the value of divorced co-parental relationships, perhaps using divorce mediation to thwart the adversarial and hostile nature of the divorce (Pinsof, 2002, p. 152).

Some single-parent families are poorly buffered against conflict and stress that may be acute or chronic. They experience multiple stresses operating simultaneously that overwhelm their capacity to cope. Poverty is a particular concern for single-parent families (Bolton & Bolton, 1987; Holman, 1983), and economic deprivation seems to be a factor when abuse occurs in these families (Gelles, 1989). Poverty also plays a role in many of the social and psychological problems associated with growing up in a single-parent household (Goldenberg & Goldenberg, 1994). Female-headed single-parent families are disproportionately represented among low-income groups. When they have adequate income and support, however, single-parent families can be as viable as two-parent families (Burden, 1986).

Many interventions with single-parent families will be ecologically based. Issues related to provision of concrete resources and social support should be built into interventions. In addition, single parents may need assistance with stress management, grief counseling, and skills related to effective child management. Finally, single parents will benefit from an enhanced informal support network including grandparents and friends.

The special tasks of parents in single-parent families are shown in the following list:

- Develop adequate social support systems.
- Resolve feelings of sadness, anger, and loneliness.
- Cope with stress, fatigue, and role overload without taking it out on the children.
- Develop child management skills that do not result in anger directed at children.
- Develop time management skills that allow for meeting children's needs as well as personal needs.

REMARRIAGE, STEPPARENTING, AND BLENDED FAMILIES: HOW MANY TIMES DO YOU HEAR ABOUT UGLY STEPFATHERS?

The privileged status of the biological nuclear family . . . contributes to the stigmatization of all nonnuclear families, but especially that of stepfamilies.

—Anne Jones, 2003

Negative stereotypes about stepfamilies, particularly when mothers are the new member, are common themes in fairy tales, yet stepparenting is commonplace and not exclusively the domain of storytellers. About one-third of all Americans will be part of a stepfamily (Jones, 2003). Despite biases and myths about stepfamilies, they are neither problematic nor inferior. As with all other families, some blended families function quite well, while others have difficulty navigating common pitfalls. Mothers most often are awarded custody, making a stepfather family the most common arrangement. Over half of families have been or will be part of a stepfamily (McGoldrick & Carter, 1999).

The process of recreating a new family based on the experience and needs of multiple individuals can be extremely complicated. The process is made even more difficult if the ex-partner is uncooperative or sabotaging of the new family unit. Embarking on a new relationship requires an "emotional divorce" from the first marriage (Holman, 1983). Divorced adults must deal with their own fears about entering into a new relationship. In addition, remarried families experience common triangles that show up on genograms (McGoldrick, 1999a); family social workers must be keenly attuned to these triangles because they can rapidly become ghosts that haunt current relationships. The first triangle is the two new partners and the previous partner. The second triangle includes the two new partners and one of the children. In fact, in previously divorced families, arguments about child rearing occur most often (Stanley, Markman, & Whitton, 2002). Each triangle is infused with potential conflict.

In stepfamilies, loneliness is often exchanged for conflict (Nichols & Schwartz, 2004). In blended families, parents may be engaged in a continuous struggle over child rearing. Conflict may occur over who assumes primary parenting responsibilities for the children and what type of parenting should occur. Rules in stepfamilies may be vague initially, with a lengthy period of time elapsing before roles, rules, and boundaries are reformulated. Children may feel confused and harbor resentment toward the stepparent whom they consider has usurped the role of the noncustodial parent. Rivalry between stepsiblings may be intense (Thompson, Rudolph, & Henderson, 2003). In addition, children's need to maintain contact with the noncustodial parent can interfere with the custodial parent's desire for a complete emotional break.

Children may have difficulty adjusting to life in a blended family. They may have trouble accepting the fact that their parents will never get together again, and loyalty to both parents may be tested. Divided loyalties are particularly likely when one parent uses the children to direct resentment at the former partner. In addition, children may fantasize about their parents eventually reuniting and try to make this happen. When there are other stepchildren entering the relationship, adjustment becomes even more complicated, since it might involve competing for affection, attention, and material possessions.

Stepfamilies face many tasks in order to accomplish successful integration (Thompson, Rudolph, & Henderson, 2003; Visher & Visher, 1982):

- Mourning losses of previous relationships;
- Arriving at a satisfactory stepparenting role;
- Redefining financial and social obligations;
- Agreeing on visitation and custody;
- Establishing consistent leadership and discipline;
- Ensuring that expectations for relationships are realistic;
- Forming new emotional bonds in the family;
- Developing new traditions;
- Dealing with sexuality in the home.

Boundaries in newly blended families need to be negotiated, and this can be a difficult task. Not only must members establish boundaries concerning physical space (sharing, property), but they must also decide how much emotional distance to maintain with new family members and agree upon roles that will work within this new family unit. Adults involved in a marital dissolution often need a clean break from the relationship, yet the presence of children demands that contact with each parent be ongoing and consistent for access to be maintained. Additionally, joining family subsystems (mother–child or father–child) will have learned to operate independently. Changes and adaptations are needed to combine the new family subsystems adequately (Nichols & Schwartz, 2004).

McGoldrick and Carter (1999) in a review of research on remarried families suggest that children fare better when:

- Custodial parents function effectively;
- There is less parental conflict;

- Children visit regularly with their noncustodial parent;
- The relationship with the ex-partner is low key and amicable;
- Nontraditional gender roles kick in; and
- Extended family is cooperative.

In addition, family integration is easier when the children are not adolescents and if there is not a new child in the new relationship.

DEATH OF A PARENT

Prior to the modern era, most marriages lasted between ten and twenty years. Death of one partner was the predominant reason for the end of a marriage (Pinsof, 2002). Divorce is now the main reason for the end of a marriage, bringing with it numerous issues. Some issues related to divorce also apply to families in which one of the parents has died (Wallerstein, 1983). Although the death of a parent in families with young children is rare (Eichler, 1997), it does happen. To children, losing a parent through divorce can seem almost as final as death. Widowhood is less likely to be associated with the dramatic drop in income that often occurs among custodial parents after divorce. However, widowed parents are less likely than divorced parents to remarry (Fustenberg, 1980). In addition, families that experience the death of one parent are likely to maintain contact with the deceased partner's family and with members of the community.

When widows and widowers with children do remarry, there is an increased likelihood of the new parent being accepted by the children if the new parent is a father. It appears that children have a harder time accepting new mothers (McGoldrick & Carter, 1999). At the same time, children need to be allowed space to grieve for the deceased parent. Triangles involving ghosts are harder to deal with (p. 422).

PARENTING BY GRANDPARENTS

Despite the mobility of many families today, grandparents often play a significant role in the lives of grandchildren. For example, many grandparents care for their grandchildren when parents are at work (Gattai & Musatti, 1999). In the past decades, parenting by grandparents was most common in African American families, but today it is increasingly common in other ethnic groups (Okun, 1996). Grandparents often assume the role of primary caretaker of children because of substance abuse or other incapacitating conditions that prevent their adult children from being custodial parents. When faced with a choice between seeing their grandchildren placed in foster care or caring for the grandchildren themselves, many grandparents feel obliged to take on parental responsibilities.

Child rearing by grandparents is not necessarily without stress and difficulty. For example, some child rearing practices of grandparents may conflict with modern parenting techniques (Okun, 1996). Also, grandparents may worry about who will care for their grandchildren if they die or become incapacitated. In addition, many older people lack financial resources to care for their grandchild and adding another mouth to feed in an already financially

| CASE 7.2 | WORKING WITH DIVERSE FAMILY STRUCTURES |

The FSW prepares herself to work with diverse family structures. Examples are a gay couple who co-parent a child, a single parent, and grandparents parenting their grand-children. Following is a case example of the latter case.

Catherine and Walter are a retired couple who became involved with Child Protective Services when their daughter, Margie, dropped off her children at the CPS office and disappeared. Catherine and Walter agreed to take custody of the children, Amy (8), Harold (6), and Linda (3). All of the members of the newly constructed family have required counseling, which was arranged by referral from the FSW to a family agency. Some of the issues experienced by the children are grief at loss of their mother; adjustment to their new parents, Catherine and Walter; adjustment to a more structured style of parenting then they had previously experienced; and adjustment to a new neighborhood. Problems experienced by Catherine and Walter included adjustment to having young children, adjusting to societal norms about how to parent that have changed from when the couple were young parents years ago, and loss of the freedom of their previous retired lifestyle.

strapped household may create additional stresses for the family. Some grand-parents may have looked forward to time on their own without any responsibilities for another person. Grandparents as parents experience a disruption in the family life cycle because they are caring for children at a time when their peers are enjoying the benefits of spare time and relief from some of their financial obligations.

Regardless of whether grandparents assume a primary or secondary care-taking responsibility for grandchildren, they often develop a strong attachment with grandchildren and play a very important role in grandchildren's development. Wilcoxon (1991) has identified five important roles of grandparents:

- *Historian* who can link children with the familial and cultural past;
- *Role model* or an example of older adulthood;
- *Mentor* or wise elder who has experienced his or her own life transitions;
- *Wizard* who is a master storyteller; and
- *Nurturer* who is the ultimate support person for familial crises and transitions.

CHAPTER SUMMARY

One way for social workers to understand families is to become familiar with issues that arise at various developmental stages. Stages of family development include marriage/partnering, birth of the first child, families with preschool children, families with school-aged children, families with teenagers, and families with young people leaving home.

The transition from each stage to the next is associated with a variety of stresses and strains for family members. Understanding these issues enables the family social worker to help families cope with changes that occur as the family matures.

EXERCISES

7.1 IMPACT OF CULTURE ON YOUR FAMILY

What is your cultural heritage? How is your cultural heritage expressed in terms of:

1. Definition of family
2. Gender roles
3. Family rituals during transitions
4. Relationship among generations
5. History of your culture

After you have described how your family expressed itself in terms of these five areas, try to sort out how much was unique to your particular family and how much culture influenced your family. What are the implications for family work?

7.2 NAVIGATING SOCIAL CLASS

Workers often overlook the values embedded in social class. These values might include beliefs about education, sex roles, politics, and education. Break into small groups and try to identify values that might be part of the: underclass, working class, professional/managerial class, business-owning class. Compare your answers with the rest of the class. What are the implications for family work?

7.3 THREE GENERATIONS OF MEN AND WOMEN

Break the class into small groups. Each student will take turns comparing gender roles in the family for the past three generations: grandparents, parents, and the present generation. How have roles changed? How have these roles affected the family life cycle?

7.4 INCLUSIVENESS

Select one example of heterosexism in society around you. Describe this heterosexism. Now select a policy or practice to revise this inherent heterosexism.

7.5 HOW YOU LEARNED

What are your unique messages and learnings about gay and lesbian families? Where did these messages come from? Whose interests do they serve? Where do you stand in regard to what you were taught growing up? How do these teachings diverge from or converge with the profession of social work? How do your beliefs reflect the political/social climate, the lack of social and institutional support, and personal beliefs, attitudes, and prejudices?

7.6   CLIMATE

Describe how each off the following influences public attitudes toward gay and lesbian families:

1. politics
2. religion
3. patriarchy
4. feminism
5. social sciences
6. research
7. therapy

7.7   ALTERNATIVES TO THE LINEAR, SEQUENTIAL MODEL OF FAMILY LIFE CYCLE

Examine the eight stages of the family life cycle. Try to mix the stages up so that they do not follow a linear and sequential path. What family circumstance could you see fitting into the new set of stages that you created?

7.8   IS RELIGION LOSING ITS HOLD ON THE FAMILY?

Historically, Judeo-Christian traditions have been very influential in regulating the family, but now the family appears to be undergoing monumental changes. Debate whether religion has lost its influence on family life.

7.9   MAKING THE RIGHT TO MARRY MORE INCLUSIVE

Divide the class into three sections. One group will develop an argument that only blue-eyed people should be allowed to legally marry. The second group will argue for the right of brown-eyed and blue-eyed people to marry. The third group will argue that everyone adult should be allowed to marry, regardless of their eye color. Make note of some of the arguments. What points that were presented were solely value based? What points had scientific merit? If research were more influential in the argument, which side would win?

7.10   SEEDS OF CONFLICT

Break into small groups. Take each of the potential areas of conflict embedded in each stage of the family life cycle and identify examples of where conflict might break out in the relationship. Role-play a couple in conflict over one of these issues and include a family social worker working with the couple to resolve the difficulty. Describe to the class what happened in the role-play.

7.11   UNDERSTANDING INTIMACY

Describe the components of a healthy intimate relationship. Divide the class into groups of four. Each group is instructed to locate two marital satisfaction inventories. What does each inventory suggest are the qualities of a satisfactory marriage? Compare the qualities and discuss in class.

7.12 HOMEOSTATASIS AND FAMILY LIFE CYCLE

Review the different phases of the family life cycle. Beside each stage, list two tasks that the family must do and potential crises that occur during each phase.

7.13 LETTING GO AND LIMIT SETTING

Break into groups of two. Role-play a parent and teenager negotiating where to let go and where to set limits. (For skill development, you might want to include a FSW helping out the parent and child.) Write down the results of this negotiation and present to the class.

7.14 ADOLESCENCE

Recall your own adolescence. How did your family values differ from values outside the home? How did you and your family navigate these differences?

7.15 YOUR ADOLESCENCE

Reflect on your own adolescence, and describe what was going on in your family and how your teen years (or those of your siblings) created changes in the family system.

7.16 LEAVING HOME

Break into groups of four or five students. Assign one student to report back to the larger class (without identifying names). Respond to the following questions:

1. At what age did you first leave home? When did you leave home for good? How often have you moved back home since you left?
2. What were the circumstances behind your leaving home? If you returned home, what were the circumstances behind this return?
3. How did your parents respond to your departure? How did your parents respond to your return?
4. How had your family changed if you returned home?

7.17 BOOMERANGING HOME

Break the class into small groups. Discuss some of the difficulties in the family that might arise when children return home. Then devise some interventions on dealing with these difficulties.[1]

---

[1]Please send your suggestions to the authors!

7.18 A Family Developmental Assessment

Based on your family of origin, complete a developmental assessment by identifying the ages of family members and outlining key developmental issues your family is facing.

7.19 Sibling Position

Take a survey of members of the class regarding birth position. Is one particular birth position overrepresented in this class of future social workers?

7.20 Social Changes Affecting the Divorce Rate

How would the following social changes affect the divorce rate?

1. longer life span
2. changing women's roles
3. changing cultural values
4. changing legal restrictions

7.21 Feminism

Many conservative thinkers argue that feminism has destroyed the family. Split the class into agree and disagree sections and debate this argument.

7.22 Marriage

Is marriage an outdated social institution? What are the benefits and disadvantages of getting married these days?

7.23 Viable Divorce

Make a list of some circumstances that make divorce a viable and preferred option in families. What actions can a family social worker take in these families?

7.24 Decisions Involved in Divorcing

Many decisions accompany the decision to divorce. List as many decisions as you can think of that a couple has to make when they divorce (including decisions that crop up as children get older). Compare your list with those of your classmates.

7.25 Developmental Challenges from Divorce

Discuss the challenges you believe a family experiences immediately after a divorce. Contrast these with what you believe to be the challenges experienced by families who have lost a parent through death. In what ways can a social worker assist the family during and after these critical periods?

7.26 GOOD AND BAD DIVORCE

Describe the qualities of a "good" divorce. Describe the qualities of a "bad" divorce. Discuss in class and compare your list with the rest of the class. What can a worker do to help a divorce be "good"?

7.27 DEVELOPMENTAL TASKS OF STEPFAMILIES

A blended family must accomplish certain tasks as the family subsystems merge. List some concrete interventions the family social worker can carry out to help the family complete each of the tasks listed in this chapter.

7.28 RESEARCH ISSUES

Examine the findings presented in this chapter concerning the family life cycle, referring to primary sources. Pose additional questions that researchers and practitioners might ask and design a study to address these issues (with the fewest amount of limitations).

7.29 DEVELOPMENTAL VARIATIONS

If your family of origin, or that of a friend, was not a typical "middle-class" family, describe how the family's developmental stages differed from the stages described in this chapter.

If a family were a container, it would be a nest, an enduring nest, loosely woven, expansive, and open. If the family were a fruit, it would be an orange, a circle of sections, held together but separable—each segment distinct. If the family were a boat, it would be a canoe that makes no progress unless everyone paddles. If the family were a sport, it would be baseball: a long, slow, nonviolent game that is never over until the last out. If the family were a building, it would be an old, but solid structure that contains human history, and appeals to those who see the carved moldings under all the plaster, the wide plank floors under the linoleum, the possibilities.

—Letty Pogrebin, 1983 (www.Bartleby.com)

8 CHAPTER | FAMILY STRENGTHS AND RESILIENCE

CHAPTER CONTENTS

Much has been written about how families get derailed, but we know much less about what families do that is right. The focus of family social work usually deals with distress and adversity, overshadowing family social workers' efforts to notice what is going right. The emphasis on what is going wrong can be all-consuming because its problems cause family pain and distress. The urgency to deal with problems relegates family strengths and health factors to the back seat of family work. Moreover, there is a paucity of research and theory about healthy relationships (Young, 2004).

However, pathologizing families has contributed to a situation where FSWs get to know families on the basis of what is negative about them. The FSW then sets out to repair the damage by eliminating certain behaviors. Nevertheless, the process of correcting problems is only one half of the equation in working with families. The other half entails recognizing what is going right, reinforcing those behaviors, and then building on family strengths and competence. Building on strengths will lead to more holistic practice with families. Families will appreciate the recognition of their positive attributes, and having a FSW acknowledge them will enhance the working relationship. It will also build self-esteem and form the basis upon which families can fall back once family work is completed and new difficulties emerge in the future. Later, families can draw on their existing strengths to make changes in family work.

Family social workers can use the ideas of risk, protection, and resilience in their practice in several ways. First, they can look at what risk factors are in play in a particular family. Recognizing risk facts is the first step to removing them. Second, FSWs can determine what factors work to protect the individual or family in that particular circumstance. Nevertheless, Fraser and colleagues strongly caution not to count exclusively on strengths or resilience to overcome adversity because they cannot completely counteract "the poisonous effects of extreme adversity" (Fraser, Richman, & Galinsky, 1999, p. 140).

ECOLOGICAL RISK AND OPPORTUNITIES

Resilience falls under the umbrella of an ecological, developmental, and relational perspective ((Hernandez, 2002). We discuss the ecological approach in Chapters 5 and 10. In this chapter we explore risk and opportunities in the different levels of the ecosystem: the micro-, meso-, macro-, and exosystems.

The family is the first school for young children, and parents are powerful models.

—Alice Sterling Honig (www.Bartleby.com)

MICROSYSTEM

In the *microsystem,* the first layer of relationships is within the family. The first set of relationships is rather small and starts with the primary caretaker, usually the mother. As the child gets older, the range of relationships expands to include fathers, siblings, and extended kin, when available. "We measure the social riches of a child by enduring, reciprocal, multifaceted relationships that emphasize playing, working, and loving" (Garbarino, 1992, p. 22). As a child gets older, his or her skills also grow to envelop peers and family friends. In the words of Marianne Neifert, "The family is both the fundamental unit of society as well as the route of culture." It represents a child's initial source of unconditional love and acceptance and provides lifelong connectedness with others. The family is the first setting in which socialization takes place and where children learn to live with mutual respect for one another. A family is where children learn to display affection, control their tempers, and pick up their toys. Finally, a family can be an ongoing source of encouragement, advocacy, assurance, and emotional refueling that allows children to grow and develop with competence into the larger world and to become all that they can. The family is a microcosm of the outside world where children learn about themselves and others. It is within the family that children learn about love, sex roles, relationships, competence, intimacy, autonomy, and trust" (www.bartleby.com). Garbarino (1992) speaks to the riches of a microsystem when he talks about large numbers of relatives, neighbors, and friends. A rich family is one where relationships are reciprocal, power is balanced, and the emotional climate is warm, responsive, positive, and affectionate (pp. 36–39).

Some families have built-in protective mechanisms that buffer them from the worst effects of a negative experience. Such families appear to surmount the risks and do well when faced with adversity. These families have an ongoing competence in the presence of intense pressure and extraordinary adversity. We are only now beginning to understand how some families are resilient in the face of such odds. Yet others are not only able to overcome trauma; they are sometimes in better shape at the other end. A couple of family qualities emerge when we speak of strengths and resilience. First, these families are flexible. They have the ability to "bounce forward" in spite of needing some assistance during their rough periods. Parents in these families provide firm but flexible leadership during difficult times as well as providing nurturance, protection, and guidance. Second, these families have strong communication and problem-solving abilities that allow them to see crisis situations clearly. At the same time, the family is able to be affectively responsive to one another and problem solve collaboratively. Research also reveals the importance of supportive individuals. Researchers note the importance of warmth, affection, emotional support, and clear-cut, reasonable structure and limits (Walsh, 1998, p. 11).

Strengths in the microsystem might include:

- Strong social networks. Networks can be a source of stress and hurt when relations are troubled, or they can be a powerful and preferred source of help, support, and connectedness.
- A sense of belonging. The most important social unit to belong to is the family. Members feel a connection to families through culture, shared religion, and rituals.
- A microsystem that expands and diversifies as the child develops. A growing child develops a hierarchy of attachment relationships, first through a primary caretaker and then expanding to other members of the primary family, extended kin, neighbors, and friends.
- Sibling relationships can be an important source of support.
- At the individual psychological and biological levels, social skills and problem-solving abilities, emotional intelligence, coping abilities, tenacity, and a sense of humor are important.
- Family characteristics such as cohesion, good community, behavior management skills, and so on.

- Family relationships. Supportive relationships with parents contribute to children who are sociable. Parents set clear and consistent rules. Parents' personal characteristics, parenting styles, disciplinary techniques, interaction patterns, quality of the parent–child attachment, and parental support influence quality of peer relations. Family support is predictive of friendship quality, and both family support and friendship quality are associated with self-esteem. Extended family relations may also help.

> *In truth a family is what you make it. It is made strong, not by the number of heads counted at the dinner table, but by the rituals you help family members create, by the memories you share, by the commitment of time, caring, and love you show to one another, and by the hopes for the future you have as individuals and as a unit.*

—Marge Kennedy (www.Bartleby.com)

Another source of strength and protection is the availability of stability and predictability offered through daily or regular routines and rituals embedded in family and school. These routines and rituals give family members necessary structure and predictability. Family routines are also important because they make daily life safe and dependable. Children must know that meals are going to be provided on a regular basis, the laundry is going to be done, and their parents will be available at a set time to help with homework. Routines have no symbolic importance but provide a secure base from which the child explores the world. Routines are observable and repetitious family behaviors that structure daily life. They differ from rituals in that they do not have the symbolic or emotional significances embedded in rituals.

"Rituals have symbolic significance in that they signify . . . collective identity and continuity" (Sandler et al., 1999, cited in Gilligan, 2004, p. 93). They also help people tune into their deepest spiritual core (Walsh, 1999). The following example illustrates the importance of a family's adherence to a ritual. While sitting in a hair salon, one of the authors overheard another patron speaking about her family rituals. She said, "I think I came from a pretty dysfunctional family, but what kept us going is that our parents took us on picnics every week. I am going to make sure that my kids also experience this ritual because it sure saved my family." What is interesting about this comment is that her family lived in a climate where temperatures can plummet to as a low as 40 below zero—but the family still followed through on its picnic ritual!

As shown by the previous example, rituals help family members develop an identity as a member of a particular family. They also help families make sense of their existence. For example, children seem to be better insulated from parental alcoholism and substance abuse when the family plans and carries out traditional family rituals. These include ceremonies, traditions, and routines, which also signify order and predictability for the child. Family social workers can value and promote opportunities for family members to mark and celebrate their identity as "family" by creating new or restoring lost rituals and routines. Family rituals not associated with a particular family problem (such as alcoholism) buffer a family from assuming a problem-saturated identity.

The role of family rituals as a positive and protective family practice has become evident over the last decade or so. Originating in religious practices, a family ritual is seen as "a symbolic form of communication that, owing to the satisfaction that family members experience through its repetition, is acted out in a systematic fashion over time" (Wolin & Bennet, 1984; cited in Viere, 2001). Like daily routines, family rituals contribute to family stability and predictability. They also give family members an identity and help them feel that they belong to a special family unit. They provide the family an anchor during times when family homeostasis is disrupted. Rituals are used to mark the loss of a life and a loved one (Walsh, 1998), and can be used to bring family members together during difficult times.

Families differ in the degree to which they adhere to rituals. Wolin (1993) casts the performance of rituals on a continuum with one pole representing a family in which there are absolutely no rituals and the other pole representing a family in which rituals are rigidly adhered to. They also suggest that four types of rituals are universal to all families: family celebrations (connected to the larger culture, such as Christmas, Ramadan, or Rosh Hashanah); family traditions (idiosyncratic to a particular family); family life cycle rituals (funerals, weddings, graduations, etc.); and day-to-day life events (dinner, bedtime etc.). Family members see rituals as symbolic.

According to Rappaport (1971), rituals consist of six components:

1. Repetition
2. Acting
3. Special behavior or stylization
4. Order
5. Evocative presentation style
6. Collective dimension

MESOSYSTEM

Parents need all the help they can get. The strongest as well as the most fragile family requires a vital network of social supports.

—Bernice Weissbourd (www.Bartleby.com)

The *mesosystem* involves the relationship between microsystems. One of the most important relationships is that between the family and school. "We measure the richness of mesosystems for the child by the number and quality of connections" (Garbarino, 1992, p. 23). Strong relationships in which important people collaborate with the child's best interest in mind open the world up for the child. The stronger these relationships, the more the child develops skills and abilities to navigate through different systems. Despite the values of independence, no family is an island. When a parent is supported at work, the security and contentment that builds within the parent is brought back home to the family. When a school values a child's input, regardless of ability, the child is happier at home. When a church congregation helps out a family when a member is ill, it relieves the burden of the family. These relationships, according to Garbarino, launch children mindfully and gently into the wider world. Families benefit when the relationships are diverse and collaborative. Communities can enhance family resilience through informal networks, social networks, and intergenerational mentoring relationships to open the space for family to participate in community life, to make significant contributions, and to take on the role of citizen.

Extended family and social support networks can provide a lifeline during times of trouble. These supportive people can give practical and emotional support. They also serve as role models and mentors. Family resilience must be supported by social and institutional policies and practices. The importance of social support networks and ongoing positive relationships, both within the family and outside, cannot be underestimated. As mentioned, it is imperative, during assessment, that FSWs make a point of identifying important people in the social network of families and their members. Important relationships that palliate the effect of stress might include a layer of positive relationships starting with the microsystem and extending to significant others outside the family. These relationships help buffer the damaging effects of trauma and adversity. Gilligan (2004) refers to this as the *scaffolding* of social support (p. 95). Scaffolding is conceptualized as both a web and a support that prevents someone from falling to the ground. It might include:

- A secure attachment to a significant other person. In an ideal world, the significant person is at least one parent but can also be a teacher, sibling, grandparent, or extended kin.
- People getting a sense of belonging to a community, culture, or other important group is also important. School offers many developmental opportunities through academics, sports, and social experiences, and teachers are mentors. Neighborhood social organizations are also invaluable sources of social support and provide a mechanism through which multiple social identities can be played out.
- As children get older, their social network expands beyond the immediate family to include friends, extended family, and teachers.
- Positive role models.

It is necessary that FSWs be aware of and work with this scaffolding of important relationships to support and strengthen their presence and ongoing functioning. Families need ongoing positive relationships with the world outside of the family walls. This includes a multiplicity of role identities and meaningful roles. When people become locked into monotonous roles, they are blocked from reaching a greater potential. Resilience is not about dwelling on problems—it is about realizing potentials. Single roles such as "mother," "student," or "breadwinner" are overly restrictive and isolating. Everyone needs to draw from a range of roles, social identities, and opportunities. FSWs should explore and encourage family connectedness to the community.

Needy neighborhoods can be strengthened through community work. From a social network perspective, family and peer relations are subsystems within a broader social ecology and they serve overlapping and differential functions with respect to child development and well-being (Franco & Levitt, 1998, p. 315). Relationships with professionals may be necessary and important but should never replace natural networks in the family's environment. In addition, Herndandez (2002) encourages the use of the "sheltering power of communities" when working with people from war-torn homelands.

EXOSYSTEM

The family does not participate directly in the *exosystem*, but its effects ripple down to the family and its members. Many of these effects come through social institutions in which families participate: schools, places of employment, churches, the social service network, neighborhoods, the city council, and so on. The city council may decide to put up extra street lights in dangerous neighborhoods or provide before- and after-school programs in local community centers. Schools might decide to provide extra tutoring for students who are struggling with academics. They might develop a zero-tolerance program for bullying. Schools might have cultural heritage days where ethnic and cultural diversity are celebrated. All of these actions will positively affect the well-being of children and their families.

MACROSYSTEM

In the *macrosystem,* larger social values create social "blueprints" (Garbarino, 1992, p. 45). Macrosystem values filter down through the various layers of the ecosystem to guide philosophies and behaviors. Social policies reflect the larger social mores. The bureaucracies and organizations of helping are often diametrically opposed to a strengths orientation (Saleebey, 1996, p. 297)—their preferred language is disease and problems. Discover the wholeness of the person. "Pursuing a practice based on the ideas of resilience, rebound, possibility, and transformation is difficult because, oddly enough, it is not natural to the world of helping and service (Garbarino, 1992, p. 297).

Political parties are about social philosophies: Should we invest in the army or should we invest in health care? Do we believe in the survival of the financially fittest? Does helping out disadvantaged families only make them more dependent or does it create a solid base for children to overcome the effects of an impoverished environment? Some of society's greatest social concerns are being fought out at the political level. How informed are voters? Some people seem to vote according to multigenerational family habits rather than really being informed of the issues. According to Garbarino, "the available data suggest that the greatest danger to children's moral development lies in the totalitarian society that commands total allegiance to the state" (1992, p. 47). The influence of the media is so pervasive that it is invisible. An important question about the media is, "In whose interest does it serve?" The media in many countries provide biased perspectives on the news and seldom look outside a country's borders to offer a range of perspectives apart from the existing party line. Therefore, the media can be a handmaiden to totalitarianism. Inasmuch as a family is enriched by diversity and strength of the relationships it has with the surrounding environment, a macrosystem is also enriched by a diversity of views. Diversity of perspectives respects pluralism.

The ecological model details how strengths and opportunities are embedded within a social context. Next we discuss the concept of risk.

RISK

In the preceding section we examined layers of the ecosystem and identified opportunities for children and their families. Risk also exists in each layer. *Risk* refers to how likely it is that an individual or family will experience a probable adverse event (Fraser, Richman, & Galinsky, 1999). A variety of factors contribute to the risk of a problem developing. For example, risk factors associated with child abuse might include caretaker depression, social isolation from friends and family, high rates of stress, lack of parenting skills, loose family boundaries (for offenders outside the family), substance abuse, and inappropriate expectations of children.

Let us now look at child sexual abuse as an example. Finklehor (1986) identifies four preconditions for child sexual abuse: a motivation to sexually abuse, overcoming internal inhibitors, overcoming external inhibitors, and overcoming child resistance. Each of these factors contributes to the risk of sexual abuse happening and together these factors comprise the risk set within the microsystem of the family. Other risk factors exist at other layers of the ecosystem. We discuss these in more detail later.

1. The offender's *motivation to abuse* must be dealt with as an individual issue that is probably beyond the expertise of the family social worker. Deviant sexual arousal will be an important focus of intervention, as will issues such as the offender's own history as a victim of abuse. Motivation to sexually abuse can be a powerful factor in sexual abuse; in fact, it is the first and foremost risk factor. Not everyone who is motivated to abuse actually abuses.

2. Addressing the offender's likelihood of *overcoming internal inhibitions* falls under the purview of a specialist, particularly when the offender has problems with substance abuse, impulse control, or psychopathology. However, the family social worker can convey to the offender that the behavior is unacceptable and that the role of the FSW is to protect the child. Potential offenders must overcome their inhibitions, and substance abuse is a powerful disinhibitor. Someone who is not inclined to sexually abuse a child would probably not do so when under the influence. We recall one stepfather who sexually abused his stepdaughter for a number of years. In therapy, he claimed he was not responsible because he was drinking at the time. The family social worker told him, "I am really glad you told me that. We now have two problems to work with—your sexual attraction to children and your drinking!"

3. The next precondition is to overcome *external impediments*—for example, another parent in the family might be present and prevent any opportunities from arising. Environmental impediments to abuse can be strengthened by building into the family necessary structures and mechanisms with

which to address the other three predispositions. This can involve teaching family members to respect personal privacy and personal boundaries. Social isolation of the family should also be addressed. Other siblings in the family should be told about the abuse (when they are old enough to understand) in order to break the secret, to see if they have been abused also, and to add another dimension of monitoring in the family. Family members can be taught about healthy sexuality and respect for gender differences. Empowerment of the nonoffending parent also is crucial.

4. *Child resistance* is another point of intervention that can be targeted by the family social worker. Children can be taught about sexual abuse and taught how to be more assertive. Children can also learn to tell someone about the abuse (preferably the nonoffending parent) or another person who will act on the information. The child's relationship with a nonoffending parent can also be strengthened to create an ally for the child.

We see from this model where several layers of risk lie. The most blatant risk is the motivation to abuse. The other factors revolve around this particular risk. Intervention for the other three factors will be rather weak and even dangerous if worked with singly, when the first precondition has not been addressed. Some of these factors work independently. Some people and some theories have placed responsibility further down the risk continuum—for example, blaming mothers for the abuse. Another case example was when a family social worker was called by child protection. A young girl's mother had just started living with a man who was released from a forensic hospital for treatment of pedophilia. Child welfare called the agency requesting that counselors see the young girl to build in protection skills. This was clearly not a viable plan when the young girl was living in the same household as a sexual abuse perpetrator.

We need to be aware of the tendency to assign risk too narrowly. Instead, it is necessary to cast our nets wider, into the other three levels of the ecosystem. For example, some families are cut off from relationships outside the family. In fact, some intrafamilial sexual abuse perpetrators and domestic violence abusers purposely control who members of the family have contact with. This behavior has the effect of cutting off family members from important relationships and information, removing the abusers from detection by the outside world. At the same time, this social isolation removes from the victims potential sources of support. This is one example of how important the mesosystem is. When a victim has a trusted teacher or coach outside the family, the opportunities for rescue are increased.

Several other examples of risk exist in the exo and macro levels. While much has been written about sexual abuse from all these different levels of the system, we give only a couple of examples here. Some practices exist in the exosystem level that might increase the risk of sexual abuse within the family. One is the decision by schools *not* to provide sex education to children, particularly when sex education includes a sexual abuse prevention component. We recall one community where the provision of sex education in the schools was proposed, which some fundamentalist groups were opposing. There were quite a few heated meetings in the community about the proposed programs. One leading opponent of the program suggested that teaching children to say no is the start of anarchy in the family because parents lose their authority over them. Eventually the program went ahead, but children were required to get parental permission to participate. This is only one example of risk in the exosystem. Can you think of other examples?

Much has also been written about the impact of macrosystem values on sexual abuse of children. The sexualization of children in the media is but one example. Patriarchy—in which male power is engrained in the social structure, giving males authority over women and children—is another example. Perhaps when Freud wrote about the Oedipal and Electra complexes, he was speaking more about the society in which he lived and less about the children who were sexually abused. Given this brief discussion about risks embedded in the ecosystem, it should be clear that assessment of risk can be quite complex. Every problem that a FSW will see in family work will be associated with a different range of risk factors—and this is where theory and research come into play.

Fraser and his colleagues (1999) caution that there is no single or direct path leading to the risk of something negative happening. However, the risk of a negative event occurring might increase as the number of factors accumulates. Possibly, the more risk factors that exist, the greater the risk of something happening. Therefore, the FSW might be able to lower the risk of an adverse event happening by intervening with some of the key risk factors that exist in a family. In the case of child abuse, the FSW might be able to teach parents new child management techniques, increase the level of social support, and help parents manage stress better. In Chapter 11 we present ways to improve parenting skills through the use of behavioral management principles. By now, most people know about the television *Super Nanny* who comes into the family home and teaches parenting techniques for very difficult child behavior. Better parenting skills might decrease the risk of child abuse or more averse child outcomes when the child gets older. When a contributing factor is stress, the FSW will work with the family to understand the source of the stress and then help the family to alleviate the stress. This might occur through relaxation training and/or helping the unemployed parent conduct a job search.

The relative influence of a risk factor varies depending upon the particular characteristics of the individuals and family. Some individuals have a high tolerance for risk factors while for others, the same risk factor might be crippling. Some people, for example, require inordinate amounts of social support from formal social agencies to function, while others are content to receive the support of one or two people. Therefore, some individuals and families are more vulnerable to negative influences. A child with a good friendship network might be less vulnerable to family conflict than a child who is isolated or rejected by his or her peer group.

As with support, risk factors are distributed throughout the ecological levels: the micro-, meso-, macro-, and exosystems. When looking at the family's ecological niche, it is also important to recognize how risk and opportunities are also distributed throughout the family's ecological network. Problems arise in the interaction of individual and family vulnerability and the impact of stressful life experiences and social contexts. Symptoms may lie in biological or sociocultural variables, creating family stress and dysfunction. Distress occurs when attempts to deal with the situation become overwhelming. The levels ecological systems are nested systems for nurturing and reinforcing resilience.

- Risk factors may be time-limited or continue. Risk contains many components: it is not certain, but is based on chance; risk is linked to harmful outcomes but not in a direct cause and effect relationship; it is a relative concept, from indicators of modestly harmful situations to those that are markers of life-threatening situations.
- Risks interrelate and are collective.
- Risk factors change with age.
- Risk may reflect structural qualities.
- Risk assessment is a prophetic tool with limits.

Based on the preceding list, it is evident that some individuals are more protected than others from the same adverse event. These are known as protective factors, and they help the individual or family compensate or overcome the negative impact of an event. In much the same way that risk factors can be cumulative, protective factors can also be cumulative.

CULTURE

Overcoming challenges is more difficult when families also face racism or poverty (Hernandez, 2002). For too long, people have been discriminated against on the basis of ethnicity and culture, and the two are related. The history of cultures and ethnicities around the world bears testament to unscrupulous regimes using culture as an excuse for oppression, discrimination, and genocide. The Holocaust, slavery, and the conquering and genocide of Aboriginal peoples across the globe are but a few examples of "man's inhumanity to man." We would like to deceive ourselves that these events occurred in another place and another time, but on a smaller scale, oppression and discrimination are occurring at home and in the present. In the face of these inhumanities, culture has provided scaffolding to those who have suffered. An examination of the history of oppression and the response to it reveals that culture has given people an identity, a community, a sense of belonging, and ways to manage lives in the face of extreme diversity.

Culture provides families with a sense of identity, a sense of belonging, and a sense of continuity. By belonging to a particular culture, people also have a natural group to reach out to in times of distress. It is therefore important that FSWs develop an awareness of their biases and ethnocentric views so that they can recognize the possibilities of strength in culturally diverse families. Historically, the approach to teaching cultural sensitivity and competence has been to offer a "laundry list" of characteristics to help workers understand the different cultures they may encounter. We now know that culture is far too complex to be understood in terms of checklists. Checklists reduce culture to a static entity rather than a dynamic and living process affecting everything from worldview, to communication styles, to food preferences, to beliefs about family. In fact, culture has many dimensions. Elsewhere (Coleman, Collins, & Collins, 2005), we attempted to identify the different dimensions of culture. We see these dimensions as strengths upon which families can develop an identity, build routines and rituals, and make valuable social connections. In the following section we build on the dimensions of culture to illustrate the strengths and risks embedded in each.

Family social workers must be able to work with clients from diverse ethnic and cultural backgrounds. Culture and ethnicity are related but not interchangeable concepts: "Culture refers to the culmination of values, beliefs, customs, and norms that people have learned, usually in the context of their family and community. Ethnicity relates to a client's identity, commitment, and loyalty to an ethnic group" (Jordan & Franklin, 1995, p. 169). Awareness of the historical background of different ethnic groups is important, as is knowledge of the customs and beliefs shared by members of each group.

The dimensions of culture include the following (Coleman, Collins, & Collins, 2005):

1. *Cultural identity:* All people identify with a particular culture. For example, Ho (1987) discusses five unifying values of the various Hispanic subgroups, though each group has distinct differences due to the melding of their Hispanic culture with that of various indigenous Indian groups. (List headings are from Ho, 1987, pp. 14–18; explanations have been paraphrased by the authors.) These five values include:
   a) *Familism:* A sense of family obligation and pride.
   b) *Personalism:* A value placed on the inner qualities of the individual's uniqueness and goodness. (*Machismo*, a related concept, refers to the male's sense of self-assurance and calm when threatened.)
   c) *Hierarchy:* A value based on social class position, including a patriarchal structure.
   d) *Spiritualism:* A belief in good and bad spirits that intervene in one's life.
   e) *Fatalism:* A belief that one cannot master the world and that one's destiny is inevitable (Ho, in Jordan & Franklin, 1995).
2. *Belief systems:* Peoples' beliefs govern their actions, but are beliefs learned through a thoughtful process of evaluation or are they propagated onto us? Certainly religion and culture have a tremendous impact on our beliefs. We might think our parents have a great influence on our belief system, but where did their beliefs come from? The impact of mass media cannot be overlooked. Beliefs about body image, type of clothes to wear, music to listen to, and so on have all been targeted by mass media. "Healthy" families have been depicted on TV shows such as *The Cosby Show* or *The Brady Bunch,* yet these depictions may be a far cry from reality and only create some mental anguish in our beliefs. An example of

incongruent reality is: Islam teaches its followers to be nonviolent, yet some people discriminate against followers of Islamic teachings and believe that they are violent people. It is very important for the FSW to take the time to find out key beliefs of family members and help these members evaluate how these beliefs are helping them or not helping them cope in our modern Western society. On another level, many minorities face war and political oppression from their homelands. Hernandez (2002) encourages workers to help people make sense out of their struggles through the development of consciousness and making meaning to inspire a sense of hope. Making meaning out of hope is also Walsh's (1998) focus.

3. *Differences between and within groups:* No culture is homogeneous. Although we refer to the "dominant" or "mainstream" culture, it is apparent that many belief systems exist in this dominant culture. But adherence to the primary beliefs demonstrates the level of belonging one feels to that particular culture. People from different cultures also differ on the extent to which they are acculturated into the dominant culture. Some people may draw strength from their cultural traditions, while others are more biculturally competent and are able to navigate different cultures with relative ease.

4. *Worldview:* Worldview gives people a way of understanding and operating in the world. For example, Ho (1987) describes the African American family as stressing "collectivity, sharing, affiliation, deference to authority, spirituality, and respect for the elderly" (p. 188). Similarly, members of different Native American tribes hold different beliefs, but there are certain common beliefs that distinguish Native Americans from members of other cultures (Ho, 1987). One of these shared beliefs is that nature is important. Native Americans believe that they are one part of the whole and they strive to appreciate and maintain a balance with other living things. Native Americans believe that all growing things and animals have spirits or souls that should be respected. The respect for nature leads the Native American to view time in terms of natural cycles or seasons. Furthermore, sharing is a traditional Native American practice, which includes bestowing one's belongings on others to honor them or to honor deceased relatives. Native American children learn to respect others' rights to be or do as they wish, and not to interfere with others. The Native American believes in good triumphing over evil; therefore, people are viewed as primarily good. Religious beliefs vary among the different tribes, but a similar emphasis is placed on rituals and ceremonies. Tribal medicine people may be consulted for treatment of physical and mental problems, rather than physicians or other health professionals. Hernandez (2002) suggests that the "psychology of liberation" can help families deal with adversity.

5. *History of a culture, including history of colonization:* Through a culture's history, people come to know who they are and how they arrived at various points in time. African Americans were uprooted from their homelands and brought to this country involuntarily, and they have experienced more societal discrimination than most other ethnic groups. Through the

harshness of their history, they have developed skills to rise above difficulties imposed on them by their oppressors. Hill (in Jordan, Lewellen, & Vandiver, 1994) identified six survival skills utilized by African Americans in a hostile society:

a) Strong kinship bonds;
b) Strong education and work achievement orientation;
c) Flexibility in family roles;
d) Commitment to religious values and church participation;
e) A humanistic orientation; and
f) Endurance of suffering.

6. *Communicating meaning and the use of language including self-expressiveness:* Perhaps one of the major sources of intercultural misunderstanding occurs because of miscommunication, yet cultures share common communication styles. Ethnic minority people using social services from agencies where there is no bilingual helper are at risk of being misunderstood or even assessed incorrectly. Use of interpreters can be problematic. For example, asking a bilingual child to interpret between the family social worker and an elderly family member can disrupt the traditional hierarchical structure of the family by putting the child in a position of power. At the same time, it may also breach generational boundaries between parents and children.

7. *History of migration:* It is very interesting to explore with families the history of their migration to this country. What were their hopes and expectations on coming here? Have they been met? There is a great deal of bravery involved in leaving behind your country of origin to move to another country that is thousands of miles away. For many immigrants, there are few family relations, friends, and other social supports in their new community. Many have to overcome language barriers, job skill challenges, and potential discrimination. The resilience of these new immigrants needs to be celebrated in family work.

8. *Beliefs about family, family structure, and kinship bonds:* The concept of "family" is expressed differently in different cultures. Ho (in Jordan, Lewellen, & Vandiver, 1994) calls attention to the high ratio of female-headed households among African American families. One cause may be high mortality rates of African American males. Consequently, families tend toward egalitarian sharing of roles. Mothers often shoulder the economic, breadwinner burden, as well as taking responsibility for childcare. The extended family network is likely to be involved in supporting the family, as is the church "family."

Similarities across subcultures may be seen in the Hispanic American family structure. For instance, the individual's needs are viewed as secondary to those of the family (Jordan, Lewellen, & Vandiver, 1994). The family system is patriarchal and hierarchical; the father is the head of the household and the parents have authority over the children. Belief in the intervention of good or bad spirits leads families to attribute mental illness to bad spirits and to rely on help from folk healers and priests.

The structure of Asian American families is hierarchical and patriarchal. Confucian philosophy and ethics "specify a familial hierarchy which demands loyalty, respect, and obedience, especially to the parents" (Jordan, Lewellen, & Vandiver, 1994). Time orientation is toward the past and present rather than toward the future. Ancestors are important to their surviving family members in that members strive to perpetuate the family's good name. Parents are influential in mate selection. Children respect and obey their parents, and wives respect and obey their husbands. The wife may have low status in the family, but educational attainment may raise her status. Families are maintained by a sense of obligation, and consequently undergo shame or loss of face if family expectations are not met. Siblings have special roles and obligations according to birth order, with the eldest son obliged to provide a home for his widowed mother. The eldest son carries the highest status among the siblings; the youngest daughter may be obliged to care for her elderly parents. Children in the roles of eldest son and youngest daughter have higher rates of stress-related illness than other children, reflecting the strains involved in carrying out their familial obligations.

In Native American families, extended family networks (which may include non-kin namesakes) are important. These groups may or may not live together in one household, but extended family groups provide support for Native American families. Support may be in the form of modeling marital and parental roles. Traditionally, marriages were arranged by two families, with the husband joining the wife's household but retaining authority with his own kin. Spousal interactions were not intimate, with the wife having lower status than her husband, to whom she was to be supportive and submissive. Today, the level of acculturation influences marital relationships. Native Americans who are most acculturated to the majority society have the most egalitarian spousal relationships. Intermarriage is common between members of different Native American groups, and between Native Americans and members of other racial groups. Divorce and remarriage are acceptable practices in Native American society. In some tribes, polygamous relationships are accepted.

9. *Beliefs about children and child rearing:* Every culture has a unique approach to childrearing. In African American families, children are treated in an egalitarian fashion and given responsibility based on age. The oldest child may be responsible for looking after younger sisters and brothers. In Native American families, children are seen as important to the renewal of tribal life, and historically have held high status. Children are disciplined and taught by extended family members in an egalitarian fashion. Corporal punishment is not used; rather, "observation and participation" (Ho, 1987) are preferred child rearing techniques. In the extended family environment, the child is surrounded by many siblings and cousins, with the older children often caring for and teaching the younger children.

10. *Family life cycle issues and cultural rituals related to life cycle:* As mentioned in this chapter, family rituals including rituals associated with

culture are important sources of family strength and resilience, offering a group identity. Some cultural rituals celebrate certain life cycle events such as weddings, funerals, and births. In addition, in some cultures, different expectations accompany the various phases of the family life cycle, such as when to leave home, whom to involve in childcare, and so on.

11. *Partnering:* The subtle and not so subtle messages about how we find a partner often have a lot to do with our cultural background. An enjoyable movie about this issue is *My Big Fat Greek Wedding,* a comedy about the family pressures to marry someone Greek, although the bride married a non-Greek. Not only is it worthwhile to explore a person's beliefs about whom they hope to partner with, but also the extended family's beliefs.

12. *Gender roles:* In Chapter 12 we explore gender issues, including gender roles. We form our beliefs on gender roles from our parents, historical context, and current social attitudes—often propagated from the mass media. Do people take on traditional gender roles? What about the new age role like the metro sexual male? Where did a person get his or her gender role beliefs? Is the person making changes to accommodate these modern times?

13. *Social values, sense of community, and social supports:* Some cultures support "rugged individualism" while others greatly value loyalty to the community. Native Americans display a cooperative spirit when interacting with others, rather than a competitive orientation. "This concept of collaterality reflects the integrated view of the universe where all people, animals, plants, and objects in nature have their place in creating a harmonious whole" (Ho, 1987).

14. *Religion and spirituality:* Religion and spirituality are important aspects of family life. We discuss these aspects briefly in this section. (For a more comprehensive discussion of religion and the family, we refer students to Walsh, 1999). Religion and family life are often deeply intertwined, and a system of values and "shared beliefs that transcend the limits of a family's experience and knowledge enables family members to better accept the inevitable risks and losses in living and loving fully" (Walsh, 1999, p. 9). Religion helps families construct or enact rituals about marriage, birth, and death that mark progression through the family life cycle. Ethnicity and religion have a tenuous link, and it is imperative that workers do not assume that the two are interchangeable. In working with the religious or spiritual dimensions of families, workers must struggle with several issues. First, they must respect families whose religious or spiritual teachings differ from their own. Second, they must find a balance in working with the family in a way that beliefs are respected, but not at the cost of family members. Perhaps this latter issue underscores the historic reluctance of helpers to enter the religious world of clients. Religion has also taken on a negative note for family workers who may have been taught that there is only one true religion (theirs!) or who may be skeptical about religion and how it has sown the seeds of national and international conflicts. Others may struggle

with the tenets of any religion that discriminates or oppresses others, such as women and gays—particularly the more conservative creeds.

Religion and spirituality often go hand-in-hand with a particular culture. Religion and spirituality are related but distinct expressions. Religion is seen as extrinsic (being imposed from outside as through religious institutions), while spirituality is intrinsic (coming from within). Religious practices serve the function of supporting family cohesion through family rituals and customs associated with religious holidays. "If, as many social scientists argue, religion has to do with two major foci of concerns—*personal meaning* and *social belonging*—then most certainly it is around the first of these that religious energies revolve primarily today" (Roof, 1999, cited in Wendel, 2003, p. 172). The concept of *lived religion* tries to understand the space between official religions and the day-to-day experience of people and is considered to be the concrete expression of the personal and sacred dimensions of human life (Wendel, 2003, pp. 173–175). In many ways, personal religion is a subjective and personal experience, although intricately tied into the institutional expressions of religion.

In some ways, religion is an institutional manifestation of ethnic and cultural heritage. Even though people are free to convert, they usually follow the religious teaching of their parents. For many years, the helping professions viewed religion as either a form of pathology to treat or something that was best left outside the therapeutic process (Wendel, 2003, p. 165). These days, spirituality is viewed from quite a different angle. In many circles, religion and spirituality are regarded as important dimensions of family work. In assessment and intervention, it is important to take both the religious and spiritual dimensions of a family into account. Addressing spirituality shows respect for a diversity of beliefs and practices. The key is to not impose religious beliefs on clients. This might be difficult since one of the tenets of many religions, Christianity in particular, is to preach to the unconverted. Family social workers should keep their religious beliefs out of family social work. The purpose is not to determine how religious a particular family is—rather, the purpose of asking is to find out about the family's world and what beliefs, social networks, and rituals guide its passage through the life cycle (Wiggins Frame, 2000). Church may be considered part of the family's extended family.

It is important to respect clients' religion and spirituality (Murray, 2002). Religion and spirituality both play a major role in clients' decisions, thoughts, and feelings about particular issues such as divorce, abortion, role of women, and child rearing. According to Walsh (1998), "suffering invites us into the spiritual domain" (p. 71). For some families, divorce can be a spiritual issue. Intermarriage of two people from different religious backgrounds can also be challenging to relationships. When we say that different religions and spiritual beliefs affect family life, we are entering into murky waters.

Research indicates that religion is a prominent factor in family relationships (Marks, 2004). Three dimensions of religious experience (religious beliefs, religious practices, and religious community) correlate with higher marital quality, stability, satisfaction, and parental involvement. There is also a connection between certain expressions of religiosity and such undesirable outcomes as prejudice, authoritarianism, abuse, and tolerance for abuse. Nevertheless, shared religious activities can contribute to intimacy and commitment in marriage. Religious practices contribute to the creation of family rituals. "Acknowledging that religion is vital to some families is one issue, but arguing that therapists *should* include and address religion in a substantive way is another . . ." (Marks, 2004, p. 228).

Asian American families usually share Confucian and Buddhist philosophies and ethics. They value living in harmony with nature and fostering interpersonal relationships. Buddhism encourages "harmonious living involving compassion, a respect for life, and moderation in behavior; self-discipline, patience, modesty, and friendliness, as well as selflessness" (Ho, 1987, p. 25).

Frame (2001) recommends developing a spiritual genogram with families for whom religion and spirituality play an important role. Such a genogram will depict a visual history of how spiritual and religious issues across generations continue to shape and affect the client's beliefs and values. When focusing a genogram on religion or spirituality, it is important to look at the family history of denomination, interfaith marriages, baptisms, first communions, events in religious communities, stable and unstable affiliations, religious closeness, divorces, religious messages, and so on. He cautions family workers to know their own religious beliefs and attitudes before working on them with others.

Spirituality provides meaning and purpose beyond ourselves, our families, our troubles. Suffering can be a spiritual issue and spirituality can help create meaning for human troubles. Spiritual resources such as prayer and meditation or the support of a spiritual or religious community can provide strength during difficult times. Crisis can help give a clear moral compass and make relationships more meaningful. Creative changes arise out of a crisis.

Discussing spirituality can create anxiety in students and seasoned practitioners about how to work with family spirituality, especially given the great diversity both within and between religions. We urge students to assume a humble and not-knowing stance, one that is equally applicable to working with cultural diversity and working with religious diversity. Griffith (1999) recommends the following stance in working with a family:

- Do not assume that you know what God means to a particular family, even if you are of the same religion.
- Do not assume that you know what a family's language about God means.
- Do not assume that a family must have the same image of God that you do.
- Do not use psychological theory to explain another's belief in God.

15. *Cultural expressions related to dress, food, music, and the arts:* Again, shared cultural expressions related to aesthetic concerns give families a sense of belonging and stability. In recent years, mainstream society has

developed a great appreciation for ethnic food. At the same time, clothing may be different and have religious or social significance.

16. *Work, education, and social class:* Social class (level of education, income, standing in the community) is important to assess, as higher status usually leads to a higher level of well-being and greater access to a range of resources. In some cases, however, families may be discriminated against by the dominant culture despite their high social standing, while at the same time being rejected by other members of their ethnic group because of their high level of acculturation into the mainstream culture. This places them in double jeopardy.

17. *Beliefs about social troubles and help-seeking behavior, including the use of indigenous and traditional healing practices:* Studies in ethnicity reveal that people differ in:
    - Their experience of emotional pain;
    - What they label as a symptom;
    - How they communicate about their pain or symptoms;
    - Their beliefs about the cause of the difficulties;
    - Their attitudes toward helpers; and,
    - The intervention they expect (McGoldrick & Giordano, 1996, p. 9).

Family social workers must be careful not to stereotype people, because individual differences exist among people of similar ethnic and cultural backgrounds. Some of these differences may be related to varying levels of acculturation. Still, certain characteristics distinguish ethnic minority cultures from the dominant or majority white middle-class culture in the United States and Canada.

1. *Ethnic minority reality:* Members of ethnic minority groups often experience poverty and racial discrimination, resulting in under-utilization of social services. Poverty and discrimination are risk factors in the macro- and exosystems that permeate a family's everyday life. These risk factors create vulnerability to stress and adversity impinging on the individual and family. The Hispanic American population has a higher percentage of poor and unemployed members than the other groups discussed here (Ho, 1987).

2. *Impact of external system on minority cultures:* Ethnic minority values may conflict with those of the majority culture on issues such as exerting control versus living in harmony with the environment, orientation to time (past, present, future), "doing" versus "being" orientation, individual autonomy versus collectivity, and the importance of nuclear versus extended family relationships.

3. *Biculturalism:* The ethnic minority person belongs to two cultures. The level of acculturation into the dominant culture is an important aspect of the assessment of families seeking outside intervention.

4. *Ethnic differences in minority status:* The status of various ethnic minority groups differs. Some groups experience more discrimination than others. For instance, refugees may receive better treatment than the descendants of

slaves do. Skin color is another determinant of status; visible minorities often experience more severe societal discrimination.

Acculturation varies among members of tribal groupings of Native Americans. Some live on reservations in primarily rural areas, where they remain isolated and may speak little English. At the other extreme are families living in urban areas, separated from their Indian heritage and totally acculturated into the majority culture. In between those two extremes are families who try to maintain a balance between their ancestral heritage and the culture of the dominant society (Ho, 1987). The family social worker must be sensitive to each family's level of acculturation, while remaining aware of Native Americans' unique historical background.

FAMILY RESILIENCE

In the field of family therapy, we have come to realize that successful interventions depend as much on the resources of the family as on the skills of the therapist.

—Froma Walsh, 1999

Most research on resilience has focused on individuals. Walsh (2003) observed that some families are shattered by crisis while others emerge strengthened and more resourceful after a crisis. Resilience in families refers to coping and adaptational processes within the family *as a functional unit* (Walsh, 1998, p. 14). Such families are able to achieve positive and unexpected outcomes when faced with adversity. Moreover, stressors affect children to the extent that they disrupt crucial family processes and relationships (Patterson, 1983, cited in Walsh, 1998). Other words to describe resilience include "self-righting capacity," and "responding with resourcefulness and tenacity when encountering extreme challenges." "To be resilient, one must be exposed to risk and then respond successfully" (Fraser, Richmond, & Galinsky, 1999, p. 137). Resilience is a dynamic process that includes a broad "class of phenomena involving successful adaptation in the context of significant threats to development" and other life course outcomes (p. 138). Resiliency is often equated with the ability to "spring back" or to rebound. Others view resilience as the ability to negotiate significant developmental challenges that confront individuals as they grow. Other definitions include: coping in the face of adversity or risk (Fraser, Richmond, & Galinsky, 1999; Walsh, 1998). The paradox of resilience is that the worst of times can also bring out our best" (Walsh, 1998, p. 10).

Resilience is not the blithe denial of difficult life experiences, pains, and scars. It is the ability to trudge on in spite of these. As much as trauma is unpleasant, it can also be instructive and chastening (Saleebey, 1996, p. 299). Resilience is the continuing identification of capacities and knowledge derived from the interplay of risks and protections in the world. No family is ever free from stress or problems. A healthy family is not a problem-free family—if that were the case, there would be no healthy families. All families face demands, stresses, challenges, and opportunities. The FSW must discard beliefs that trauma leads to pathology and that a toxic environment will necessarily lead to immutable difficulties. Believe that families have the capability to self-correct.

Resilient families have strength when under stress, when in crisis, and this strength helps them overcome adversity. Previously, families were considered to be contributors to risk but not to resilience. "Resilience came to be viewed in terms of an interplay of multiple risk and protective processes over time, involving individual, family, and larger sociocultural influences" (Walsh, 2003, p. 2). Resilient families function well despite the risk factors they face. Believing in strength and resilience can help family workers join with family members who are averse to labels of pathology.

Resilience is a complex process involving the biological, psychological, and social factors that fight against the negative effects of stressful events and help families and individuals adapt to difficult life events. The hallmarks of resilience are initiative and perseverance and are maintained by hope and confidence. Hinton (2003) argues that the need for risk and protection must exist for resilience to be realized. Both individuals and systems can be resilient and include (1) the ability to change or adapt to negative life circumstances— overcoming the odds, (2) the capacity to bounce back—sustained competence under stress, and (3) the ability for a firm engagement with the risk factor under question (Hinton, p. 38), recovery from trauma, and successful adaptation despite adversity.

When assessing a family from a resilience framework, the FSW will therefore need to blend an ecological and developmental perspective to understand family functioning within the context of the broader sociocultural environment. Because resilience is a *process* rather than a static characteristic or cluster of traits, it best emerges within supportive contexts and relationships. Resilience involves the interaction between nature and nurture. Family social workers who work with resilience are keenly attuned to the central importance of significant relationships with kin, intimate partners, and mentors such as coaches or teachers, who support efforts, believe in potential, and encourage them to make the most of their lives (Walsh, 2003, p. 2). A family resilience perspective recognizes parental strengths and potential limitations. Recognizing both strengths and limitations balances assessment and family work. It requires changing the deficit-based lens perspective that views people as damaged or dysfunctional to viewing them as challenged by life situations.

Resilience is more than having the ability to manage difficult challenges, shouldering a burden or surviving an ordeal (Walsh, 2003, p. 13). Embedded in resilience is the potential for personal and relational transformation and growth that rises out of successfully dealing with adversity. One central tenet of both crisis theory and resilience theory is that families can emerge stronger and more resourceful after a crisis because dealing successfully with one situation generates the ability to deal with similar difficulties in the future. That is, families learn skills in one crisis that can be transferred to similar situations in the future.

Walsh (1999, p. 24) offers a framework with which to understand family resilience:

KEYS TO FAMILY RESILIENCE

Family Belief Systems

- Making meaning of adversity
- Positive outlook
- Transcendence and spirituality

Organizational Patterns

- Flexibility
- Connectedness
- Social and economic resources

Communication Processes

- Clarity
- Open emotional expression
- Collaborative problem solving

Walsh (1998, pp. 45–78) contends that family belief systems are the "heart and soul" of resilience. They include making meaning of adversity, having a positive outlook, and transcendence and spirituality. Each of these areas is discussed briefly in the following list. For a more in-depth discussion we refer you to her book.

- *Making meaning of diversity:* Families must believe in the importance of the family, and the family must provide caring for its members. Crisis then becomes a shared challenge in which each family member contributes to its solution. Members believe in one another and they also believe in the family. They also trust one another. Resilient families are also in a continuous process of growth and change throughout the family life cycle and accept the fluid and ever-changing nature of the family. Family social workers need to understand the "meaning of family" for each of the members. Through ongoing family transactions, they try to make sense of adversity, and how they make sense of it will determine what they do about it. Difficulties emerge when families become locked into a rigid explanation or belief.
- *Positive outlook:* For resilient families, crises are seen as challenges and opportunities that they will overcome the through perseverance. Such families endure hardship courageously and hold onto hope and the belief that things will be better in the future. Mistakes then become a launching ground from which new learning springs. In addition, humor within the family aids coping. According to Walsh (1998), resilient families, as the "Serenity Prayer" exhorts, take initiative to deal with their problems but accept what they cannot change.
- *Transcendence, spirituality, and transformation:* Transcendent beliefs provide meaning and purpose beyond our selves, our families, and our

adversities (Walsh, 1998, p. 68). As mentioned previously in this chapter, families also fare best when they are connected to larger supportive social systems. Spirituality, also discussed earlier, can also give families the tools and belief systems with which to deal with adversity. Finally, families can learn and grow through struggles and pain.

Walsh (1998) also discusses "family shock absorbers": flexibility; stability; capacity for change; counterbalancing stability and change; connectedness; balancing unity and separateness; clear boundaries; and shared leadership providing nurturance, protection, and guidance.

STRENGTHS: CREATING AN ECOLOGICAL NICHE

Strengths based, resilience oriented approaches are needed to shift focus from how families have failed to how they can succeed.
—Froma Walsh, 1998

Family strengths-based practice is defined as "the set of relationships and processes that support and protect families and family members, especially in times of adversity and strengths" (Myers, 2003). Gilligan (2004) suggests that sometimes clients may be competent and successful in facets of their lives that we fail to see. Being able to identify and work with family strengths is both an attitude and a skill. Saleebey suggests that "strengths may lie in unlikely places." Develop an awareness and respect for positive qualities and abilities, talents, resources. Marsh (2003) suggests the need for concrete tools with which to recognize family strengths. In Chapter 5 we presented the family categories schema used to identify how families are functioning in the areas of: (1) problem solving, (2) affective responsiveness, (3) affective involvement, (4) communication, (5) role behavior, (6) autonomy, (7) modes of behavioral control, and (8) general functioning. This framework can help family social workers focus on the positive qualities of a family by identifying strengths and challenges.

As such, family strengths might include such relationship qualities as closeness, concern, caring, and positive communication. Families are able to draw on successful coping strategies to manage challenges and stresses in daily life. Factors related to positive child development include parental well-being, including physical and mental health, common shared family activities such as household chores and routines, parental involvement in children's activities, positive communication patterns. These are all factors captured in the family categories schema discussed in Chapter 5.

Walsh (1998) adds several other qualities to this list:

- Crediting positive intentions.
- Praising efforts and achievements.
- Drawing out hidden resources and lost competence.
- Finding strengths in the midst of adversity.
- Building empathic connections with and between family members.

All of these qualities fit well into the areas covered by the categories schema. FSWs should keep their eyes and their ears open to identifying strengths alongside of assessing problems.

One pitfall of professional helpers is to view themselves as the most important influence in a family's life. Gilligan (2004) agrees, arguing that help flows from many sources. The role of the FSW is to help release positive processes that are trapped behind a wall of despair and feelings of being overwhelmed. Reflecting on the work from Miller, Hubble, and Duncan (1995), we point out that while the quality of the relationship with the worker is an important contributor of change, the most powerful influences on the change process are client factors. Some of these factors have been discussed in this chapter, and they include personal characteristics, belief systems as well as a strong social support network. This means that FSWs might not be the exclusive or even the primary source of help. The worker's task, more than helping, may be to see where help is flowing, or potentially flowing, in the client's context. What is the client doing well? What are other people doing well?" (Walsh, 2003)

To focus on a strengths-based practice, FSWs need four skill sets:

1. *The ability to identify and use strengths:* Identifying and using strengths is both an attitude and a behavior.
2. *Cultural competency:* Cultural competency provides family social workers with an openness and sensitivity to hidden reserves within a cultural framework. It also involves knowing how to use these cultural assets to the benefit of the family.
3. *Interpersonal sensitivity and knowledge:* This involves where to look in the family's life for assets.
4. *Relationship-supportive behavior* (Green, Mcallister, & Tarte, 2004).

Family strengths and family health are closely connected concepts. As such, Hettler (1984, cited in Myers, 2003) proposed a six-dimensional model of healthy family functioning:

1. Physical
2. Emotional
3. Social
4. Intellectual
5. Occupational
6. Spiritual

Similarly, the Wheel of Wellness model posed by Sweeney and Witmer (1991, cited in Myers, 2003) sees health as stemming from interrelated and interconnected life tasks that include spirituality, work and leisure, friendship, love, and self-direction. Self-direction was further divided into: (1) self-worth, (2) sense of control, (3) realistic beliefs, (4) emotional responsiveness and management, (5) intellectual stimulation, (6) problem solving and creativity, (7) sense of humor, (8) exercise, (9) nutrition, (10) self-care, (11) gender identity, (12) cultural identity, and (13) stress management. These life tasks interact dynamically with a variety of life forces: family, community, religion, education, government, media, and business/industry. Use the wheel to assess the wellness of the family and develop appropriate interventions.

What is necessary for a worker to work from a strengths-based perspective? First, workers must develop an attitude that believes in the value of potential. It means empowering families to take action on their own behalf. Empowerment should minimize the sense and reality of family and community powerlessness. FSWs need to help people discover the strength within themselves, their families, and their community. Clients possess many strengths, and helping professionals have often overlooked the massive and frequently unappreciated resources and competencies that groups and families have to offer. Fostering client strengths will inspire confidence and spur client motivation. Moreover, families will be more likely to continue independent development and growth when work focuses on identified family abilities, knowledge, and skills. Working with strengths puts social workers in a collaborative role with clients because family workers recognize that clients are experts on their own situations. Because the FSW works from an ecological niche, s/he is fully aware that the family's environment is full of resources.

Assessment and mobilization of family strengths should focus on the positives related to many areas, including:

- Relationships, emotional content of caring, positive gender roles, parental caring toward their children, maternal/paternal physical and emotional care, positive family events, supportive peer relationships, family history of success in conflict management
- Individual family member skills such as cognitive or intellectual ability, optimism, a belief in self-responsibility through an internal locus of control, competent parenting behaviors, support and cohesion within the family, positive mentoring relationship, supportive social environments
- Personal characteristics such as a sense of humor, motivation, sense of direction, inner strengths and resources, close relational ties with others
- Access to community resources such as health, education, and social services, and the skills to navigate in these community resources
- The ability to recognize and remember difficult life experiences and to learn from these experiences

The worker should pay particular attention to the multigenerational family system as it moves across the life cycle. At each developmental stage, the balance shifts between stressful events that heighten vulnerability and protective processes that enhance resilience as well as the influence of family, peers, and other social forces. A family resilience framework focuses on family adaptation around nodal events, including both predictable, normative transitions, and unexpected untimely events (Walsh, 2003, p. 4).

It is important to note the concurrence of symptoms with recent or impending events that have disrupted or threatened the family. Frequently, individual difficulties coincide with stressful transitions. In looking at stressful events it is important to explore how family members handled the situation, including their proactive stance, their immediate response, and their long-term survival strategies.

No single model of family health and resilience fits all; what matters the most in dealing with adversity is effective family processes. Family assessment typologies tend to be static and acontextual, offering only a snapshot of interaction patterns but lacking a contextual view in relation to the family's resources and constraints and their emerging challenges over time.

Successful resolution of problems means tapping into family strengths.

KEY STRATEGIES

1. Look at the family belief systems, which influence how that family understands their problems. The perception and understanding of reality emerge through family and social transactions. These perceptions help determine family processes and approaches to crisis situations. "Adversity generates a crisis of meaning and potential disruption of integration" (Walsh, 2003, p. 6). A family's resilience is encouraged through adopting beliefs that build upon opportunities to resolve problems and encourage growth. One helpful question in this regard is to ask family members what their theory is about what caused their particular difficulty. A second question might be to ask them what they believe needs to happen for their difficulties to become better.

    Positive beliefs play a role in how a family functions. Stories and narratives about difficulties are the building blocks of meaning and will reveal how a family understands itself and its difficulties. "Groups who suffer the domination of broader social institutions or suppression of their own cultural devices under the dominant culture frequently do not have their stories heard, not only in the wider world, but also in their own world" (Saleebey, 1996, p. 301). Certainly one of the characteristics of oppression is having one's stories and beliefs buried through ignorance and stereotypes.

2. The family social worker can help the family make meaning out of their personal difficulties. Strong and healthy families have strong attachments with one another and approach problems as a shared challenge. Family relationships give them strength. They are also able to recognize and place problems within the context of an unfolding process over time and they believe that their family continually changes and grows over time. They can be helped to understand family life cycle transitions as meaningful personal and family milestones, which are transitions, anticipated, welcomed, and celebrated rather than problem-saturated family events to be avoided and dreaded. When they encounter difficulties, healthy families avoid blaming, shaming, or pathologizing. The FSW can help families move in these directions and help them see their difficulties as understandable, manageable, and meaningful. At this time, the worker's role is to clarify the nature of problems and available resources, keeping family members well connected so that they can turn to one another for support. Resilience is strengthened by mutual support, collaboration, and commitment. At the same time, strong families respect others' differences, separateness, and boundaries.

3. The family social worker can help the families reframe their difficulties as positive by embracing hope and a belief that the future is bright. A skill of the FSW is to help the family overcome feelings of futility and failure, because when families lack hope they stop trying and instead become passive and pessimistic. Optimism can be fostered in a family through the positive outlook of the family worker where the family can recognize and celebrate their strengths, and discover new options for them to problem solve. At the same time, it is important not to dismiss their real and probably justifiable despair. It is important for the FSW to empathize with their despair but at the same time validate their strengths and potential.

4. Keep a realistic perspective on the problem. Even when working from a strengths-based perspective, it is important to acknowledge the reality of a family's difficulties. Pain and distress are important. Nevertheless, the problem should not become the identity. Family assessment and service plans must incorporate strengths as well as problems. The strength's perspective honors the power of the family to self-correct and right itself with the help of the environment. The worker must also inject hope and a belief that the family difficulties can be overcome. This can be done in a spirit of collaboration, with the worker and family participating in problem definition. Together they develop knowledge, access tools, and set out goals, within an atmosphere of respect.

Saleebey (1996), in response to criticisms that a strengths perspective is naïve or even "Pollyanna-ish," contends that practicing from a strengths perspective does not mean ignoring the real difficulties that families face. Rather, he argues:

> In the lexicon of strengths, it is as wrong to deny the possible as it is to deny the problem . . . it does deny the overwhelming reign of psychopathology as civic, moral, and medical categorical imperative. It does deny that most people are victims of abuse or of their own rampant appetites. It denies that all people who face trauma and pain in their lives inevitably are wounded or incapacitated or become less than they might. . . . The appreciations and understandings of the strengths perspective are an attempt to correct this overwrought and, in some instances, destructive emphasis on what is wrong, what is missing, and what is abnormal (p. 297).

Saleebey advocates for balance and cautions against the tendency to see nothing but the negative. Families must also be assessed from the angles of what they can do: their capacities, talents, competencies, possibilities, visions, beliefs, hopes, and potentials. It means going an extra step and zeroing in on what people know and what they are capable of doing. It also means counting and using individual, family, and community resources.

Current work in the helping professions points to the use of language during the helping process. Within the strengths perspective, the use of language is very important. Saleebey (1996) encourages us to "use a dictionary of helping," a dictionary that includes the use of such words as *empowerment, skills, hope, support, ability,* and *knowledge.* Using such a dictionary will alert us to what

| CASE 8.1 | LOOKING FOR STRENGTHS |

Sometimes family social workers must focus on family problems because these problems create a dangerous situation within the family or the community. However, even families with the most serious problems also have strengths, and it is important that the FSW acknowledge these. An example follows.

Kim and Tsi were reported to the FSW because of the neglect and possible abuse of their two small children, Pearl (3) and Jade (2). The mother was a stay-at-home mom and the father worked as a mechanic's assistant in a garage until the garage closed and left him unemployed. At the time of the report, he'd been unemployed for six months, and the couple's meager savings was almost gone. Both parents were feeling the stress of the situation and were fearful of being evicted from their small, two-bedroom apartment. This situation resulted in Tsi being depressed and withdrawn, while Kim was angry at her husband for not getting up and going job hunting every day. This created an environment where the children were left unattended, and an unconfirmed report from a neighbor that the children were being spanked too frequently and too severely.

During the assessment, the FSW looked for strengths as well as problem areas. She knew that finding the couples' strengths would indicate areas that could be used to shore up the couple's coping responses. Some of the strengths she reported were social supports, including extended family members nearby who were willing to help, and church attendance with caring members and friends willing to help. The church also had a mother's day out program that could offer respite care for the children. A local community center offered parenting courses that could work with the parents on appropriate parenting and disciplinary techniques. Individual strengths of the parents noted in the assessment included the Tsi's good work record and training to be a mechanic. Both Tsi and Kim were willing to come in to work with the FSW and looked forward to the help they would receive.

---

is going right and what the possibilities are and lead us to understand that people are experts in their own lives.

At the same time, the worker and the family can use humor, encourage healthy loyalty within the family, support independence, and foster insight to help families learn from their difficulties.

Risk and protective factors outlined at the beginning in this chapter interact with one another to determine how well a family will respond to a threatening event. Saleebey (1996) adds "generative factors" to the mix—remarkable and revelatory factors that, taken together, dramatically increase learning, resource acquisition, and development, accentuating resilience and hardiness. The ingredients of resilience include family competence or functioning over time, nature of adversities faced, individual and social assets, environmental protections and challenges, context in which stress is experienced, and individual perception and definitions of stressful situations. People are more motivated to change when their strengths are acknowledged and supported. In addition to asking family members what their problems are, the FSW can inquire as to what strengths they bring to the family and what they think are the strengths of other family members. The worker creates a language of strength, hope, and movement" (Kaplan & Girard, 1994, cited in Saleebey, 1996).

CHAPTER SUMMARY

The focus of this chapter was to help the FSW to start thinking about family strengths and resilience. These strengths can be placed in an ecological approach along with risk factors, paying attention to micro-, meso-, macro-, and exosystems. We also emphasize the need to examine family members' beliefs as a source of both strength and risk. The impact of culture and ethnicity on beliefs is very important and must be understood by the family social worker.

EXERCISES

8.1 YOUR ETHNIC BACKGROUND

What is your own ethnic background? List five beliefs that stem from your unique background that you see as strengths. How have these beliefs helped you and your family?

8.2 MIGRATION

Break into dyads and interview each other, exploring the history of the other person's family's migration to this country. What hopes and expectations did they have and were they met?

8.3 PARTNERING

What messages were you given as a teenager on who you could or could not date? What beliefs do you have on this issue? Discuss with your classmates the different messages and beliefs.

8.4 DESCRIBE A HEALTHY FAMILY

Describe from TV what would be a healthy family. In your own words, describe what you think is a healthy family. Is it ever possible to have a perfect family? Why or why not?

8.5 EXPLORING RESILIENCE

Split into groups of two. Each student will recall a difficult time in his or her family of origin and share this experience with a partner. The student will then talk about the strengths within the family that helped the student and the family deal with the difficulty.

8.6 WHEN RELIGIOUS VALUES CLASH WITH EQUALITY

We are all familiar with religious values that go against the teachings of a particular religious group. Some examples include the role of women, the condemnation of gay and lesbian relationships, abortion, and so on. Select one such issue to debate. Divide the class randomly into two sections and debate the following statement: "It is more important to respect the religious beliefs of the family than it is to free a single family member from religious beliefs that oppress that individual." Then discuss how workers can respect and work with religious values in family social work.

8.7 A SPIRITUAL GENOGRAM

Do a three-generation genogram of your family, with particular emphasis on religious adherence and spirituality. What does this genogram say about you and your family? What are the implications for family social work?

8.8 RESILIENCE AND YOU

Reflect on a difficult period in your life—a difficult time that you overcame. Identify four individual qualities, four family qualities, and four social qualities that helped you deal with this difficulty. Keep the nature of the difficulty to yourself, but provide the class with a list of the qualities that helped you.

ASSESSMENT WITH THE ENTIRE FAMILY

In Chapter 9 we present guidelines for effective assessment and intervention. We also present a very different lens to understand a family problem, in particular, the different ways that family members, in collaboration with the FSW, can view and define a problem. Finally, we expand upon systems theory with the assessment of circular patterns in a family.

EFFECTIVE ASSESSMENT AND INTERVENTION

The FSW assesses and intervenes in ways that help the family system change. This change often involves not only change in internal family interactions but also changes in the family's interactions with larger systems. Change is not always a steady process, and the FSW's interventions with a family can be obstructed in various ways. Assessment and intervention will be more effective if the FSW keeps the following considerations in mind:

1. Maintain culturally sensitive practices.
2. Focus on the family's needs.
3. Respect clients' autonomy.
4. Avoid fostering dependency.
5. Reassess clients' resistance.
6. Maintain professional distance.
7. Set reasonable expectations.
8. Use both a micro and macro focus.

CULTURALLY SENSITIVE PRACTICE

Throughout this book we emphasize the need for family social workers to be able to work with clients from diverse ethnic and cultural backgrounds. Culture and ethnicity are related but not interchangeable concepts: "Culture refers to the culmination of values, beliefs, customs, and norms that people have learned, usually in the context of their family and community. The term 'ethnicity' relates to a client's identity, commitment, and loyalty to an ethnic group" (Jordan & Franklin, 1995, p. 169). Awareness of the historical background of different ethnic groups is important, as is knowledge of the customs and beliefs shared by members of each group.

Family social workers must be careful not to stereotype people, as individual differences exist among people of similar ethnic and cultural backgrounds. Some of these differences may be related to varying levels of acculturation. Still, certain characteristics distinguish ethnic minority cultures from the dominant or majority white middle-class culture in the United States and Canada. Ho (1987) outlines six characteristics: ethnic minority reality, impact of external systems on minority cultures, biculturalism, ethnic differences in minority status, ethnicity and language, and ethnicity and social class.

1. *Ethnic minority reality:* Members of ethnic minority groups often experience poverty and racial discrimination, resulting in under-utilization of mental health services.
2. *Impact of external systems on minority cultures:* Ethnic minority values may conflict with those of the majority culture on issues such as exerting control over versus living in harmony with the environment, orientation to time (past, present, and future), "doing" versus "being" orientation, individual autonomy versus collectivity, and the importance of nuclear versus extended family relationships.

3. *Biculturalism:* The ethnic minority person belongs to two cultures. The level of acculturation into the dominant culture is an important aspect of the assessment of families seeking mental health services.

4. *Ethnic differences in minority status:* Status of various ethnic minority groups differs. Some groups experience more discrimination than others. For instance, refugees may receive better treatment than the descendants of slaves. Skin color is another determinant of status; populations of darker skin color often experience harsher societal discrimination.

5. *Ethnicity and language:* Ethnic minority people seeking mental health services from non-bilingual helpers are at risk of being misunderstood or even misdiagnosed. Use of interpreters is fraught with problems; for instance, asking a bilingual child to interpret between the family social worker and an elderly family member can upset the hierarchical structure of the family by putting the child in a position of power.

6. *Ethnicity and social class:* Social class (level of education, income, standing in the community) is important to assess, as higher status usually leads to a higher level of well-being and greater access to resources. In some cases, however, individuals may be discriminated against by the dominant culture despite their high social-class standing while at the same time being rejected by other members of their ethnic group because of their high level of acculturation into the mainstream culture. (List headings are from Ho, 1987, pp. 14–18; explanations have been paraphrased by the authors.)

Initial family work techniques for FSWs to use with minorities are those that promote bonding between the social worker and the family. It is extremely helpful for the FSW to show genuine interest about cultural issues for the family, which involves asking questions about the family's background in a curious and empathic manner. Most families are quite willing and comfortable talking about their cultural background and are pleased that the FSW shows this kind of interest in them.

In order to engage the family, the social worker may adopt the family's verbal and nonverbal communication style and relevant metaphors. Other family systems techniques that may be used include behavioral methods such as social skills training. For instance, specialized treatment packages are available to help families learn better communication, problem solving, or anger management techniques (see Franklin & Jordan, 1999).

Focus on the Family's Needs

Sometimes it may be difficult for the FSW to focus on the family's needs, particularly when the FSW's schedule conflicts with that of the family. The FSW may want to schedule a home visit at 4 P.M. so as to finish the work day by 5 P.M., but the client family may prefer to meet with the FSW at 8 P.M. to give the parents a chance to relax after the day's work and spend time with their children. Similarly, the client's behavior or choices may be inconvenient or at odds with the FSW's beliefs. For example, one client insisted on living with her unemployed boyfriend in a high-crime area rather than moving in with her mother in a safer neighborhood. The client got more emotional support from her boyfriend than from her mother. Even though the FSW would have preferred to meet with the client in a safer location, she recognized that her client fared better with her boyfriend than with her mother.

RESPECT CLIENTS' AUTONOMY

Clients have a right to make their own choices. The role of the FSW is to sustain and encourage clients to make personal decisions. It can be difficult for the FSW to avoid stepping in and making decisions for the client, particularly if the client's choices are self-destructive, such as refusing to leave a dangerously abusive relationship. Encouraging people to make their own decisions increases their competence and control over their lives because people learn by experience. As one FSW said, "When we support clients by helping them access community resources and by continuing to help them improve their skills, clients become increasingly able to make appropriate decisions and to change destructive life patterns."

In accepting clients' right to make their own decisions, the FSW must always remember that the client is a separate individual with the right to control his or her life. The FSW cannot accept responsibility for client actions. The FSW also must differentiate between his or her personal values and life goals and those of the client, remembering that the goal ultimately is to help the client learn skills. Indeed, effective professionals encourage client self-exploration and self-direction. If the FSW has trouble separating his or her personal needs from those of the client, a supervisor can assist in the self-examination process. For example, the FSW may highly value college education and the client may not. It is important for the client to choose their life direction not the FSW for them.

AVOID FOSTERING DEPENDENCY

A third consideration for FSWs involves client independence. Sometimes the client must depend on the social worker, but excessive dependency can be counterproductive. During periods of stress and crisis, clients may rely on FSWs to help them make and carry out decisions. For example, one FSW helped a depressed client obtain professional counseling. The client needed assistance in finding an appropriate therapist and setting up an appointment. The social worker responded by spending most of a home visit phoning therapists and scheduling the first appointment, though customarily the FSW would just provide information and support to encourage her client to initiate contact.

While occasional dependency may be acceptable, the FSW should avoid fostering unnecessary dependency. Encouraging clients' independence will strengthen existing competencies and help them develop additional competencies. Family social workers who regularly allow clients to become dependent will harm rather than help clients. One FSW left a family party when a client called her and asked her for a ride. This was not an emergency situation, and the FSW did not place appropriate limits on her professional role. Helping the client find her own transportation would have been more valuable for this client, encouraging her to develop independent coping skills. During the FSW's working relationship with a family, the type and amount of dependency will vary. The goal is for clients to become self-reliant. Keeping this goal in mind helps the social worker judge what level of dependency is appropriate and what is not.

REASSESS CLIENTS' RESISTANCE

A fourth consideration for FSWs involves client motivation. Some clients may appear unmotivated to comply with program expectations or to work toward other life goals that are important. Often social workers label this behavior as resistant, but it may occur because of conflict between the FSW and the client over the goals to be accomplished. The FSW who feels frustrated over low motivation should ask, "Are these the client's goals, my goals, or goals of the agency?" Perhaps the goals are not culturally appropriate or personally meaningful to the client. If so and if the selected goal will benefit the client, the FSW may try to present it in a way that is acceptable to the client. If the goal does not appear to be of benefit to the client, the expectation should be dropped.

Resistance may be a message from the client that the FSW is over-stepping the boundaries of the relationship. Resistance can also signal that the issues being discussed are central to the client. If the family is not making progress toward establishing goals, the FSW should attempt to discover what barriers may be preventing them from trying to achieve these goals. Two major barriers to goal attainment are lack of resources and skills. Perhaps helping the client problem solve to overcome or remove the barriers will enable the family to move toward its goals.

If the family is not complying with a required goal in an involuntary program, such as court-ordered treatment for child abusers, program policy and legal procedures will guide the FSW's response. If a client in a voluntary program does not want to attend parent meetings, however, the FSW may change her or his expectations for this family. Alternatively, the FSW may occasionally encourage the client to attend the meetings while focusing attention on other aspects of the program to which the family is attracted.

MAINTAIN PROFESSIONAL DISTANCE

A fifth consideration for FSWs is the nature of their relationships with families. Over time, relationships will change. For example, as positive feelings grow between the FSW and the family, boundaries may become blurred and the relationship may begin to resemble a personal friendship. The FSW may become truly fond of the family and deeply committed to helping. Although positive regard for clients is essential for developing a good working relationship, it should not become confused with friendship. The FSW needs to maintain an appropriate emotional distance. Maintaining this distance is important for several reasons.

The FSW needs to remain objective and goal-focused to help the family become independent and effective. Appropriate distance between family members and the social worker encourages the family to view the FSW as a role model for behavioral change.

On another level, maintaining a professional relationship with a family is a form of self-protection for the FSW. The circumstances of the family's life could become overwhelming for an FSW who becomes too emotionally involved or takes personal responsibility for solving the family's problems. Failure to establish clear boundaries with families can leave the FSW feeling burdened by distressing family situations. Focusing on understanding how the family may feel, without over-identifying, helps the FSW function professionally and effectively.

SET REASONABLE EXPECTATIONS

A sixth guideline for FSWs is to help families feel competent, rather than inadequate. Families may feel that bringing the social worker into their home places them in a vulnerable position, regardless of the purpose of the program. Additionally, families may feel overwhelmed by expectations they fear that they cannot meet. Though the FSW focuses on encouraging and positively reinforcing family strengths, family limitations must also be acknowledged. The FSW must take care to avoid creating feelings of inadequacy.

A MICRO AND MACRO FOCUS: AN ECOLOGICAL INTERVENTION

The FSW needs to move beyond just working with changing internal family interactions, a micro focus, to helping change macro-level interactions—that is, looking at the interactions a family has with systems outside the family unit. Ecological theory is helpful for this.

The type of ecological interventions required will arise from an assessment of the family's relationship with its environment, as portrayed in its ecomap. The ecomap is the blueprint for planned change and is the first stage in deciding upon an action (Hartman & Laird, 1983). Not only does an ecomap organize information visually, it also outlines family themes and targets for change. As was mentioned in Chapter 5, the family must be involved in creating the ecomap. The FSW can ask family members, "What does the ecomap mean to you?" Focusing on the ecosystem will also remove the problem from the level of individual blame. We should point out here that the goal of ecological intervention is to teach clients how to problem solve for themselves, rather than relying on the FSW to do it for them (Kinney, Haapala, & Booth, 1991).

Typically, the social worker should focus on environmental problems first (Kaplan, 1986). This will help the family deal first with less-threatening issues, while assisting them in locating community supports. The type of ecological interventions used depends upon the issues, client skills, and available resources. For example, one FSW reported that the following resources were either not available to clients or difficult for them to locate: mental health treatment, housing, day care, low-skill basic jobs, transportation, legal services, and religious programs (Goldstein, 1981). Social workers in a different program found that emergency housing, homemaker services, group homes, parent aides, impatient drug and alcohol treatment, and respite care were difficult to obtain (Kohlert & Pecora, 1991). The social worker must also help families develop creative ways to use formal and informal resources. Sometimes families merely lack information about where resources exist. Other times, family members may have the knowledge, but lack the skills to get connected to resources. In such cases, the FSW will have to help the family get connected (Helton & Jackson, 1997). The ultimate goal is to help clients learn how to get needs met on their own, even though it often is tempting and perhaps easier to take care of clients' needs rather than encouraging self-sufficiency (Kinney, Haapala, & Booth, 1991).

Hepworth and Larsen (1993) list the following ecological interventions that FSWs can perform for families:

- Supplementing resources in the home environment;
- Developing and enhancing support systems;
- Moving clients to a new environment;
- Increasing the responsiveness of organizations to people's needs;
- Enhancing interactions between organizations and institutions;
- Improving institutional environments;
- Enhancing agency environments;
- Developing new resources.

DEFINING PROBLEMS

The goal of problem definition is to explore, identify, and define dynamics within and beyond the family in a way that opens up possibilities for change. Problem definition is very important because the way we define problems can create very different directions for family work. Each member of the family has a unique perspective on the problem, and every perspective is important. For example, a problem defined by the family as a child spending too much time "hanging out with friends," may be a "conforming" issue for the parents, an "independence" issue for the target child, and an "exclusion" issue for siblings.

Developing a clear understanding of family problems is necessary for devising interventions. Thus, how the FSW and the family jointly view a problem is crucial. This viewpoint or definition of the problem will direct our intervention. Most problem definitions follow a systemic view. Yet these systemic views can be radically different. The following list describes six ways to view problems, along with related intervention models, most of which are discussed in future units of this manual. The way you define a problem often depends on: how the family initially defines the problem; how you prefer to define problems—that is, the theoretical perspective you are most comfortable with; the mandate of your agency and how the agency views problems—for example, some agencies are heavily oriented toward solution-focused counseling and define problems to fit their view; and finally, and hopefully ultimately, the problem will be defined jointly between the family and yourself in a way that both you and the family feel offers the most opportunities to create positive change.

1. A traditional analytic view is that the *symptomatic person is the problem*. This traditional analytic view has it roots in individual psychopathology, in which problems are viewed inside people. Nearly all counselors involved in individual counseling somewhat subscribe to this view. However, the influence of a more generalist, ecological view has expanded the exclusive focus on individual psychopathology to take more into account the effect of larger social systems on an individual's well-being.

   Imagine you have the Smith family referred to you because of concerns around their 13-year-child being noncompliant, argumentative, and "throwing temper tantrums." The traditional analytic view would say, for example, that the child has anger management problems and low self-esteem issues. Because of this individually oriented assessment of the problem, the preferred treatment approach would be individual counseling for the child, focusing on anger management techniques and discussion of self-esteem issues.

2. The social systems assumption is that *the family is the problem* (the basic systems view). Family systems theory had great influence in the 1960s and 1970s, changing the way many counselors viewed problems. Instead of viewing problems as being within an individual, problems were seen as systems problems, that is problems evolving from relationship patterns within the family. The primary system of concern and influence on a person was the family. Thus the social systems assumption was that the family is the problem—particularly, the way family members relate to each other. Major family therapy models that ascribed to this view included the communicative model and structural family therapy models.

   For example, the Smith family has difficulties in dealing with anger and relating to each other in ways that give each other support. By defining the anger as a family systems problem, the treatment approach would involve family counseling, focusing on how the family as a whole supports one of its members to deal with anger. More appropriate ways for the family to express anger and its accompanying hurt would be put into place.

3. The Mental Research Institute in Palo Alto assumption is that *the attempted solution is the problem* (an interactional view). This is a rather interesting view that could be simplified by saying, "if what you are doing does not work, stop doing it and try something different!" If yelling at your children to do their homework is not working, try something different. If nagging to get your partner to help with household chores is not working, try something different. Thus, if what you considered to be a solution to a problem—that is, yelling as a solution to not doing homework or nagging as a solution to not doing household chore—is not working, then these so-called solutions become the problem and they need to be

changed. Behavioral family therapy becomes a helpful model to look at alternative behaviors (solutions) to help achieve desired family changes.

For example, a family yelling and arguing (their attempted solution) increases the family members' anger instead of decreasing it. Family counseling would be offered, but the focus would be on changing the family behavioral and relational patterns of withdrawing to more adaptive behaviors. A typical maladaptive pattern occurs when parents are experiencing a child with temper tantrums. Parents arguing or yelling at the child only "feeds" the temper tantrum. Yelling only increases the tension in the room, although parents might discharge energy initially. Instead, the parents need to "starve" temper tantrums. I suggest a rather radical approach: instead of yelling or arguing, parents physically hug (comfort) the child and then give the child a choice of continuing to be hugged, talking nicely about what is bothering him or her, or going to his or her room to get control of the temper tantrum. Thus instead of yelling/arguing at the child, the parents learn to take control by giving choices to help the child learn more appropriate ways of seeking attention and taking control of temper tantrums.

4. The Milan group says *the problem is the solution* (a functional cybernetic view). The Milan group was one major school of strategic family therapy. It viewed problems as having some sort of function in the family system. Thus, within the family relationships or systems there was some reason for or function for the problem. It was therefore important to assess and hypothesize what function the problem was having and then turn this function around to make the problem the solution.

For example, by being angry the Smith family will learn the value of affective closeness—that is, family anger will led to forgiveness and thus force the family to become affectively close. Again, given this definition of the problem, family counseling would occur. The family would be made aware of the "payoff" or function the anger has on the family, which involves attempting to force the family to be more affectively close. The family would be supported in becoming routinely affectively close without the need for anger to force them to be so.

5. Michael White, a social worker from Australia, and his colleague David Epson from New Zealand offer a very unique narrative model view of a problem in which *the symptom (problem) is a restraint* (evolutionary cybernetic view; i.e., the direction of interaction between the problem and solution is important).

For example, the Smith family, at times, allows anger to take control of the family and will need to become more vigilant as a family unit to keep anger away. (Anger or yelling is verbalized as an external entity). The focus in family counseling would be to help the family become aware of the power or influence anger/yelling has on the family. The family would be encouraged to make greater efforts in doing behaviors that have been successful in minimizing the impact anger has on them—for example, doing family recreational activities, family talk times, and so on. Temper tantrums are also a very good issue to externalize.

6. Maturana sees *the distinction as the problem* (the structured determined view). Anger/yelling can be seen as overwhelming or as a challenge. Whether the family defines anger as a negative (i.e., overwhelming) or as a positive challenge (a call for affective attention) will open different possibilities for change. It is sort of like whether you view yourself as an optimist or a pessimist. Do you make the distinction that the glass is half empty or half full? When you wake up in the morning do you say to yourself, "I do not want to get out of bed—I hate going to work," which may lead to a more negative approach to the day, or do you get up in the morning and say, "What a beautiful morning, I am going to have a great day!" which may lead to a positive approach to the rest of the day?

    In a family counseling process the family would be encouraged to redefine anger in a way that opens up opportunities for them. For example anger can help people truly appreciate the times in the family that anger is not present. The adolescent girl feeling angry could be defined differently (restoried), to reflect that she is a very sensitive, caring child, deeply involved and moved by what is happening in the family. By seeing herself no longer as an angry person but as a very sensitive, caring child deeply involved and moved by what is happening in her family, she can receive the support she needs to continue to try to be a respectful, compliant, confident adolescent without self-doubt and blaming others.

    In the Smith family anger can be viewed as a call (albeit a loud one) for attention. By providing immediate affective support, positive attention is given, and the need to receive affective support by continued anger decreases. The hope is that family members will learn that if they want affective support they just need to ask for it instead of having to yell or get angry to receive it. Thus, when adolescents feel angry, hurt, or into self-doubt, they do not need to resort to anger outbursts but instead can just ask for the support and comfort they so often need.

CIRCULAR PATTERNS

In addition to the preceding six ways to define problems, another very helpful way to assess families is to look for circular repetitive patterns. Repetitive circular patterns were discussed in detail in Chapter 2. Here, we focus on intervention into these patterns through stimulating interaction and lineal, circular, strategic and reflexive questions. Patterns are particularly relevant when we see problems within the social systems assumption that "the family is the problem."

Recognizing patterns is the cornerstone of family systems theory. By patterns, we mean that the same behavior happens repeatedly and becomes quite predictable. The ways that families function are often both predictable and patterned. Thus, the family social worker needs to pay attention to the ongoing, repetitive patterns of communication between family members.

Predictable patterns contribute to family system stability so that the energy of family members is not wasted on mundane tasks. We know who is going to ask the children to do the dishes, put them to bed, or get them to do their homework. We are also quite certain about how the children are going to respond to these requests. When systems are stable, the familiar patterns within a family play an important role in keeping the family on an even keel. Family patterns also reveal patterns of affiliations, tensions, and hierarchies within the system (Minuchin, Colapinto, & Minuchin, 1998). Some family patterns are determined by ethnicity and culture. Behavior is explained through these ongoing, repetitive patterns, which both trigger and maintain behavior.

When a family has trouble, it is often because their repetitive patterns have produced inertia without providing an adequate response to the issue at hand. In this way, *the solution becomes the problem.* Because the patterns are habits, family members feel secure in the stability they provide. The habitual patterns might be hurtful to individuals and harmful to the family system, but because family members are unaware of or unskilled in other ways of responding, they are unable to change, and the family is described as being stuck.

STIMULATING INTERACTION

To assess circular patterns, it is useful to observe a repetitive circular pattern occur in the actual family interview. We do this through "stimulating inter-action" (similar to "enactment"). The FSW can wait for spontaneous family events to arise where a pattern evolves or the worker may set the stage to encourage family members to play out their usual family patterns. "Effective enactments empower the family, allowing them to express their usual ways of functioning and to explore new pathways on their own" (Minuchin, Colapinto, & Minuchin, 1998, p. 49).

The FSW asks two people in the family to face each other and stimulates interaction by having them enter into a dialogue over a particular issue. For example, with the Smith family the worker might introduce the interaction by asking the mother and father to face each other and try to resolve the problem they had last evening about a parenting issue of disciplining the children.

The family worker then sits back and closely observes their communication for approximately five minutes (which is the usual length to time to observe a pattern of communication). A practical definition of a pattern is a circular sequence of communication that occurs three times. The Smith couple will likely start talking, and the family worker might notice Mrs. Smith looking more depressed, quiet, and withdrawn, and Mr. Smith looking uncertain, anxious, and wanting to be quiet and withdraw. Working with one person at a time, the worker elicits from each member his or her thoughts/feelings/behaviors. It is important for the three to be connected. As one person describes his or her thoughts/feelings/ behavior, the other person must sit and listen without saying anything.

After the family worker has a cognitive understanding of the pattern (after it is repeated three times, or over a five-minute interval), it is important to stop the maladaptive pattern and work with the dyad. If, on the other hand, the couple is communicating in an adaptive way, let them continue! Adaptive communication is what they need to do, and they should be encouraged in their efforts. For example, if the Smith couple is able to share their parenting concerns, listen to each other, and develop realistic plans, let them do so! After they complete an adaptive interchange, commend the efforts of the dyad and help them become aware of their adaptive circular communication. Unfortunately, most families who initially come to counseling are likely to demonstrate maladaptive communication. It is now important to contract with the family if they want to change the maladaptive pattern.

LINEAL, CIRCULAR, STRATEGIC, AND REFLEXIVE QUESTIONS

Beyond stimulating interaction, the FSW can also assess circular patterns through the use of questioning. Karl Tomm (1987a, 1987b, 1988) describes four types of questions that are appropriate for family interviewing: lineal, circular, strategic, and reflexive. According to Tomm, questions can be used for therapeutic and assessment purposes. Selecting an area for examination needs to be done carefully, and "every question and every comment may be evaluated with respect to whether it constitutes an affirmation or challenge to one or more behavior patterns of the client or family" (Tomm, 1987a, p. 4). For example, starting the interview by asking, "What problems would you like to discuss today?" will bring out different responses from asking, "What positive things have happened to you over the past week?" The FSW must carefully note clients' reactions to the questions being posed.

Lineal questions ask for information and assume a basic cause-and-effect sequence. Lineal questions attempt to define problems and seek explanation. Examples of lineal questions include the following:

*   What brings you in today?
*   How long have you been experiencing these problems?
*   What is making you depressed?

Circular questions are based on circular causality and the connections among family members. Circular questions help the FSW to learn about ongoing patterns of family interaction and the effects that family members' behaviors have on one another. Circular questions demonstrate to the family that issues do not belong with individual members—everyone is connected to "the problem" regardless of whether or not they have a "symptom" themselves.

Circular questions are meant to create change, whereas lineal questions are intended to elicit information (Wright & Leahey, 1994). Circular questions are aimed at developing explanations for problems and identifying relationships between individuals, ideas, beliefs, and events. They can be used to change cognitive, affective, and behavioral domains of family functioning. Circular questions are useful for assessing the role of the presenting problem within the family. Each person is asked questions related to the definition of the problem, including who says what to whom. Examples of circular questioning include the following:

*   When Melissa said that she was upset with you, how did you react?
*   When you hear your husband yelling at the kids, how does that make you feel?

Strategic questions are directed at change, based upon the social worker's assessment of the situation. The underlying intent of strategic questions is to correct behavior. Such questions challenge or confront patterns within the family. Examples of strategic questioning follow:

- Can you try to see it his way?
- When are you going to tell him what you think?

Reflexive questions ask clients to become self-observers. Reflexive questioning is based on the belief that change depends on the efforts of clients, not the social worker. Examples of reflexive questioning follow:

- What do you plan on doing about finding a new job?
- What do you think you can do to improve your school grades?
- When your mother gets into a fight with your sister, what does your father usually do?

INTERVENTION IN CIRCULAR MALADAPTIVE PATTERNS

In order to work with circular causality, it is important to first recognize recurring behavior and interactions involving circular interaction patterns. Refer to examples in Chapter 2, Figure 2.1. It will be helpful for the worker to draw on a piece of paper the family's circular patterns, especially ones revolving around a selected issue. A flipchart may be especially useful so everyone in the family will have the same visual map of the circular pattern. Remember, the simplest patterns consist of feelings-behavior-feelings-behavior and around and around.

1. Clarify with the family these patterns, pointing out the relationship between affect or feelings and behavior. For example, father scolds child, child feels hurt, child pouts, father feels frustrated, father scolds, and around the pattern goes. It is helpful for a family to see how they go around in these maladaptive circles.
2. When this is done, help clarify any family rules or myths that perpetuate these patterns—for example, a myth that the only way a child will listen to a parent is when the parent yells at the child.
3. When clarifying a circular pattern with a family, it is necessary to explore underlying feelings and any additional behaviors.
4. Point out evidence of emotional distress and get members to label specific feelings. When feelings are out in the open, particularly fears and hurts, they can be directly faced.
5. Encourage the family to provide each member with reassurance and support.
6. Help the family develop understanding of each other by bringing their circular patterns out in the open and including underlying feelings.

7. After the dysfunctional patterns have been identified, the worker should then get the family to think of helpful *adaptive* patterns to deal with problem situations.
8. Help the family negotiate simultaneous change.
9. Reinforce family member's constructive suggestions.
10. Coach family members in trying out new adaptive behaviors and assign realistic tasks explicitly as homework (Tomm & Wright, 1979).

DETRIANGULATION

In Chapter 2 we discussed how triangulation often occurs in families. See also Figure 9.1. What is important now is for the family social worker to stop triangulation by "detriangulation" of the family members. Detriangulation involves strategies through which the family worker disrupts one triangle and opens up the family members to new, more functional alliances or triangles. Carter and McGoldrick (1999) suggest that detriangulating involves "unlocking compulsory loyalties so that three dyadic relationships can emerge from the enmeshed threesome" (p. 441). Often dysfunctional triangles are shown through an intense relationship between a parent and a child, often in opposition to the other parent. Four possible methods of detriangulation are available for the FSW.

1. One way of detriangulating is to point the triangle out to the three people. People cannot change what they do not know about. Therefore, labeling the process brings to awareness what is happening.
2. Another method of detriangulation is ensuring that family members interact as dyads. This involves making certain that a third person does not jump into conflictual relationships, but instead allows the two other family members to work out the conflict on their own.
3. Another method is through reversal, or getting one person in the triangle to do the opposite of the pattern. For example, if a teenager acts out every

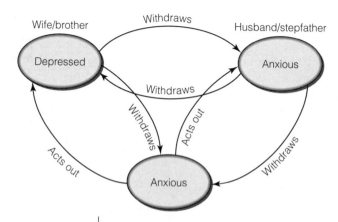

FIGURE 9.1 | TRIANGULATION

time the parents begin an argument, the teenager would be instructed to instead go to his or her bedroom to study for an hour and let the parents work out their issue.

4.　Detriangulation also can occur by shifting alliances (i.e., who does what with whom). If the mother is always the one trying to get a child to comply with a command, change can be accomplished by having the father gain the child's compliance. When a couple is triangulated with a child as a means of avoiding issues in their relationship, they might be instructed to spend a certain amount of time together talking about whatever is on their minds that day without the third party present. If they need the assistance of a third party to bring an issue to resolution, they might be encouraged to talk with a different adult, including the family worker. Ideally, the couple should learn to deal with their issues directly and honestly. Alternatively, another adult family member could act as a supportive advice giver, removing the children from the conflictual relationship. In this way, members are guided into new functional attachments with nuclear or extended family members.

WORKING WITH INVOLUNTARY CLIENTS

Clients often enter family work reluctantly. Some are visibly resistant. Clients who are experiencing problems such as sexual abuse, family violence, or substance abuse often show strong resistance at the onset of family social work. Resistance by clients is not surprising, because many people enter family social work feeling anxious, frightened, or ashamed. In addition, parents often feel like failures when a problem attracts agency attention.

Families may also be resistant to the actions of a particular agency because of past experience or because of what the agency represents to them. Some families may have been involved with other agencies without seeing any change in their problems. Clients may be concerned about possible breaches of confidentiality or anticipated lack of agency understanding of their situation. As a result, they may choose to be minimally compliant, doing only enough work to get by. Most involuntary clients are resistant clients, but not all resistant clients are involuntary.

Involuntary clients typically receive services from an agency without asking for them. They may not be motivated to engage in family social work, and they may refuse to work toward the goals that the FSW or agency has identified. They often arrive at an agency because they have been forced to receive help by public officials. In this light, assessment of involuntary clients should be done carefully because of the possibility that the problems are dangerous, illegal, or both.

Willingness to become involved in family work varies from one family to another. Even voluntary clients fall along a continuum of motivation for services. At one extreme end of the continuum are clients who are legally mandated to receive service and who do not believe they have a problem. Somewhere in the middle are those who believe they have a problem but do not want to enter treatment to make the necessary changes. The ideal clients recognize that they have a problem and want to change their circumstances to eliminate the problem.

Family members often show varying degrees of reluctance toward acknowledging a problem and engaging in the necessary work to produce change. An especially complex situation occurs when there is some form of victimization within the family and the perpetrator does not want to change.

Involuntary clients are often mandated to receive agency intervention because of problems involving child welfare, mental health, or criminal justice. An overarching issue often is substance abuse. For all these categories of problems, laws exist to force clients into treatment against their will. When clients enter treatment against their will, they are likely to be resistant.

Even when there is no legal mandate forcing clients into treatment, some clients become involved because of pressure from family members or friends. For example, the spouse of a substance abuser may threaten to leave unless the person goes into treatment. Children usually have little leverage to force the family into work unless the child's behavior becomes so problematic that it is difficult to ignore, as when a child becomes suicidal or runs away from home. When some family members are resistant to family work, they are likely to hamper the progress of the rest of the family.

In another common scenario, some family members agree that there is a problem, but they believe that the problem belongs to someone else in the family. This is a very common stance among families in which teenagers are "acting out." The challenge for the social worker is to help all family members understand their roles in the development of the problem.

Clients usually look for one of two outcomes from family social work. Some just want to eliminate the pain created by the problem, and in the process they want to be "nurtured." These clients may be satisfied once the initial stress has been alleviated, and they may avoid making difficult or lasting changes. Other clients want to change their lives in concrete ways. They are willing to work hard to achieve needed changes in their lives. These are the most rewarding clients for family social workers.

Involuntary or otherwise resistant families usually benefit from a clear contract stating the expected outcomes of their actions. The FSW's task is to convey that despite the involuntary nature of their involvement in the work, some choices remain, and every choice is associated with an anticipated outcome. For example, those who are ordered into work for reasons of abuse but refuse to become involved may find that the FSW has written a letter to the court or that their children have been placed in foster care. Ultimately, the social worker can empathize with clients' anger and fears about family social work and discuss how the involuntary nature of the work affects everyone.

Families need to know that participating in family social work is their choice. When families understand that there are certain issues over which they have control, their resistance may decrease. The FSW should emphasize that freedom from unwanted agency intervention will occur when the conditions of the court order or contracted work are met. The contract should contain some recognition of client self-determination and state the conditions under which the family will become free from agency and legal intrusion.

Work with involuntary clients should begin by focusing on specific, concrete changes. Clients should be informed that some conditions of the work are not negotiable, and they need to understand the specific conditions for termination.

As uncomfortable as it may be, family social workers must clearly describe the conditions linked to involuntary family social work. For example, if the social worker is required to prepare a court report, families should know about this at the outset. Clients must know what is expected of them as well as what is negotiable. When clients do not want to work, the family social worker can point out that the family has a right not to participate but that nonparticipation involves some consequences. In summary, the family social worker must discuss the nature of the problem, his or her role, nonnegotiable requirements, procedures mandated by the referral source, negotiable requirements, and choices available to the clients (Hepworth & Larson, 1993).

Family social workers should keep in mind that motivation is the flip side of resistance. Motivation is present when families have a sincere desire to change something in their lives. Resentment and negativity undermine motivation. When clients feel blamed by the social worker and agency for their problems, without any concomitant understanding or empathy, they may view the FSW as a threat. Family social workers must be prepared to face clients' feelings of hostility and anger and to respond openly to the negative feelings. Arguing usually accomplishes little and can escalate clients' hostility and resentment. Since resistance to work may be part of a family's general style of dealing with outsiders, empathic responses by the family social worker can provide an example of appropriate behavior. We suggest not confronting client perceptions until trust and acceptance have developed. Direct confrontation about responsibility for problems during the assessment phase is likely to produce defensiveness rather than lead to change (Ivanoff, Blythe, & Tripodi, 1994).

By recommending that FSWs not confront client perceptions early in the work, we are not saying that FSWs should collude with client dysfunction. The single most important skill for working with family resistance is being able to identify when it may be counterproductive to push an issue with the family (Brock & Barnard, 1991). Appropriate work with resistant clients entails looking for windows of opportunity to induce change. Sometimes clients may block the development of a working contract by insisting on pushing through their own definition of the problem. Social workers may be able to find a common ground somewhere between the FSW's and the client's definitions of the problem. Once the initial barriers are broken, many FSWs discover that clients gradually drop their defensiveness in defining the problem. Social workers need to remember that defensiveness serves a protective function for clients, and this protective stance can be dropped only after clients feel safe. Overcoming resistance usually involves finding out about the FSW and evaluating him or her (Lum, 1994).

Work with involuntary clients can be just as effective as work with voluntary clients (Ivanoff, Blythe, & Tripodi, 1994, p. 57). The most positive results seem to be related to the quality of worker–client interaction. One last word of advice is in order: a wise worker must be able to recognize the difference between a resistant family and an ineffectual intervention.

GOAL SETTING

As soon as key problems have been identified, the next step is setting goals. Clear, specific, concrete, and measurable goals, consistent with the family's beliefs and interests, should be itemized in contract form. Goals should be significant to the family and also be achievable and realistic, determined by the family's commitment and resources. A reasonable length of time for achieving goals should be established and an evaluation date set. An explicit understanding of approaches to be used and the responsibilities of various family members and of the FSW also should be a component of the contract. At this time, the social worker should reinforce the importance of regular attendance at the family sessions because some family members may continue to resist intervention (Nichols & Schwartz, 2004).

Intrinsic to family social work is self-determination—the principle that clients have the right and responsibility to determine what they will do. To arrive at a goal statement, the social worker and family must determine the *desired end state*—that is, a description of how the family would like to get along with each other (Bandler, Grinder, & Satir, 1976). To arrive at the desired state, all must understand what the current state is, as well as the resources necessary for arriving at the intended destination. Families should not be manipulated or coerced to accept goals that they do not believe are important. Goals, interventions, and responsibilities may need to be modified in response to changing circumstances.

To assist families with goal setting, FSWs will need to accomplish the following tasks:

1. Recognize that family members are more receptive to change during times of crisis.
2. Move from global, abstract goals to concrete and specific goals.
3. Define clear, concrete, and measurable goals.
4. Help the family identify goals that they would like to achieve first.
5. Assist family members to negotiate with each other regarding behavioral changes.
6. Identify skills and strengths of the family.
7. Obtain a commitment from the family.

If goal setting is done correctly, the work will progress with focus and purpose. Family social work goals stated in clear and specific terms forecast what will be happening once the goals are achieved. In other words, goals identify what the family wishes to accomplish. Although goal setting is ongoing and continuous, the most productive time to set goals is after the problems have been identified and explored. Until the FSW and the family have a shared understanding of the situation, goal setting will be premature.

CONTRACTING

From their first meeting, the FSW and the family will have expectations about what they want to accomplish and how objectives will be met. Contracting can be done on a short-term or long-term basis. For example, short-term verbal or written contracts can help a family get through a crisis (Kinney, Haapala, & Booth, 1991), while long-term contracts focus on results that occur over an extended period of time, such as improved grades in school. The family social work contract is a concrete agreement that specifies goals of the intervention and the means by which to achieve them. The contract should state specific problems, the goals and strategies to alleviate them, and the roles and tasks of the participants.

A contract is an explicit agreement "concerning the target problems, the goals and strategies of . . . intervention, and the roles and tasks of the participants" (Maluccio & Marlow, 1975). Contracts may begin as recommendations from the social worker to the family about what needs to be done to resolve the problem (Nichols & Schwartz, 1998). They should not be developed hastily; it will take at least a couple of interviews for the FSW to assess the situation and establish a bond with the family.

Contracting should also cover important procedural details such as when and where meetings will take place, how long they will last, what records will be kept, rules governing confidentiality, and who will attend sessions.

Essential to contracting is ongoing accountability between the family and the FSW. Family members are not passive recipients of service; rather, they must be active participants in the entire process. Egan (1994) outlines four basic features of a family contract:

1. The contract will be negotiated, not declared, by the parties involved—that is, helper and family;
2. The contract will be understandable to all involved parties;
3. An oral or written commitment to the contract will be obtained;
4. The contract will be reviewed as the work progresses. If necessary, the contact will be revised.

The FSW is responsible for initiating and structuring discussion about contracting. The first step is to identify common ground between the needs of the family and the services that can be provided. Time constraints limit the social worker's availability for work with a family and must be taken into account. In addition, the mandate of an agency will place further constraints on how social workers enter into contracts with client families. Finally, FSWs should not contract to provide services that are beyond their competence or exceed the agency's capacity and resources.

As mentioned, contracts can change as the work progresses, reflecting the dynamic nature of family social work. Essentially, every time the FSW and family agree on an activity, they have formulated a contract. As the work moves forward, the contract will become increasingly complex, and may eventually address issues in the FSW–family relationship.

| CASE 9.1 | WORKING WITH OTHER HELPERS |

Wanda and Kenneth came to the FSW because Kenneth's ex-wife had moved out of the state with his two-year-old son, Johnny, and refused to allow Kenneth to see the boy. Kenneth reported that his ex-wife, Nola, was angry with him about their divorce and was jealous of his new wife, Wanda. Nola had envisioned that she and Kenneth would remarry until Wanda came upon the scene. Wanda reported that not only was Nola angry with the couple, but that both of their families (and some of their friends) were upset about the union. Wanda said this is because she is somewhat older than Kenneth and divorced herself. Both families have religious beliefs against divorce and they have had much difficulty accepting the untraditional age difference between the newlyweds.

The FSW's assessment revealed a need for legal aid to deal with the custody and visitation issues, as well as family counseling for the extended family issue. Since Wanda and Kenneth did not have a great deal of money, the FSW referred the couple to an attorney service that provided help on a sliding fee scale basis according to family income. The FSW then referred the couple to a family counseling center associated with their religious denomination to help with the family issues.

A contract makes the family and the FSW accountable to one another. Each assumes an active role and responsibility to fulfill agreed-upon tasks and to work toward negotiated goals. The contract should identify reciprocal obligations and ways to evaluate change.

CHAPTER SUMMARY

In this chapter we focused on assessment of the entire family, moving into six different ways to define family problems. Of particular importance is for the family social worker to be continually culturally sensitive. Intervention targeted changing circular patterns through stimulating interaction; the use of lineal, circular, strategic, and reflexive questions; and detriangulation. We also discussed working with involuntary clients, including the need for the family social worker to develop goals and set contracts with all families.

The family social work relationship is established to achieve certain goals. Goal setting allows the work to develop and retain its purpose. Goals should specify what the client wishes to achieve through family social work, as well as the methods that will be used. Goals should meet the following criteria: they should be measurable, set within a reasonable time limit, consistent with the client's values and abilities, and under the client's control. Strategies for setting goals include identifying general intentions, defining the specifics of the goal, and setting goals that can be reached within a measurable period.

Contracting occurs at the end of the assessment phase. The contract is an agreement between the client and the FSW outlining the goals of the relationship and the means to be used to achieve these goals. The contract can be oral or written and should be negotiated early in the work, but it may change as the work progresses. Without a contract, there is often confusion because the FSW and the family are proceeding without a shared understanding of the work to be accomplished. Contracts are limited by time constraints and agency mandates. Effective contracts specify what needs to be accomplished and how, the roles of the FSW and the client, and procedural details such as when and where meetings will take place.

EXERCISES

9.1   TARGETING ASSESSMENT ISSUES

Break the class into groups of three and brainstorm issues and questions that might be asked in an assessment interview. Report back to the main group. Assign a class member to collate the lists given by all the groups. This list can be distributed to the entire class for future reference.

9.2   REFRAMING A PROBLEM FROM INDIVIDUAL TO FAMILY FOCUS

Select one possible family problem that a FSW might see in family work. How might this problem be considered an individual problem? Now create a scenario where you reframe this problem as a "family problem." How might family members resist this reformulation of the "problem"?

9.3   RESISTANCE IN PROBLEM DEFINITION

Identify one possible problem where an individual in a family is the reason for initiating family work. How can the FSW redefine the problem into a family issue without stimulating resistance in the family?

9.4   ROLE PLAY

Break into groups of six again. One person will play the role of family social worker to interview a family in which a teen-aged child has been charged with possession of drugs (marijuana). The family consists of Katie (mother), Bobbie (father), Phil (14-year-old charged with drug possession), Jackie (16-year-old perfect daughter), and Jimmy (a typical 8-year-old). The court has ordered the family into therapy. All family members are angry with Phil for putting the family through this turmoil. Family members do think that they play a role in the problem. First, role-play to deliberately create resistance in the family. After 5 to 10 minutes, work with this resistance to diminish it and engage to work with their problems. Compare the two approaches. What is different between the two role-plays? Report back to the class.

9.5   CIRCULAR CAUSALITY

Reflect upon a well-established relationship in which you are currently participating, or a relationship from your childhood. Try to identify an ongoing circular pattern of interaction between you and the other person. Label your own thoughts, feelings, and behaviors, then try to do the same for the other person. How does circular causality work when there seems to be a power imbalance?

9.6 ONGOING PERSONAL CIRCULAR CAUSALITY

Examine one of your ongoing relationships. Identify an ongoing circular pattern of interaction with that significant other. It does not matter where you start to identify the pattern. (You might want to work together with this person). Start with one individual and identify, thoughts, feelings, and behaviors, and then move to the second person and do the same. Draw the pattern on a piece of paper, drawing the diagram one step at a time. How does circular causality work?

9.7 WORKER TRIANGULATION AND ETHICAL ISSUES

Divide the class into two sections. One section will argue for the worker to keep a secret disclosed by one family member. The other section will argue that keeping the secret colludes with family dysfunction. Debate in class. Then formulate an agency policy for dealing with the issue.

10 CHAPTER | THE INTERVENTION PHASE

INTERVENTION PHASES

Many family social workers feel comfortable in the engagement, relationship building, and assessment phases of family work, They may experience the most self-doubt when specific family changes have been targeted. In Chapter 10 we discuss many practical changes inducing skills that family social workers can use with families. These skills are not to be used mechanically by family social workers. Rather, they must be used selectively, based on the assessment of a particular family. The intervention phase formally starts after the family social worker has engaged the family and completed a thorough assessment, goals have been set, and a clear contract has been made. We first look at micro skills that can be used on a moment-to-moment basis to help families and family members alter their behaviors and repetitive ways of functioning. These skills include focusing, using examples, confronting, enactment, externalizing the problem, and the use of metaphor. We then examine sub-phases of intervention, which include contracting, crisis intervention, ecological intervention, and problem solving. Other skills that are presented specifically depend upon specific family dynamics such as problematic family alliances, working with enmeshed families, examining family rules, multigenerational issues, and boundary problems. We also discuss issues related to working with minority families.

The contract is a partnership in which the FSW and the family work together to achieve agreed-upon goals. The role of the FSW in the intervention stage is to provide support, education, and concrete assistance (see more on roles in the following section). Ways of helping may include assisting the family to restructure daily routines, teaching family members to communicate more directly and effectively, developing new parenting strategies, altering circular patterns, and offering feedback and support as clients learn and practice new behaviors. It should be noted that many interventions will involve action rather than simply talking (Kaplan, 1986). Workers should be versatile in developing a range of skills that are comprehensive and multidimensional.

As mentioned previously, family social work is a partnership between the FSW and the family, characterized by knowing and accepting one another, and working together to achieve agreed-upon goals. The FSW supports family members as they risk looking at themselves and at family interactions to increase awareness and change behaviors. The FSW becomes an important presence in the life space of the family, addressing issues relating to the difficulties that the family faces. As mentioned, the selection of intervention techniques will relate directly to how the problem is defined. For example, if the family social worker believes that sexual abuse within the family is the result of family dynamics, the intervention would be to change family dynamics. On the other hand, if the worker believes that sexual abuse within the family is the result of the perpetrator's sexual attraction to children, intervention will be much different (Coleman & Collins, 1990), as will be the worker's determination of whether or not the family work has been successful. The worker might help the family restructure daily routines, model skills, provide support and encouragement, and help family members communicate more directly and effectively, or even help the mother access concrete resources after the father has been ordered out of the home.

In the process of joining, learning, and separating, a number of intervention issues emerge. First is the importance of remaining focused on family issues. The family social worker engages in this work for professional reasons and the experience can create personal feelings of satisfaction, pleasure, and, at times, frustration. In the course of family work, FSWs experience times when their self-esteem is heightened, skills are improved, and insight is gained. However, these are the indirect result of serving the family rather than being sought directly by the FSW.

Munson (1993) identified four phases of interviews with families and has also used the phases to look at integration of process and technique. In the first phase, the worker identifies the interaction *style* of the family and matches it to the style of the family. This enables the worker to join with the family. In the second phase, the worker *enables* family members to express themselves. The third phase involves a worker–family *encounter* during which family patterns of relating and behaving are clarified. In the final phase of an interview, the worker *shifts the dysfunction,* during which alternative ways of interacting are created.

ROLES AND OBJECTIVES OF THE FAMILY SOCIAL WORKER

Historically, professional helpers have approached families and individual clients from an "expert" position. With presumably more knowledge and experience than clients, professionals worked with families to solve problems, make decisions, and show families ways to be more effective parents. As an expert, the helping professional carried out this role as an authority, detached from the family, and families were not considered partners in a change process. Power and knowledge were the domain of the professional helper. In the process, the helper gave and the family received. The giving–receiving pattern created power imbalances that interfered with motivation, commitment, and goals.

Changes in social workers' roles and expectations emerged out of shifts in perception of the family and effective helping. Today, the family is not a passive recipient of intervention, but is an active partner and participant throughout the entire change process. Nor does the family social worker know better than the family (Wood & Geismar, 1986). The family, within parameters determined by society, must define its own needs, setting priorities, and stating preferences for services. Consequently, the family social worker is a collaborator, facilitator, and negotiator. These multiple roles demand that workers be well educated. Indeed, to fulfill these roles, family social workers must use multiple helping skills and be competent in a range of domains pertinent to their role. The role of family collaborator and partner requires that workers reject canned "expert" solutions to predefined problems. Families have both the right and the responsibility to identify their special concerns and goals in relation to their family situation and to play an active role in their resolution.

To better help families, family social workers must understand their own family issues and interpersonal relationships in order to develop mutual respect and partnership with the individual families. Broadening the focus beyond the individual to embrace the entire family unit is a profound shift in perspective for many professionals whose educational background and inclination motivate them to advocate for children, at times in an *adversarial* role to the family. The shift from an individual to a family perspective requires them to incorporate a belief in family competence into the decision-making and problem-solving process.

In partnership with families, family social workers use seven roles as a springboard from which to stimulate change: empathic supporter, teacher/trainer, consultant, enabler, mobilizer, mediator, and advocate.

1. In the role of *empathic supporter,* the guiding philosophy of a family social worker is to identify and reinforce family strengths while recognizing family limitations or lack of resources. Acknowledging strengths enables the FSW to join with the family and develop a bond that will increase trust, motivation, and optimism to work toward change. While every family has strengths, social workers have unfortunately often been preoccupied with dysfunction and pathology, perhaps reinforcing dysfunction by focusing primarily on problems. For example, despite negative parenting practices, most parents care deeply about their children. Such caring should be highlighted to create the foundation for dealing with targeted problems.

2. The *teacher/trainer* role allows the FSW to cultivate areas where the family is deficient or lacking in skills or knowledge. Viewing family problems as the result of skill deficits (or even more palatably, as new skills to be learned), rather than as evidence of pathology, makes families more open to working on problems in a nondefensive manner. Problem areas may include deficits in communication, parenting skills, problem solving, anger management, conflict resolution, values clarification, money management, and skills of daily living.

    The teaching role often plays out in parent training interventions. Sometimes the teaching role involves helping parents substitute verbal and physical punishment with more positive and constructive parent–child interactions. Other times, the family social worker teaches parents to work more effectively with difficult child behavior by reinforcing positive behavior and discouraging negative or annoying behavior. Through such teaching activities, parents can become therapists for their children.

3. The family social worker as *consultant* is an advisor to the family for specific problems that arise. For instance, the family generally may function well but may find adolescence a particularly difficult time for which they need specialized help. The FSW, as a consultant, can offer valuable information to parents on typical or "normal" teenage behavior. In the process, parents gain deeper insight about their adolescent's needs and will be less inclined to consider their child a problem in future interactions. The family social worker can also provide ongoing feedback to parents and children who may be isolated or otherwise lack mechanisms to obtain such feedback from other sources.

4. The *enabler* role allows the family social worker to expand opportunities for the family that might not otherwise be accessible. For instance, an immigrant family may not be familiar with the various services appropriate

for their special needs. Informing a family about available services and helping them to use these services will empower the family. The empowerment that family members experience when accomplishing a task can pave the way for future successes.

5. The family social worker as *mobilizer* captures the worker's unique position in the social network of helping resources. A social worker, knowledgeable about helping systems and community support networks, activates and manages the involvement of various community groups and resources to serve families. The FSW can mobilize community agencies to work with a family. When school poses challenges to children, for example, the FSW can coordinate with school and family activities and communication to establish additional opportunities for a struggling student.

6. In the *mediator* role, the family social worker addresses stress and conflict between individuals and systems. Mediation can occur at any level of the system. The FSW can mediate solutions when the family is in conflict with the community, or at a narrower level, mediate between family members who are in conflict. When a family member has an antagonistic relationship with a landlord or neighbor, the FSW can also attempt to resolve the conflict.

7. The family social worker also acts as an *advocate,* a role that requires activism on behalf of client families. The FSW is in a unique position to understand how family problems may be rooted in conditions within the broader societal context. Consequently, community activism and political action give family social workers the means with which to work for social and legislative reform benefiting clients.

INTERVENTION TECHNIQUES

Family social workers can use a variety of techniques to assist client families to gain new insights and ultimately to practice new behaviors. These techniques include: observation, focusing, use of examples, confrontation, refraining, enactment, externalizing the problem, use of metaphors, and contracting.

OBSERVATION

Systematic observation, a formal procedure used both in research and in practice to record actual behavior, may be used when objective information about the presence of events is needed. The family may be helped by seeing the frequency data collected about a particular problem, such as how often tantrums occur. Systematic observation helps parents learn to manage the behavior of hyperactive children or children with other behavior problems, and may be employed to help abusive parents develop positive, effective behavior management techniques. Changing from a punitive, aversive parenting style to a more positive, reinforcing way of responding can be facilitated by self-monitoring procedures, such as teaching parents to count the number of times they respond positively or negatively to their child. Helping a parent learn to record words that a child with a speech problem says during part of the day may be an important part of an assessment of speech difficulties. Having a parent learn to record the number of times a particular physical therapy routine is carried out could be very important for increasing compliance with a treatment program.

Listening and observation form the foundation of qualitative family assessment. Observation as a clinical skill for a FSW cannot be overemphasized. Without open and accurate observation, the activities that follow will have no substance. Observation allows the worker to obtain accurate information essential for understanding families—some of which is not explicit. However, unless mindful use is made of observation, much can be lost. Descriptions of family events and dynamics by family members may be contradictory; other times, family members may be unable to describe what is going on because they lack verbal skills or because they do not understand what is happening. Additionally, through independent observation of what is happening in a particular family, the family social worker can piece together independent viewpoints into a unified whole. Thus, through observation, or "listening with the eyes," the FSW notices the physical characteristics and nonverbal behaviors, energy level, emotions, and congruence between verbal and nonverbal expression.

Observation enables the FSW to develop a comprehensive understanding of the ways the family experiences the world. The worker must listen to both the content and the process in the family. The FSW observes, for example, to subtle issues related to themes of power, authority, and ambivalence about seeking or receiving help. Difficulties in discussing socially stigmatized topics and inhibitions concerning the direct and full expression of powerful feelings are particularly crucial to look out for (Shulman, 1992). Since FSWs are likely to pick up indirect communication from nonverbal rather than verbal communications, they must observe these closely. Observations of family dynamics supplement information obtained from the verbal flow of an interview as well as from any assessment tools used by the family worker.

Family social work provides special opportunities for observation. In contrast to an office setting, FSWs have the opportunity to conduct an ecological assessment of the individual and the family and the community. The worker makes mental notes about the community by becoming aware of the broader environment where the family lives, noting such things as access to community services (including transportation and medical and educational agencies), neighborhood safety, and recreational and cultural opportunities. Such information helps place into perspective discussions with the family and also provides a knowledge base to draw upon when making linkages to about resources.

Once in a home, observation has added importance because the family worker is witness to the physical environment of the family. Seeing the organization of the home and materials available to meet basic needs allows the worker to understand more about client strengths and coping strategies, resources, and limitations imposed by the home environment. Before entering the home, the worker might create a checklist for what to look for, given the special circumstances of the family. Certainly, observations of the physical environment will be affected by special circumstances (Holman, 1983). For example, a family in severe economic crisis may live in a dilapidated house, with inadequate plumbing, mattresses on the floor, or an infestation of vermin. One family worker worked in a small home where the family owned six large dogs. The day after each visit, the worker noticed marks on her body, suggesting flea bites. Alternatively, an impoverished house may suggest depression and apathy. Similarly, when working with parents of an active child, the FSW may observe that there are few children's materials available and wonder about parental knowledge of child development or their ability to purchase stimulating toys. Family social workers often formulate hypotheses about families and later try to validate or refute them. In the preceding example, a hypothesis about parents' lack of knowledge of child development might be discarded if the home was equipped with child-appropriate materials, including books, toys, and play equipment.

Besides informing the FSW about environmental and physical resources, home observation provides opportunities for observing how family members interact in their daily routine. In office meetings, professionals may interact with only one member of the family, while in-home sessions allow FSWs to speak with the entire family. Contributions of individual family members' well-being or dysfunction may be noticed and clues obtained for what assistance is needed. Careful observation also strengthens documentation and other record-keeping demanded by many programs.

Overall, observation skills provide information for many intervention decisions made. Cultural and ethnic differences also need to be factored into observations of the family. Some cultures have extended family living with them, and others find it disrespectful for certain family members to be in the same room or to address directly. Ultimately this information should be obtained in a way that remains sensitive to and respectful of the fact that the worker is a visitor in the home of the family. Such information should not be used to condemn or make value judgments on lifestyles.

Family social workers need to observe the social functioning of the family. Social functioning is best understood by looking at the social roles that family members perform. Individual behavior and adjustment reflects how well family members perform their social roles. Geismar and Ayres (1959) proposed four areas of role performance within the family and four outside the family. Internal roles include:

- Family relationships and family unity
- Childcare and training
- Health practices
- Household practices

External family roles include:

- Use of community resources
- Social activities
- Economic practices
- Relationship of the family to the social worker

Focusing

After the family worker has made observations of the family and its environment, the worker then needs to focus on particular issues. Focusing involves paying attention. To do this, both the client and the FSW must ensure that time is used productively. While tangents are sometimes productive, most often they are unproductive. It is therefore important to recognize when clients shift topics or steer the discussion elsewhere. It is possible to focus on the client, on the main theme or problem, on others, on mutual issues, on the interviewer, or on cultural/environmental or contextual issues. Based on prior knowledge of the problem and the client, the FSW can develop a list of relevant and promising areas to be explored. However, anticipating problem areas is not always possible. Sometimes clients are scattered or overwhelmed.

Use of Examples

Examples help the FSW explain, describe, or teach a concept to a family. Generally, examples should be compatible with experiences of the family's life. Examples can be used to accomplish several objectives. They offer reassurance that others have faced the same challenges. A family social worker may tell a worried parent whose child is about to begin kindergarten, "Many parents have these concerns. One mother told me that with each of her five children, she felt some worry as they began kindergarten." Examples can illustrate alternative ways of dealing with a difficult situation. The FSW may tell a parent, "Once when I talked with another mother about a similar situation, she told me that she had tried letting her child take a nap in the afternoon. Your situation sounds similar. Does her decision seem like it would work for you, too?"

Examples can help clients feel at ease with something that has made them uncomfortable. The FSW may say, "I remember a mother who tried three different ways to help her child learn to use the toilet before the child was trained. Like her, you may find that the second or third effort will work, even though the first one did not." Examples in the form of interesting stories are valuable teaching aids because they are likely to be remembered longer than generalized statements.

Confrontation

Confrontation is a useful skill for family social workers, but its effectiveness has been questioned because it can be either growth promoting or damaging to a client. Confrontation often is viewed as hostile, unpleasant, demeaning, and anxiety provoking (Brock & Barnard, 1991). FSWs may be reluctant to use confrontation because of potentially harmful consequences, such as the client pulling out of counseling or escalating anger. Yet confrontation can be helpful under some circumstances. The level of confrontation should be chosen carefully: "Don't use a cannon when a pea shooter would suffice!" Similarly, confrontation is not a verbal hit-and-run; rather, it is used constructively to bring about change.

The goal of confrontation is to raise awareness by presenting information that the client is overlooking or failing to identify. The FSW must find a way to make new information palatable or acceptable to the person being confronted. While confrontation can be a difficult skill to master, particularly for FSWs who are ambivalent about its use, it can also generate change quickly.

A useful guideline in deciding whether to confront clients is to determine what purpose confrontation will serve. Is confrontation planned because the FSW is impatient and unwilling to allow the client to move at his or her own pace? Does the FSW enjoy confrontation or want to impose her or his personal values on the client? Conversely, is confrontation desirable because the FSW is attuned to client feelings and wants to create change? Confrontation often is most useful only after other skills have failed.

Confrontation requires tenacity and tact on the part of the FSW, who must be willing to bring into the open an unexpressed feeling, idea, or issue. Without confrontation by the FSW, family members may persist in behavior that is self-destructive or harmful to others. Confrontation, when used appropriately and in a caring manner, benefits the client. Brock and Barnard (1991) suggest that the difference between a well-executed confrontation and a confrontation that is demeaning or hostile can be perceived in the social worker's tone of voice.

Confrontation is appropriate in addressing repetitive client problematic behavior that has not changed through other efforts. For example, the client may be avoiding a basic issue that is troubling or creating dysfunction within the family. Confrontation may assist a family member to recognize self-destructive or self-defeating behaviors or to acknowledge the possible consequences of behaving in a particular way. Further examples of appropriate situations for confrontation include incongruent behavior during an interview that affects the quality of the counseling relationship; failure to assume responsibility for oneself; visible discrepancies between thoughts/feelings and words/behaviors; and unrealistic or distorted perceptions of reality.

The purpose of confrontation is to point out discrepant aspects of the client's verbal and nonverbal behavior, bringing them to conscious awareness. The primary function of confrontation is to create disequilibrium in order to permit new behaviors to develop. While confrontation does not solve the actual problem, it does prepare the client to work on the problem.

Confrontation is most effective when a strong client–FSW relationship has been established. A general guideline is the stronger the relationship, the more effective the confrontation. One positive outcome of effective confrontation is a deepening of the client–worker relationship. By using attentive listening and empathy skills to tune in to the client's reaction to confrontation, the FSW may help the client to gain a greater insight and motivation for change. For example, a worker might say, "I get a sense that you are bothered by what I just said." Because of the high emotional intensity of confrontation, it should not be used at the end of a session, when feelings should approach a more even keel.

Confrontation has varied effects, depending on whether the client has the personal and social resources to cope with the information being presented. A client with well-developed defenses may block the impact of confrontation, and the FSW should recognize these defenses and discuss them. Even though some people react poorly to feedback, a social worker who is not honest is colluding with maladaptive behavior.

Successful confrontation occurs in two stages: formulating the confrontation statement and addressing the response of the client. The social worker should prepare for possible reactions such as withdrawal, defensiveness about the FSW's observations, denial, discrediting the feedback, arguing, or finding someone else to collude with.

The following sentence shells can be used for formulating confrontational statements:

"On the one hand, you say _____, and on the other hand you do _____ " (Used to confront discrepancies between words and actions)

"I am puzzled (confused) about what you just said/did . . . could you please help me understand?"

"I don't get it . . ."

Effective confrontation requires that the social worker point out discrepancies, inconsistencies, or contradictions between the client's words and actions. In describing these discrepancies, the FSW must avoid judgmental or evaluative speculations and conclusions. Following a confrontation with an empathic response will increase its effectiveness as a motivator for change.

LEVELS OF CONFRONTATION

Level 1: Giving in to the client. At this level, the FSW either ignores the problematic behavior or makes a weak attempt to confront and then withdraws at the first sign of resistance. At this level, the FSW may be overly concerned about being disliked or being attacked, or may not be committed enough to the relationship to become involved.

Level 2: Scolding. The social worker coerces the client into changing by shaming, attempting to induce guilt, or nagging. The FSW risks losing self-control and may even give the client a lecture about acceptable behavior. At this level, confrontation can be demeaning and manipulative.

Level 3: Describing ineffective behavior. The social worker describes the behavior that is hurting the client or others and identifies possible reasons for the behavior. The FSW may attempt to empathize by conveying a message about how difficult it is to face and take self-responsibility for the behavior, yet the message is straightforward and does not involve lecturing or giving in.

Level 4: Identifying negative consequences of behavior. The social worker identifies ineffective behavior patterns and examines feelings. The FSW also helps the client to identify possible negative consequences of continuing the behavior.

Level 5: Levels 3 and 4, plus soliciting commitment to change. This level incorporates components of Levels 3 and 4 but also challenges the client to accept responsibility for the problem and for making changes. Changes will occur only if the client honestly agrees with the social worker.

REFRAMING

Refraining removes a situation from an old context (set of rules) and places it in a new context (set of rules) that defines it equally well (Becvar & Becvar, 1996). In a reframe, positive interpretations are assigned to problematic behaviors and responses (Satir & Baldwin, 1983). The technique is most successful if the FSW is able to persuade the family that the reframe is plausible and more accurate than the former interpretation (Brock & Barnard, 1991). When problems are understood in a more positive light, new responses are likely.

What makes reframing such an effective tool of change is that once we do perceive the alternative class membership(s) we cannot so easily go back to the trap and the anguish of the former view of "reality"; it is almost impossible to revert to our previous helplessness and especially our original hopelessness about the possibility of a solution (Watzlawick, Weakland, & Fisch, 1974).

Social workers should use reframing selectively. Not all issues should be reframed. For example, sexual abuse should never be reframed as the perpetrator's attempt to show affection.

EXAMPLE OF REFRAMING   A hyperactive child can be reframed as a challenging, energetic child. Instead of relying on medication, parents may plan more physical activities to help the child "burn off" excessive energy.

ENACTMENT

An enactment is an attempt to bring a family conflict from outside the interview into the here-and-now of the interview. It is useful when a critical family incident has occurred in the family worker's absence. Thus, a problematic scenario is actively created during an interview. In an enactment, family members demonstrate how they deal with the issue while the therapist observes and assesses interaction. Alternative solutions can then be devised.

EXAMPLE OF ENACTMENT   The FSW might say, "You described an argument between yourselves last night as parents. I would like you now to move your chairs and face each other and carry on with this argument. I would like to see if you can resolve this issue now and I will help you to do so."

EXTERNALIZING THE PROBLEM

Externalizing the problem as an intervention is credited to Michael White, an Australian social worker, and his colleague David Epston from New Zealand. It involves separating the problem from the person to allow the problem to be viewed outside the person. "Externalizing is an approach to therapy that encourages the persons to objectify and at the same time personify the problems that they experience as oppressive. In the process, the problem becomes a separate entity and thus external to the person or relationship that was ascribed as the problem" (White & Epston, 1990, p. 38), giving the family a better opportunity to gain control over the problem. The process of separating the person from the oppressive problem is achieved by using externalizing language or activities to locate the problem outside the person.

The FSW begins the intervention by asking the family to describe how much influence they have over the problem and how much influence the problem has over them. This is called a relative influencing question (White, 1989). "The problem becomes the problem, and then the person's relationship with the problem become the problem" (White & Epston, 1990, p. 40). When families view problems from this vantage (i.e., a double description), their perspective widens. By changing the perception and meanings attached to the problem, there is a greater potential to arrive at a solution (Brock & Barnard, 1991).

EXAMPLE OF EXTERNALIZING THE PROBLEM   Instead of stress being perceived as an internal problem, it can be defined as an external stress monster that occasionally enters one's life. The family worker than can explore when the family member is most vulnerable to this stress monster and also when the family member is able to keep the stress monster out of their lives.

Externalizing the problem can be used in a number of situations. Brock and Barnard (1991) suggest that externalizing the problem is an especially effective tool in working with addictions in the family. Thus, alcohol becomes the "enemy" that the family shares together.

USE OF METAPHOR

A metaphor is "a figure of speech in which a word or phrase literally denoting one kind of object or idea is used in place of another to suggest a likeness or analogy between them" (Satir & Baldwin, 1983, p. 244). Metaphors are used to help clients understand abstract concepts. They provide information in a nonthreatening way and give families some distance from a threatening situation.

EXAMPLE OF USE OF METAPHOR   To help families understand how a crisis can destabilize the family system, the FSW may compare the family to a mobile that gets out of balance when objects are added or moved around.

CONTRACTING

Contracting, which was mentioned in the preceding chapter, can include contracts between family members. Two types of commonly used contracts are *quid pro quo* (QPQ) and good faith (Jackson, 1972). In the QPQ contract, one person agrees to exchange a behavior for one desired by another family member. For example, a mother might agree to drive her daughter and friends to the mall if the daughter washes the dishes without being told. The good faith contract, by contrast, is not dependent on the behavior of another family member. A person is rewarded after contract conditions are met. For instance, if a child completes her homework all week, she can invite a friend over to spend the night on the weekend. In both types of contracts, the FSW can help family members to make the conditions of the contract as clear and specific as possible.

ECOLOGOCIAL INTERVENTION

The type of ecological interventions required will arise from an assessment of the ecomap described in Chapter 5. The ecomap is the blueprint for planned change and is the first stage in deciding upon an action (Hartman & Laird, 1983). Not only does an ecomap organize information visually, it also outlines family themes and targets for change. The ecomap should be created with the family. Family attention can be directed to address the question, "What does this mean to you?" Focusing on the ecosystem will also remove the problem from the level of individual blame. We should point out at this point that the goal of ecological intervention is to teach clients how to do for themselves, rather than relying on the FSW to do it for them (Kinney, Haapala, & Booth, 1991).

Typically, the worker should focus on environmental problems first (Kaplan, 1986). This will help the family problem-solve around less threatening issues, while at the same time build in supports for the family. The type of ecological interventions used depends on the issues, client skills, and resources available in the community. For example, one author reported that the following resources are either not available or are difficult to access for family-centered workers: mental health, housing, day care, low-skill basic jobs, transportation, legal services and religious programs (Goldstein, 1981). In another report, workers found that emergency housing, homemaker services, group homes, parent aides, in-patient drug and alcohol treatment, and respite care were also difficult to obtain (Kohlert & Pecora, 1991). The worker must also help families develop creative ways to use formal and informal resources. Sometimes families will merely lack information about where resources exist. Other times, family members may have the knowledge but lack the skills to get connected to resources. In this case, the family worker will have to help the family get connected (Helton & Jackson, 1997). The ultimate goal is to help clients learn how to get needs met on their own. It is tempting and perhaps easier to do for the clients instead of teaching them to do for themselves (Kinney, Haapala, & Booth, 1991).

Hepworth and Larsen (1993) presented a range of ecological interventions for families. They include:

- Supplementing resources in the home environment;
- Developing and enhancing support systems;
- Moving clients to a new environment;
- Increasing the responsiveness of organizations to people's needs;
- Enhancing interactions between organizations and institutions,
- Improving institutional environments;
- Enhancing agency environments; and,
- Developing new resources.

CRISIS INTERVENTION

There are many types of crises that a family social worker may encounter when working with a family, and sometimes a crisis can be used to the advantage of the family. At times this means that the worker might want to create a crisis, and at other times the worker will want to defuse one (Brock & Barnard,

1991). Two methods exist to defuse a crisis: the FSW can become triangulated into a relationship, and the FSW can return the family to the past. One way for the worker to become triangulated is to get the member to direct exclusive attention toward the worker by using empathic statements. Taking the family into the past helps the family to recall similar crises and helps them to realize that despite the present crisis being consuming, they have experienced crises in the past and have used skills to get themselves out of those crises.

Regardless of the situation, it is crucial that the worker remain calm throughout the interview. The best approach toward clients in crisis is a straightforward approach.

There are many different models of crisis intervention, and we present a common model below (Gilliland & James, 1993):

1. Defining the problem: In defining the problem, the skills discussed in Chapter 5 provide a requisite base upon which to do crisis intervention.
2. Ensuring client safety: The immediate needs of the client must be attended to.
3. Providing support: Sometimes the support will be in the form of referral to other helping sources.
4. Examining alternatives: Alternatives should build on the strengths of the clients.
5. Making plans.
6. Obtaining a commitment.

Workers will not always want to avoid a crisis. For example, family workers may sometimes want to induce a crisis to destabilize families. There are many ways of doing this, such as removing a child from the home. At times, families may be too complacent or may lack the motivational anxiety necessary to create change. One method of creating a crisis is by amplifying an issue in the family (Brock & Barnard, 1991; Minuchin, 1974). The worker might draw attention to a piece of interaction from an interview and magnify its significance. Alternatively, the worker might be able to change the meaning a family member attaches to a particular experience and work from the assumption that a change in how a client sees a problem will also promote a change in behavior (Brock & Barnard, 1991).

HOW TO TEACH PROBLEM-SOLVING SKILLS

Family social work focuses on systemic interventions on the family as a unit rather than on individual members. Systemic intervention is linked with a problem-solving and communicative intervention. Because the systemic intervention focuses on the family as a unit, the problem-solving intervention teaches members to negotiate solutions to their problems that are acceptable to all. Seven steps in problem solving include: problem definition, goal selection, solution generation, consideration of consequences, decision making, implementation, and evaluation. Teaching clients to problem solve requires a shift on the part of the FSW who is now no longer the "expert" but the facilitator. As facilitator and consultant, the FSW teaches the family to develop solutions to their own problems rather than relying on outside help.

STAGES OF PROBLEM SOLVING

1. Problem definition describes a problem situation. A situation is a problem when its resolution is not automatic. It also involves discovering how each person contributes to the problem.
2. Goal selection describes what each person wants to happen.
3. Generation of solutions as a result of brainstorming will lead to identification of a number of alternative responses that may lead to resolution of the specific problem.
4. Consideration of positive and negative consequences of any solution could relate to time; money; personal, emotional, and social effects; and include possible immediate and long-term effects.
5. Decision making is based on weighing the proposed solutions and consequences and deciding which one is best for the individual at that time. Decision making involves consideration of a person's priorities and values and contracting a solution.
6. Implementation requires carrying out actions called for by the proposed solution.
7. Evaluation must review the results of problem solving and decide whether it met the goals and, if changes are necessary, selection of another option (go back to number 3).

Developing Problem-Solving Skills

Disorganized and unskilled families often lack skills to be able to solve problems adequately. Families must learn how to deal with immediate problems and develop skills to solve problems for the future when the worker is no longer around. Problem solving entails seven steps to help families arrive at solutions to their problems.

The problem-solving approach not only focuses on helping people resolve present difficulty, it also involves teaching clients the skills solve problems by learning strategies for dealing with present and future concerns. Thus, a problem-solving emphasis is on helping families learn more effective ways of becoming independent and self-reliant.

Teaching clients to problem solve demands that the family social worker serve as a facilitator rather than an expert. The shift from expert to facilitator starts at the point of problem and goal definition. Previously, workers defined client problems for them and then imposed solutions. Conversely, the current problem-solving model empowers clients and families to actively identify their own needs and goals. When a family has difficulty doing so, the FSW simplifies the process. In some situations, if a family can only vaguely define a difficult situation, the FSW may initially take a more active role in identifying a problem, gradually involving the family. The overarching goal is to empower the family to assume this responsibility as they develop the skills to do so.

In considering solutions to problems, however, family social workers will often have more knowledge about topics than does the family, thus placing the FSW in a position to offer help. The shift in philosophy to facilitator does not mean that such information will not be shared. Rather, it means that clients will be encouraged to generate unique solutions on their own and consider consequences. In decision making, the FSW will at times need to state an opinion, or even ask specifically that something be done; usually, however, the worker encourages the family to decide. Clients develop more independence as they improve their coping and decision-making skills.

In the early stages of problem solving, more direction from the FSW may be necessary. Later, the family social worker becomes less directive as the client assumes more responsibility. One program described how services to families changed over time: at first, "doing for," then "doing with," and, finally, "cheering on." A related technique is contracting (Jordan & Cobb, 2001).

SOLUTION-FOCUSED PROBLEM-SOLVING QUESTIONS

The solution-focused approach offers some very useful questions that can be asked to help families solve their problems (DeJong & Berg, 2002). The following are some of these questions the FSW could ask a family:

1. What resources does your family have right now?
2. What would you like to stay the same?
3. What will you notice in your family when things are getting better?
4. What will each family member be doing differently?
5. Are there times when the above is already happening to some (even a small) extent, and what is different about these times?
6. What would be the first sign that the family is moving in that direction?
7. How will your family know that they are making progress?

These questions can help a family discover that small changes lead to larger changes in a positive problem-solving process.

HOW TO TEACH COMMUNICATION SKILLS

Healthy communication is an important aspect of family work because dysfunctional communication can interfere with effective problem solving (Kaplan, 1986). Effective problem solving requires that healthy communication among family members be congruent, direct, honest, and clear (Satir, 1967). By examining family communication, workers will be able to see how family members experience their relationships with one another, how they express intimacy, and how they convey information (Satir & Baldwin, 1983). Thus, work with communication in families entails fostering new skills. These skills may be taught by instruction or through worker modeling (Bodin, 1981).

Changing dysfunctional communication is a three-step process:

1. Family members should discuss communication;
2. Then analyze their behaviors and emotional responses; and
3. Look at the impact of the interaction on relationships (Watzlawick, Beavin, & Jackson, 1967).

Metacommunication is "communication about communication" or a "message about a message" (Satir, 1967). Most communication is a request (Satir, 1967). Metacommunication is useful to check out the meaning of what another has just said and is particularly useful in working with families. While families communicate a lot, they seldom spend time looking at underlying messages to one another (Hepworth & Larsen, 1993). Discussions of metacommunication are most effective if done in the here-and-now when the interaction is fresh in the mind of the family members. The FSW will have to pay close attention to the ongoing family interaction, stop the communication process, and then engage the family in a discussion of the events that just occurred. The goal is to get the family to replace dysfunctional patterns of communication with healthier communication.

Systemic intervention also focuses on the family interaction, particularly communication strengths and deficits. Training to improve families' communication emphasizes both verbal and nonverbal skills (Granvold & Jordan, 1994). Verbal communication skills include listening and empathizing, "I" statements, leveling, and editing.

Listening and Empathizing

Family members can be taught to actively listen, or paraphrase, what the speaker said in order to communicate that the message was received. For instance, the wife says to her spouse, "I feel angry right now because you were late and did not call." Her husband, using active listening says, "You are mad because I did not telephone to say I would be late." Problems could arise if instead the husband said, "You are always trying to control me by nagging. Get off my back." Compare the two different responses. Which response demonstrates more healthy communication? Rather than getting in an argument, the listener in the first example has restated the angry message and communicated to his wife that he heard what she said, thus supporting her communication. Also, if the paraphrase is incorrect, the speaker has an opportunity to give feedback and clarify her message. This type of listening communicates empathy to the speaker.

Use of "I" Statements

Use of "I" statements to communicate a message, especially a message likely to put the listener on the defensive, can help members reduce family conflicts. The angry spouse in the previous paragraph can say, "You are a thoughtless bum, you come home late all the time and never call!" Alternatively, she can use an "I" statement to express the effect of her husband's behavior on her feelings. For example, "When you come home late and don't call me, it makes me feel angry and frightened, because I worry about your safety." The general format for making "I" statements is, "I feel (*speaker's feeling*), when you (*family member's behavior*), because (*compelling rationale*)."

Developers of one family-centered, home-based model provide the following guidelines for using "I" messages (Kinney, Haapala & Booth, 1991):

- Describe behavior not persons.
- Use observations, not inferences.

- Use behavioral descriptors, not judgments.
- Avoid the use of generalizations such as never, always, etc.
- Speak for the moment.
- Share ideas, and do not give advice

If the listener uses active listening to be empathic, the speaker might offer a solution, such as, "Could we make a deal that I won't worry if you are less than an hour late, and that you agree to call if you will be more than an hour getting home?" The listener might modify the solution or offer an alternative one until a mutually agreeable solution is found. Active listening and use of "I" statements can be modeled and practiced with the FSW giving feedback.

The FSW also may be alert to communication deficits in the interaction. For instance, a family member may talk too loudly or softly, too quickly or slowly, or use a tone of voice that is monotonous and boring or excitable or hostile (Gambrill & Richey, 1988). The FSW also may watch for ways to help members improve their nonverbal communication. For example, members may practice communicating with relaxed posture, with a warm and smiling facial expression, and appropriate eye contact (Hepworth & Larsen, 1986).

WORKING WITH ENMESHED OR DISENGAGED FAMILIES

Satir and Baldwin (1983) describe an exercise called "Ropes" that provides clients with a concrete, visual depiction of family relationships. Each family member ties a short rope around his or her waist. Longer ropes form links between family members. This exercise helps families to recognize the complexity of family relationships. It can be used with any family as a starting point for discussing relationships and boundaries.

ESTABLISHING BOUNDARIES

In working with enmeshed families, FSWs strive to strengthen boundaries between family members and increase the autonomy of individuals (Nichols & Schwartz, 2004). The social worker encourages family members to speak for themselves. While one person is speaking, the FSW must not allow interruptions from other members of the family.

In much the same way, FSWs can help families to establish boundaries around sibling or parental subsystems. For example, topics such as sex or money may be declared off-limits to children. Similarly, children should be allowed time and space for play, without parental interference.

Disengaged families avoid interaction and intimacy; therefore, the FSW must challenge their efforts to circumvent conflict. Family members must begin to make more contact with each other, even if such contact is conflictual at first.

Sometimes, dealing with boundary dynamics is as simple as changing "who does what with whom." For example, one family social worker worked with a family where the father took on the role of a rather stern disciplinarian of his teenage son. The mother, seeing this and trying to add some balance to the father's role, would never discipline the son. They had unknowingly created a "bad parent, good parent" dynamic that was not working for anyone in the family. One parent was over-involved while the other was disengaged. Instead, the mother, who was quite capable and competent in her parenting skills, was given the role of being the disciplinarian of their son and the father was instructed to take on the role of a supportive parent to the son, including behind-the-scene support to his wife in her new parenting role. This simple change of roles produced positive results; the son was quite comfortable, compliant, and understanding of his mother's role as disciplinarian and created a new positive relationship with his father.

DEALING WITH DYSFUNCTIONAL FAMILY ALLIANCES

Family dysfunction may be created by dysfunctional family alliances. These include, but are not limited to, a disengaged marital relationship, enmeshed relationships, triangulated relationships (often a child triangulated into a marital relationship), or inappropriate relationships with members outside the family unit (Hepworth & Larsen, 1993). Goals of altering these structures of relationships can include: to break down a problematic relationship, to strengthen or create underdeveloped relationships, to reinforce functioning relationships, and to loosen enmeshed relationships. Before any of these goals are worked on, the family must first be able to describe these relationships, understand their impact on the family, and finally, decide to change them. A well-constructed genogram should highlight the nature of these relationships and alignments and can be used to alter them. Family sculpting, discussed in Chapter 5, is another way of pointing out the structure of family relationships. After family members recognize how relationships are structured in their family, they will be prepared to discuss what they want to change, how these things can be changed, and the consequences to individuals and the family unit of changing them.

A strong parental alliance is necessary for family well-being, and workers should try to enhance the parental alliance by getting parents to arrive at an agreement on parenting standards. The FSW must help parents who are not united in their parenting standards in an interview. In a consultation outside the hearing range of the children, the parents can be asked how they are going to handle a specific child-related issue that has emerged. Once the parents have arrived on a decision, the parents should act upon their decision together. If similar issues arise between interviews, a homework assignment can be for the parents to consult in a private room and then to return and conjointly act upon the issue.

WORKING WITH FAMILY RULES

Every family has rules that govern behavior. Some family rules are explicit, while others are unspoken. Openly discussing these rules makes it possible to revise them. Satir poses several questions to ask when looking at family rules: Are the present rules impossible to follow? Are the rules up to date and relevant to a changing situation? What are the rules governing roles of males and females? What rules surround the sharing of information? What are the family rules about what members can say about what they feel, see, and hear (Satir & Baldwin, 1983)?

In discussing rules with a family, the social worker must help the family to examine their rules. When the rules are unclear, they need to be brought out into the open. When rules are outdated or unfair, the social worker must help the family make a decision about whether to keep such rules. The FSW can start by emphasizing that all families operate according to a set of rules, many of which are unspoken. An example of a family rule is that everyone is supposed to eat dinner together. After making certain that family members know what the term *family rule* means, the FSW can then begin to discuss rules. The social worker should have an idea of what areas the discussion of family rules should cover. For example, in a family in which the activities of children are not monitored or supervised, the FSW may direct discussion to rules concerning parental involvement with the children.

Rules involve both instrumental basic family living rules, rules around communication, and rules around boundaries. For example, instrumental rules include rules around dinner time, who does the dishes, curfews, and so on. Communication rules are around how family members express themselves, particularly the expression of feelings. What rule is there around the expression of anger, as an example? Boundary rules are about who does what with whom. Who helps children with their homework? Who goes to parent–teacher interviews? Who disciplines which child? It is very important that all family members have an opportunity for input into the articulation of these rules to create a flexible, fair set of rules that they are then more likely to be compliant with. Ultimately, the parents will have the final say, yet it is very important to involve the children if you want compliance. The FSW can help with this process to keep the negotiations from becoming a control issue or a heated debate and instead encouraging a supportive, working together process for a family.

GUIDELINES FOR INTERVENTION WITH MINORITY FAMILIES

The International Association of Psychosocial Rehabilitation Services (IAPRS) established a goal of developing culturally competent services. Cultural competence refers to sensitivity and responsiveness to different cultures. Recognition of ethnic and cultural differences should include efforts to adapt treatment to fit the culture and ethnicity of the family and community context in which services are delivered. To achieve cultural competence in service provision, the IAPRS (1997) recommends:

1. Inclusion of culturally competent concepts in organizations' mission statements, policies, procedures, and practices.
2. Inclusion of cultural competence standards and indicators in organizations' research and evaluation programs.

3. Inclusion of cultural competence training programs in organizations' operations.
4. Quantity and quality of support given to staff members who belong to under-represented minority groups.
5. Increased bilingual/bicultural staff from target ethnic and cultural groups.
6. Increased number of volunteers, board, and staff from target ethnic and cultural groups.
7. Increased number of chapters, agencies, and staff who attend multicultural activities, conferences, and seminars.
8. Increased number of clients served from ethnic and cultural target groups.
9. Increased self-, family, and community referrals from ethnic and cultural target groups.
10. Reduced incidence of agency dropouts, emergencies, and rehospitalization among members of targeted ethnic and cultural groups.
11. Increased documentation of advocacy activities specifically against cultural, sexist, ethnic, and disability discrimination.
12. Increased meetings between agency representatives and cultural and ethnic community leaders.
13. Increased involvement of family, especially extended family as defined by the cultural or ethnic group, in the rehabilitation process.
14. Availability of services and brochures that are language-appropriate.
15. Agency environment reflecting the target ethnic and cultural group(s) served.
16. Increased number and type of multicultural activities that occur in the agency.
17. Increased number and type of culturally appropriate modalities, alternative approaches, and innovative methods.

Family work techniques for FSWs to use with minorities are those that promote bonding between the social worker and the family. In order to engage the family, the social worker may adopt the family's verbal and nonverbal communication style and relevant metaphors. Other family systems techniques that may be used include behavioral methods such as social skills training. For instance, specialized treatment packages are available to help families learn better communication, problem-solving, or anger management techniques (see Franklin & Jordan, 1999).

Intervention with African American Families

Lewellen and Jordan (1994) found that feelings of family empowerment and satisfaction with services were related to successful family intervention. Further, trust and communication style were important variables. African Americans, in comparison to other ethnic groups, reportedly were more sensitive to such matters as insensitivity of the family worker. Members of this group reported less trust in the establishment, including mental health service providers. Lack of trust may result in guarded communications and defensive interactions with the family social worker. Specific recommendations for working with

African American families include the following (Jordan, Lewellen, & Vandiver, 1994, p. 32):

1. Offer services to the extended family network or to groups of families who support each other.
2. Take into account the needs of single, female heads of households, including transportation problems, accommodation to work schedules, and babysitting needs.
3. Consider flexible hours for meetings so that extended family members may attend. Also, consider transportation and lodging needs for extended family.
4. Services should be brief and time-limited to encourage attendance of families who may distrust the mental health system.
5. Treatment focusing on psychoeducational and social skills methodology may be used, as well as direct communication with the family about treatment issues.
6. The family social worker must be willing and able to acknowledge racism and issues that may impede self-disclosure by African American family members.
7. African American family members value mutuality and egalitarianism; thus, the family social worker should provide services that respect the client family and include the family in the decision-making process.

INTERVENTION WITH HISPANIC AMERICAN FAMILIES

Intervention issues for Hispanic American families may be identified by looking at families according to their level of acculturation:

> Group 1, newly arrived immigrant families, need concrete services such as language instruction, information, referral, and advocacy. Efforts must be made to reach out to these families as they may not access services on their own due to language and cultural barriers.
>
> Immigrant-American families may require conflict resolution, problem-solving, or anger management training due to intergenerational conflicts.
>
> Immigrant-descent families are more comfortable seeking traditional mental health services. They likely speak both Spanish and English in the home and are acculturated into the dominant culture (Padella et al. and Casas & Keefe in Jordan, Lewellen, & Vandiver, 1994, p. 33).

The family social worker may be considered as equal to a healer, priest, or physician by the Hispanic American family, depending on the family's level of acculturation. In fact, the family may have consulted a priest or folk healer first, before seeking services from an agency.

Jordan, Lewellen, and Vandiver (1994, p. 34) make the following recommendations for work with Hispanic American families:

1. Time-limited treatment which includes the family and extended family, due to the importance and insularity of the family;
2. Content sensitive to the family's level of acculturation, beliefs, hierarchy, and traditions;

3. Treatment sensitive to role confusion and conflict the newly arrived family may be experiencing; thus, techniques including communication skills, negotiation training, and role clarification may be important;
4. Treatment sensitive to the family's need for education, information, and referral services;
5. Inclusion of folk healers, priests, or other nonrelative helpers.

INTERVENTION WITH ASIAN AMERICAN FAMILIES

Jordan, Lewellen, and Vandiver (1994) suggest techniques to enhance service provision to Asian American families. Because hierarchy is important to Asian American families, treatment plans should include high-status members of the family or community. The family social worker may be seen as an authority figure and can use this status to implement positive family changes. The social worker must be sure to show respect for members of the family. Services offered within the family's neighborhood are believed to increase client participation in treatment.

Clear communication between the family social worker and family members is essential. The social worker should avoid using slang, jargon, or regional expressions. Also, if an interpreter must be used, he or she should be sensitive to the family's culture and social class. Treatment should include psychoeducational techniques. The entire family may be included in the treatment, with deference shown by the family social worker to the elderly members. Other families in the community, in centers, churches, or temples, may be utilized in support/social groups for treatment of problems such as severe and persistent mental illness.

INTERVENTION WITH NATIVE AMERICAN FAMILIES

Ho (1987) makes the following recommendations for treating Native American families in a sensitive manner:

1. Provision of concrete services may be necessary for Native American families experiencing difficulties due to lack of food, housing, or other necessities. Provision of necessities helps the social worker to engage with family members.
2. The family social worker's communication with the Native American family should be "open, caring, and congruent . . . (and delivered) in a simple, precise, slow, and calm" manner (Ho, 1987, p. 94).
3. To get to know the Native American family, the FSW should observe their communication patterns and styles and note how members of the extended family network interact with one another. "To do this, the family social worker needs to be attentive, talk less, observe more, and listen actively" (Ho, 1987, p. 95).
4. Mapping techniques may be used to learn about the extended family.
5. The Native American value of the collective indicates the need for mutual establishment of treatment goals.

6. Problem solving may be facilitated by "(a) social, moral, organic reframing/relabeling; (b) mobilizing and restructuring the extended family network; (c) promoting interdependence as a family restructuring technique; (d) employing role model, educator role, and advocate role; (e) re-structuring taboos for problem solving; and (f) collaborative work with medicine person, paraprofessional, and therapist helper" (Ho, 1987, p. 99).

DIFFERENT CULTURES WORKING TOGETHER

This book does not debate whether workers from a different culture should work with other cultures. Rather, we argue for the necessity of cultural competence. We summarize here cultural issues presented by Coleman, Unrau, and Manyfingers (2001). Much heterogeneity exists within cultures (Weaver, 1997b; Weaver, 1999; Thomason, 1991) and proposing that a single approach can meet the needs of *all* families within a particular ethnic or cultural group risks stereotyping, as well as collapsing a particular culture to a single form (Gross, 1998). We must be attuned to the dangers of overlooking or ignoring spiritual, language, social structure, and political differences across ethnic communities or risk over-generalizing cultural knowledge or using this knowledge inappropriately and ineffectively with minority families (Sue & Zane, 1987; Weaver, 1997b). Intervention cannot be singularly designed so that individual differences are disregarded. As Gross (1998) suggested, "all the study in the world about a given culture or subculture might not lend a hint of explanation of the behavior or attitudes of a single member of that culture or subculture" (p. 9).

Working with families in a culturally sensitive way necessarily means that workers must understand clients from both a larger group and an individual level. Gross (1998) points out the necessity of understanding the "grand narratives" of a particular culture from the vantage of individuals and "micro narratives" from within that particular culture. For example, the grand narratives of Native people include respect for people, land, and creatures; giving high esteem to elders; noninterference into the lives of others, including in child rearing efforts; and interconnectedness and interdependency (Coleman, Unrau, & Manyfingers, 2001; Weaver 1997b). These grand narratives of Native peoples reveal how they value cooperation and group harmony. Their story, however, has been altered by individuals of the dominant culture cultural to suggest that Native Americans are co-dependent rather than interdependent, and enmeshed rather than interconnected (Weaver, 1997a). Therefore, effective family work demands that workers relate to families on two levels, based on cultural grand narratives and micro narratives. Micro narratives deserve their own place in intervention and they can only be uncovered by listening with humility and openness—not by reading about diversity (Gross, 1998). Thus, family workers must observe and listen to each client family, using the grand narratives as a cultural backdrop to working with any single family (Coleman, Unrau, & Manyfingers, 2001). Because it is impossible to know everything about a specific cultural group (and even about your own cultural group) or family, workers can use assessment and interviewing skills to find out essential information about each one (Weaver & Wodarski, 1995).

Understanding the history of ethnic groups goes hand in hand with understanding and accepting diversity within a particular culture (Weaver, 1999). The history of many cultures has been checkered by periods of intense pressure to assimilate into the dominant culture, by assuming its traditions, values, and beliefs, making traditional ways of being undervalued or unacceptable. Many people of different ethnic or cultural heritages have been made to feel ashamed of their traditional ways of living. Historically, assimilation has disrupted the traditional behaviors and beliefs of many groups, disrupting child rearing practices, isolating people from different cultures from traditional helping networks (Cross, 1986). Indiscriminate placement of ethnic minority children, such as African Americans or Native Americans, deprives the children of their cultural and spiritual heritage as well as important linkages to their past.

Exposure to insensitivity to cultural nuances has created historical trauma with implications for how ethnic peoples might respond to helping services (Weaver & Yellow Horse Brave Heart, 1999). The trauma brings with it deep-rooted distrust of social workers who may be viewed as coercive authority figures (Miller & Pylpa, 1995; Schacht, Tafoya, & Mirabala, 1989; Thomason, 1991; Weaver, 1997b). Negative opinions of social workers may exist in part because of a history of social work interventions that have been culturally insensitive and damaging to people and their traditions (Coleman, Unrau, & Manyfingers, 2001; Weaver, 1997a). Social workers, as representatives of the dominant group, have historically imposed values upon minority groups which were insensitive and oppressive, amounting to cultural genocide. While members of the profession today feel shame about their historical activities as agents of the state, and seek to redress these historical injustices, members of cultural minorities still associate the profession with past injustices. New social workers are sometimes startled to discover that their efforts to develop a mutually respectful and trusting relationship with minority clients are met with distrust and suspicion. Talking to families about their personal experience with social workers is the first step in discovering what injustices they have experienced.

At the same time, it is important to remember that not everyone is connected to their cultural heritage to the same degree (Joe & Malach, 1998; Weaver, 1999). Factors such as location of residence, interracial marriages, and child welfare placement of children may help to explain varying degrees of attachment and adherence to traditional practices. At the same time, many people incorporate traditional and nontraditional practices in their daily living (Joe & Malach, 1998), and even for people who are very traditional, some traditions do not enter daily activities.

FAMILY   The starting point for family social workers is to understand what "family" means to different cultural groups. The dominant culture emphasizes the rugged individual and the nuclear family form. The conceptualization of these two entities forms the basis that determines who is eligible to receive family social work services. The dominant view of the family eclipses the practices of cultures that include larger family networks in their definition of family. In

Native American families, for example, the immediate family grows at marriage, because for that culture the concept of "in-law" does not exist and those marrying into a family become included as full family members (Sutton & Broken Nose, 1996). Depending upon the specific culture, extended kin can reach beyond blood relatives to include elders, neighbors, ancestors, or family friends. In part, these more inclusive family systems reflect different cultures' beliefs that value group orientation, interdependence, and interconnectedness, which embraces a cluster of relationships, beginning with the family, and expanding to include others (McCormick, 1996). In addition, community membership and connectedness is valued among many cultures, reflecting the importance of collaborative relationships rather than family privacy and individualism. This value is apparent when group consensus emerges as a major influence in decision making (Joe & Malach, 1998).

Extended family also plays a central role in raising children in many cultures. Family social workers should be prepared to ask about who is involved in a particular family, using genograms as a primary tool. In some cultures, the primary child–adult relationship may not be between child and parent in a family, and may instead include grandparents or aunts and uncles (Cross, 1986; Pimento, 1985; Red Horse, Lewis, Feit, & Decker, 1978). Community elders and members of older generations may be powerful sources of influence for children, families, and the community as a whole. In some cultures grandparents may play a dominant role in childcare responsibilities and parents may seek advice from elders and other esteemed members of their cultural community. An initial task for family social workers is to map out the family network with a family and then be prepared to include aunts, uncles, cousins, grandparents, and possibly neighbors as targets of intervention as well as potential resources for alternative childcare providers (Red Horse, Lewis, Feit, & Decker, 1978). Child welfare workers have recently begun to appreciate the potential of extended family as foster families in which children know the people they are being placed with and with whom they feel more connected. One family social worker was relieved to discover that an involved aunt was willing to foster her two nieces who were locked out of their house by an irate father. The two girls felt secure and wanted when their aunt offered to take them in.

Family social workers therefore need to understand what "family" is within particular cultures, as well as the specific worldview that families in a culture hold in terms of their relationships with others. Added to these two perspectives is how families from different cultures integrate generations, making it necessary for family social work to include multiple generations into family social work interventions. Genograms provide a starting point for family social workers to bridge cultural gaps between a worker and a family. Genograms should capture the "broad" definition of extended family, spanning three or more generations, to depict traditional clan systems. The three-generation genograms also capture the degree of cultural disruption a family has experienced.

With an expanded definition of family among some cultural groups, family social workers must be open to the possibility of extended families *sharing* the responsibility for childcare. It is possible for childcare responsibilities to be divided among family members. For example, an uncle or aunt might assume

CASE 10.1	MULTIGENERATIONAL PATTERNS

One of the new multigenerational family patterns seen with increasing frequency may be referred to as the "sandwich generation," that is, parents with responsibilities for caring for their elderly parents as well as their young children. A case example of a typical sandwich generation family follows.

Alice is a remarried mother of two stepchildren from her husband's previous marriage and a baby with her husband, Ray. The two older children are twins, Kathy and Ricky (14 years old), and the baby is Heather, who is 6 months old. The twins came to live with the family when their biological mother's alcoholism was revealed; she is currently in a treatment facility. Soon after the twins came to live with Alice and Ray, Alice's mother moved in with the family. Bess, 78 years old, fell and broke her hip. After surgery and rehabilitation, she was unable to live alone, thus the move to be with her son and his family.

The FSW's role is to help the family address the multiple problems experienced by the family. These include the custody of the twins and living/visitation arrangements with their parents once the mother gets out of the treatment facility. Other possible areas for intervention include adjustment of all to the stepfamily arrangement, to the new baby, and to the grandmother moving in. Some stepfamily issues likely to be a concern include marital issues and sibling rivalry. The grandmother may experience loss of identity, lack of peer support, and role confusion.

the primary role as disciplinarian, whereas grandparents might be relied upon for spiritual guidance.

At a practical level, the family social worker service delivery should identify extended family members who have had success with parenting and include them in service plans where improved parenting is a targeted area of concern. Other important members of the cultural community, such as spiritual leaders, can also be involved in the planning and implementation of the intervention (Williams & Ellison, 1996), taking into consideration issues of confidentiality and parental self-determination (Joe & Malach, 1998; Schacht, Tafoya, & Mirabala, 1989). Family workers should also be aware that some families prefer to work with members outside of their cultural community because they do not want others to know about their personal issues. Another option is to find culturally appropriate parenting sessions offered by a community agency.

CHAPTER SUMMARY

This chapter introduced the family intervention phase. During the intervention phase of family social work, the FSW provides support, education, and concrete assistance. Effective intervention requires that the social worker focus on the family's needs, respect client autonomy, avoid fostering dependency, reassess client resistance, maintain professional distance, and set reasonable expectations.

Specific intervention techniques available to the FSW include use of examples, confrontation, reframing, enactment, use of metaphors, and contracting. Intervention techniques should be chosen to meet the needs of the family.

The FSW needs to recall the assessment phase and use the ecomap when presenting ecological interventions.

Family social workers frequently encounter families who are experiencing crisis. It is important that the FSW remain calm and help the family sort out its challenges.

Systemic interventions help FSWs and families to think about the family as a whole. Systemic interventions are particularly helpful in teaching problem-solving and communication skills to families.

Family members need to find a balance between disengaged and enmeshed relationships. The FSW can help families set rules that will bring them closer to achieving this balance.

Finally, guidelines for intervention with minority families—African American, Hispanic American, Asian American, and Native American—were presented.

EXERCISES

10.1   ROLES OF FAMILY SOCIAL WORKERS

Family social workers can assist families in a variety of circumstances. Consider each of the seven roles that a family social worker might assume. Give an example of a situation where each role might be used and provide an example of what the family social worker can do to fill the role.

10.2   FOCUSING ON THE CLIENT

Think of a specific person with whom you have had difficulty interacting (not necessarily in the context of social work). List some things you could do to establish rapport with this person. Next, list some ways you could show this person that you are focusing on him or her, rather than on yourself.

10.3   USE OF EXAMPLES

Develop three examples that would help you to explain a concept or practice to a client. With a partner, practice using examples to explain one of these concepts (such as using time-outs) to a client.

10.4   USE OF CONFRONTATION

List three situations in which confrontation would be a helpful intervention. With a partner, role-play the use of confrontation with a client.

10.5   COMMUNICATION SKILL TRAINING

Caitlyn Jones is a 15-year-old girl who is having trouble in school. Her older brother and sister left home before they had finished high school. Her brother

Ryan got into trouble with the law, and her sister Jamie became pregnant at age 17 and moved in with her boyfriend's family. Caitlyn's parents, Bob and Kerrie, are worried that Caitlyn will also leave home early and drop out of school. Caitlyn feels she has been pressured by her parents to do well in school. She has been struggling with her classes and is fearful of failure. Write some "I" statements Caitlyn could use to communicate her feelings to her parents, as well as some active listening responses her parents could offer. With three other students, role-play a session with the Jones family (one student should play the FSW and the other three should be Caitlyn, Bob, and Kerrie). Negotiate some solutions to Caitlyn's problems.

10.6 PROBLEM-SOLVING APPROACH

Keeping in mind the Jones family described in the previous exercise, outline the steps of a problem-solving intervention for this family.

10.7 CIRCULAR CAUSALITY ROLE-PLAY

Role-play with two other students who are to play two people in a family who are having a problematic pattern of communication. The FSW should instruct the dyad by saying, "I would like to see how the two of you resolve differences." Members of the dyad then turn and face each other and start to interact over an issue (select an issue relevant to the dyad). This should take at least 5 to 10 minutes to explore. The FSW then clarifies what each person in the dyad is feeling and thinking, and resultant behavior. The worker then focuses on the second person's thoughts/beliefs/feelings, ending with a description of the behavior of the second person.

The next step is to connect the behaviors to the thoughts/beliefs/feelings of the first person. Once this is done, the worker can start the pattern anew until people understand how they impact the other person. The next step is to ask, "Well, how is this ever going to change?" and let the individuals develop a concrete approach to what they are going to do to solve their difficulties.

INTERVENTIONS AT THE CHILD AND PARENTAL LEVELS

A BEHAVIORAL FAMILY APPROACH

Interventions at the family and parental level are the focus of Chapter 11. These interventions are based on principles of behavioral intervention. A behavioral family approach is compatible with the family life cycle. Phases of family development require that members adapt to a continuously changing and maturing family system. The behavioral approach involves continuous reeducation or relearning, and is particularly effective with younger children

(Thompson, Rudolph, & Henderson, 2003). However, the basic premises are also useful for later stages of the family life cycle and child development. Reeducation requires that parents develop a positive relationship with their children so that they can guide the children through challenging developmental phases. For instance, adolescence is a time when teens are moving toward adulthood. The teen is an adult one minute and a child the next, requiring flexibility, sensitivity, and guidance by the parent.

Behavioral family social work has several advantages over traditional intervention. It is useful for chaotic families that require a structured series of intervention strategies for parents to carry out in their daily family life (Kilpatrick & Holland, 1995). In office settings, the behavior or events may appear too briefly, infrequently, or too removed from the child and family's other life experiences (Gordon & Davidson, 1981). It also avoids pathologizing families. Rather, behavioral family social work casts problems as a lack of skill that can be learned.

Behavioral family work grew out of the observation that behaviors are shaped and maintained by relationships in the environment, particularly those in the family. It therefore follows that behavior can be changed by changing environmental contingencies (rewards and punishment) that maintain the problematic behavior and prevent the appearance of prosocial behaviors. Since parents are most in control of significant contingencies in the child's environment, particularly when the child is young, they are in the best position to create behavior change with the child. Thus, change occurs first with the parent and later with the child. Essentially, parents are their child's therapists.

Under these conditions, the FSW consults with parents, teaching them to intervene directly and immediately in the child's behavior. Parents live with the child and are a stable, continuous treatment resource. If parents learn to deal consistently with their child even when the FSW is not present, an environmental context for ongoing behavior change will be established. This fundamental principle of social learning theory can be used by parents with varying degrees of parenting skills.

Assumptions

Behavioral family interventions look at ongoing family relationships and interactional patterns rather than the intrapsychic life of individual family members. In behavioral terms, communication is a powerful consequence of behavior, either positive or negative. Through a positive worker–family relationship, the worker models appropriate social behavior, coaches parents in developing positive communication skills, and helps them structure a set of behavioral contingencies to be used consistently in family interactions (Bloomquist, 1996; Kilpatrick & Holland, 1995). Given the premise that parents are the best therapists for their children, planned changes in parental behavior should be followed by changes in child behavior and vice versa.

Behavior problems are seen as learned responses that become set and intensified with ongoing reinforcement. Much of the reinforcement in families is unintentional because members are seldom aware of how behavior is reinforced and maintained. Being self-aware and tracking child behavior is difficult for many parents to do for extended periods. Without awareness, however, imposed consequences may produce unintended effects. For example, scolding may reinforce a child's behavior because the child receives attention from the parent. Other times, parents might ignore or reinforce behavior inconsistently, making it difficult to extinguish or eliminate the behavior. Many parents do not know how to use behavioral consequences effectively. In such instances, parents fail to follow through on threats. Punishment may be delayed, defusing its effectiveness and confusing the child, and other times, the level of punishment does not match the level of the problematic behavior by being either too mild or too severe.

Similar to the circular interactions described in Chapter 2, parents who respond negatively toward their children are also most likely to have children behave negatively in return. In some families, negative behavior receives more attention than prosocial behavior. Thus behavioral intervention attempts to modify problem interaction and alleviate presenting symptoms. Ideally, changes in negative behavior by either the parent or the child will cause a spiral of positive family interactions. Ultimately, treatment needs to be tailored to fit the specific circumstances of specific families. The goal is to increase rewarding interactions by producing positive behavior change, decrease the rate of coercion and aversive control, and teach effective communication and problem-solving skills.

Under the premise of behavioral family work, behavior should change when contingencies or reinforcements are altered. Before this can happen, FSWs must do a careful, detailed assessment with the family to understand the specifics of the problem and to find out how often (i.e., the baseline frequency) the problem behavior occurs before change is attempted. Then the FSW must devise strategies to change the contingencies of behavior in each family. During information gathering, the task is to identify antecedents and consequences of the problem behavior. Problems must be defined in concrete, observable, and measurable ways. Based on this information, strategies are designed to alter the antecedents or consequences of the behavior. It is important to remember to measure the problem behavior before the intervention and after.

Figures 11.1 and 11.2 illustrate other types of measurements: time sampling (percent of time), duration recording, and frequency of behavior (see Jordan et al. in Grinnell & Unrau, 2005).

PRINCIPLES AND PROCEDURES

The behavioral family approach is based upon the principles of behavior modification and social learning theory, which explain how behavior can be increased, decreased, or maintained, and how new behaviors can be learned. We believe that understanding these principles are essential for anyone who works with families. The social learning approach offers families a structured method for dealing with a range of family problems. Family workers not familiar with social learning approaches will not be as effective as they could be when working with parents.

Frequency of behavior shown in Week 1 by _____

Problem behavior _____

Date	Frequency	Total	Time	Comments

FIGURE 11.1   │   TIME SAMPLING AND BEHAVIOR FREQUENCY RECORDING

Duration of behavior shown in Week 1 by _____

Problem behavior _____

Date	Length of time behavior observed	Total time	Additional observations

FIGURE 11.2   │   BEHAVIOR DURATION RECORDING

The basic principles of behavior analysis address the effects on behavior of its antecedents and consequences. Though most attention has been focused on consequences of behavior, especially on the positive consequences or reinforcement, it also is important to recognize the effects of changing the immediate environment. This environmental focus can be used to make homes safe for young children. For instance, we put fences around playgrounds to keep children safe and we remove dangerous objects from their reach. A FSW who brings toys or other activities to keep one child entertained while she talks to the parent and sibling changes the child's environment positively. What we say to each other can also be an antecedent condition that increases the likelihood that a behavior will occur. Parents who know how to give clear and unambiguous directions and follow through on them, for example, will likely see more cooperation on the part of their children than parents who give confusing, conflicting directions.

Behavior also is influenced by its consequences. Positive, reinforcing consequences increase the likelihood that behavior will be repeated, while negative consequences decrease the likelihood of reoccurrence. Many parents naturally use positive consequences, for example, when they praise and encourage a child who is learning to walk or talk. But as child behavior becomes more complex or problematic, parents often need help in knowing which behaviors require attention and which should be ignored or punished. Parents may unintentionally become negative in their interactions with children because of lack of skill or frustration, and may need help in learning to change unpleasant interactions into more positive and enjoyable ones.

Teaching parents to use reinforcement effectively is important in parent training, after parents learn to judge the appropriateness of the child's behavior by integrating knowledge of child development and behavior principles. Furthermore, the general family work guidelines discussed earlier also are important to include when teaching parenting skills. For example, the FSW may discover that the parents' needs and problems may interfere with their ability to parent and must be addressed. Also, the systems perspective presented earlier reminds the FSW to consider the effects of intervention on other family members. Similarly, the child's behavior is influenced by family subsystems, which must be considered when intervening with parent–child relationships, such as the widowed grandmother who lives with the family and is trying to take over the parental role. A broader ecological view goes beyond asking what consequences could change a child's behavior to asking questions about environmental conditions. For example, does the physical environment (including the interfering grandmother) make it possible for the child to comply with parental requests?

Just as behavioral management principles are important to both family social work and to parent training, so are problem-solving skills. Problem-solving skills are necessary for competence in parenting. Also important is conducting parent training in the parents' home rather than in a clinic or other institutional setting.

TECHNIQUES

Because we cannot present in this book every detail necessary for family social workers to master the knowledge and skills for using behavioral management principles, we urge the reader to obtain this information elsewhere as preparation for family work. Several excellent, comprehensive parent-training programs exist to help parents deal with many child-management problems. The procedures are especially important for parents of children with handicapping conditions and parents who abuse or neglect their children. Following are a few of the many behavioral techniques that families find helpful.

Teaching is a tool that can be used successfully with many families. In one study, a parent reported liking learning the different ideas on how to handle behaviors—for example, breaking power struggles by offering choices. In the same study, another parent said, "I learned how to intervene, trying different techniques of discipline" (Coleman & Collins, 1997).

Teaching should be based on an assessment of each situation and used to show to families how to use a specific skill. Steps involved in teaching include:

1. Giving the members a rationale for learning the skill;
2. Demonstrating the skill; and
3. Having clients practice the skill, after which they receive feedback (Brock & Barnard, 1991).

TEACHING FAMILY COMMUNICATION SKILLS: AN EXAMPLE   Family communication is a skill that underpins most aspects of family functioning. Bloomquist (1996) suggests a three-step model in teaching communication skills:

1. Introduce family communication skills to the family (e.g., being direct, honest, and open, focusing on the here-and-now, attentive listening, using "I" statements, do not interrupt, do not yell, do not be verbally abusive, etc.)
2. Practice the skills in the family. One way is to role-play both the "do's" and the "don'ts" so everyone knows the difference and can readily identify the skills that are acceptable. The family worker can model these skills before the family role-plays. All members of the family should take turns practicing these skills. A videotape can be used to help the family observe what they are doing.
3. Use the family communication skills in real life. The worker might want to enact or stage the "real" problem initially—that is, select a problem pertinent to the family—and then have the family demonstrate their new communication skills while talking about it.

TEACHING CHILD COMPLIANCE   Bloomquist (1996) also provides a step-by-step method to obtain child compliance. A child is compliant when he or she listens to and obeys parents' directives. Both parents and children learn new behaviors:

1. Give effective commands. The commands should be specific and one-step so that the child knows exactly what is being asked of him or her. Commands that are vague, in the form of questions, multiple, or accompanied by a rationale are to be discouraged.
2. Use effective warnings. If the child is not compliant with the command, the parent can use a warning that takes the form "If . . . then . . ." The warning should be given only once.
3. Give effective positive or negative consequences to the child for compliant or noncompliant behavior. Praise can be used for compliant behavior and negative consequences can be used for noncompliant behavior.
4. Parents are to try and stay cool and avoid power struggles if the child is not compliant.
5. Persevere until the child knows that the parent means business. Perseverance is necessary because compliance is seldom secured the first time a parent

uses these techniques. In fact, it may take a long and exhausting time before the pattern of behaviors becomes engrained.

6. Be consistent. Make certain that the parents respond the same way each time the child shows a particular behavior.
7. A chart can be used for younger children.

The idea of learning new skills can be offered as a way of overcoming problems; for many families this will be new because the stereotype of counseling is to analyze the past (Kinney, Haapala, & Booth, 1991).

There are several ways to teach clients. In *direct instruction,* the worker presents information directly to clients. In *modeling,* the worker performs the behavior in front of the clients, and in *contingency management,* clients are taught to manage contingencies of reinforcement—that is, support change through rewarding behaviors and by ignoring or punishing behaviors that they want to change (Kinney, Haapala, & Booth, 1991).

People will be more prepared to learn once they recognize that learning occurs every day. However, they may want to understand the rationale, particularly how using a particular skill will benefit them. Once the family has understood these issues, they will be prepared to have the skill broken down into manageable pieces. Demonstrations of the skill need to be accurate. After the worker shows the skill, the family members should be asked to describe what they observed step-by-step. Because a skill involves a series of complex behaviors, the worker should break down the skill into manageable parts and have the clients learn components of the skill one step at a time. Teaching and demonstrating skills can be identified "on-the-spot" in the home. Workers can capitalize on teachable moments and use a crisis or other timely events to inject a teaching moment. Parents make use of teaching and report that it is a helpful intervention (Coleman & Collins, 1997). The final stage of teaching is having the individual or family practice the skill and receive feedback on their performance. At this stage, the worker should offer positive comments and corrective feedback to the client.

Positive reinforcement is the process whereby appropriate behaviors are recognized and reinforced, thus increasing the probability of these behaviors occurring in the future. Unfortunately, parents often notice only inappropriate behaviors and do not take the time to recognize "good" or prosocial behavior, thus failing to positively reinforce these good behaviors with praise and sometimes even a type of enjoyable reward. For example, a child who just spent one hour completing his or her homework and reading should be praised for the effort and invited to spend time with his or her parents watching a favorite TV show. It is often helpful to have children select what they would like to have as a reinforcement and then create a chart. Ideas for reinforcement, apart from spending time with a parent (discussed in the following paragraph), might include being allowed to do a favorite activity, staying up later, praise, or having a friend sleep over. We recommend using social reinforcers (such as praise or time spent with a parent doing a favorite activity) over material reinforcers (such as money or a new bike).

A form of positive reinforcement is the parent spending time with a child and being involved. Such social and privilege reinforcers are quite effective with children. Parental involvement fulfils the dual purpose of positively rewarding children for their behaviors *and* increasing affective involvement of family members: ". . . positive reinforcement of good behaviors is related to well-behaved children" (Bloomquist, 1996, p. 52). Positive activity scheduling with a child involves listing activities that parents and children enjoy doing together, scheduling time together, having the parent "notice" good behavior by praising, describing good behavior, and touching (p. 53). In order for behavior to be rewarded, *it must first be noticed!* To do so, parents must be aware of their own minute-to-minute behavior with the child. Parents must understand the concept of positive reinforcement before they can use it. They must also be willing to put their own responses under a microscope so that they know what they need to change and how.

Negative reinforcement involves applying consequences that strengthen or maintain a behavior through their *removal*. For example, a parent yelling is a negative reinforcement to get child to comply. Compliance in this case might be to do homework. If the parent stops yelling before the child complies and the child continues to avoid doing homework, the parent has taught the child that avoiding homework is acceptable and that s/he has won. Alternatively, if a child stops a particular behavior (in this case avoiding homework) in order to avoid more aversive parental behavior, the parent learns that yelling is effective. Negative reinforcement is not to be confused with punishment.

Punishment involves the use of an aversive punishment *immediately* after the behavior occurs. We strongly believe that positive consequences are preferable to punishment and should be used whenever possible. Examples of punishment include taking away privileges, grounding, or time-outs. We do not recommend the use of spanking as a form of punishment. Spanking teaches children that physical violence is acceptable to get one's way. It also creates fear of the parent.

Extinction is a behavioral technique designed to eliminate undesirable behavior. Clients are instructed to withhold attention from the individual who is behaving inappropriately and not reinforce the problematic behavior through inadvertent types of reinforcement. Extinction is useful for behaviors such as whining, crying, tantrums, and sleep disorders (Thompson & Rudolph, 1992). Extinction is a slow method. The annoying behavior must be *consistently* ignored, all family members must cooperate with the extinction plan, and parents must persist even when the method does not produce immediate results (Davis, 1996).

Time-out is an indispensable parenting technique used to weaken problematic behaviors of children. When used correctly, parents substitute time-out for physical discipline. Parents often observe that children's behavior tends to spin out-of-control paralleling the loss of parental patience. Time-out entails removing the child from a stimulating environment and placing the child into a setting that is low stimulation. During time-out, parents have a chance to regain composure while the child calms down. A quiet place for children can be a chair or a quiet room. The child's bedroom should be avoided for time-out—its use as a time-out space can contribute to bedtime difficulties because the child associates the bedroom with upsetting incidents.

Time-out is useful when children fail to follow rules set by parents and can be a consequence of breaking a rule. At the point where the rule has been broken and the consequence is imposed, the parent should immediately place the child in the time-out spot. The length of time in the spot will depend upon the child's age, but should only range from between 5 and 15 minutes at one time. Workers might want to use the following teaching sequence before implementing the time-out procedure. Davis (1996) recommends the following tips in using time-outs:

- Decide which behaviors qualify for time-outs. Then, parental expectations should be specified as clearly as possible to the child. Typically, time-outs can be used for temper tantrums or other noncompliant behavior.
- Determine in advance which quiet settings would be the most appropriate for time-out.
- Decide at what point the time-out will be used. We recommend that a time-out be used after the child has been warned about the impending consequence if the parent's orders are not complied with. If the child violates the order, the time-out should be imposed immediately, even if the child protests and backs down.
- Let the child know in advance what behaviors are acceptable and which ones are unacceptable. Then explain to the child the purpose of the time-out calmly.
- Do not argue with the child when imposing a time-out. Do not talk with the child except to explain the purpose of the time-out and why it is happening.
- At times, particularly the beginning of using time-outs, the child may have to be physically taken to the time-out spot. The parent must be prepared to take the child back if he or she leaves prematurely. Parents should realize children often resist the time-out procedure when it is first implemented and ensuring that the child remains in the quiet spot can be both frustrating and a drain of energy for the parent. Thus, parents may have to remain physically close to the child but distant enough not to stimulate the child's behavior further. Parents need to be assured that once the child becomes accustomed to the consistent use of time-outs, the child will become more compliant.

Role-playing allows the client to act out a real-life situation and develop skill and confidence with difficult situations. It is appropriate for times when the client has difficulty being assertive because of the newness of the situation. For instance, a parent offended by the abrupt manner of her child's school teacher may be reluctant to ask the teacher questions about the child's school performance. During the role-play, the FSW may take on the role of school teacher while the mother asks the teacher questions. The mother may then try out both roles. For instance, she can be the mother asking the teacher pertinent questions; she can then take the role of teacher while the FSW models some additional questions the mother could ask.

Role-playing is used often with families. Through a role-play, clients start to see how their behavior is viewed by others and receive feedback about these behaviors (Thompson & Rudolph, 1992). Role-playing is useful for skill development and for playing out a scenario to determine the consequences of a particular behavior. Role-playing can also be used to depict problem situations outside the here-and-now setting, such as a problem with a neighbor or a boss.

There are several ways of using role-playing with a family. One way of staging a role-play is for the worker to play a role with the person playing themselves. Another method is to have people reverse roles and play a problem scenario. The latter method is useful to help people understand the other person and develop empathy skills. Finally, role-playing can be used to rehearse skills relevant to a situation, much the same as rehearsing for a play before performing in front of a live audience.

To role-play, clients are asked to bring a problematic situation into the interview and are asked to re-create it in the interview. Feedback can then be given to the family member about the scenario.

Role-play is a safe form of behavioral rehearsal, involving practicing a new behavior without the fear of consequences. During behavioral rehearsal, the worker and significant others provide feedback to the client. After the behavior is practiced in a safe environment, the client will then do the actual behavior in the real world (Davis, 1996).

Rule setting involves parents setting rules for their children, knowing what situations to set rules for, and learning how to enforce these rules when children are not compliant. Parents must learn a set of procedures for setting rules that ensures that they *consistently* follow through with rules and establish *consequences* for children who are noncompliant. Rule setting and enforcement can be broken down into several manageable steps.

- First, parents must convey to the children specifically what the rules are and the rationale for each rule. The explanation must match the cognitive ability of the child.
- Then parents should offer an alternative to the child's behavior and the child should be informed of the consequences of not following through on the rules.
- If the behavior persists, the parent must firmly tell the child that if the behavior occurs again, there will be a consequence (the consequence should be clearly spelled out).
- If the behavior continues, the parent must then stop the child and impose the consequence *immediately*. This procedure must be followed every time the child breaks a particular rule. Consistency is imperative. Imposing a consequence one time but not another will only confuse the child. Additionally, inconsistent enforcement of rules does not produce behavior change with children.

Modeling is demonstration of a specific behavior for family members. This technique is particularly useful when the family cannot imagine themselves carrying out a particular action or when they cannot begin an activity. It is also useful when a family member lacks necessary skills to take action or is hesitant to try out a new behavior. Examples of situations appropriate for modeling include demonstrating a job interview, asking a spouse to help with childcare, or comforting a sad child.

Family workers can model effective behaviors for parents. Other models may occur through videotapes or peers and adults who have experienced similar problems but have developed the skills to deal with those problems. In Chapter 4 we discussed a range of communication skills that workers can use to work with families. The family social worker can model these skills to the family with the expectation that the family will start to identify with the counselor's communication style and use the skills with one another in the family.

After modeling the behavior, the FSW should encourage the client to perform and practice the behavior. Doing so assures that the client understood what was modeled and that the client can imitate the behavior of the family social worker. The FSW can provide corrective feedback if necessary. Such practice helps ensure that the client will remember the behavior and provides the FSW the opportunity to correct any errors in the client's performance as well as to reinforce and encourage the client's behavior.

Self-control training is useful for individuals who are able to assume some responsibility for their own behavior. Self-control training is useful for anxiety reduction, school refusals, stuttering, and to some extent, hyperactivity. Steps involved include:

1. Selecting the behavior to be changed;
2. Recording for approximately one week when the behavior occurs, the setting, and the antecedents and the consequences;
3. Setting a realistic goal;
4. Changing the antecedents and the setting related to the behavior;
5. Altering the consequences that reinforce the behavior;
6. Recording what happens; and,
7. Devising a plan to ensure that the changes continue.

Assigning homework involves sending an assignment home with families. Change begun in family interviews does not stop when an interview ends—families should continue to change after the interview. One way of doing this is for the family to be given homework to work on between sessions. Assignments can take many forms, but have a threefold purpose:

1. To get family members to behave differently;
2. To collect information about family behavior outside the interview; and
3. To emphasize self-responsibility to create change.

Assignments should be based on the work done in an interview and are useful in bridging gaps between sessions. They should be geared toward the ability and motivation of the family and must be clearly spelled out. Assigning homework to families will get them used to being responsible for behavior change and will prepare the family for when the worker is no longer available to nudge them along. Examples of homework include letter writing, making telephone calls, charting behavior, and continuing to use an agreed-upon parenting technique. Another example of a homework assignment is having family members keep track of how often a certain behavior occurs. Keeping track of the behavior can help family members become aware of how often a behavior occurs and, in doing so, the family will be involved in monitoring progress made in family work (Kinney, Haapala, & Booth, 1991).

Selection of what homework to assign is very important and should relate to the assessment of the family and work that is being done. For example, if the family is socially isolated, a homework assignment could be for the family or any number of its members to use a community resource or nurture an outside relationship.

For homework to be effective, the FSW must start the next interview with a review of how the homework went. Occasionally workers will discover that the family did not do the homework assignment. In this case, it will be necessary to find out what prevented the family from doing the assignment. Reasons may range from open resistance to not understanding the instructions. When homework is assigned regularly, families eventually learn to expect assignments at the end of every interview (Hartman & Laird, 1983).

Stress reduction includes progressive relaxation, a useful technique to deal with generalized anxiety or anxiety that is situation specific. For generalized anxiety, the person is taught the skills of relaxation. For situation-specific anxiety, the person learns to relax while visualizing anxiety-provoking situations. In deep muscle relaxation, the individual relaxes the muscles, one group after another, until a state of deep relaxation is achieved. Typically, people are instructed to start by tensing and releasing their toes, and then gradually move the tension and relaxation to major and minor muscle groups up the body. Muscle tension should occur for about 5- to 10-seconds at a time. There are tapes or scripts that can teach progressive relaxation. Alternatively, the worker can script a relaxation session.

Contingency contracting is useful in working with children because it relies heavily upon input by all concerned parties. Though mutual negotiation, a contract is developed to indicate which behaviors individuals will perform and when. Usually the contract is formally written and involves who is to do what for whom, under what circumstances, when, and where. Rewards are then placed in the contract to ensure that if the contract is successfully carried out by all parties, they will follow through on mutually positive rewards specified. All parties in the contract must be clear on what they will give and what they will get if the contract is followed.

Contingency contracting can be broken down into five steps (Thompson & Rudolph, 1992):

1. Problem to be solved is identified;
2. Data are collected to find out baseline frequency;
3. The counselor and client set mutually agreed-upon goals;
4. Methods for obtaining the goals are selected;
5. Techniques are evaluated for observable, measurable change.

Ryan's Homework Program

Mon. Tues. Wed. Thurs. Fri.

Brings books home from school.

Starts homework at 7:00 P.M. without arguing.

Keeps television off during homework.

Stays in one room to do homework until 8:00 P.M.

Ryan gets:

    1 point for bringing home books from school

    3 points for starting homework without arguing

    2 points for keeping television off during homework time

    1 point for remaining in one room to complete homework

Total points

    I, _____ agree to do my homework regularly based on the conditions set above. I understand that I will earn points based on the agreement above. When I earn _____ points, I will be able to cash them in for _____.

Mother's signature   Father's signature

Child's signature

FIGURE 11.3 | EXAMPLE OF A CONTRACT NEGOTIATED BETWEEN A PARENT AND CHILD TO COMPLETE HOMEWORK

Teenagers in particular may find contingency contracting useful (see Figure 11.3). The contract is used for families to specify appropriate behaviors and corresponding rewards and consequences. Both the teen and parent have input into what behaviors they want included, and disputes may be negotiated. When first beginning to use contracting, simple issues should be selected.

Assertiveness training teaches family members how to say what they need to say in an appropriate manner—that is, they are neither aggressive nor passive. Conflicts in families often occur because members do not know how to disagree appropriately and do not know how to be assertive, resulting in passive or aggressive behavior. When members are passive, others can easily intrude on their rights. Aggressive members intrude on the rights of passive members and often learn to get their needs met through anger. Teaching assertiveness skills helps family members deal with one another, and the skills are also useful outside the family.

Evidence Base of Behavioral Family Interventions

Children usually behave differently from setting to setting, suggesting that adults determine what type of behavior is permissible in each setting. An exception is aggressiveness that remains constant wherever the child is; that is, a child who is aggressive at home will more likely be aggressive with peers. Interventions when children are young are most successful. Children with behavior problems also exert an enormous amount of control over their environment. They have difficulty "faking" good behavior and develop habitual patterns of problem behavior.

Behavioral family work has been used for such diverse problems as temper tantrums, hyperactivity, homework problems, bed-wetting, disobedience, delinquency, and aggressive behavior (Alexander & Parsons, 1973; Baum & Forehand, 1981; Foster, Prinz, & O'Leary, 1983; Webster-Stratton & Hammond, 1990). Others have used behavioral family work to teaching parenting and child management skills to parents who physically abuse their children. Behavioral treatment is effective for teaching child management techniques (Sandler, VanDercar, & Milhoan, 1978; Wolfe, Sandler, & Kaufman, 1981) and self-control techniques (Denicola & Sandler, 1980; Isaacs, 1982).

Parents of children with behavior problems have poorly developed parenting skills compared with parents of children who are functioning adequately (Patterson, 1982). However, it is more positive to view parents as having skill deficits rather than as pathological, because parents can learn new skills.

Intervention with child problems requires careful assessment and evaluation, and clearly operationalized techniques. Behavioral family work is an educative experience where parents are taught to understand and consistently apply behavioral skills with their children.

Besides teaching new skills, family social workers must pay attention to the environment in which families live. Some families experience more stress than others, and stress is disproportionately distributed among poorer families. They differ from other families in accessing resources that help them mediate stress. These families have fewer community, financial, and personal resources. Accordingly, they may feel alienated from mainstream society and lack trust in formal helpers. When they do connect with community supports, the experience is likely to be negative. Lack of support networks allows problems to grow because the resources are lacking to handle crises on the spot. Information, concrete resources, and emotional support may be absent. These families tend to be isolated, with limited contacts with people outside the family. Aversive events dominate family life in these families, making it difficult for them to tune into daily family events effectively. Unless an ecological approach is taken, parent training may be undermined.

The central premise of behavioral family social work is that behavior is maintained by its consequences, and rewards strengthen the connection between a stimulus and a response. This means that negative behaviors should not be reinforced but positive behavior should be (Nichols & Schwartz, 2004). In coercive families both positive and negative reinforcement mechanisms are present, but most seem to reinforce the wrong thing in that parents of aggressive children reward deviant behavior and punish prosocial behavior (Patterson, 1982; Patterson & Fleischman, 1979). In addition, abusive parents rely excessively on aversive methods of behavior control and fail to use consistent and positive child management techniques (Denicola & Sandler, 1980). Modifying "microanalytic" interactions between parents and children may reduce the risk of child abuse and other negative behaviors.

Currently, much of the behavioral family work is derived from the Oregon Social Learning Center where G. R. Patterson and colleagues (1982) examined microanalytic interactions within families and noted how responses shape the interaction. Microanalytic interactions resemble the circular patterns of interaction described in Chapter 2, although the model is more linear in that it sees a difference between an antecedent event and consequences. It primarily focuses on the here-and-now and makes minimal use of history.

Antisocial children have fewer house rules, and parental permissiveness is often related to aggressive behavior. Aversive parental behavior suppresses prosocial behavior and accelerates ongoing coercive behavior. Parents of antisocial children are more likely to give aversive consequences for coercive child behaviors (i.e., spanking, yelling). Thus, abused children have higher rates of coercive behavior than other children. Negative reinforcement increases the likelihood of high-intensity negative responses. For example, the child stops throwing a tantrum in the grocery store when the parent agrees to buy her candy.

PARENTING SKILLS TRAINING

Parent training, unlike other models of family work, accepts parents' definition of the child as the problem. Parent training assumes that the problem identified by the parents should be targeted for change. However, while the model explicitly states that the child is the focus of change, parents must learn to respond differently to their children. Parent training helps parents to become aware of antecedents and consequences of their child's behavior and to exert control over them. Parent training can occur in a group session outside the home or with individual families either in the home or the office.

ASSUMPTIONS

Parent training is based on the behavioral principles reviewed earlier in this chapter and can help parents in the following ways:

1. It can help parents learn to anticipate the needs and rhythms of a child. For example, stimulating a child before bedtime is unwise for the parent. Similarly, taking the child for his or her baby pictures while the infant would normally be napping is not recommended. The stimulation must be age-appropriate.
2. It can help new parents to understand how much self-sacrifice parenting requires. Parents must recognize that their previous lifestyle is changed

forever once children arrive. Each stage of child development also requires a change in parental lifestyles. One cannot parent and party at the same time. Sleep may become scarce.

3. Parents can learn to understand the stresses on their relationship that come with raising children. While the parents' relationship may become closer, there will be times when they feel unloved, unwanted, isolated, or rejected. The couple must be helped to discuss the effects on their relationship openly—including changes in their energy levels and sex life. They also need to openly discuss concerns about being effective parents. Financial worries also have to be addressed rather than ignored.

4. Parents should recognize that some of their concerns may not be addressed immediately. Waking up four times a night to feed the baby decreases the likelihood of an active sex life for the parents. Similarly, staying awake waiting for a teenager to come in at night can also be draining. Sleeping patterns will probably not change until the baby begins to sleep through the night. However, despite the inability of parents to change the situation, being able to talk about their frustrations and needs is still necessary for them.

5. Parents should recognize that frustrations, financial worries, and lack of sleep can result in many conflicts and feelings of frustration. Thoughts of hitting the child or leaving a partner are common. If they remain just thoughts, they are normal. However, these become problematic if acted upon.

6. Parents must recognize that they need to learn to love their children. The bond between the parents and the child is not automatic; it takes time and work to make it happen. An important aspect of the parent–child relationship is the match of temperaments. An active baby is a challenge for calm, slow-moving parents. Conflict with an older child may also create much resentment in the parent–child relationship.

7. Parents should recognize that they may need assistance to appreciate the joys of parenthood. When parents are bogged down in the daily stress of parenting, they may miss some pleasures that a child can give to his or her parents. Thus, parents must learn to balance the work and responsibility of childcare with the ability to play with their children.

8. Parents must recognize that unresolved personal issues will create additional stress. Distinguishing between ongoing personal or couple issues is important. Naturally, different issues will require different interventions. For example a woman who has suppressed childhood memories of sexual abuse may suddenly have flashbacks and bouts of anxiety when a daughter is born or when the daughter reaches a certain age. These types of stresses cannot be dealt with in the context of a developmental crisis.

PRINCIPLES AND PROCEDURES

Parent training relies on checklists, observation in the home, and interviews. Following is a suggested step-by-step plan for implementation of parent training.

Step 1: Develop a clear definition of the problem. In problem identification, behavior related to the presenting problem is broken down into concrete, observable, and measurable terms. Problem definition looks at three phases in relation to the problem. First, workers and parents identify what event precedes the behavior. These are known as *antecedents* and they provide important information about the cues that occur immediately before the behavior. Second, assessment of the problem describes behavior concretely. Third, assessment involves the *consequence* of the behavior such as the parental response, identifying responses that keep the behavior going.

The entire family should be included in problem identification and understand the role they play in provoking or reinforcing the behavior. However, it is advisable that input by parents be the focus of the first interview. Should the child be included in this first information collecting interview? Initially, the presence of the child may interfere with finding out critical pieces of information (Gordon & Davidson, 1981). Until parents understand the problem differently, having the child present for the initial problem identification may be detrimental to the child. Parents may also want to speak in private or refer to the child negatively during this first interview. Thus, until the behavior is reframed and understood by the parents as a learned behavior, the child may be labeled as "bad" or as the "problem."

A useful starting point in understanding the behavior would be to ask parents to describe a typical day, asking for detailed and concrete information. Checklists or charts may be used to capture the family's behaviors. At the second meeting, including the child might be useful so that parent–child interactions may be observed. When assessment is conducted in the agency, some agencies have observation rooms with two-way mirrors where colleagues can form a team to help in observing family interactional patterns.

Parents can identify a problem child easily but might have more difficulty identifying antecedents to the behavior. In other words, the parents may have labeled the child as "bad," but be unable to provide specific examples of when the behaviors occur. The FSW must help parents describe the specific problematic behavior; for example, if the child throws tantrums, what specifically does he do when he throws a tantrum (cry, yell, hit, throw things, etc.) and how often (per day, week, etc.) does a tantrum occur? The behavior must be understood in terms of frequency, intensity, duration, consequences, and social context. Parents should describe what they consider to be the sequences of interactions that contribute to problematic behavior. It is important that the behavioral sequences in the problem be described by concrete behavioral descriptions followed by a concrete description of the interactions between parent and child.

Step 2: Observe and measure behavior. After the specific behavior targeted for change is identified, the FSW must establish ways to observe and record the frequency and duration of the behavior. It is important that everyone involved know the baseline frequency (i.e., the frequency of the behavior before intervention) of the behavior to determine if there has been improvement. In this stage, the family social worker must teach the parents to observe and record the actual behavior as well as the antecedents and consequences. The FSW and parent can use behavior checklists and questionnaires.

Observing and recording the behavior must occur with every family on the FSW's caseload. Parents require training to recognize when the behavior is occurring and especially when the behavior is *not* occurring. Parents must also examine their own behaviors that occur before and after the behavior of the child—that is, occasions when they provide positive and negative attention to the child or when they ignore the child. Ultimately, the FSW wants to make certain that the behavior of the child matches the behavior of the parent and vice versa. Once parents are taught to observe and count child behaviors and to be aware of their subsequent responses to these behaviors, parents will become more "self-conscious" and understand their contributions to the child's misbehavior.

FSWs who work in client homes are able to do this. It must be remembered that the manner in which problems are reinforced can be complicated because of remote reinforcers that keep behavior going. For example, parents may model aggressive behaviors to their children but spank the child for aggressive behavior, confusing the child. Events that occur outside the family home may also reinforce the child's problem behavior—for example, peer encouragement to skip school. Problems outside the home will require meetings and planning with significant others to make certain that the response to the behavior is consistent. The focus of family intervention is on changing the parent–child interactions. Focusing on efforts that the families are making is important rather than criticizing what they are doing wrong.

Material reinforcers (toys, coins) can be used in addition to social reinforcers (praise or time spent together). Determining what reinforcers should be used for the family is important because not everyone responds to the same rewards. However, many families that family social workers see lack material resources to use as reinforcers. In addition, when social reinforcers are used, the child learns to value relationships.

In sum, parents are instructed to conduct a "three-term contingency" measurement (Gordon & Davidson, 1981) that includes: (1) observing the antecedents of the behavior (that is, the events that set the stage for the behavior); (2) a description of the behavior; and, (3) the consequences of the behavior (that is, the specific events that follow the behavior). Parents should record observations over a one-week period, during which time they will develop insight into the events. Insights gained by the family during this information gathering phase will be an impetus for change.

Step 3: Design an intervention. Measurement should not be limited to assessment but must continue throughout intervention to determine whether the intervention is being applied correctly and to see if the intervention is producing the desired results. The intervention must match the circumstances of the family, and be flexible and individualized for every family and every problem. The following four guidelines will help in selecting a treatment (Gordon & Davidson, 1981): (1) Decide how realistic environmental control is given parental resources; (2) Assess the quality of the marital relationship for parents' ability to work as a team; (3) Identify personal issues for the parents, such as depression or substance abuse, that could interfere with the ability to follow through on a treatment plan; and (4) Assess the child's ability to cooperate with the intervention plan. Be aware that "environmental noise" (stress) may interfere with the intervention.

Then, decide which behaviors should be increased and which should be decreased. Positive reinforcement accelerates behaviors that might not occur frequently. Reinforcers selected must be valued by the child, and workers will find that children are remarkably willing to let parents know what reinforcers should be used in their program. During intervention, parents must learn to respond *immediately* (with positive reinforcement, punishment, ignoring, etc., depending on whether the behavior is to be increased or decreased) to the child's display of the problem behavior. When reinforcing behaviors are to be increased, reinforcements might be gradually withdrawn over time with the expectation that the desired behavior will become more durable once it is well established. Changes in child behavior will be the parents' own reward. However, the FSW may ask parents to think of ways to reward themselves also (a night out without the children, for example); parents of children with behavior problems often experience little joy because they are over-focused on the children and their own relationship.

Behavior can be diminished by applying contingent punishment and extinction. One example is time-out, where the child is isolated at the point a problem behavior is shown. Other ways of diminishing behavior include verbal reprimands or ignoring the behavior. Time-out can be replaced by positive reinforcement—for instance, children can earn tokens or points for good behavior.

Step 4: Prepare the family to encourage the new behaviors to continue. Evaluations of most interventions have usually looked at whether treatment creates initial changes but seldom consider whether improvements persist (i.e., maintenance). Many therapists rely upon a "train-and-hope" approach, assuming that changes made during intervention will remain intact long after treatment has stopped or even permanently (Stokes & Baer, 1977). For parents to continue their new techniques over time, they must learn to use skills in different settings and in new contexts or situations (Foster, Prinz, & O'Leary, 1983). Parents must also learn to maintain these new changes despite facing environmental stressors that could erode gains made in treatment (Steffen & Karoly, 1980). Thus, an important part of the intervention should account for keeping the positive changes going when the FSW is no longer present. Parents can be asked directly about what they have learned and how they expect to keep the changes going.

The family social worker can work with parents to devise a checklist specific to the child's problem behavior. Observed behavior could include temper tantrums, working on homework, completing household chores, or staying dry at night, just to name a few. Many of the observed behaviors will occur at home, and often in the parents' presence.

Parents should be taught how to observe and record the following aspects of their child's behavior:

- Count how many times a behavior occurred within a particular time period. The time period selected can be short or long, depending upon the problem. For example, if a child is to do homework between 7:00 and 8:00 every evening but avoids homework by leaving the room, going to the bathroom, or playing with pets, the parent can observe and record the avoidant behavior during the one-hour period. Alternatively, if the parent has been instructed to record the occurrence of a child's temper tantrums, the length of time needed to observe the child's behavior could be as long as a day or more. The family social worker and the parent can develop a chart for recording frequency of behavior.
- Note how long a behavior lasted. Some behaviors can be measured by how long they last. For example, a parent may record how long it takes a child to comply with the parent's request to do the dishes.
- Record the severity of the behavior. In this type of observation, the family social worker must help the parent devise a scale to measure a particular behavior. Examples could include how well a child washes the dishes or how loud a child's whining is in reaction to a parent's denial of a privilege.

Parents also need to become aware of events that precede the target behavior, as well as how they respond to the behavior.

Case 11.1 addresses parent training used with Harry and Lisa Fryer, a young couple with three-year-old twins.

TECHNIQUES

The following are some parenting skills that the family social worker can help parents learn:

1. Help parents learn to provide a variety of stimulating experiences for their children. The experiences must be age and context appropriate and involve shared parent–child activities such as reading, playing games, and recreational activities.
2. Help parents learn to reinforce a child's attempts to be independent. The child's development of a positive identity should be supported by the parents. The overarching developmental task of childhood is to separate from the parents and move toward maturity. Parents may find this developmental phase difficult to handle as they fear for the child's safety. Other parents may believe that attempts at independence are a sign of rejection. Also, studies suggest that parents allow more independence to male children than they do to female children, so parents must be aware of gender differences.
3. Help parents recognize that the demands on them do not decrease during early family developmental stages, but rather the demands increase. For

CASE 11.1	PARENT TRAINING

Harry and Lisa were sixteen-year-old high school juniors when their twins were born. Their inexperience at parenting was addressed by the family social worker (FSW), Joyce Perdue. Mrs. Perdue's assessment revealed that Lisa was the primary caregiver while Harry worked in a local grocery store. Lisa reported that the twins were unmanageable much of the time. She reported that the children refused to take naps or go to bed at night without a tantrum. When they were awake, the twins either fought with each other or teamed up against their mother to get into mischief, according to Lisa. For instance, while Lisa talked on the phone one day last week, Tina drew pictures on the living room wall with crayons while Tommy climbed the bookcase, sending books and knickknacks crashing to the floor.

Harry tried to provide Lisa with some relief after he got home from work, but he was frustrated by the twins' lack of compliance with their parents. Harry said that the twins were "basically healthy and happy but totally out of control."

Mrs. Perdue helped the couple apply rewards for compliant behavior. For example, the twins could earn a Popsicle for dessert after lunch, or a trip to the park. The couple learned that rewarding the twins' good behavior was likely to increase it. The FSW also helped Lisa and Harry learn to use extinction whenever possible, discouraging negative behavior by ignoring it. In situations when extinction was not possible, the Fryers learned to use time-out. For instance, when Tina and Tommy fought with each other, the parents were to redirect their behavior by putting each child in a time-out chair.

The Fryers learned these new parenting behaviors by observing Mrs. Perdue as she modeled them. Lisa and Harry then practiced the behaviors while Mrs. Perdue observed and offered feedback. As the couples' parenting skills improved, Mrs. Perdue warned the couple that they might see an increase in the twins' undesirable behaviors before positive changes occurred. This was exactly what happened. But the Fryers continued using their new skills and gradually observed an improvement in the twins' behavior. Mrs. Perdue then helped the parents to establish a few simple rules to provide a routine for the twins and to guide their behavior. These rules included no hitting others or destroying others' property, bedtime at 8:30, and so on. The Fryers reported a much calmer and happier family life as their parenting skills improved.

---

instance, having a second child is not just twice the work of having one child, but seems to increase work exponentially.

4. Help the parents recognize that the child has a need to be both independent and dependent at the same time. This can be confusing for parents and children alike. Family life can be quite confusing because of this.

5. Help parents recognize that if they work outside the home, they may feel torn between the needs and demands of their job and those of their family. Guilt is a common feeling for parents who are in this situation, especially mothers who may feel pressures from husband, extended family, and neighbors to sacrifice their personal life for their child and family. Men do not usually experience this type of pressure.

BEHAVIOR PROBLEMS AND PARENT–CHILD CONFLICT

Parent–child conflict is often encountered by family social workers. Between one-third and one-half of all family social work referrals for children and adolescents may involve behavioral problems (Kadzin, 1991). Parent–child conflict may be symptomatic of a child with behavior problems or indicative of general family distress and poor parenting skills. Behavior problems take different forms, depending on the age of the child and situational and personality factors, but can include noncompliant behavior, temper tantrums, aggression, argumentativeness, refusing to obey curfews, running away from home, engaging in criminal behavior, or abusing alcohol and other drugs. Parents of acting-out children often feel alone and exhausted.

Generally, intervention in families with parent–child conflict involves a five-phase process (Forgatch, 1991):

1. *Tracking behavior:* Parents should pay close attention to child behaviors. In particular, they should learn to distinguish between compliant and noncompliant child behaviors. The parents need to respond appropriately to desirable behaviors and avoid reinforcing problematic behaviors.
2. *Positive reinforcement:* When the child behaves acceptably, the parents should respond with praise or rewards such as increased privileges.
3. *Teaching appropriate discipline:* If the child's behavior is not appropriate, the parents can apply a consequence such as time-out or loss of privileges.
4. *Monitoring children:* Parents should be taught to monitor their children's whereabouts, companions, and activities.
5. *Problem solving:* Problem-solving intervention strategies are discussed in Chapter 10. Use of problem-solving skills can help parents find solutions for their current difficulties and prevent the occurrence of future problems.

Parent–child conflict is often associated with children's behavior problems. Severity of conflict depends on the issues and personalities involved. In conflictual situations, parents are often desperate and children may be angry, rebellious, or sad.

Baynard and Baynard (1983) outline a three-step program to assist families who are experiencing parent–child conflict.

1. Have each parent make a list of the child's behaviors that are causing conflict. If there are two parents, they should make separate lists and then combine them.
2. Ask parents to cut the lists apart and separate the items into piles: one for the child, one for the parent(s), and one for items that overlap. Into the child's pile go the behaviors that will not affect the future life of the parents, even though they may have consequences for the child. Into the parent's pile go the behaviors that could have consequences for the parents. Items for the child's pile could include watching too much television, dressing sloppily, and fighting with siblings. Items for the parent's pile could include criminal activities by the child such as theft, vandalism, or assault. Items

from the overlapping pile should be sorted and moved to either the child's pile or the parent's pile. In sorting through the child's problematic behaviors, parents need to consider which ones they can control and which ones they cannot.

3. Help parents learn not to take responsibility for items in the child's pile. Parents must convey to their children a sense of trust that children can make the right decisions.

ASSISTING PARENTS IN SETTING RULES

The following principles of natural and logical consequences have been identified by Grunwald and McAbee (1985):

1. The consequence should be directly related to the behavior.
2. The consequence should be meaningful to the child.
3. The consequences of the behavior should be known ahead of time.
4. The child should be aware that there is a choice between appropriate behavior and behavior that will lead to negative consequences.
5. The consequence should take place as soon as possible after the behavior has occurred.
6. The consequence should usually be of short duration.
7. The consequence should not be a lecture; rather, it should involve some action.
8. As many family members as possible should agree to the action.

AVOIDING PITFALLS IN BEHAVIORAL INTERVENTIONS

In applying behavioral interventions, family social workers must be careful to avoid some common pitfalls. For example, Johnson (1986) suggests that defining problems as interactional may cause some clients to feel that the entire family is an object of blame. Also, certain interventions may seem to favor one family member over another, rather than treating family members equally.

In one study, parents discussed their perceptions of alliances and power imbalances that may develop during family social work. First, parents expressed concern about the possibility of having their parental power undermined by the FSW. Second, alliances between the social worker and family members were sometimes viewed as problematic; for example, if the FSW formed alliances with children, parents perceived these alliances as collusion against parental authority. Conversely, other parents were pleased when the FSW developed a working relationship with a child, because they felt that the child was receiving special attention (Coleman & Collins, 1997). Family social workers must be prepared to discuss alliances and power issues openly with clients so that potential problems can be avoided.

The following FSW behaviors can interfere with the success of behavioral interventions and should be avoided:

- Blaming individual family members or the entire family for difficulties
- Taking sides or aligning with individual family members
- Telling clients what to do instead of helping them arrive at their own solutions
- Relying on negative consequences rather than positive reinforcement
- Using technical language that the family cannot understand

By becoming familiar with how people learn and by developing skill in balancing family and individual needs, FSWs can help create an atmosphere in which all family members feel heard and understood, expectations are expressed in straightforward language, and family members participate actively in the process of change.

FAMILY PSYCHOEDUCATIONAL INTERVENTIONS

Family psychoeducation is included here because of its emphasis on family behavioral skills techniques combined with education and social support interventions. The following material is from *Family Treatment* (Janzen, Harris, Jordan, & Franklin, 2006, pp. 57–59).

ASSUMPTIONS

The goals of family psychoeducation are to educate families about their problems and to improve families' interactions with each other and with their community. Family psychoeducation was developed to intervene with individuals diagnosed with a mental illness and their families. An educational component was combined with other skills techniques and social support interventions to round out the model. Skills such as communication or problem-solving training are included to improve the families' functioning. Support is included to identify and connect families with other individuals experiencing similar problems. Since its initial use with individuals with a DSM diagnosis, family psychoeducation has been used with many other problems and types of families. Examples of problems for which psychoeducational intervention has been used include child ADHD, anorexia, diabetes, and other health problems. The intervention also is used with family problems such as anger control and conflict resolution.

Family psychoeducation assumes that the family is healthy and functional and has strengths to bring to the table that will help the family improve. This is in contrast to previous theories that blamed family members for their ill member's problems. Names associated with the development of this model are Falloon, Hogarty, Anderson, Reiss, and Johnson. These clinician-researchers theorized that families could successfully learn to cope in the face of problems. Their research shows that families who react to a family problem with criticism, hostility, and over-involvement make the problem worse, and conversely, families who have good communication and problem-solving skills will help the family and its members to successfully solve their problems.

PRINCIPLES AND PROCEDURES

The FSW's role in family psychoeducation is to educate families, to provide skills training, and to connect families with resources in the community. Roles needed, therefore, include educator, therapist, case manager, and advocate. The FSW also is charged with motivating and encouraging families, modeling new skills, and assigning homework for family practice. Family psychoeducation may be done with one family at a time or with groups of families meeting together.

TECHNIQUES

Assessment in family psychoeducation focuses on identifying the level of skills in the family (i.e., communication, conflict resolution, etc.). Qualitative and quantitative techniques may be used to further explore areas of family functioning. For instance, a genogram may help to explore family patterns of an illness that may be the focus of the family psychoeducational treatment. Alcoholism, for example, may be a dysfunctional family pattern that can be revealed by a mapping technique. Quantitative techniques may help to operationalize problems further. Using the example of alcoholism, a standardized scale to measure alcohol and drug usage may be helpful.

Education is the delivery of information in a didactic way. This component is often delivered in groups by the FSW or another expert (i.e., physician or other professional). The educational component may be offered prior to or simultaneously with other components of family psychoeducation.

Case management is connecting families to appropriate community resources. Examples include job training, housing, support groups (i.e., AA), or any other resource that may meet the families' needs. The FSW must have a comprehensive knowledge of resources in his or her community.

Family therapy techniques used by the FSW are usually skills oriented. Examples of particularly useful skills are communication, conflict resolution, anger management, marital enhancement, and problem solving. Some family members may require skills such as job training and other life skills, such as medication maintenance.

EVIDENCE BASE FOR FAMILY PSYCHOEDUCATION

The many family psychoeducation research studies have focused on families involved with the mental health system. Lambert's meta-analysis shows the effectiveness of family psychoeducation with affective disorders, major depression, and anorexia (2004). A review by Franklin and Jordan (1999) showed this model to be effective, with improved family and patient outcomes with all family types regardless of background.

CASE 11.2	PSYCHOEDUCATION

The FSW received an intake on a family facing the mother's diagnosis of HIV. The mother, Elena, had watched as her husband Alejandro's health deteriorated from AIDS. He died two years ago, leaving Elena with one son, Joaquin, age 12. The FSW made a home visit to interview Elena and Joaquin after reviewing the steps of family psychoeducation. The FSW felt this intervention model to be appropriate because the intake indicated that the family was suffering with both health and psychological issues; the evidence-based literature she reviewed confirmed the efficacy of this approach with HIV-AIDS. Following is a brief review of the family social work in each phase of psychoeducation.

Assessment: The FSW focused on identifying the family's level of skills (i.e., communication, conflict resolution, etc.). Qualitative and quantitative techniques were used to further explore areas of family functioning. An ecomap (qualitative technique) was used to assess the family's level of community and family support. A health inventory and social support inventory (quantitative techniques) were used to operationalize problems further.

Education: Elena and Joaquin attended a three-session workshop on HIV-AIDS along with other families.

Case management: The FSW served as the case manager for Elena and Joaquin, connecting them with appropriate community resources. The FSW connected Elena and Joaquin with medical resources and an HIV-AIDS family support group that meets monthly.

Family therapy techniques: The family therapy techniques used by the FSW were determined from the assessment, which revealed Joaquin's anger and Elena's need for parent training. This family may eventually need skills training such as medication maintenance, depending on the course of Elena's illness.

CASE 11.3	FOCUSING ON CHILDREN

The FSW made a visit to the home of Cliff and Claire, a middle-aged African American couple, and their four children. The children were Able (14), Fontana (12), Selena (6), and Foster (4). The family was reported for suspected child abuse by neighbors. The FSW found the couple to be somewhat suspicious of the FSW and the agency; they said that they had been reported before and that the neighbors were "out to get them."

In doing her assessment, the FSW looked for risk factors of child abuse/neglect to confirm or disconfirm the report. Some of the factors she looked for included isolation from family or other support systems; negative interactions within the family; inappropriate parental expectations of the children and/or lack of parenting skills; and high rates of stress. In her investigation of these issues, the FSW found that Cliff and Claire had very little knowledge of child developmental stages or parenting skills. The teenagers, typically, were testing boundaries. The two younger children were acting out, possibly because of the stress between the teens and their parents. Intervention focused on these issues.

CASE 11.4	INCORPORATING EVERYONE'S PERSPECTIVE

Alice and Ray are part of the "sandwich generation." They are parenting Ray's two children from a previous marriage, twins Kathy and Ricky who are 14 years old. Together the couple has a six-month-old baby, Heather. The twins came to live with the family when their biological mother's alcoholism was revealed; she is currently in a treatment facility. Soon after the twins came to live with Alice and Ray, Alice's mother moved in with the family. Bess, 78 years old, fell and broke her hip. After surgery and rehabilitation, she was unable to live alone, thus she moved in with her son's family.

It is important when doing family social work to obtain the perspectives of all family members. Using this family as an example, the FSW found that Alice feels the twins have been spoiled by their mother and that they are undisciplined. She is angry with Ray for not being stricter with the two children. Alice is also angry with Grandmother Bess's interference with parenting and other matters. Ray, on the other hand, feels that the children have been through a difficult time with their alcoholic mother and that they need a gentle hand. He also feels that his mother is elderly and harmless. He is mostly amused and just ignores her when she "meddles." The twins' perspective of the family situation is that their new stepmother is "wicked" and that she is "out to get them," clearly preferring the baby to them and to their interests. They feel their father is weak for not standing up to Alice and they miss their mom. They see Grandma Bess as the only adult who will stand up for them.

It will be the FSW's role to help the family negotiate these differences in perspective. Techniques such as problem-solving, conflict resolution, and communication training, as well as anger control, may be useful.

CHAPTER SUMMARY

This chapter presented some techniques for helping families to better handle the stresses and problems of day-to-day living and strategies to develop a positive family climate. Interventions included behavioral family therapy, family psychoeducation, and parent training. As families transition through normal developmental stages, parents can help this family maturation process by creating a positive parent–child relationship and learning techniques to shape their child's behavior in a positive direction.

EXERCISES

11.1 BEHAVIORAL FAMILY APPROACH EXERCISE

Imagine that your supervisor asks you to see a client family named Smith. The Smiths are experiencing problems with a teenage daughter, Christina, aged 13. The problems center around Christina's desire for more independence. She would like to go to the mall and stay out late with her friends on Saturday, but her parents (Tom and Julie) are worried that she is not old enough for this responsibility. Additionally, Christina feels that her father is too bossy and domineering, while her mother is a "doormat." Christina reports that her father actually spanked her when she sneaked out of school early to go to the mall with her friends. Christina also tells you that her brother Thomas, age 14, is allowed to go to the football game with friends without adult supervision every Friday night. She does not believe this to be fair.

Team up with a partner and use the steps of the behavioral family approach to address the Smith families' issues.

Step 1: Problem definition

Step 2: Behavioral observation

Step 3: Design an intervention

11.2   Family Psychoeducation Exercise

Identify a client you know about and design a family psychoeducational plan, including education, skills training, and identification of supportive resources.

11.3   Practice a Role-Play

List some appropriate situations for which role-playing would be a helpful technique. Pick one of these and practice it with a partner.

11.4   Parent Training

Design a plan for intervening with a single-parent mother who is having trouble with her acting-out teenage son.

11.5   Modeling

List three situations in which modeling would be a helpful technique. Pick one of these and practice it with a partner.

11.6   Behavioral Intervention with a Family

Break into groups of three or four students. Divide a piece of paper into two columns. On the top of one column, write "Do's" and on the top of the second column write "Don'ts." Devise a list of skills that can be used in communication skills training with families. Compare your list with the rest of the class, discuss the lists, and then compile a complete list based on everyone's responses.

INTERVENTIONS WITH COUPLES AND GENDER SENSITIVE INTERVENTION

CHAPTER 12

CHAPTER CONTENTS

COUPLE WORK

When working with families, the FSW often will become aware that marital issues are directly effecting the couples' parenting efforts. Further marital issues can affect children's well-being. "There is convincing evidence that marital distress, conflict, and disruption are associated with a wide range of deleterious effects on children in families" (Gottman, 1999, p. 4). The focus of this book is on family work, not family therapy nor marital therapy, and we suggest that beginning FSWs refer couples to a marital therapist if they wish marriage counseling. However, in our work as FSWs we still need to be able to focus on the marital dyad to help the couple become more supportive of each other in their joint parenting efforts.

Satir (1967) considered the parents the "architects of the family." Quite simply, this means that parents define and determine many of the characteristics of the family unit. Parents create the family structure and rules that govern a family. Parents need to teach children healthy ways of functioning. A major way of teaching children healthy ways of functioning or behaving is for the parents to model these healthy behaviors. If parents expect children to cooperate with each other it is important for parents to model cooperation between themselves.

Satir identified two central themes about parents within a family: (1) "The marital relationship is the axis around which all other family relationships are formed. The mates are the architects of the family. (2) A pained marital relationship tends to produce dysfunctional parenting" (1967, p. 2). Often the FSW will meet just with the couple and focus on their relationship and how they communicate with each other and support each other to be consistent in their parenting. Parenting skill training with just the couple present (see Chapter 11) is also a role the FSW performs. Family social work with couples is fairly basic, and more advanced couples work needs to be done by a family therapist. Basic family work is primarily educational and supports couples to model the behaviors they expect from their children.

Family rules created to help families function in a healthy manner need also to be followed by the parents. For example, if a rule is that children should not hit each other, this should be a family rule of "no hitting family members," including between parents. If a rule is "no swearing" by the children, the parents can themselves model a no-swearing policy. Likewise, a family rule of "no yelling" may be put into place, and it is very important for the parents to model this no-yelling behavior. It really follows the adage "practice what you preach." We are aware that at times there are different rules and behavioral expectations for adults then for children, but many rules and behavioral expectations can be applied by the family as a whole and modeled by the parents. How children learn to share feelings, deal with anger and stress, and solve problems can be learned by observing the parents. Parents need to demonstrate healthy ways of communicating and problem solving to act as models of these behaviors to their children.

When two people who experience personal problems get together and hope that these problems will get better because of the relationship, difficulties can result with the children. They might expect that a certain child will fulfill personal needs, or alternatively, they might need a child to satisfy their relationship (see more on triangulation in Chapter 9). It is important to get an idea of the history of the marriage (or relationship). How did they meet? What did they like about one another? How did they make decisions about their relationship? What was their relationship like before children came along? Eventually, the worker can find out about significant people in their lives and perhaps even locate issues that have been passed down the generations. FSWs should be attuned to negative interactions between the parents because these interactions demonstrate negative child outcomes (Stanley, Markman, & Whitton, 2002).

John Gottman (1999) has studied marriages extensively and identified behaviors that predict divorce. The predictors of divorce exist in all relationships; however, in happy marriages, the behaviors occur less often. Based on extensive research, Gottman offers the following threats to marriages.

- Negativity outweighing positivity during disagreement.
- Four Horsemen of the Apocalypse: criticism, defensiveness, contempt, and stonewalling. These Four Horsemen are particularly corrosive to relationships. Contempt does not exist in satisfying relationships.
- Emotional disengagement, underlying tension and sadness, and the absence of positive affect.
- Conflict on "perpetual issues" is "gridlocked" or characterized by emotional disengagement.
- "Repair" attempts fail.
- Harsh start-up of conflict discussions.
- Refusal of husband to accept influence by the wife. (Wives typically accept influence from the husband.)
- Absence of de-escalation attempts.
- Little positive affect (p. 68).

Few people have studied what makes a healthy marriage. We assume that health is the absence of problems or the absence of pathology. Yet as family social workers, we need to stress the importance of sharing love and caring in a family and minimizing—or indeed stopping—criticism, defensiveness, contempt, and stonewalling in order to have healthy families. The couples have to be the leaders and models in this regard.

GENDER SENSITIVE PERSPECTIVE

An underpinning philosophy we now employ when working with families as well as couples is a gender sensitive perspective. We let families and couples know that it is a philosophy and approach we strongly believe is important in today's Western society. We are aware that we are imposing our bias, and not all couples/families will accept this view, but we believe the concept of equality is still important to share with families and couples.

We believe a gender sensitive perspective is useful with the marital and parenting subsystems as well as the family as a whole. Our rationale for a gender sensitive perspective is that we have found it highly conducive to understanding and engaging couples in the counseling process. It helps us be very sensitive to people's feelings and who they are.

We first present issues in work with couples and the gender sensitive conceptual framework. The later part of the chapter is somewhat an extension of behaviorally focused interventions from Chapter 11, in which we focus in greater depth on parenting skill training within a gender sensitive context.

GENDER SENSITIVE INTERVENTION

Gender sensitive intervention is linked with support and education, as well as problem solving. Key elements of this approach involve helping families to:

- Recognize and change the destructive consequences of stereotyped roles and expectations;
- Avoid the promotion of dependency and submissiveness for women and children;
- Encourage women to build positive self-esteem and encourage men to become actively involved in child and household duties.

Intervention using a gender sensitive perspective does not advocate neutrality for the family social worker, as does traditional family therapy. Gender sensitive family work occurs with worker and client family being on an equal footing. Family members are empowered to gain a positive understanding of their skills and abilities, changing the whole family in a positive way. This is congruent with the overall approach taken throughout this book that the family worker actively supports family members. Support and education, as well as problem solving and contracting, support the goals of feminism.

Applying this supportive approach while utilizing a gender sensitive perspective helps families through education about current gender issues and gender realities. Young girls still grow up in a world that gives them very different messages from the ones that boys receive about their value, roles, and life opportunities. Yet traditional therapy often fails to take this social context into account when dealing with women's (and girls') problems. One therapist may treat a woman's depression and anger in response to an abusive relationship as a symptom of an individual psychiatric problem, encouraging her to adapt to the problems rather than to change her situation. It is important that family social workers understand families, and women in particular, in a modern social context and not from a traditional psychiatric model. The FSW can teach a woman to differentiate between her problem and someone else's problem, helping her to realize that every failed relationship in her life is not her fault. Women have been socialized to take responsibility for family relationships and the well-being of individual family members.

Family social work helps families recognize and change the destructive consequences of stereotyped roles and expectations in the family. Traditional therapists have assessed the mental health of women and men differently. Healthy women are expected to be more submissive, less independent, more easily influenced, less competitive, more excitable and emotional, more conceited about their appearance, less objective, and less interested in math and science than are healthy men. For women, the most significant barrier to finding a good worker has been the male standard of behavior that traditionally guides what is "healthy" and "normal." It is imperative that FSWs present themselves in the beginning stage of family work as not following traditional views, but as defining adult relationships as egalitarian. In the intervention phase, this translates to having adults equally participate in child rearing and in household tasks.

Gender sensitive family work avoids promoting dependency and submissiveness for women and children. Women often feel that their role is to nurture and support others rather than to express themselves, and have been taught to take care of others first. As a result, they often have difficulty recognizing their own needs. Exhausted working women are trying to keep up with all the demands of work as well as home demands, resulting in stress and burnout. At the same time, gender sensitive family work recognizes the importance of relationships to women and at the same time makes certain that the emphasis on relationships does not oppress women or allow others to manipulate them.

For women who have been abused, health and well-being starts with recognizing their will to survive. Placing women's issues within a larger social context also boosts women's self-esteem. Effective family social work helps women build self-esteem, stand up for themselves, and assume greater control over their lives. It gives women choices and opens up opportunities otherwise denied to them and at the same time encourages men to value their roles of equal partner and parent. Men in the process, are encouraged to become actively involved in parenting and household responsibilities. Client strengths and competence are emphasized. Indeed, the key to helping women and families is to focus on strengths rather than weaknesses. In family or couple work, this means giving equal consideration to the skills, aspirations, and careers of women.

A gender sensitive FSW working with couples who are experiencing a troubled marital relationship should explain that there are two key ingredients for a successful marriage:

1. A good marriage requires a supportive, nurturing relationship involving genuine commitment and caring for each other. This is an indirect way of saying that partners need to develop intimacy to achieve marital satisfaction. As mentioned earlier, the major reason given for marital divorce was feeling unloved in the relationship.
2. A satisfying marriage also requires equal or at least a negotiated sharing of instrumental tasks within the household. When children are present, there should be equal sharing of parenting tasks such as assisting children with homework, taking children to dental appointments, and spending creative play-time with children. Both parents need to understand that the time and energy they invest in childcare pays big dividends in terms of family functioning. Furthermore, the male's role in raising children has to be enhanced to that of an equal partnership with the female. This means that women

also need to avoid making men feel incompetent when caring for children, and men need to become active partners in doing household tasks such as cooking and laundry.

PROBLEM SOLVING WITHIN A GENDER SENSITIVE INTERVENTION PERSPECTIVE

A problem-solving intervention approach complements a gender sensitive perspective. Because gender sensitivity assumes equality of family members, given developmental and personal capacities, problem solving encourages participation of all members in solving common family problems. What affects one member affects everyone. Problem solving helps members negotiate solutions to problems that are acceptable to everyone in the family.

In teaching families about problem solving, family social workers help families identify concerns and goals, set priorities, and develop a plan for working toward resolution. Problem solving is an essential component of individuals' and family members' well-being, and the use of this model can enhance a family's ability to independently address its own needs.

In the course of personal and work life, family members have goals as well as problems or stresses. Problem-solving strategies can be used to reach goals, meet challenges, or deal with stresses and problems. Problem solving is one way of coping with life's events. Given the same stressful circumstances, one person may cope by denial or avoidance while another copes through effective problem solving. Parents may be taught the problem-solving process so that they will have a better understanding of the processes and strategies involved in thinking through a problem and carrying out proposed solutions.

The social work profession has a long history of using a problem-solving approach. The problem-solving model is based, in part, upon an assumption that parents' day-by-day situations are often as complex and demanding as those of many professionals. Therefore, the preparation and training given to many professionals in problem solving is appropriate for parents. Problem-solving skills are an important part of social work training as workers are taught how to identify, assess, and intervene with client problems. A second assumption is that teaching parents problem-solving skills helps assure that parents have the necessary skills for developing positive parent–child relationships.

HISTORICAL CONTEXT

Historically, men have held more public and private power than women. Men wrote laws, controlled property and money, and were recognized as heads of households, while women did most of the work within the home and received little recognition, power, or respect for their contributions. These patterns have been changing within the last few decades as growing numbers of women have entered the workforce and the political arena, but imbalances of power remain. Because of longstanding patterns of gender inequity, family social workers are likely to encounter situations in which women are oppressed and abused.

Expecting women to adapt to oppressive situations is inappropriate; instead, family social workers should empower them to assume greater control over their lives. Empowering women might entail helping them find ways to change or leave oppressive and abusive relationships and to gain a broader awareness of the options available to them. Accordingly, gender sensitive interventions are well suited to family social work, particularly work with families in which women have been oppressed or abused by their partners.

Gender sensitive family social workers question some of the views held by traditional family therapists, including their emphasis on circular causality, particularly when applied to power imbalances. They disagree with the idea that women contribute to their own abuse. Instead, they attribute the abuse to imbalance and misuse of power.

To implement a gender sensitive approach with clients, FSWs must be willing to question their personal assumptions about men and women and gender roles. They need to become familiar with the ways in which society reinforces unequal treatment based on gender. Gender sensitive social workers take an ecological perspective when understanding family dynamics, recognizing the influence of a family's social environment on its internal functioning. Many families have absorbed messages about gender stereotypes and inequalities from the larger society. Finally, gender sensitive social workers recognize that changes in families can slowly lead to changes in society and that social change can improve life for families.

A FEMINIST CRITIQUE OF FAMILY SYSTEMS THEORY

Gender sensitive family social work uses a feminist perspective to understand how families function. The feminist perspective has been described as "an attitude, a lens, a body of ideas about gender hierarchy and its impact rather than a specific model or a grab-bag of clinical techniques" (Carter, 1992, p. 66). Feminist theory is a philosophical foundation upon which family social workers can base gender sensitive interventions without perpetuating patriarchal assumptions about the role of women in families and in society. Feminist theory, as it applies to family social work, advocates sensitivity to the problems created when rigid, traditional gender roles are assigned to family members (to the woman's detriment) or when power is not balanced or abused. It also sheds light on the fact that gender has an influence in male–female relationships (Rampage, 2002). Feminist social workers recognize the detrimental effects of power imbalances and gender-based inequality in family relationships.

Feminists have challenged some of the basic assumptions of traditional family therapists, noting the influence of cultural and historical biases on the development of family theory (Nichols & Schwartz, 2004). Feminist theorists have criticized sexist biases of the pioneers of family therapy, who failed to question the value of characteristics in which males are socialized (rationality, independence), while discounting characteristics (such as nurturing and interconnectedness) typically associated with female socialization. Early family theorists also endorsed a "normal family structure," often based on gender inequality. Early theorists, for example, spoke about instrumental roles (which should be assumed by males) and affective roles, typically assumed by women. When the roles were reversed, family therapists advocated "putting the pants back on the men!" Advocates of feminist social work practice believe this male-constructed view of the world associates female characteristics with weakness, passivity, masochism, and inferiority.

During the 1980s, feminists began to criticize family systems theory for some of its sexist biases, particularly the assumption that if all participants in the system contribute to a problem, they do so from positions of *equal* power. In particular, feminists challenged family systems concepts of circular causality, neutrality, complementarity, and homeostasis. These concepts were discussed in Chapter 2. Feminists consider circular causality (implying that members are locked in an equal and never-ending, repetitive pattern of mutually reinforcing behaviors) to be a sophisticated way of blaming victims and rationalizing the status quo (Goldner, 1985a). Circular causality was considered particularly problematic in its explanation of abuse or other problems associated with power imbalances. Indeed, McGoldrick (1999b) noted that "the conundrum of responsibility without power has long characterized women's lives" (p. 107).

When used to explain situations of family violence, circular causality implies that the perpetrator and victim are equally involved in producing and maintaining "the problem." The most sexist use of circular causality was to "punctuate" the circular pattern by suggesting that the sequence to wife abuse often starts with the woman nagging the man. Not only were women blamed for the abuse, they were also blamed for starting the sequence of events that culminated in their abuse. Feminist therapists took a different stance, challenging mainstream family theory by insisting that women are *not* equally responsible for their own abuse because they have little power in the family system. They argue that using circular causality to explain abuse subtly removes responsibility from the abuser while implying that the victim contributes to the problem by playing into the interaction pattern resulting in abuse.

Similarly, the family systems idea of the worker being neutral during family work ignores and even condones differences in family members' power. Feminists disagree with the idea that social workers should avoid holding one family member responsible for a problem and suggest that those who abuse power are ultimately responsible. Through neutrality, they argue, traditional helpers contribute to the maintenance of the status quo.

Feminists also challenge *complementarity*—the belief that gender differences are acceptable because men and women play separate but equal roles in family life. According to traditional views, men are responsible for the economic well-being of the family while women are responsible for the care giving of family members. In other words, under the traditional model, wives are responsible for almost everything that keeps the family operating smoothly, such as housework and childcare (Eichler, 1997). Feminists point out that while the homemaker role is valued in the abstract, the actual work is denigrated (Pogrebin, 1980). Moreover, women are socialized to assume responsibility for the emotional well-being of the family. Goldner (1985a) alerts us to this bias: "We think of mothers as gatekeepers, regulating the interaction between the family and the outside world, and also as switchboards, regulating communication patterns within the family" (p. 39).

A major concern about gender bias in family work is the longstanding tendency of the helping professions to blame mothers for the problems of other members or the family as a whole because family well-being is seen as the responsibility of women. Ironically, they are responsible for family well-being even though they lack power. Mothers have been considered the central (and often only) socialization agent of children (Mackie, 1991), ignoring the role of fathers in childcare. Because of this ascribed responsibility, when sexual abuse happens it is her responsibility. Mother blaming is both pervasive and disturbing (Caplan & Hall-McCorquodale, 1985). Difficulties such as attachment disorders (Bowlby, 1969), schizophrenia (Weakland & Fry, 1974), and sexual abuse (Trepper & Barrett, 1986) have all been placed on the doorstep of poor "mothering." Mothers have also been blamed for participating in their own abuse. In the literature, mothers are described as either over-involved or remote. They are either incompetent or over-competent. They are either over-emotional or cold. Women cannot win. Either way, women are responsible for the ills of the family. In the development of child problems, mothers are described as contributors to the disorders, but repeatedly, fathers are ignored, even when the problem originates from the father, as in the case of sexual abuse. Mothers have also been blamed for the difficulties of adult men (Caplan & Hall-McCorquodale, 1991).

Another fundamental tenet of family systems theory is that the family, as a living organism, attempts to maintain a balance or homeostasis. This view of family functioning obscures or eliminates individual responsibility, because all behavior is seen as an attempt by the family as a unit to maintain homeostasis. Family homeostasis and mother blaming work together to entrench the anti-woman bias evident in family systems theory. On one hand, mothers are responsible for the problems of the family, but homeostasis is used to excuse or obscure power abuses by male family members.

Family social workers should take special note of how homeostasis has explained family problems, particularly when the problem involves victimization. For example, family systems theorists who discuss the causes of intrafamilial sexual abuse have interpreted the father's behavior in positive terms (i.e., a misguided attempt to show affection), while suggesting that mothers should be assessed for inhibited sexual desire. Such theories reveal a not so subtle gender bias. Not only are fathers given positive intent for the abuse, mothers become responsible for maintaining homeostasis. Again, in the words of Goldner (1985a), "Insofar as all roads lead to Mom, her excesses and deficiencies will indeed make an enormous difference in how life flows around her and how the children develop" (p. 40).

POWER IMBALANCES IN FAMILY RELATIONSHIPS

One of the strongest critiques of family therapy by feminists is the assertion that by failing to challenge the imbalance of power in families, family therapy has sanctioned this imbalance (Dye Holten, 1990). Because feminist practice is primarily concerned with power and how it is distributed, feminist theory is particularly concerned with inequality in family relationships. A fundamental aim of feminism is to ensure that power in family relations is fairly distributed.

One source of inequal power is the law, which gives husbands, wives, mothers, fathers, and children certain rights and obligations. A second source of power is the gender norms established by society. While gender power is changing as traditional role definitions change, these changes seem to be more apparent in well-educated, middle-class households. Changes in gender roles may create confusion in families, and members may face conflicts as roles change. A third source of power involves access to knowledge and resources. People can increase their personal power base by improving their formal education and obtaining more resources, such as money, information, or social support. Women usually have less economic power than men, and economic dependency becomes especially potent with the arrival of children (Mackie, 1991; McGoldrick, 2002). However, when wives have greater status or money than their husbands, divorce is more likely to occur.

Personality differences influence the distribution of power in family life. Members with high self-esteem, for example, are likely to have more power than those with low self-esteem. People who are outgoing, talkative, and assertive are also considered to have greater power and control than those who are not.

Another important source of power involves factors such as age and the life stage. Changes in life situations that affect personal power are sometimes difficult to understand and constitute potentially stressful life events. For instance, an unemployed husband may not have the same status and power he enjoyed while working. The loss of power from a change in life situations may be accompanied by sadness, anger, or both. Power differences may also shift at retirement when men lose social power because they are no longer as involved in public spheres of life.

A final source of power influencing family members concerns "emotional factors." Family members vary in their ability and willingness to give or withhold love and affection. Motives also vary on this dimension, with some family members exerting control with manifestations of love, affection, dominance, force, denial, or rejection.

Not all power discrepancies in families are destructive or undesirable. For example, parents should have more power than their children. We see many families these days where children have much more power in their families than they can responsibly handle. Ineffective parenting and failure to discipline appropriately leaves many children with excessive power. The challenge to possessing personal power in a relationship is to use this power *responsibly* and not just assume that because it comes with a particular family *role*, power can be used in any way one wants. Every family and family member have unique configurations of power based on age, sex, education, personality, and life situation. Couples need to be acutely aware of these factors in exercising power with each other. In addition, family workers should be keenly attuned to power issues within the families with whom they are working.

Power is not diminished or lost when shared. In fact, shared power helps to balance families, and family satisfaction is highest when all family members get to share in the family's power. Gottman and Notarius (cited in Rampage, 2002, p. 264) observe that a balance of husband–wife power is related to marital quality and marital satisfaction. A family council or regular marital review is one way families can equalize power distribution. Emotionally healthy families use power to support one another, while troubled families use power to distort, control, or dominate. Appropriate use of power helps members reach their potential and provides maximum benefit to family members.

Regardless of how power relates to gender in the family, social workers need to be sensitive to issues of power. Gender sensitive FSWs strive to model egalitarian relationships with families. Rather than taking an authoritarian role, they work to empower family members, modeling the benefits of sharing power rather than appropriating it for oneself.

The Ecological Orientation of Gender Sensitive Practice

In assessing family problems, gender sensitive family social workers recognize the influence of the economic, political, and social environments in which people live, as well as the prevailing social attitudes and expectations that frame gender roles. By recognizing the social context of gender roles and associated traits, FSWs can better understand why men abuse their partners emotionally and physically. Additionally, they realize that women may remain in abusive relationships because of feelings of powerlessness, helplessness, and lack of control over their lives.

Until recently, traditional family systems therapists have failed to connect family problems to socially prescribed gender roles and power imbalances, and thus have not acknowledged how the interactions between family members are affected by the larger social system (Goodrich, Rampage, Ellman, & Halstead, 1988, p. 12). Feminists point out that trying to assess a family's problems without regard to ecological embeddedness "is like watching a parade through a key hole" (Goldner, 1985a, p. 34).

The larger social context needs to be considered when looking at family dysfunction. Feminists suggest that cultural values and beliefs about gender influence how families function, with the larger cultural context playing a role in wife battering and child abuse.

FAMILY VALUES AND FAMILY VIOLENCE: A CRITIQUE

Why is an understanding of values and beliefs about families important? Don't families just exist independent from other families? Shouldn't families just do the best they can and face the consequences of not fulfilling social obligations? As with any clinical practice, workers must understand the wider social context of their practice and understand how larger social values might influence their practice. In this critique, we use the example of family violence to show how workers have colluded with three social values and how this collusion has skewed workers' understanding of abuse in the family. In a study of family violence from colonial times to the present, Pleck (1987) suggested that three central societal values have hindered attempts to eliminate family violence. These values include beliefs about family privacy, family stability, and conjugal and parental rights.

FAMILY PRIVACY

Over time, there has been lack of agreement about how much families should be left to their own devices without outside intervention from the state. This fundamental question concerns all family social workers who must grapple with the intrusiveness of their work. Many family social workers work for state-based agencies and have a legal mandate to enter homes. Some of the value placed on family privacy is based on the belief that intimate family relationships should be free from state intrusion and interference. As stated by Pleck (1987), "Modern defenders are likely to argue that the family has a constitutional right to privacy or insist that the home is the only setting where intimacy can flourish, providing meaning, coherence and stability in personal life" (p. 8). To what extent should family social workers intrude into resistant families?

In the same fashion, behavior within families is often viewed differently from behavior outside the family. "When we think of the family, and then think of the world that surrounds it, we tend to think in terms of contrasts" (Goldner, 1988, p. 24). For example, abuse of family members is sometimes attributed to family dynamics, but similar behavior directed toward a neighbor is viewed as assault. Separate government agencies exist to deal with abuse inside and outside of the family, and one cluster of theories explain violence outside the home while another cluster describes violence within the home.

Social isolation has become the downside of family privacy. Many families seen by family social workers are socially isolated, making access to social resources difficult. Privacy removes families from scrutiny and keeps family members from potential sources of social support and information.

Family social workers must identify their personal beliefs about family privacy and decide what impact their beliefs and agency mandates may have on working with families. When families are involuntary, the family social worker must cross the line concerning privacy. If a family social worker is uncertain about how to deal with issues of privacy, he or she may be governed by politeness and apology instead of dealing with family problems. Drawing artificial boundaries around the family inhibits family work.

Efforts to safeguard family privacy affect social work practice, especially when abuse is suspected. Notions about privacy may protect abusers from legal consequences and prevent victims of family violence from using resources to escape the abuse.

FAMILY STABILITY

Keeping families together is a central goal of family social workers. When working with people involved in abuse, however, FSWs may be forced to choose between two basic values: the autonomy of the family and the protection of children (Giovanonni, 1982). Making this choice is difficult because the measure of success for family social workers is often keeping the family together. However, family social workers are often faced with the difficult choice of protecting vulnerable family members, necessitating that children be removed from the home. Maintaining family autonomy becomes a line drawing exercise and the mandate of the agency might determine where family workers draw the line.

Traditionally, one way of ensuring family stability has been to reinforce established gender roles by keeping the male at the "head." Encouraging the independence of women has been viewed as a threat to the family unit (Cherlin, 1983). Strong women have the resources to manage on their own and they are not economically dependent. Gordon contends that "the concept of the autonomous family, in fact, as it is manipulated in contemporary political discourse, is generally used in opposition to women's rights as autonomous citizens" (1985, p. 218). Family social workers need to examine their personal biases about gender roles to consider what it means to empower *every* member of the family unit. Family social workers must decide whether the goal of preserving family stability meets the needs of every family member, particularly those who are vulnerable. Does failure to preserve the family make the intervention a failure?

The desire to maintain family stability has frequently led family social workers to make mothers the focal point of intervention, because traditionally women have assumed responsibility for family well-being. A mother may feel pressured to keep the family together even at great personal emotional cost. Moreover, the family's economic welfare may be at risk. As recounted by Goldner (1985a), "She knows that she has much more at stake and much more to lose if things don't work out than the man she married . . . the breakdown of the traditional family has too often meant a new kind of freedom for men and a new kind of trap for women" (p. 41).

CONJUGAL AND PARENTAL RIGHTS

From a feminist perspective, marriage is a relationship based on an unequal distribution of power, usually with the male as the dominant partner. "Truly, position is power" (Munson, 1993, p. 362). The husband is often the primary wage-earner, and his position is validated politically, socially, and economically. He is usually physically more powerful, a fact that makes potential abuse of his power threatening to other family members. In patriarchal societies such as ours, both women and children have historically been considered possessions of the father, making them vulnerable to boundary violations and violence (Armstrong, 1987; Nelson, 1987). Feminists consider the traditional husband as the benefactor of the marital relationship at the expense of the wife.

Power hierarchies within families are influenced by both gender and age. These factors play an important role in how families are structured (Goldner, 1988), providing fundamental organizing principles of family life. Power comes from socially endorsed *conjugal and parental rights*. Just as there are special privileges and power imbalances outside the family, there are "private" power imbalances and special privileges inside the family. Women have power over children, and men have power over women (Mackie, 1991).

SOCIALIZATION AND GENDER ROLES

Families provide a socializing environment for children. Influences on children's gender role socialization are pervasive. Some of the influences are subtle, while others are blatant. Family social workers need to be attuned to biases involved in child rearing and to recognize how sexist biases handicap both male and female development. Mothers and fathers interact with their children differently. For example, mothers are more likely to feed, clean, and protect children whereas fathers tend to play with them more (Mackie, 1991). Similarly, mothers often are more involved in the daily routine of childcare and discipline, even when women work outside the home. Nevertheless, fathers are most responsible for the sex typing of the children. Researchers have noted that fathers are more likely than mothers to reinforce stereotypical gender behavior in children.

Children are often treated differently based on gender. Parents cuddle female infants and talk to them, and they handle male infants less gently and play with them more. Boys are more likely to be spanked as a form of discipline, whereas girls are more likely to be verbally reprimanded. Achievement is expected more from male children than from female children. Parents are also more likely to punish behavior that deviates from social expectations of the child's gender and reward behavior that fits the mold of the specific gender. For example, parents are more likely to discourage independent activities of girl children and to discourage dependence in male children. If parents observe a male child struggling with a problem, they are inclined to let him find his own solution. With a female child, they are more likely to take over and solve the problem instead of letting her develop the skills of doing it alone. Boys are often pressured to cover up or deny feelings of sadness and vulnerability (Pollack, 1998).

How parents relate to one another also affects children's perceptions of their own gender. For example, Pogrebin (1980) suggests that how the family allocates roles regarding household tasks and paid employment affects children's competence, their ability to overcome stereotypical notions, and their occupational choices.

Feminists note that despite the fact that many families are headed by dual-career couples, role arrangements within the family often have remained static or at best have progressed very slowly. Most people acknowledge that men *should* contribute equally to domestic duties, but the reality is different. In the words of Eichler (1997), "There is an amazing inelasticity in men's contributions to household tasks; no matter how much there is to do, men do the same amount" (p. 60). Thus, women often continue to shoulder the burden of family and household responsibilities even when they also hold jobs outside the home.

To be gender sensitive is to be aware of the different behaviors, attitudes, and socialization experiences associated with growing up male or female, especially differences in power, status, position, and privilege within the family and in society in general. Gender sensitive family social workers strive to empower clients and enable them to move beyond prescribed sex roles to roles in which they have expanded options.

DIVISION OF LABOR IN FAMILIES

Relationships between men and women often shift after the birth of the first child. A woman who remains at home with an infant, even for a short period, often falls behind her spouse with regard to career advancement and salary. The man becomes the "breadwinner," while the woman assumes the traditional role of housekeeper and mother. Child rearing removes women from public roles while men gain public power, and public power is easily translated into private power.

Marriage and parenthood have different effects on men and women. Regardless of the labor status of the partners, females continue to do most of the work within the home. Domestic involvement encompasses housework, childcare, emotional support of family members, and maintenance of the family's social status (Mackie, 1991). Traditional norms dictate that the first priority of women will be the family.

Domestic responsibilities are not distributed evenly in the family. This appears to be related to conjugal power. Housework and childcare limit the amount of time in which a parent can pursue personal interests and career development. Men "help" out with the housework, while women have the primary responsibility for ensuring that jobs get done. In addition, men are said to "baby-sit" their own children. There are indications, however, that women's movement into the workforce has increased their conjugal power (Mackie, 1991).

Men's lives can be broadened and enriched when they participate in nurturing children and assume responsibility in family relationships. Unfortunately, some men resist changes in their roles. One explanation for the increase in divorce rates over the past two decades is that more women have been refusing to take sole responsibility for familial nurturing and communication, household tasks, and childcare. Instead, they expect their husbands to share these duties. Only when a male assumes equal responsibility for these tasks can the marital and parental relationship evolve into an equal partnership. At the very least, the distribution of roles needs to be negotiated between the two people. Dissatisfaction develops when a woman anticipates an equal partnership, with which her partner may verbally agree, but little change actually occurs.

The challenge of getting men to take housework and parenting seriously has been described as "troublesome, problematic, and complex" (Braverman, 1991, p. 25). In the 1990s, most wives worked approximately 1.5 hours more each day than their husbands, including part-time jobs, housework, and childcare. This amounts to an extra month of 24-hour days per year. Only about 20 percent of husbands share equally in housework and childcare (Carter, 1992). In order to preserve marriages, husbands and wives have constructed myths that support the egalitarian ideal of marriage, while in reality playing stereotypical, traditional roles (Carter, 1992). For example, the wife is responsible for laundry, while the husband tends the car—hardly an equitable arrangement. Laundry consumes approximately four hours per week, while responsibility for the car demands only four hours a month. Women have changed their roles drastically, but male roles seem to have remained static.

Gender sensitive social work seeks to empower women to assume greater control over their lives, rather than to adapt to oppressive circumstances. The following example illustrates a gender sensitive approach to assisting a family.

Jorge and Liz Martinez have four children, ages 9, 7, 5, and 3. The family came to the attention of the family social work agency when neighbors reported that the oldest child, 9-year-old Anabella, was left home as primary caretaker while both parents worked. The FSW, John Preston, learned that Mr. Martinez worked as a city employee and Mrs. Martinez was employed full-time as a legal secretary. Both were required to work long hours, putting in overtime several nights a week. Mrs. Martinez reported feeling overwhelmed by her schedule. In addition to her job, she was responsible for the care of home and family. She turned to her daughter Anabella for help.

Mr. Martinez felt that his wife should take care of the household, as his mother had done when he was growing up. He believed that his contribution to the family was to keep a stable job and bring home a weekly paycheck, as well as maintain the yard and make car repairs. After all, Mr. Martinez explained, his own mother had raised nine children, kept a spotless home, and never complained.

The FSW asked Mr. and Mrs. Martinez to make a list of the tasks they performed and the amount of time involved in each. Mr. Martinez was surprised to discover that doing the laundry took his wife 4 hours per week, while maintaining the cars took him only 4 hours per month. The FSW also helped Mr. Martinez reassess his traditional expectations of family life in the context of a nontraditional household with a full-time working mother. Although Mr. Martinez still did not feel comfortable doing "women's work," he began to understand the bind his wife was in. The family did not have much extra money, but they decided to pay Mr. Martinez's 16-year-old niece to baby-sit and do light housekeeping after school.

RECOMMENDATIONS FOR GENDER SENSITIVE FAMILY SOCIAL WORK

Gender sensitive practice promotes equality between men and women. The FSW strives to help family members examine their assumptions about gender roles as a prerequisite for deciding which aspects to keep and which to discard.

Within the context of marital relationships, a gender sensitive philosophy embraces equality in decision making and shared participation in household tasks and childcare. FSWs help families to understand the connection between socially constructed gender roles and family dynamics.

Family social work that is gender sensitive is action oriented, not merely nonsexist. Whereas nonsexist counselors attempt to avoid reinforcing stereotypical thinking about gender roles, proactive gender sensitive family social workers help clients to recognize how their own perceptions have been affected by internalizing these stereotypes. Clients are better helped when they have an opportunity to perceive and overcome social and political barriers.

The following guidelines will be helpful for FSWs who aim for gender sensitive practice:

- Do not focus solely on mother–child interactions. Doing so reinforces the belief that children's problems are the mother's responsibility. Instead, make every effort to include fathers in the intervention, to ensure that both parents are actively involved in the lives of the children.
- Do not make mothers responsible for the only change that occurs in the family. Integrate intervention to include both parents when looking at parenting, taking histories, and changing individual behaviors. Fathers must be included in all aspects of assessment and intervention. If you are concerned about how fathers will be receptive to the intervention, especially that they may not participate in making changes, discuss the situation with your supervisor and with the family.
- Make gender-related issues with families explicit. Help clients negotiate the division of household and childcare tasks between parents (Goldenberg & Goldenberg, 1996).
- Explore the distribution of power within the family, and be especially alert to signs of abuse of power, such as evidence of domestic violence. When abuse exists, take every precaution to first protect the victim before working with family dynamics.
- Look for the strengths of women, rather than concentrating on pathology.
- Integrate the sociopolitical status of gender into family work (Good, Gilbert, & Scher, 1990). Do not merely assume that any family member should or should not do something just because of gender. Males can do laundry, just as females can work outside the home. Male children can be as involved in household chores as female children.
- Be attuned to your personal biases. This involves confronting personal agendas and becoming aware of blind spots related to gender (Brock & Barnard, 1991). Remember that some of your opinions were formed subtly over a lifetime of socialization. You might not even be aware of what your gender biases are. Families improve more when social workers are warm and actively structure interventions with families (Green & Herget, 1991).
- Realize that family structures take different forms and that no monolithic family structure is superior to all others. Single-parent families are not deformed, and children can thrive just as well in these family structures as in two-parent families. Judgments about the desirability of family structure and composition must be made in terms of the effects on family members, rather than adherence to rigidly prescribed gender roles.

- Recognize that increasing equality will require that one family member relinquish some power and privilege. The member who benefited the most from the inequality may resist relinquishing power.

- Despite all we discussed above, recognize that some families may prefer adhering to traditional gender roles. This may be based on religious or cultural beliefs. In working with these families, the family social worker should not impose different beliefs on them. However, the family social worker must be certain that every family member is satisfied with the current role division, rather than having it enforced on them by the most powerful family member.

- Encourage individual family members to take pride in their contributions to family life. Women's work is as essential as men's work. Look for the positives and build upon them. If a man assumes a nurturing role, even for a short period, notice it and make positive comments, connecting his behavior with the well-being of other family members.

INTERVENTION STEPS

Couple and gender sensitive intervention seems complicated because a large part of it involves the FSW integrating the philosophy and concepts presented in this chapter into practice. Yet there are some concrete skills that will help in applying these interventions.

1. Introduce yourself to the couple or family and during a window of opportunity explain that you believe in a gender sensitive perspective in your practice. Explain what this means: specifically, that you believe in treating family members equally and with respect, and believe that couples should be a partnership of equals and not one person dominate over another due to past societal norms. Ask for questions and respond to them as best you can.

2. Model treating the couple and/or family members as equal, making sure that you try to spend equal time listening to each family member, not allowing one member to dominate the family work.

3. It is very important that the FSW takes the time to engage all family members, including what it is like to be who they are because of their gender. Spend the time to listen to and understand the client on gender issues. What is it like to be a woman in the year 2006? What is it like to be a man? How do gender roles play out in this particular family and how satisfied are family members with these gender roles? What particular pressures are they feeling today given their gender? What roles and expectations do they have of each other and how do they feel about these roles and expectations? Be aware of the language you use in discussing gender-sensitive practice. Some family members, for example, may dislike or feel threatened by the term "feminism."

4. Encourage the couple to openly talk about gender roles and expectations with each other. Coach them in the discussion. Topics they may need to negotiate include issues such as money, control, equity, sex, sharing of feelings, couple time together, housekeeping, discipline, and childcare.

CASE 12.1	EVALUATING MARITAL WORK

Johnny and June had been married for 10 years, with no children born into the family, when June was diagnosed with depression. The FSW determined that a psychoeducational approach was best for this particular case. The intervention focused on educating June and Johnny about the wife's illness and arranging support systems, medication, and cognitive therapy for June's depression, as well as marital counseling for the couple. A single-subject design was used to evaluate the case.

Measurement included weekly monitoring using a social support inventory completed by both of the couple, a medication maintenance chart and a depression inventory for June, and a martial satisfaction inventory for the couple. The FSW also used a 10-point rating scale to do independent ratings of June's mood and the couple's rating scale at the weekly treatment sessions. The measures allowed for ongoing monitoring and evaluation of treatment progress, so that treatment modifications could be made as needed.

5. Create structure in assigning housekeeping chores and expectations to help the couple negotiate getting these chores done. Do the same with childcare responsibilities. This might involve challenging the traditional arrangements of child rearing and housekeeping tasks and negotiating a more balanced distribution of these tasks.
6. Use "teachable moments" to educate the couple on gender equality, including shifting the power balance between men and woman. Some family/couple problems may be defined in such a way to include dimensions of power and gender.
7. Support positive changes, particularly changes that alter gender roles—for example, a husband taking responsibility for helping children with school work. We need to support the move away from gender-specific rules and roles.

CHAPTER SUMMARY

A family social worker needs to be gender sensitive, working with the family in a supportive and educational role. Gender sensitive and problem-solving approaches can be implemented simultaneously for effective interventions with families.

The gender sensitive perspective captures an attitude regarding the impact of traditional gender roles on problems experienced by families. Traditional family therapists endorse a systems view of family functioning in which members share equal responsibility for family problems, but gender sensitive FSWs recognize unequal power distributions and strive to empower women and children who have been victimized by inequitable family power arrangements.

Family social workers seek to understand gender roles within the economic, political, and social contexts in which families exist. Gender sensitive

FSWs strive for political, economic, and social justice for women and children, whom they perceive as unequal partners in family life.

Feminist theory acknowledges the core inequality that is inherent in most spousal relationships. Sources of gender-based power include the legal system, societal norms, educational and financial resources, personality differences, life circumstances (age, location, or life stage), and emotional factors.

Gender sensitive social workers seek to empower families by increasing their awareness of available options. Parents can be encouraged to share equally in childcare and household tasks, raising their children in a nonsexist atmosphere that recognizes each individual's capabilities and contributions to family life.

EXERCISES

12.1   DIFFERENT PERSPECTIVES ON FAMILY PROBLEMS

Think of a family with whom you are familiar. How would you assess this family's problems? Redefine the problems to include dimensions of power and gender.

12.2   FAMILY VALUES

Define what is meant by "family values." Where did this definition come from? Who benefits from this definition? Who is disadvantaged by this definition? How would social life be different if only one monolithic family form existed?

12.3   EFFECTS OF SOCIETAL VALUES ON FSWs AND CLIENTS

Three central societal values influence the FSW's role: family privacy, family stability, and conjugal/parental rights. List three of your beliefs concerning each value. Describe some of the effects these beliefs may have on your work with clients.

12.4   GENDER ROLES

Think about your family of origin. How did your family encourage traditional gender roles for its members? How was flexibility of roles encouraged?

12.5   NONSEXIST CHILD REARING

Describe behaviors that you consider inappropriate for girls but appropriate for boys, and vice versa. For example, some people would find it inappropriate for male children to play with dolls. Indicate why each behavior is inappropriate.

12.6   DIVISION OF LABOR BASED ON GENDER

Based on your own family of origin, complete the following list of household chores, allocating percentages to each parent. Put a checkmark next to each task that you feel should be assigned on the basis of gender.

	Percent Done by Mother	*Percent Done by Father*
Task		
Buy groceries.		
Prepare meals.		
Discipline children.		
Stay home when children are sick.		
Shop for children's clothes.		
Vacuum the house.		
Take children to doctor.		
Attend school functions.		
Volunteer at the school.		
Attend parent-teacher interviews.		
Help children with homework.		
Manage finances.		
Do the dishes.		
Do the laundry.		
Clean bathrooms.		
Discipline children.		
Change beds.		
Feed pets.		
Maintain lawn.		
Maintain car.		
Put children to bed.		
Other (describe)		

12.7 A Healthy Marriage

Break into groups of four. List the qualities of a healthy marriage. Compare the qualities to the red flags identified by Gottman. Present your findings in class.

12.8 Critique Systems Theory

Based on your personal experience, critique systems theory. What principles do not make sense to you? What principles make sense to you? How well do the principles fit for different cultures? For genders?

12.9 Different Perspectives on Family Problems

Think of a family with whom you are familiar. How would you assess this family's problems? Redefine the problems to include dimensions of power and gender.

13 CHAPTER | THE TERMINATION PHASE

In this chapter we examine issues related to termination, including who takes the initiative to terminate: the family, the FSW, or both. Because the decision to end family work does not necessarily mean that the family will stop contact with all agencies, referral is an important component of the termination process. Specific suggestions for phasing out and concluding family social work follow.

Ideally, termination is the final phase of family social work. We say "ideally" because sometimes families do not reach the final phase of the helping process with the worker but end family work before a mutually agreed-upon time has been reached. Sometimes even the most realistic and sensible goals have not been met because of premature termination.

Ending family work constructively sets the stage for continued positive change, yet termination is often overlooked as an essential part of the helping process (Kaplan, 1986). The central focus of termination is evaluating whether work with the family has resolved the presenting problem. A related purpose is ensuring that progress will be sustained—a process that can occur only if families develop the skills they need to resolve future problems independently after the FSW's involvement has ended.

Family social work is often short-term (sometimes between four and ten sessions) because many families seek assistance during periods of crisis and are motivated only to solve their immediate problems. Other families allow the family social worker into their home because they have been pressured to work on specific issues, but are at best reluctant or ambivalent about receiving help. If the family work is terminating because the worker is leaving the agency, the family will need to understand this. Plans for termination or transfer to another helper should be negotiated with the family early in the helping process in the contracting and goal-setting phases. Some agencies automatically impose time limits on family social work, making the termination date clear and explicit. The FSW should initiate the countdown to the final appointment in advance of the last scheduled contact by periodically reviewing with the family the progress to date. Nevertheless, families may need the social worker's help to work through a number of important issues during the termination stage: denial, anger, sadness, and letting go.

The most ideal time to terminate family work is when the presenting problem has been resolved and both the family and the social worker are satisfied with the outcome. In practice, however, termination often occurs in unanticipated ways. Some families drop out of a program or terminate before the desired outcome has been achieved. Moreover, when work is unsatisfactory or is not going anywhere, despite repeated efforts to restart the process, the FSW should end the relationship after holding one final session to review what happened.

When the work has been successful, clients may experience a range of emotions as they approach termination. Most authors emphasize feelings of separation and loss, implying that a planned termination produces a grief reaction. We believe that this case may be overstated, yet social workers may find that some clients are reluctant to terminate. They may bring up new problems or claim that the old problems have worsened. Other clients, especially involuntary clients, may welcome the end of the working relationship.

Social workers also react to termination in a variety of ways. Some may be hesitant to stop services. Termination for these social workers will be easier when they acknowledge limits to their responsibility for people's lives (Gambrill, 1983). FSWs should accept that after the end of family work, responsibility for decision making rests with the family. Other times, a social worker may have become quite close to the family and feel saddened that the relationship is coming to an end. It is important for family social workers to reflect on their feelings about terminating with a particular family. These feelings will reveal a lot about the nature of the relationship and the work that was achieved.

PLANNING FOR TERMINATION

Successful termination requires skill on the part of the FSW. The first step is for the FSW to discuss impending termination with the family at the outset of work, usually during contracting and goal setting. It is important for the FSW to recognize limitations and functions of family social work, including understanding differences between family social work and family therapy. Defining clear goals at the outset will help clarify when termination should occur.

In the initial contact with the family, the FSW might give them an agency phone number and request that they phone if for any reason they cannot be present for a scheduled appointment or if they wish to terminate family work at any time. Although some worker–client relationships may end abruptly or unexpectedly, the best time for termination is when it is anticipated and planned for from the beginning of the work. The manner in which termination is handled can influence how well the family maintains changes and improvements made during the helping relationship. Satisfactory termination of a helping experience also may predispose a family to seek help again if they need it. The FSW needs to help the family identify goals to be achieved after family social work ends, and explain the different roles of other helpers compared with those of the family social worker. Identifying community resources that can support the family after termination and helping the family link to these resources also occurs at this time.

Generally, the process of termination should parallel the end of each family meeting. For example, about ten minutes before ending an interview the FSW can tell the family that ten minutes remain, address unfinished business, and use the remaining time to summarize the session. At this time, the FSW can identify the strengths of the family and its members. Arrangements for the next session can then be made. Again, remind the family to phone the agency number if for any reason they cannot attend a scheduled appointment. Every week the social worker and family will repeat the process of reviewing what family members have achieved and how the family can continue making progress (Kinney, Haapala, & Booth, 1991). Termination of the overall working relationship follows similar steps, except that there will be no further sessions. Summarization should cover what happened in family work from the beginning to end. At this time, the family worker should encourage the sharing of feelings concerning termination.

POSSIBLE REACTIONS TO TERMINATION

Much has been written about ending helping relationships, most of it focusing on negative aspects. For the majority of clients and their social workers, however, termination is essentially positive because it is often used to focus upon accomplishments. Positive reflection will increase clients' self-confidence and reinforce feelings of personal competence. The family social worker should not be reluctant to credit the family for its efforts in resolving problems. Families may be eager to try out new skills learned in the helping relationship. Similarly, when social workers feel they have achieved their designated goals with clients, the FSWs' self-esteem increases, renewing them for future work.

Problems with termination can arise if the FSW is unwilling to discuss termination with the family or avoids discussion of family members' feelings about stopping the family work. Problems can also emerge when the FSW has not maintained clear boundaries with the family. For a family social worker who has become over-involved, termination may spark anxiety. The FSW may grieve the loss of the relationship or worry about the family's future welfare. While most terminations produce a mixture of feelings, family social workers who have maintained professional objectivity and boundaries will be able to deal with their emotions more effectively than those who have not. Of course, it is inappropriate for a social worker to end a professional relationship only to strike up a personal relationship with a former client.

Family social workers often establish intense and meaningful relationships with families and may feel hesitant about initiating termination. Termination means letting go and moving on. The FSW's feelings can range from grief to joy or include a mixture of both. The FSW should not minimize the role that family social work played in creating change. Terminating with some families may bring relief, while discontinuing with others may elicit feelings of sadness and loss. Through experience, the FSW will anticipate feelings to address at the time of termination. Family members' feelings can range from pride and satisfaction to anger, sadness, or regret. The FSW can recognize signs suggestive of difficulty at terminating: for example, a client may predictably cancel appointments as the date of each appointment draws closer. It may be difficult to schedule a final meeting when family members have canceled several times previously. Sometimes the FSW will need to remind the family that time is running out before conducting one final appointment.

Clients may try to obstruct termination in the following ways:

- They may become overly dependent on the social worker.
- They may report that former problems are starting to reappear.
- They may introduce new problems.
- They may find substitutes for the social worker (Hepworth & Larsen, 1993).

Most of these concerns can be anticipated by contracting at the beginning of the family work and by exploring the family's feelings about termination near the end. Referrals to other agencies and nurturing informal support networks are two important ways of easing termination. Families may be especially reluctant to terminate when goals have not been met. Short-term programs seem especially vulnerable to family dissatisfaction with the services. A parent in one short-term program stated, "I disliked the shortness of it. We're quite dysfunctional. In order to get a habit established, we needed long-term help" (Coleman & Collins, 1997).

Alternatively, termination can be a time of celebration, especially when concrete, positive change has occurred. The FSW should be aware of the limits of family social work and encourage the family to transfer to another helper if and when appropriate. Rituals associated with closure and evaluation should promote a sense of satisfaction with progress made.

PREMATURE TERMINATION AND DROPOUTS

Sometimes families terminate indirectly. Some may simply not be at home for a scheduled meeting, and others may call and cancel at the last minute. They may be difficult to get hold of after a failed appointment and the family social worker begins to suspect that the family is avoiding further contact. Other times individual family members do not show up for a scheduled meeting with the FSW (Barker, 1981). Another hint that families are considering dropping out is when instead of expressing dissatisfaction with family social work, they talk about practical problems of participating in family sessions, such as missing work, having to reschedule other appointments, and so on. When the social worker begins to notice a pattern forming (two consecutive missed appointments), we suggest raising the topic for discussion, if the worker is able to make contact with them.

The difference between families who stop work prematurely and those who merely drop out is that premature terminators try to give the social worker notice and a reason for leaving. It should be remembered that as many as 40 percent of families terminate work after six to ten sessions (Worden, 1994), but perhaps fewer for home-based services. Premature termination may be associated ecological factors like lower household income and ethnicity (Clarkin & Levy, 2004; Kadzin, 2004). It is thus very important during the initial stages of family work for the FSW to explore income issues as well as ethnicity with the family. For example, a worker must be keenly attuned to cultural differences throughout the family work and discuss the impact of cultural differences on family work as issues emerge. Indeed, a major thrust of this book has been the micro and macro ecological systems approach as well the importance of diversity, ethnicity, culture, and spirituality in a family's life (see Chapter 5). The FSW needs to show understanding of these factors and discuss them with the family at the onset of family work in order to engage a family. These factors also need to be raised with sensitivity and understanding in the termination process.

When a family announces its decision to terminate, the FSW should acknowledge the decision and elicit information about the rationale for termination. In such cases, the work may be stopped because of client absences, resistance, the social worker's inability to take the family further, or personality conflicts between family members and the social worker. Information garnered from clients will help the FSW differentiate between timely, appropriate termination and inappropriate or premature termination.

One type of premature termination occurs when clients display sudden improvement; this is referred to as a "flight into health" (Tomm & Wright, 1979) or "faking good." Families may "fake good" when they view change as threatening and they make superficial changes to get the worker out of their lives.

They may tell the FSW that their problems have been resolved, and there may even be a temporary cessation of problems lasting for a short period of time. If the family specifically states that they would like to end work, but the FSW believes that termination would be premature, the FSW should move into the *recital* step of termination to review problems and even renegotiate a new contract. In doing so, the FSW and family can encapsulate the changes, identify problems that still exist, and sort out what goals need to be achieved. Eliciting specifics of the family decision may be helpful. The FSW can try to find out when the family decided to quit and what factors prompted the decision. What is most important is that the goals of the family worker be congruent with those of the family.

While termination can sometimes be averted, at other times premature termination may be unavoidable. In such cases, the FSW must accept the decision to terminate without applying inappropriate pressure, even though the FSW disagrees with the family's decision (Tomm & Wright, 1979).

Avoiding premature termination can be more difficult with court-mandated clients, who often wish to avoid any work beyond what has been required by the court. They may suddenly become resistant the day a court order ceases to exert authority over them. One way to prevent this outcome is to encourage family members to discuss their reaction to being ordered into treatment at the outset. Court-mandated families who drop out of family work must also face the consequences of their decisions. Premature termination may mean that child welfare authorities or the courts will have to be notified.

In an ideal world, termination takes place after the presenting problems have been resolved. The family's ability to cope with problems, not avoid them, is an important indicator of readiness to terminate. Movement toward termination occurs smoothly if the beginning and middle stages of treatment have concluded successfully. Effective family social workers often set mini-goals and suggest that progress toward a goal be evaluated within a specified number of interviews. However, the most important decision for family social workers concerns when to end. Ideally, termination should occur after goals have been met. In some agencies, the FSW must assess whether the family needs further help or whether they can resolve problems on their own. Regardless of how termination occurs, the social worker should initiate an honest discussion of everyone's perceptions of what was achieved during family social work.

PRACTICAL TERMINATION STEPS

Termination can occur in several ways (starting with early or premature termination) to a completed mutually agreed-upon termination:

1. Clients decide not to follow through with an initial meeting or do not show up for the initial meeting.
2. The family structure has changed since referral—for example, separation of parents or removal of identified child client into care.

3. Family has an initial family meeting but does not return.
4. Direct withdrawal, usually via a telephone call stating clients' decision to terminate with or without stating reasons.
5. One or more family members resist attending family sessions.
6. Clients show active resistance, questioning the process and outcomes. One or more clients may be openly uncooperative or hostile.
7. Sessions seem to reflect no progress. Termination should be by mutual consent.
8. Repeated cancellation of appointments or failure to keep them without formal withdrawal by clients.
9. Termination by mutual agreement following successful resolution of presenting problem(s).
10. Termination on clients' initiative at the end of a contractual period of specified length. Contracting for a specified period provides a time framework that may make intervention efficient.

Let's look at each of the termination ways presented in this list.

1. Clients decide not to follow through with an initial meeting or do not show up for the initial meeting.

    Some clients have been on a waiting list for weeks, or even months prior to your initial contact and may have found an alternative agency to obtain their counseling needs. For some, the situation has improved (a crisis has passed), and counseling is no longer desired by the family. Alternatively, when an appointment has been set up, one or more of the family members convinces the family they no longer require counseling. Some families use counseling as a threat to get members to change their behaviors! It is still important to terminate appropriately with these families. This is done by simply informing the family that if they would like your services in the future they should feel free to recontact the agency (i.e., keep the door open for them).

2. The family structure has changed since referral—for example, separation of parents or removal of identified child client into care.

    Some family structures can change significantly, which affects the initial referral problems. Separation of parents, removal of identified child client into care, or an adolescent child moving out of the home to live with relatives or live on his or her own are all examples we have come across. It is useful for the family social worker to invite the remaining family members to a family meeting to discuss the changes on the family structure as well as any other family concerns they may have. However, the family worker should let the family know that if in the future they would like family work, they should recontact the agency, and also provide phone numbers of other agencies that an identified child who has left the home can contact if he or she wishes some help.

3. The family attends an initial family meeting but does not return.

    It is important to have a follow-up phone call with the family or you will be left wondering if you have done something wrong in your initial meeting. Indeed, you may have not engaged the family into the family social work process and not "connected" with the family. It is important to find this out and either invite the family to return to discuss your role and their expectations of you and the process, or to refer the family to another resource for help. The family's failure to return after an initial family meeting may not be due to you not connecting with the family; instead, the family may state that the one session was enough.

One or more family members may feel that the family worker did not "connect" with them and thus believe that the counseling would not be helpful. Others may state that the family situation has changed and they do not feel further family work is necessary. Some families say that the particular service does not meet their specific needs, that another service would meet their needs better, and that they have sought help elsewhere. Again, in the follow-up phone call support whatever position the family takes and offer your service at another time is they so desire it.

4. Direct withdrawal, usually via a telephone call stating clients' decision to terminate with or without stating reasons.

Again, it is helpful to yourself and to the agency to find out reasons behind the termination. If it is because the agency does not meet the needs of the family, the agency mandate might have to change to accommodate this particular family. If clients feel they did not connect with you, you may need to look at your engagement skills. It also could signal that the family crisis has passed. Whatever the reasons, it is important to invite the family to return if they so wish at a later date.

5. One or more family members do not want to attend family sessions.

Although it is more difficult to work with a family without all members living in the home involved, it is not impossible to still be helpful. Remember from Chapter 2 on systems theory that change in one part of the system will effect change on other parts of the system. Thus, even if one family member does not want to attend, system changes may still positively affect this member. Nevertheless, the FSW needs to explore with the family the reasons for one or more family members not wanting to attend family sessions. This may prove to be a very helpful focus of a family meeting because it does say something about how the family organizes itself as well as how it solves problems. In this case, the central problem becomes one or more family members not wanting to attend family sessions. How does the rest of the family feel about this? How do they communicate their concerns with each other? What commitment do they have to work on family issues and to each other? How does this family plan to resolve this issue? These questions can lead to a most interesting and helpful family social work meeting.

6. The family shows active resistance, questioning process and outcomes. One or more clients are openly uncooperative and may be hostile.

Often clients are resistant when they have not felt understood and felt that their feelings, such as fear and anger, have not been validated. It is important to spend the time "joining" (see Chapter 4 on skills) not just at the content level but also at a feeling level. At the content level, it is important to clarify their expectations and hopes for family work as well as your role with them. Yet it is equally important to show all family members that you understand their frustrations, fears, concerns, and reluctance for this work. Feelings need to be brought out into the open and validated. It is helpful to try to normalize family issues (see Chapter 7 on developmental issues) and to point out their strengths to convey hope (see Chapter 8 on the strengths perspective). Any time in the family social work process when a client seems resistant, it is very important to immediately address their underlying concerns and feelings, or you have the potential of loosing the family to premature termination.

7. The sessions seem to reflect no progress. Termination should be by common consent.

It is important to routinely ask the family for feedback about whether they see that progress is being made or not (a form of formative evaluation, Chapter 5). At the end of every family meeting you can ask if the meeting was helpful or not. We suggest that some of the time in at least every fourth family meeting should be spent discussing what progress has been made. If the family believes no progress is being made, either a new contract of problems and goals need to be set (see Chapter 6 on problem definition and contracting) or mutually agreed-upon termination should be considered. Remember that if you and the family decide to terminate, you should offer your services at a later date and inform the family of other services that may be of help to them.

8. Repeated cancellation of appointments or failure to keep them without formal withdrawal by clients.

Cancelled appointments can be very frustrating for family social workers because they have set aside the time to meet with the family. When a pattern occurs (we define a pattern as something that happens at least three times), we suggest phoning the family and openly discussing whether being involved in family work is really realistic at this period in the family's life. At this time, the FSW can "normalize" the difficulties some families have in their very busy lives in committing themselves to the often time-consuming family work process, and can graciously suggest that family work be terminated until the family feels they are in a better position to agree to regular appointments.

9. Termination by mutual agreement following successful resolution of presenting problem(s).

There is little to be gained by continuing family work when the presenting problem has been successful resolved. A major focus of family work is to teach families problem-solving skills (Chapter 10). It is hoped that the experience and skills gained in solving the presenting problem will not only positively affect other problems and family dynamics, but also can be applied to other problems in the present and in the future.

10. Termination on clients' initiative at the end of a contractual period of specified length. Contracting for a specified period provides a time framework that may make intervention efficient.

Termination at this time is the ideal. It is when we have an opportunity with a family to terminate the family social work process constructively.

STEPS FOR TERMINATION

Five steps are required for constructive termination: (1) recital; (2) inducing awareness of change; (3) consolidating gains; (4) providing feedback to the FSW; and (5) preparing the family to handle future problems.

1. *Recital*—As the helping process draws to a close, the social worker and each family member should be given an opportunity to comment on their experience in family work with an emphasis on discussing what has changed (Bandler, Grinder, & Satir, 1976; Worden, 1994). Doing so will help family members understand what changes have been made and what has happened to produce these changes. Lum (1992) calls this *recital,* a technique that involves reviewing important incidents of family work. Recital resembles summarization.

If negotiated goals have not been achieved or additional problems have emerged, the recital may point to the need for referral to a different agency or to another social worker within the same agency. In either case, the family should summarize their perceived progress to date so that they will be able to help the new social worker understand the situation. In a planned referral, the FSW will speak personally with the new social worker after receiving the family's permission.

As mentioned earlier, routine and ongoing review of the family's progress throughout intervention will make the final summarization easier (Barker, 1981; Tomm & Wright, 1979). Negotiating for a predetermined number of sessions alerts families to the eventual end of intervention and sets a contract to track change. While an open-ended contract may be more typical, we suggest a time-limited, well-developed focus for work, allowing for flexibility with regard to the frequency and duration of sessions. Periodic reviews give family members an opportunity to express satisfaction or dissatisfaction with the progress being made and also allow the family and the social worker to make changes as the work proceeds.

2. *Inducing awareness of change*—After family members have discussed with the FSW their reactions to the social work process, they can receive feedback from the worker's perspective. As the FSW and family compare their perceptions of the process, family members will develop both a conceptual understanding and the tools with which to produce further change. These reflections can be a powerful source of self-esteem for family members.

Professional helpers want to be effective, and many have entered social work to fulfill a sincere desire to promote healthy social and family functioning. Because of this, they may develop a sense that credit for the change belongs to the social worker. It is unfortunate that failures are usually attributed to clients, while successes are claimed by social workers. Pinpointing the source of the change can be difficult because change often involves being in the right place at the right time, doing the right things with the right people. In fact, for years researchers have been trying to isolate factors that create change. Regardless of where the FSW believes the change originated, it is essential for the family to receive credit for making the change (Wright & Leahey, 1994). To accomplish this, the FSW can ask family members what *they* did to create the change (Brock & Barnard, 1991). Social workers need to be humble in discussing their contributions. When family members are reminded of their own part in creating change, they will feel competent to meet future challenges.

It is natural for social workers to accept praise—success is a major source of professional gratification. Nevertheless, the family social worker's professional responsibility is not complete until termination has been conducted satisfactorily. Families struggle with the pain, conflict, and pressure of their problems and deserve credit for making changes. When change occurs with a child, parents should recognize that they are primary caretakers for the child in the present and future. Giving recognition for progress increases the chance that the positive effects of family social work will persist. To do otherwise conveys the message the family cannot manage without the social worker.

If a family is distressed by lack of progress at termination, social workers must find a balance when discussing negative and positive aspects of the work. Negatives should be presented as goals to work toward in the future. Social workers may also want to explore with their supervisors possible reasons why the sessions were not successful. Perhaps the goals were too high or unrealistic. Resistance to change may have been increased by the FSW's inability to understand the family members' hesitancy. In many cases, social workers have explained lack of movement by claiming that families were unmotivated, rather than trying to understand how they may have contributed to the problem.

Social workers need to acknowledge difficulties in working with families. Overburdened families sometimes will not benefit from complex or fancy interventions. It is important that the FSW believe the family has worked hard despite making little change. It is also important for the social worker to reinforce family strengths. Even though we are encouraging family social workers to credit families for change, the FSW can also relish successes. Family social work is rewarding when the family social worker is a partner in the change process.

In Figure 13.1 we present a checklist for termination. Social workers and client families can complete the checklist together to determine whether termination issues have been addressed. The checklist consists of 16 factors that are useful in evaluating clients' readiness for ending family social work. If a family, together with the family social worker, can answer "Yes" to most of these statements, then termination is appropriate and timely.

3. *Consolidating gains*—The third step of termination is talking about the future, emphasizing how to maintain and build upon the goals achieved. Helping the family develop strategies for attaining future goals is an excellent method for consolidating gains (Lambert & Ogles, 2004). When

	Yes	No
The presenting problem has been eliminated	❑	❑
It has been made manageable or tolerable for the family	❑	❑
The changes made can be measured effectively	❑	❑
Positive changes have been made in psychosocial functioning	❑	❑
Family members are communicating more effectively	❑	❑
Family members are safe from abuse	❑	❑
Formal support networks are available, and the family knows how to use them	❑	❑
The family has an adequate informal network upon which to call when in need	❑	❑
Family or individual members have been referred for specialized services in the community	❑	❑
The family has agreed to be referred to specialized services	❑	❑
The family has learned skills to function in their daily routine	❑	❑
Basic physical needs of all family members are being met	❑	❑
The social worker and family have evaluated the family's progress to date	❑	❑
The family is satisfied with the service rendered	❑	❑
All family members are better off as a result of the work	❑	❑
The family has gone through recital of the changes they have made	❑	❑
Family members have acknowledged the role they have played in creating change	❑	❑

FIGURE 13.1 | CHECKLIST FOR TERMINATING FAMILY SOCIAL WORK

appropriate, the FSW can help the family make a transition to other community supports.

Reviewing family accomplishments is also an important component of the FSW's self-evaluation. Client behavior is one factor in determining a successful outcome, but other factors are also important. The FSW can note the professional learning accomplished while working with the family. The FSW's professional development is advanced through learning new skills or improving existing skills, regardless of whether the case outcome is positive or negative. The FSW may articulate the learning in various ways: "I persevered," "I learned how to work with a suicidal individual," or "I have developed more skills in teaching parents how to manage difficult child behavior."

Termination should be viewed as a transition, not an end. Describing termination in this way to clients produces the sense of a new beginning and a recognition of all that has been accomplished. Participating in a helping relationship requires faith—in oneself, in families, and in the helping process. Family social workers may not witness clear evidence that they have helped families change or achieve desired goals, but their efforts may make some important differences in their clients' lives. Additionally, some interventions may have no immediate impact, but may exert an influence in the future. Some of the greatest benefits to families may come in the form of increased confidence, new skills, or supportive social networks that enable clients to see themselves differently and help them respond to challenges later. Believing that their efforts have not been in vain diminishes the regrets FSWs feel about ending their work with a family.

4. *Providing feedback to the FSW*—It is important to provide formal closure to the intervention by holding a face-to-face discussion. During the final session, evaluation of case outcomes may be conducted. Gurman and Kniskern (1981) recommend evaluating the progress of the entire family unit, as well as the subsystems that may have been experiencing problems (e.g., the marital subsystem and individual family members' functioning). The first step involves evaluating with the family their perceptions of success. The FSW can ask family members, "What did you find most helpful during our work together?" and "What did you want to happen that did not occur?" It gives the family an opportunity to highlight the highs and lows of the process and also shows them that the social worker is receptive to feedback. The social worker should not react defensively to feedback, but should express appreciation and inform family members that their contributions will help the FSW in future work with families. Additionally, measurement instruments or other assessment tools may be used one last time to provide comparative data to add to the evaluation.

5. *Preparing the family to handle future problems*—A final step in termination is to ask the family to anticipate upcoming changes or challenges that could cause setbacks (Nichols & Schwartz, 2004). The social worker should ask the family to describe how they plan to handle such situations. The FSW can also use this theme to reinforce family strengths and newly developed skills. Another method of preparing families for the future is to gradually extend the time between family meetings and thereby encourage the family to lessen their reliance on the program.

Some agencies expect social workers to make a follow-up visit to clients after termination. Such a follow-up can provide a "booster shot" during a time when the family is vulnerable to relapse. Follow-up services can help families through transitional periods (Lum, 1992). During vulnerable periods, the FSW may become reinvolved with a family for a brief period of time to prevent the family from slipping into old patterns. Vulnerable periods depend upon family characteristics and the type of problem experienced.

Case 13.1 illustrates a successful termination of family social work.

CASE 13.1	TERMINATION

Lindy Stein and her parents Mary and Todd participated in family social work with their family social worker (FSW), Betty Chess. The family initially became involved with the FSW agency when 15-year-old Lindy ran away from home and was gone for a week. Prior to running away, Lindy was truant from school on numerous occasions and rebellious toward her parents and her teachers. Her grades had dropped from an A average to Cs and Ds, and she had been charged as a minor in possession of alcohol.

Mrs. Chess determined during the assessment that Lindy was reacting to her parents' separation and subsequent divorce. The divorce was difficult for the couple, who were angry with each other and had put Lindy in the middle of their fighting. Lindy's behavior was a response to her frustration and her inability to communicate her needs and feelings to her parents.

Mrs. Chess intervened by helping Lindy learn to communicate her feelings to her parents. As Mary and Todd began to realize how their conflicts were affecting their daughter and contributing to her problems at school and at home, they recognized the need to arrive at a truce. Mary and Todd consequently agreed to allow Mrs. Chess to refer them for family counseling so that they could effectively co-parent Lindy.

As Mrs. Chess prepared the family for termination, she set aside time for the Steins to provide a recital of their experience in family work, followed by her own summary of the family's gains. Holding a termination session allowed Mrs. Chess to provide closure and to receive feedback from the family. She asked them to evaluate what had been most and least helpful during family social work. At the end of the termination session, Mrs. Chess asked the family to anticipate future problems and to describe how they planned to address them. This review of the skills learned allowed Mrs. Chess the opportunity to congratulate the family on their improved communication skills. Mrs. Chess referred the family for counseling to enable the Steins to consolidate their gains and to continue to improve their interactions. She also reminded the Steins that they could schedule "booster sessions" with her whenever they felt the need for follow-up services.

When becoming involved at a later date with families, the FSW can refer to follow-up contacts as "consultations" or "booster shots." Family members are likely to work through their problems more quickly if they feel that they are in charge of the changes, with the family social worker serving as information provider and encourager on a short-term basis. The social worker must take care to identify the consultation as a sign of health rather than an indication of failure.

TIMING OF TERMINATION

The best time to decrease the frequency of sessions is when progress has been made, goals have been reached, and the family shows signs of stability. Most families agree to termination when they can identify improvement in their problem-solving capacity. If families find termination difficult to accept, the FSW may ask a paradoxical question such as, "What would each of you have to do to bring the problem back?" to give family members a better awareness of the changes made (Tomm & Wright, 1979).

The frequency of sessions may need to be decreased when a family seems overly dependent on the social worker. At times paraprofessionals have acted in a supportive capacity with family members only to become their major support system because other supports have not been nurtured. To avoid fostering dependency the FSW can mobilize formal and informal supports for the family while concurrently decreasing the frequency of sessions. If the family resists decreasing the frequency of sessions, the FSW should discuss concerns and solicit support from all family members (Tomm & Wright, 1979). Family members may worry that if appointments are discontinued altogether, they will be unable to cope. By asking, "What do you think will happen if we stop meeting?" and by openly discussing family members' anxieties, the FSW can often prevent the worst-case scenario from occurring.

HOW AND WHEN TO REFER CLIENTS TO OTHER PROFESSIONALS

Referral to other professionals may be necessary for a variety of reasons. Specific skills are needed by the FSW to assist families in making a smooth transition from one professional to another. Major reasons for referring families to other professionals include the following:

- A family may need assistance from a specialist. It is unrealistic to expect family social workers to be experts in all areas. Assistance from other professionals may be needed when problems are complex. Referral can be either for consultation or for in-depth treatment. The role of the FSW after referral will vary from that of a treatment collaborator to that of a former helper. For example, if an adult within a family is sexually abusing a child, it is important that specialists in offender treatment be consulted. The FSW may refer the family for consultation with a psychiatrist but may continue to meet with the family until the consultation is complete.
- A family member may have a problem that should be assessed at an institution with the resources available to assess and treat the particular problem.
- A family moves out of the social worker's catchment area but needs continued assistance. Referral to a social worker in the new area may be indicated.

Family social workers should not think of themselves as inadequate if they must refer a family. Referral requires extensive knowledge of resources within the community as well as good counseling skills with families.

Clients need to be prepared prior to referrals. The FSW must explain the reasons for referral and how the family may benefit from it. For example, if the FSW has determined that the family's problems include a family member's alcoholism, the family social worker can refer the individual alcoholic and the family for addiction treatment. To facilitate the referral, the FSW can provide a summary for the new helper and possibly give a copy to the family. Selecting an appropriate referral source is essential, and colleagues and supervisors can offer suggestions about which agencies can best meet the family's needs.

For families who have established rapport with their social workers, referral to other helpers may be difficult. The comments of a mother about what she did not like about a family social work agency illustrate this difficulty:

> We did not like being turned over to someone else. We are not machines; we are people. [FSW] had established an excellent rapport, she was trusted, she was effective, and when *they* thought she was done, she was pulled out without consultation. Not any consideration to the workability of the dynamic. These are intimate, profoundly personal issues . . . if I don't like them, I don't want them in my family . . . I want to accept help, but I'm simply not a case, I'm a human being . . . It's really detrimental to take out someone who is working well with a family . . . if [FSW] had stayed six months, [child] would never have been in placement for a year and it would have saved [the Agency] thousands of dollars (Coleman & Collins, 1997).

As this mother's comments show, switching to a different FSW can be difficult for some families. They may be emotionally attached to the first social worker and not want to go through the stages of trust building and engagement another time. Referral may be more effective if the FSW participates in the family's first meeting with the new social worker. This personalizes the referral and helps alleviate family members' anxieties about starting with someone they do not know and must learn how to trust. Before the actual referral, family social workers should encourage family members to express concerns or ask questions about the upcoming referral. Likewise, the new helper should clarify with the family why the referral was made and attempt to clear up any misconceptions the family may have. Thus, referral is smoothest if both the family and the new helper are given adequate explanations.

EVALUATING RESULTS OF FAMILY SOCIAL WORK

Although positive and even dramatic results may be obtained during family social work, success is measured by the positive changes that are maintained or continue to evolve weeks and months after termination. We encourage social workers to obtain follow-up information from the family. A focus on outcome directs the FSW to orient work toward change, to focus on problems that can be realistically changed, and to think of how the family will cope on their own (Haley, 1976). In a follow-up contact, the FSW should explain that this is a normal pattern of practice (e.g., "We always contact families with whom we have worked to get information on how they are doing"). It is also important to follow up with a clear and specific purpose in mind, such as reinforcing changes made in family work. To reinforce an emphasis on outcome, we suggest conducting follow-up sessions face-to-face.

The degree of change achieved in family social work should be assessed at all levels: individual, parent–child, marital, and family system. Gurman and

Kniskern (1981) suggest that a "higher level of positive change has occurred when improvement is evidenced in systemic (total family) or relationship (dyadic) interactions than when it is evidenced in individuals alone" (p. 765). That is, change in individual family members does not logically require change in the family system, but stable change in the system does require both individual change and relationship change; relationship change also requires individual change.

Another measure of outcome is evaluation of practitioner performance. The competence of the FSW is central to the success of family social work. Just as setting goals for family behavioral change assists in the change process, so too does setting goals for one's professional performance assist in your change process to becoming a more skilled worker (see Figure 13.2).

CASE 13.2 | TERMINATION

Johnny and June (see Case 12.1), were seen by the FSW for 12 weeks after June was diagnosed with depression. The couple also required marital counseling. A psychosocial intervention was introduced; the treatment plan included education for the couple about depression, arrangement of social support systems, establishment of regular medication and cognitive treatment for June, and marital counseling for the couple. The data collected during the treatment allowed the FSW to make a judgment about termination of the treatment.

Measurement included weekly monitoring using a social support inventory completed by both of the couple, a medication maintenance chart and a depression inventory for June, and a martial satisfaction inventory for the couple. The FSW also used a 10-point rating scale to do independent ratings of June's mood and the couple's rating scale at the weekly treatment sessions.

The scores on the inventory were recorded on a graph (see Chapter 6) and treatment was terminated when scores were at a satisfactory level.

I developed the following new skills in working with this family:

Skills in working with specific problems areas:

New techniques of intervention:

Self-awareness of strengths and problem areas:

With this family, my best work involved:

With this family, I could have done the following better:

I learned the following about my family practice:

FIGURE 13.2 | FAMILY SOCIAL WORKER'S SELF-EVALUATION FORM

CHAPTER SUMMARY

In this chapter we described the process of terminating the family social worker's relationship with a client family. Termination involves summarizing the family's accomplishments, reviewing problems that remain, and making decisions about further work, follow-up, or referral. Termination may occur for three reasons: termination is predetermined and time-limited; the family's goals have been accomplished; or the family or the FSW decides not to continue.

Steps for successful termination include (1) recital of the family social work process with the client family, (2) inducing an awareness of change, (3) consolidating gains for the social worker and the family, (4) providing feedback from the family to the FSW, and (5) preparing the family to handle future problems. If termination is described as a transition rather than an ending, it may seem more palatable both to the family and to the FSW.

Contracting for a specific number of sessions at the beginning of family work sets time limits to encourage completion of goals. When adequate progress has been made, the FSW can begin to decrease the frequency of sessions as a way to help the family prepare for termination. Referral to another professional may be necessary in some cases.

Giving families credit for the positive changes they have made is an excellent way to increase clients' self-esteem, feelings of competence, and motivation for independence. When families have made little progress during family work, the FSW can acknowledge family members' positive efforts toward solving their problems. The FSW may seek supervision or consultation for help in determining the causes of a lack of progress. Implementing systematic evaluation and follow-up procedures helps the FSW to analyze his or her performance and set goals for improvement.

EXERCISES

13.1 REASONS FOR TERMINATION

List some reasons for advising a family to terminate family social work.

13.2 SUGGESTIONS FOR THE FUTURE

Using a family from your field placement or work setting as an example, list some suggestions you could make to help the family maintain positive gains after termination.

13.3 REEVALUATION AND FOLLOW-UP PROCEDURES

List some procedures that would help you evaluate the effectiveness of your work with a family.

REFERENCES

Ackerman, N. (1958). *The psychodynamics of family life.* New York: Basic Books.

Adams, J., Jaques, J., & May, K. (2004). Counseling gay and lesbian families: Theoretical considerations. *Family Journal: Counseling and Therapy for Couples and Families, 12*(1), 40–42.

Adler, A. (2003). Cited in J. Prochaska & J. Norcross (Eds.), *Systems of psychotherapy: A transtheoretical analysis* (pp. 63–100). Pacific Grove, CA: Brooks/Cole.

Ahrons, C. (1999). Divorce: An unscheduled family transition. In B. Carter & M. McGoldrick (Eds.), *The expanded family life cycle: Individual, family, and social perspectives* (3rd ed.) (pp. 381–398). Needham Heights, MA: Allyn & Bacon.

Alessandria, K. (2002). Acknowledging white ethnic groups in multicultural counseling. *Family Journal: Counseling and Therapy for Couples and Families, 10*(1), 57–60.

Alexander, J., Holtzworth-Munroe, A., & Jameson, P. (1994). The process and outcome of marital and family therapy: Research review and evaluation. In A. Bergin & S. Garfield (Eds.), *Handbook of psychotherapy and behavior change* (4th ed.) (pp. 595–630). Toronto: Wiley.

Alexander, J., & Parsons, B. (1973). Short-term behavioral intervention with delinquent families: Impact on family process and recidivism. *Journal of Abnormal Psychology, 81*(3), 219–225.

Alexander, J., & Parsons, B. (1982). *Functional family therapy.* Monterey, CA: Brooks/Cole.

Allen, M., & Yen, W. (1979). *Introduction to measurement theory.* Monterey, CA: Brooks/Cole.

Almeida, R., Woods, R., Messineo, T., & Font, R. (1998). The cultural context model: An overview. In M. McGoldrick (Ed.), *Revisioning family therapy: Race, culture, and gender in clinical practice* (pp. 414–431). New York: Guilford.

Anastasi, A. (1988). *Psychological testing.* New York: Macmillan.

Anderson, C. (1999). Single-parent families: Strengths, vulnerabilities, and interventions. In B. Carter and M. McGoldrick (Eds.), *The expanded family life cycle: Individual, family, and social perspectives* (3rd ed.) (pp. 399–416). Needham Heights, MA: Allyn & Bacon.

Anderson, S., Russell, C., & Schumm, W. (1983). Perceived marital quality and family life cycle categories: A further analysis. *Journal of Marriage and the Family, 45,* 127–139.

Arad, D. (2004). If your mother were an animal, what animal would she be? Creating play-stories in family therapy: The animal attribution story-telling technique (AASTT). *Family Process, 43*(2), 249–263.

Armstrong, L. (1987). *Kiss daddy goodnight: Ten years later.* New York: Pocket Books.

Arnold, J., Levine, A., & Patterson, G. (1975). Changes in sibling behavior following family intervention. *Journal of Consulting and Clinical Psychology, 43*(5), 683–688.

Assembly of First Nations. (1994). *Breaking the silence: An interpretive study of residential school impact and healing as illustrated by the stories of First Nations individuals.* Ottawa, ON: First Nations Health Commission.

AuClare, P., & Schwartz, I. (1987). Are home-based services effective? A public child welfare agency's experiment. *Children Today, 16,* 6–9.

Bailey, K. (1987). *Methods of social research.* New York: Free Press.

Balaguer Dunn, A., & Michael Levitt, M. (2000). The genogram: From diagnostics to mutual collaboration. *Family Journal: Counseling and Therapy for Couples and Families, 8*(3), 236–244.

Baltimore, M. (2000). Ethical considerations in the use of technology for marriage and family counselors. *Family Journal: Counseling and Therapy for Couples and Families, 8*(4), 390–393.

Bandler, R., Grinder, J., & Satir, V. (1976). *Changing with families.* Palo Alto, CA: Science and Behavior Books.

Barker, R. (1981). *Basic family therapy.* Baltimore: University Park Press.

Barker, R. (1995). *The social work dictionary* (3rd ed.). Washington, DC: NASW.

Barlow, C., & Coleman, H. (2003). Suicide and families: Considerations for therapy. *Guidance and Counseling. 18*(2), 67–73.

Barlow, C., & Coleman, H. (2004). After suicide: Family responses to social support. *Omega: Journal of Death and Dying, 47*(3), 187–201.

Barsky, A. (2001). Understanding family mediation from a social work perspective. *Canadian Social Work Review, 18*(1), 25–46.

Barth, R. P. (1990). Theories guiding home-based intensive family preservation services. In J. K. Whittaker, J. Kinney, E. Tracey, & C. Booth (Eds.), *Reaching high-risk families: Intensive family preservation services* (pp. 89–112). New York: Aldine de Gruyter.

Bateson, G., & Jackson, D. (1974). Some varieties of pathogenic organization. In D. Jackson (Ed.), *Communication, family, and marriage* (pp. 200–216). Palo Alto, CA: Science and Behavior Books.

Baum, C., & Forehand, R. (1981). Long-term follow-up assessment of parent training by use of multiple outcome measures. *Behavior Therapy, 12,* 643–652.

Baum, N. (2003). Divorce process variables and the co-parental relationship and parental role fulfillment of divorced parents. *Family Process, 42*(1), 117–131.

Baynard, R., & Baynard, J. (1983). *How to deal with your acting-up teenager.* New York: M. Evans.

Beavers, W. (1981). A systems model of family for family therapists. *Journal of Marriage and Family Therapy, 7,* 299–307.

Beavers, W. (1988). Attributes of a healthy couple. *Family Therapy Today, 3*(1), 1–4.

Beavers, W., Hampson, R., & Hulgas, Y. (1985). Commentary: The Beavers System Approach to family assessment. *Family Process, 22,* 85–98.

Becker, K., Carson, D., Seto, A., & Becker, C. (2002). Negotiating the dance: Consulting with adoptive systems. *Family Journal: Counseling and Therapy for Couples and Families, 10*(1), 80–86.

Becvar, D., & Becvar, R. (1996). *Family therapy: A systemic integration.* Boston: Allyn & Bacon.

Beels, C. (2002). Notes for a cultural history of family therapy. *Family Process, 41*(1), 67–82.

Bending, R. (1997). Training child welfare workers to meet the requirements of the Indian Child Welfare Act. *Journal of Multicultural Social Work, 5*(3/4), 151–164.

Berliner, K., Jacob, D., & Schwartzberg, N. (1999). The single adult and the family life cycle. In B. Carter & M. McGoldrick (Eds.), *The expanded family life cycle: Individual, family, and social perspectives* (3rd ed.) (pp. 362–380). Needham Heights, MA: Allyn & Bacon.

Berry, M. (1997). *The family at risk.* Columbia, SC: University of South Carolina Press.

Besa, D. (1994). Evaluating narrative family therapy using single-system research designs. *Research on Social Work Practice, 4*(4), 309–325.

Beutler, L., Machado, P., & Allstetter Neufelt, A. (1994). Therapist variables. In A. Bergin & S. Garfield (Eds.). *Handbook of psychotherapy and behavior change* (4th ed.) (pp. 229–269). Toronto: Wiley.

Bitter, J. (2004). Two approaches to counseling a parent alone: Toward a Gestalt-Adlerian integration. *Family Journal: Counseling and Therapy for Couples and Families, 12*(4), 358–367.

Blacker, L. (1999). The launching phase of the life cycle. In B. Carter & M. McGoldrick (Eds.). (1999). *The expanded family life cycle: Individual, family, and social perspectives* (3rd ed.) (pp. 287–306). Needham Heights, MA: Allyn & Bacon.

Bloom, M., Fischer, J., & Orme, J. (2005). *Evaluating practice: Guidelines for the accountable professional* (5th ed.). Boston: Allyn & Bacon.

Bloomquist, M. (1996). *Skills training for children with behavior disorders.* New York: Guilford Press.

Blum, H., Boyle, M., & Offord, D. (1988). Single-parent families: Child psychiatric disorder and school performance. *Journal of the American Academy of Child and Adolescent Psychiatry 27*, 214–219.

Bolton, F., & Bolton, S. (1987). *Working with violent families: A guide for clinical and legal practitioners.* Beverly Hills, CA: Sage Publications.

Borstnar, J., Mocnik Bucar, M., Rus Makovec, M., Burck, C., & Daniel, G. (2005). Co-constructing a cross-cultural course: Resisting and replicating colonizing practices. *Family Process, 44*(1), 121–132.

Bostwick, G., & Kyte, N. (1988). Validity and reliability. In R. Grinnell (Ed.), *Social work research and evaluation* (3rd ed.) (pp. 111–126). Itasca, IL: F.E. Peacock.

Bowen, M. (1971). The use of family theory in clinical practice. In J. Haley (Ed.), *Changing families: A family therapy reader* (pp. 159–192). New York: Grune & Straton.

Bowen, M. (1978). *Family therapy in clinical practice.* New York: Jason Aronson.

Bowlby, J. (1969). *Attachment.* New York: Basic Books.

Brant, C. (1990). Native ethics and rules of behaviour. *Canadian Journal of Psychiatry, 35*, 534–539.

Braverman, L. (1991). The dilemma of homework: A feminist response to Gottman, Napier, and Pittman. *Journal of Marital and Family Therapy, 17,* 25–28.

Bredehoft, D. (2001). The framework for life span family life education revisited and revised. *Family Journal: Counseling and Therapy for Couples and Families, 9*(2), 134–139.

Brendel, J., & Nelson, K. (1999). The stream of family secrets: Navigating the islands of confidentiality and triangulation involving family therapists. *Family Journal: Counseling and Therapy for Couples and Families, 7*(2), 112–117.

Breunlin, D. (1988). Oscillation theory and family development. In C. Falicov (Ed.), *Family transitions: Continuity and change over the life cycle.* New York: Guilford.

Brock, G., & Barnard, C. (1992). *Procedures in marriage and family therapy.* Boston: Allyn & Bacon.

Burden, D. (1986) Single parents and the work setting: The impact of multiple job and homelife responsibilities. *Family Relations, 35,* 37–43.

Caffrey, T., & Erdman, P. (2000). Conceptualizing parent-adolescent conflict: Applications from systems and attachment theories. *Family Journal: Counseling and Therapy for Couples and Families, 8*(1), 14–21.

Caffrey, T., Erdman, P., & Cook, D. (2000). Two systems/one client: Bringing families and schools together. *Family Journal: Counseling and Therapy for Couples and Families, 8*(2), 154–160.

Callard, E., & Morin, P. (Eds.). (1979). *Parents and children together: An alternative to foster care.* Detroit: Wayne State University, Department of Family and Consumer Studies.

Caplan, P., & Hall-McCorquodale, I. (1985). Mother-blaming in major clinical journals. *American Journal of Orthopsychiatry, 55,* 345–353.

Caplan, P., & Hall-McCorquodale, I. (1991). The scapegoating of mothers: A call for change. In J. Veevers (Ed.), *Continuity and change in marriage and the family* (pp. 295–302). Toronto: Holt, Rinehart & Winston of Canada.

Carich, M., & Spilman, K. (2004). Basic principles of intervention. *Family Journal: Counseling and Therapy for Couples and Families, 12*(4), 405–410.

Carlson, J., Kurato, Y., Ruiz, E., Ng, K., & Yang, J. (2004). A multicultural discussion about personality development. *Family Journal: Counseling and Therapy for Couples and Families, 12*(2), 111–121.

Carmines, E., & Zeller, R. (1979). *Reliability and validity assessment.* Sage University Paper Series on Quantitative Applications in the Social Sciences, 07–017. Beverly Hills, CA: Sage.

Carter, B. (1992). Stonewalling feminism. *Family Therapy Network, 16*(1), 64–69.

Carter, B., & McGoldrick, M. (1988). *The changing family life cycle: A framework for family therapy* (2nd ed.). New York: Gardner Press.

Carter, B. (1999). Becoming parents: The family with young children. In B. Carter and M. McGoldrick (Eds.), *The expanded family life cycle: Individual, family, and social perspectives* (3rd ed.) (pp. 249–273). Needham Heights, MA: Allyn & Bacon.

Carter, B., & McGoldrick, M. (Eds.). (1999). *The expanded family life cycle: Individual, family, and social perspectives* (3rd ed.). Needham Heights, MA: Allyn & Bacon.

Carter, B., & McGoldrick, M. (1999a). Overview: The expanded family life cycle. In B. Carter & M. McGoldrick (Eds.). (1999). *The expanded family life cycle: Individual, family, and social perspectives* (3rd ed.) (pp. 1–26). Needham Heights, MA: Allyn & Bacon.

Carter, B., & McGoldrick, M. (1999b). The divorce cycle: A major variation in the American family life cycle. In B. Carter, & M. McGoldrick (Eds.), *The expanded family life cycle: Individual, family, and social perspectives* (3rd ed.) (pp. 373–380). Needham Heights, MA: Allyn & Bacon.

Carter, C. S. (1997). Using African–centered principles in family preservation services. *Families in Society: The Journal of Contemporary Human Services, 78*(5), 531.

Cherlin, A. (1983). Family policy: The conservative challenge to the progressive response. *Journal of Family Issues, 4*(3), 417–438.

Clarkin, J., & Levy, K. (2004). The influence of client variables on psychotherapy. In M. Lambert (Ed.), *Handbook of psychotherapy and behavior change* (pp. 194–226). New York: John Wiley & Sons.

Cobb, N., & Jordan, C. (2001). Competency-based treatment of marital discord. In H. Briggs & K. Corcoran (Eds.), *Social work practice* (pp. 169–198). Chicago: Lyceum.

Coleman, H., & Collins, D. (1990). The treatment trilogy of father-daughter incest. *Child and Adolescent Social Work Journal, 7*(40), 339–355.

Coleman, H., & Collins, D. (1997). The voice of parents: A qualitative study of a family-centered, home-based program. *The Child and Youth Care Forum (Special Edition on Research in the Field of Child and Youth Care), 26*(4), 261–278.

Coleman, H., Collins, D., & Collins, T. (2005). *Family practice: A problem based learning approach.* Peosta, IA: Eddie Bowers.

Coleman, H., Unrau, Y., & Manyfingers, B. (2001). Revamping family preservation services for native families. *Journal of Ethnic and Cultural Diversity in Social Work, 10*(1), 49–68.

Collins, D. (1989). Child care workers and family therapists: Getting connected. *Journal of Child and Youth Care, 4*(3), 23–31.

Collins, D., Thomlison, B., & Grinnell, R. (1992). *The social work practicum: An access guide.* Itasca, IL: F.E. Peacock.

Coltrane, S. (1998). *Gender and families.* Thousand Oaks, CA: Pine Forge Press.

Conoley, C., Graham, J., Neu, T., Craig, M., O'Pry, A., Cardin, S., Brossart, D., & Parker, R. (2003). Solution focused family therapy with three aggressive and oppositional-acting children: An N = 1 empirical study. *Family Process, 42*(3), 361–374.

Coontz, S. (1996). The way we weren't: The myth and reality of the "Traditional Family." *National Forum, 76*(4), 45–48.

Corcoran, K., & Fischer, J. (2000). *Measures for clinical practice, Volume 1, Couples, families, and children* (3rd ed.). New York: Free Press.

Courtney, M. (1997). Reconsidering family preservation: A review of *Putting Families First. Child and Youth Services Review, 19*, 61–76.

Crichton, M. (1995). *The lost world.* New York: Ballantine

Cross, T. (1986). Drawing on cultural tradition in Indian child welfare practice. *Social Casework, 67*(5), 283–289

Curtner-Smith, M. (1995). Assessing children's visitation needs with divorced noncustodial fathers. *Families in Society, 76*(6), 34–348.

Davis, K. (1996). *Families: A handbook of concepts and techniques for the helping professional.* Pacific Grove, CA: Brooks/Cole.

Davis, L., & Proctor, E. (1989). *Race, gender, and class: Guidelines for practice with individuals, families, and groups.* Englewood Cliffs, NJ: Prentice Hall.

DeJong, P., & Berg, I. (2002). *Interviewing for solutions.* Pacific Grove, CA: Brooks/Cole.

Dekovic, M., Janssens, J., & VanAs, N. (2003). Family predictors of antisocial behavior in adolescence. *Family Process, 42*(2), 223–235.

Denby, R., Curtis, C., & Alford, K. (1998). Family preservation services and special populations: The invisible target. *Families in Society, 79*(1), 3–14.

Denicola, J., & Sandler, J. (1980). Training abusive parents in child management and self-control skills. *Behavior Therapy, 11*, 263–270.

Doherty, W. (2003). A wake up call: Comment on "Lived Religion and Family Therapy." *Family Process, 42*(1), 181–183.

Doucet, A. (2001). "You see the need perhaps more clearly than I have": Exploring gendered processes of domestic responsibility. *Journal of Family Issues, 22*(3), 328–357.

Duval, E. (1957). *Family transitions.* Philadelphia: Lippincott.

Dye Holten, J. (1990). When do we stop mother-blaming? *Journal of Feminist Family Therapy,* 2(1), 53–60.

Early, T., & Glen Maye, I. (2000). Valuing families: Social work practice with families from a strengths perspective. *Social Work, 45*(2), 118–130.

Eckstein, D. (2001). Counseling is the answer . . . counseling is the answer . . . But what is the question? 25 questions for couples and families. *Family Journal: Counseling and Therapy for Couples and Families, 9*(4), 463–476.

Eckstein, D. (2002). Walls and windows: Closing and opening behaviors for couples and families. *Family Journal: Counseling and Therapy for Couples and Families, 10*(3), 344–345.

Efron, D., & Rowe, B. (1987). *Strategic parenting manual.* London, Ontario: J.S.S.T.

Egan, G. (1994). *The skilled helper.* Pacific Grove, CA: Brooks/Cole.

Eichler, M. (1988). *Nonsexist research methods: A practical guide.* Boston: Allen & Unwin.

Eichler, M. (1997). *Family shifts: Families, policies, and gender equality.* Toronto: Oxford University Press.

Eisenstein-Naveh, A. (2003). The center for children and families at risk: A facilitating environment. *Family Journal: Counseling and Therapy for Couples and Families, 11*(2), 191–201.

Elizur, Y., & Ziv, M. (2001). Family support and acceptance, gay male identity formation, and psychological adjustment: A path model. *Family Process, 40*(2), 125–144.

Ellis, K., & Eriksen, K. (2002). Transsexual and transgenderist experiences and treatment options. *Family Journal: Counseling and Therapy for Couples and Families, 10*(3), 289–299.

Epstein, N., Baldwin, D., & Bishop, D. (1983). The McMaster family assessment device. *Journal of Marital and Family Therapy, 9,* 171–180.

Epstein, N., Bishop, D., & Levin, S. (1978). The McMaster model of family functioning. *Journal of Marriage and Family Counseling, 4,* 19–31.

Etchison, M., & Kleist, D. (2000). Review of narrative therapy: Research and utility. *Family Journal: Counseling and Therapy for Couples and Families, 8*(1), 61–66.

Falicov, C. (1999). The Latino family life cycle. In B. Carter & M. McGoldrick (Eds.), *The expanded family life cycle: Individual, family, and social perspectives* (3rd ed.) (pp. 141–152). Needham Heights, MA: Allyn & Bacon.

Finkelhor, D. (1986). Sexual abuse: Beyond the family systems approach. In T. Trepper & M. Barrett (Eds.), *Treating incest: A multiple systems perspective* (pp. 53–66). New York: Haworth.

Fischer, J., & Corcoran, K. (1994). *Measures for clinical practice.* New York: Free Press.

Fischler, R. (1985). Child abuse and neglect in American Indian communities. *Child Abuse & Neglect, 9,* 95–106.

Fitzpatrick, M., & Reeve, P. (2003). Grandparents raising grandchildren—a new class of disadvantaged Australians. *Family Matters, 66,* 54–57.

Fong, R. (1994). Family preservation: Making it work for Asians. *Child Welfare, 73,* 331–341.

Forehand, R., Sturgis, E., McMahon, R., et al. (1979). Parent behavioral training to modify child noncompliance: Treatment generalization across time and from home to school. *Behavior Modification, 3*(1), 3–25.

Forgatch, M. (1991). The clinical science vortex: A developing theory of antisocial behavior. In D. Pepler & K. Rubin (Eds.), *The development and treatment of child aggression* (pp. 291–315). Hillsdale, NJ: Lawrence Erlbaum Associates.

Foster, C. (1993). *The family patterns workbook.* New York: Jeremy P. Tarcher/Perigree Books.

Foster, S., Prinz, R., & O'Leary D. (1983). Impact of problem-solving communication training and generalization procedures on family conflict. *Child and Family Behavior Therapy, 5*(1), 1–23.

Frame, M. (2001). The spiritual genogram in training and supervision. *Family Journal: Counseling and Therapy for Couples and Families, 8*(1), 72–74.

Franco, N., & Levitt, M. (1998). The social ecology of middle childhood: Family support, friendship quality, and self-esteem. *Family Relations, 47,* 315–321.

Franklin, C., & Corcoran, K. (2003). Quantitative clinical assessment methods. In C. Franklin & K. Corcoran (Eds.), *Clinical assessment for social workers: Quantitative and qualitative methods* (pp. 71–94). Chicago: Lyceum.

Franklin, C., & Jordan, C. (1992). Teaching students to perform assessments. *Journal of Social Work Education, 28*(2), 222–243.

Franklin, C., & Jordan, C. (1999). *Family practice: Brief systems methods for social work.* Belmont, CA: Brooks/Cole.

Fraser, M. (1997). *Risk and resilience in childhood: An ecological perspective.* Washington: NASW Press.

Fraser, M., Richman, J., & Galinsky, M. (1999). Risk, protection, and resilience: Toward a conceptual framework for social work practice. *Social Work Research, 23*(3), 131–143.

Fraser, M., Pecora, P., & Haapala, D. (1991). *Families in crisis*. Hawthorne, NY: Aldine de Gruyter.

Fulmer, R. (1999). Becoming an adult: Leaving home and staying connected. In B. Carter & M. McGoldrick (Eds.), *The expanded family life cycle: Individual, family, and social perspectives* (3rd ed.) (pp. 215–230). Needham Heights, MA: Allyn & Bacon.

Furstenberg, E. (1980). Reflections on marriage. *Journal of Family Issues, 1*, 443–453.

Gabor, P., & Collins, D. (1985–86). Family work in child care. *Journal of Child Care, 2*(5), 15–27.

Gabor, P., & Grinnell, R. (1995). *Evaluation and quality improvement*. Boston, MA: Allyn & Bacon.

Gambrill, E. (1983). *Casework: A competency-based approach*. Englewood Cliffs, N.J: Prentice-Hall.

Gambrill, E. (2006). *Social work practice: A critical thinker's guide* (2nd ed.). New York: Oxford.

Gambill, E., & Richey, C. (1988). *Taking charge of your social life*. Belmont, CA: Behavioral Options.

Garbarino, J. (1992). *Children and families in their social environment* (2nd ed.). New York: Aldine de Gruyter.

Garbarino, J., & Gilliam, G. (1987). *Understanding abusive families*. Lexington, MA: D.C. Heath and Company.

Gattai, F., & Musatti, T. (1999). Grandmothers' involvement in grandchildren's care: Attitudes, feelings, and emotions. *Family Relations, 48*, 35–42.

Gavin, K., & Bramble, B. (1996). *Family communication: Cohesion and change*. New York: Harper Collins.

Geismar, L. (1978). Family disorganization: A sociological perspective. *Social Casework, 69*, 545–550.

Geismar, L., & Ayres, B. (1959). A method for evaluating the social functioning of families under treatment. *Social Work, 4*(1), 102–108.

Geismar, L., & Krisberg, J. (1956). The Family Life Improvement Project: An experiment in preventive intervention. *Social Casework, 47*, 563–570.

Gelles, R. (1989). Child abuse and violence in single-parent families: Parent absence and economic deprivation. *American Journal of Orthopsychiatry, 59*(4), 492–503.

George, L. (1997). Why the need for the Indian Child Welfare Act? *Journal of Multicultural Social Work, 5*(3/4), 65–175.

Gilligan, R. (2004). Promoting resilience in child and family social work: Issues for social work practice, education and policy. *Family Process, 23*(1), 93–104.

Giovanonni, J. (1982). Mistreated children. In S. Yelaja (Ed.), *Ethical issues in social work*. Springfield, IL: Charles C. Thomas.

Gladow, N., & Ray, M. (1986). The impact of informal support systems on the well-being of low-income single-parent families. *Family Relations, 35*, 57–62.

Gold, J., & Hartnett, L. (2003). Confronting the hierarchy of a child-focused family: Implications for family counselors. *Family Journal: Counseling and Therapy for Couples and Families, 12*(3), 271–274.

Gold, J., & Morris, G. (2003). Family resistance to counseling: The initial agenda for intergenerational and narrative approaches. *Family Journal: Counseling and Therapy for Couples and Families, 11*(4), 374–379.

Gold, L. (2003). A critical analysis of fusion in lesbian relationships. *Canadian Social Work Review, 20*(2), 259–271.

Golden, L. (1999). Therapeutic stories with an ethnic flavor. *Family Journal: Counseling and Therapy for Couples and Families, 7*(4), 406–407.

Goldenberg, H., & Goldenberg, I. (1994). *Counseling today's families*. Pacific Grove, CA: Brooks/Cole.

Goldenberg, I., & Goldenberg, H. (1996). *Family therapy: An overview* (4th ed.). Pacific Grove, CA: Brooks/Cole.

Goldenberg, I., & Goldenberg, H. (2000). *Family therapy: An overview* (5th ed.). Belmont, CA: Brooks/Cole.

Goldner, V. (1985a). Feminism and family therapy. *Family Process, 24*(1), 31–47.

Goldner, V. (1985b). Warning: Family therapy may be hazardous to your health. *The Family Therapy Networker, 9*(6), 18–23.

Goldner, V. (1988). Generation and hierarchy: Normative and covert hierarchies. *Family Process, 27*(1), 17–31.

Goldstein, H. (1981). Home-based services and the worker. In M. Bryce & J. Lloyd (Eds.), *Treating families in the home: An alternative to placement*. Springfield, IL: Charles C. Thomas.

Good, G., Gilbert, L., & Scher, M. (1990). Gender-aware therapy: A synthesis of feminist therapy and knowledge about gender. *Journal of Counseling and Development, 68*, 227–234.

Goodrich, T., Rampage, C., Ellman, B., & Halstead, K. (1988). *Feminist family therapy: A casebook*. New York: W. W. Norton.

Gordon, L. (1985). Child abuse, gender, and the myth of family independence: A historical critique. *Child Welfare, 64*(3), 213–224.

Gordon, S., & Davidson, N. (1981). Behavioral parent training. In A. Gurman & D. Kniskern (Eds.), *Handbook of family therapy* (pp. 517–553). New York: Brunner/Mazel.

Gottman, J. (1999). *The marriage clinic*. New York: W. W. Norton & Company.

Gottman, J., & Levenson, R. (2002). A two-factor model for predicting when a couple will divorce: Exploratory analyses using 14-year longitudinal data. *Family Process, 41*(1), 83–96.

Granvold, D., & Jordan, C., (1994). The cognitive-behavioral treatment of marital distress. In D. Granvold (Ed.), *Cognitive and behavioral treatment: Methods and applications* (pp. 174–201). Pacific Grove, CA: Brooks/Cole.

Green, R., & Hergret, M. (1991). Outcomes of systemic/strategic team consultation: III. The importance of therapist warmth and active structuring. *Family Process, 30,* 321–336.

Green, B., Mcallister, C. & Tarte, J. (2004). The strengths-based practices inventory: A tool for measuring strengths-based service delivery in early childhood and family support programs. *Families in Society, 85*(3) 326–335.

Greeno, C. (2003). Measurement, or how do we know what we know? Topic one: Validity. *Family Process, 42*(3), 433–434.

Griffith, M. (1999). Opening therapy to conversations with a personal God. In F. Walsh (Ed.), *Spiritual resources in family therapy* (pp. 209–222). New York: Guilford Press.

Grinnell, R., & Unrau, Y. (Eds). (2005). *Social work research and evaluation: Quantitative and qualitative approaches.* (7th ed.) New York: Oxford.

Grold, K. (2000). The openness to therapy assessment. *Family Journal: Counseling and Therapy for Couples and Families, 8*(1), 85–90.

Gross, E. (1995). Deconstructing politically correct practice literature: The American Indian case. *Social Work, 40*(2), 206–213.

Gross, G. (1998). *Gatekeeping for cultural competence: Ready or not? Some post and modernist doubts.* Paper presented at the 16th Annual BPD Conference, Albuquerque, New Mexico.

Grunwald, B., & McAbee, H. (1985). *Guiding the family: Practical counseling techniques.* Muncie, IN: Accelerated Development.

Gurman, A. S., & Kniskern, D. P. (1981). Family therapy outcome research: Knowns and unknowns. In A. S Gurman & D. P. Kniskern (Eds.), *Handbook of family therapy* (pp. 742–776). New York: Brunner/Mazel.

Hackney, H., & Cormier, L. (1996). *The professional counselor: A process guide to helping* (3rd ed.). Toronto: Allyn & Bacon.

Hahn, R., & Kleist, D. (2000). Divorce mediation: Research and implications for family and couples counseling. *Family Journal: Counseling and Therapy for Couples and Families, 8*(2), 165–171.

Haley, J. (1971). Approaches to family therapy. In J. Haley (Ed.), *Changing families: A family therapy reader* (pp. 227–236). New York: Grune & Straton.

Haley, J. (1976). *Problem-solving therapy*. San Francisco: Jossey-Bass.

Hanson, S. (1986). Healthy single-parent families. *Family Relations, 35, 125–132.*

Harper, K., & Lantz, J. (1996). *Cross-cultural practice in social work with diverse populations.* Chicago: Lyceum.

Harris, S., & Dersch, C. (2001). "I'm just not like that": Investigating the intergenerational cycle of violence. *Family Journal: Counseling and Therapy for Couples and Families, 9*(3), 250–258.

Hartman, A., & Laird, J. (1983). *Family-centered social work practice.* New York: Free Press.

Helton, L., & Jackson, J. (1997). *Social work practice with families: A diversity model.* Boston: Allyn & Bacon.

Hepworth, D., & Larsen, J. (1993). *Direct social work practice.* Chicago: Dorsey Press.

Hernandez, M., & McGoldrick, M. (1999). Migration and the life cycle. In B. Carter & M. McGoldrick (Eds.), *The expanded family life cycle: Individual, family, and social perspectives* (3rd ed.) (pp. 169–184). Needham Heights, MA: Allyn & Bacon.

Hernandez, P. (2002). Resilience in families and communities: Latin American contributions from the psychology of liberation. *Family Journal: Counseling and Therapy for Couples and Families, 10*(3), 334–343.

Herndon, M., & Moore, J. (2003). African American factors for student success: Implications for families and counselors. *Family Journal: Counseling and Therapy for Couples and Families, 10*(3), 322–327.

Hetherington, E., Cox, M., & Cox, R. (1978). Play and social interaction in children following divorce. *Journal of Social Issues, 35*, 26–49.

Hill, J., Fonagy, P., Safier, E., & Sargent, J. (2003). The ecology of attachment in the family. *Family Process, 42*(2), 205–221.

Hines, P., Preto, N., McGoldrick, M., et al. (1999). Culture and the family life cycle. In B. Carter and M. McGoldrick (Eds.), *The expanded family life cycle: Individual, family, and social perspectives* (3rd ed.) (pp. 69–87). Needham Heights, MA: Allyn & Bacon.

Hinton, M. (2003). *A qualitative study of resiliency in women with a history of childhood sexual abuse.* Unpublished Masters thesis, Faculty of Social Work, University of Calgary.

Ho, M. K. (1987). *Family therapy with ethnic minorities.* Newbury Park, CA: Sage Publications.

Holman, A. (1983). *Family assessment: Tools for understanding and intervention.* Newbury Park, CA: Sage.

Horejsi, Heavy Runner Craig, & Pablo, J. (1992). Reactions by Native American parents to child protection agencies: Cultural and community factors. *Child Welfare, LXXX*(4), 329–42.

Hudak, J., Krestan, J., & Bepko, C. (1999). Alcohol problems and the family life cycle. In B. Carter and M. McGoldrick (Eds.), *The expanded family life cycle: Individual, family, and social perspectives* (3rd ed.) (pp. 455–469). Needham Heights, MA: Allyn & Bacon.

Hudson, W. (1982). *The clinical measurement package: A field manual.* Homewood, IL: Dorsey Press.

Hudson, W. (1985). Indexes and scales. In R. Grinnell (Ed.), *Social work research and evaluation* (pp. 185–205). Itasca, IL: F.E. Peacock.

Hughes, J., & Stone, W. (2003). Family and community life. *Family Matters, 65*, 40–47.

Hunter College Women's Studies Collective. (1995). *Women's realities, women's choices* (2nd ed.). New York: Oxford University Press.

International Association of Psychosocial Rehabilitation Services. (IAPRS). (1997). PSR standards and indicators for multicultural psychiatric rehabilitation services. *PSR Connection,* Issue 4, 7.

Isaacs, C. (1982). Treatment of child abuse: A review of the behavioral interventions. *Journal of Applied Behavior Analysis, 15*, 273–294.

Ivanoff, A., Blythe, B., & Tripodi, T. (1994). *Involuntary clients in social work practice.* New York: Aldine de Gruyter.

Jackson, D. (1972). Family rules: Marital quid pro quo. In G. Erickson & T. Hogan (Eds.), *Family therapy: An introduction to theory and technique* (pp. 76–85). Monterey, CA: Brooks/Cole.

Janson, G., & Steigerwald, F. (2002). Family counseling and ethical challenges with gay, lesbian, bisexual, and transgendered (GLBT) clients: More questions than answers. *Family Journal: Counseling and Therapy for Couples and Families, 10*(4), 415–418.

Janzen, C., Harris, O., Jordan, C., & Franklin, C. (2006). *Family treatment: Evidence-based practice with populations at risk.* Belmont, CA: Brooks/Cole.

Jaques, J. (2000). Surviving suicide: The impact on the family. *Family Journal: Counseling and Therapy for Couples and Families, 8*(4), 376–379.

Jencius, M., & Duba, J. (2002). Creating a multicultural family practice. *Family Journal: Counseling and Therapy for Couples and Families, 10*(4), 410–414.

Jencius, M., & Duba, J. (2003a). Searching for the ideal parents: An interview with Al Pesso and Diane Boyden. *Family Journal: Counseling and Therapy for Couples and Families, 11*(1), 89–97.

Jencius, M., & Duba, J. (2003b). The marriage of research and practice: An interview with John Gottman. *The Family Journal: Counseling and Therapy for Couples and Families, 11*(2), 216–223.

Joe, J., & Malach, R. (1998). Families with Native American roots. In E. W. Lynch and M. J. Hanson (Eds.), *Developing cross-cultural competence: A guide for working with children and families* (2nd ed.). Baltimore: Paul H. Brookes.

Johnson, D., & Johnson, F. (1994). *Joining together* (5th ed.). Boston: Allyn & Bacon.

Johnson, H. (1986). Emerging concerns in family therapy. *Social Work, 31*(4), 299–306.

Johnson, T., & Colucci, P. (1999). Lesbians, gay men, and the family life cycle. In B. Carter and M. McGoldrick (Eds.). *The expanded family life cycle: Individual, family, and social perspectives* (3rd ed.) (pp. 346–361). Needham Heights, MA: Allyn & Bacon.

Jones, A. (2003). Reconstructing the stepfamily: Old myths, new stories. *Social Work, 48*(2), 228–236.

Jongsma, A., & Datilio, F. (2000). *The family therapy treatment planner.* New York: Wiley.

Jordan, C., & Cobb, N. (2001). Competency-based treatment for persons with marital discord. In K. Corcoran (Ed.), *Structuring change* (2nd ed.). Chicago: Lyceum Books.

Jordan, C., & Franklin, C. (2002). Treatment planning with families: An evidence-based approach. In *The Social Workers' Desk Reference*. Al Roberts and Gilbert Greene, Editors. New York: Oxford.

Jordan, C., & Franklin, C. (2003). *Clinical assessment for social workers: Quantitative and qualitative methods* (2nd ed.). Chicago: Lyceum.

Jordan, C., Franklin, C., & Corcoran, K. (2005). Measuring instruments. In R. Grinnel & Y. Unrau (Eds.), *Social work research and evaluation: Quantitative and qualitative approaches* (7th ed.) (pp. 114–131). New York: Oxford.

Jordan, C., Lewellen, A., & Vandiver, V. (1994). A social work perspective of psychosocial rehabilitation: Psychoeducational models for minority families. *International Journal of Mental Health, 23*(4), 27–43.

Juhnke, G., & Shoffner, M. (1999). The family debriefing model: An adapted critical incident stress debriefing for parents and older sibling suicide survivors. *Family Journal: Counseling and Therapy for Couples and Families, 7*(4), 342–348.

Kadushin, A. (1992). *The social work interview.* New York: Columbia University Press.

Kadzin, A. (2004). Psychotherapy for children and adolescents. In M. Lambert (Ed.), *Handbook of psychotherapy and behavior change* (pp. 543–589). New York: John Wiley & Sons.

Kaplan, D., & VanDuser, M. (1999). Evolution and stepfamilies: An interview with Dr. Stephen Emlen. *Family Journal: Counseling and Therapy for Couples and Families, 7*(4), 408–413.

Kaplan, L. (1986). *Working with the multiproblem family.* Lexington, MA: Lexington Books.

Kaslow, N., & Celano, M. (1995). The family therapies. In A. Gurman & S. Messer (Eds.), *Essential psychotherapies: Theory and practice* (pp. 343–402). New York: Guilford Press.

Kerlinger, F. (1979). *Behavioral research.* Toronto: Holt, Rinehart & Winston.

Killian, K. (2002). Dominant and marginalized discourses in interracial couples' narratives: Implications for family therapists. *Family Process, 41*(4), 603–618.

Kilman, J., & Madsen, W. (1999). Social class and the family life cycle. In B. Carter and M. McGoldrick (Eds.), *The expanded family life cycle: Individual, family, and social perspectives* (3rd ed.) (pp. 88–105). Needham Heights, MA: Allyn & Bacon.

Kilpatrick, A., & Holland, T. (1995). *Working with families: An integrative model by level of functioning.* Boston: Allyn & Bacon.

Kim, J. (2003). Structural family therapy and its implications for the Asian American family. *The Family Journal: Counseling and Therapy for Couples and Families, 11*(4), 388–392.

Kinney, J., Haapala, D., & Booth, C. (1991). *Keeping families together: The Homebuilders Model.* Hawthorne, NY: Aldine de Gruyter.

Klein, N., Alexander, J., & Parsons, B. (1977). Impact of family systems intervention on recidivism and sibling delinquency: A model of primary prevention and program evaluation. *Journal of Consulting and Clinical Psychology, 45*(3), 469–474.

Kleist, D. (1999). Single-parent families: A difference that makes a difference? *The Family Journal: Counseling and Therapy for Couples and Families, 7*(4), 236–244.

Kliman, J., & Madsen, W. (1999). Social class and the family life cycle. In B. Carter & M. McGoldrick, (Eds.). *The expanded family life cycle: Individual, family, and social perspectives.* (pp. 88–105). Needham Heights, MA: Allyn & Bacon.

Kohlert, N., & Pecora, P. (1991). Therapist perceptions of organizational support and job satisfaction. In M. Fraser, P. Pecora, & D. Haapala (Eds.), *Families in crisis* (pp. 109–129). New York: Aldine de Gruyter.

Kozlowska, K., & Hanney, L. (2002). The network perspective: An integration of attachment and family systems theories. *Family Process, 41*(2), 285–312.

Kramer, L., & Radley, C. (1997). Improving sibling relationships among young children: A social skills training model. *Family Relations, 46*(3), 237–246.

Krechmar, M., & Jacobvitz, D. (2002). Observing mother-child relationship across generations: Boundary patterns, attachment, and the transmission of caregiving. *Family Process, 41*(3), 351–374.

Lambert, M. (Ed.). (2004). *Bergin and Garfield's handbook of psychotherapy and behavior change* (5th ed.). New York: Wiley.

Lambert, M., & Bergin, A. (1994). The effectiveness of psychotherapy. In A. Bergin & S. Garfield (Eds.), *Handbook of psychotherapy and behavior change* (4th ed.) (pp. 143–189). Toronto: Wiley.

Lambert, M., & Ogles, B. (2004). The efficacy and effectiveness of psychotherapy. In M. Lambert (Ed.), *Handbook of psychotherapy and behavior change* (pp. 139–193). New York: John Wiley & Sons.

Lambert, S. (2005). Gay and lesbian families: What we know and where to go from here. *Family Journal: Counseling and Therapy for Couples and Families, 13*(1), 43–51.

Langsley, D., Pittman, F., Machotka, P., & Flomenhaft, K. (1968). Family crisis therapy: Results and implications. *Family Process, 7*(2), 145–158.

Laszloffy, T., & Hardy, K. (2000). Uncommon strategies for a common problem: Addressing racism in family therapy. *Family Process, 39*(1), 35–50.

Lawson, D., & Brossart, D. (2004). The developmental course of personal authority in the family system. *Family Process, 43*(3), 391–409.

Lawson, G., & Foster, V. (2005). Developmental characteristics of home-based counselor: A key to serving at-risk families. *Family Journal: Counseling and Therapy for Couples and Families, 13*(2), 153–161.

Ledbetter Hancock, B., & Pelton, L. (1989). Home visits: History and functions. *Social Casework, 70*(1), 21.

LeMasters, E. (1957). Parenthood as crisis. *Marriage and Family Living, 19*, 325–355.

Lewandowski, C., & Pierce, L. (2004). Does family-centered out-of-home care work? Comparison of a family-centered approach and traditional care. *Social Work Research, 28*(3), 143–151.

Lewellen, A., & Jordon, C. (1994). Family empowerment and service satisfaction: An exploratory study of families who care for a mentally ill member. Unpublished manuscript. The University of Texas at Arlington.

Lewis, J. (1988). The transition to parenthood: 1. The rating of prenatal marital competence. *Family Process, 27*(2), 149–166.

Lewis, R. (1991). What are the characteristics of Intensive Family Preservation Services? In M. Fraser, P. Pecora, & D. Haapala (Eds.), *Families in crisis* (pp. 93–108). Hawthorne, NY: Aldine de Gruyter.

Lum, D. (1992). *Social work practice and people of color: A process-stage approach.* Pacific Grove, CA: Brooks/Cole.

Mackie, M. (1991). *Gender relations in Canada.* Toronto: Harcourt.

Magnuson, S. (2000). The professional genogram: Enhancing professional identity and clarity. *Family Journal: Counseling and Therapy for Couples and Families, 8*(4), 399–401.

Magnuson, S., & Shaw, H. (2003). Adaptations of the multifaceted genogram in counseling, training, and supervision. *Family Journal: Counseling and Therapy for Couples and Families, 11*(1), 45–54.

Magura, S., & Moses, B. (1986). *Outcome measures for child welfare services: Theory and applications.* Washington, DC: Child Welfare League of America.

Main, F., Boughner, S., Mims, G., & Logan Schieffer, J. (2001). Rolling the dice: An experiential exercise for enhancing interventive questioning skill. *Family Journal: Counseling and Therapy for Couples and Families, 9*(4), 450–454.

Maluccio, A., & Marlow, W. (1975). The case for the contract. In B. Compton and B. Galaway (Eds.), *Social work processes.* Homewood, IL: Dorsey.

Mannes, M. (1993). Seeking the balance between child protection and family preservation in Indian child welfare. *Child Welfare, 72*, 141–152.

Mannis, V. (1999). Single mothers by choice. *Family Relations, 48*(2), 121–128.

Marks, L. (2004). Sacred practices in highly religious families: Christian, Jewish, Mormon, and Muslim perspectives. *Family Process, 43*(2), 217–231.

Marsh, D. (1999). Serious mental illness: Opportunities for family practitioners. *Family Journal: Counseling and Therapy for Couples and Families, 7*(4), 358–366.

Marsh, J. (2003). Arguments for family strengths research. *Social Work, 48*, 147–149.

Marshall, T., & Solomon, P. (2004). Provider contact with families of adults with severe mental illness: Taking a closer look. *Family Process, 43*(2), 209–216.

Maslow, A. (1968). *Toward a psychology of being.* New York: Van Nostrand Reinhold.

Mason, M. (2005). Theoretical considerations of "resistant families." *Family Journal: Counseling and Therapy for Couples and Families, 13*(1), 59–62.

Masson, J. (1994). *Against therapy.* Munroe, ME: Common Courage Press.

May, K. (2001). Theory: Does it matter? *Family Journal: Counseling and Therapy for Couples and Families, 9*(1), 37–38.

May, K. (2003). Family therapy theory: What is important in the training of today's family counselors? *Family Journal: Counseling and Therapy for Couples and Families, 11*(1), 42–44.

May, K. (2004). *How* do we teach family therapy theory? *Family Journal: Counseling and Therapy for Couples and Families, 12*(3), 275–277.

May, K., & Larson Church, N. (1999). Families and communities: Building bridges. *Family Journal: Counseling and Therapy for Couples and Families, 7*(1), 51–53.

McClurg, L. (2004). Biracial youth and their parents: Counseling considerations for family therapists. *Family Journal: Counseling and Therapy for Couples and Families, 12*(2), 170–173.

McConnell Heywood, E. (1999). Custodial grandparents and their grandchildren. *Family Journal: Counseling and Therapy for Couples and Families, 7*(4), 367–372.

McCormick, R. (1996). Culturally appropriate means and ends of counselling as described by the First Nations people of British Columbia. *International Journal for the Advancement of Counselling, 18*(3), 163–172.

McGoldrick, M. (1999a). History, genograms, and the family life cycle. In B. Carter & M. McGoldrick (Eds.), *The expanded family life cycle: Individual, family, and social perspectives* (3rd ed.) (pp. 141–152). Needham Heights, MA: Allyn & Bacon.

McGoldrick, M. (1999b). Women throughout the family life cycle. In B. Carter & M. McGoldrick (Eds.), *The expanded family life cycle: Individual, family, and social perspectives* (3rd ed.) (pp. 106–123). Needham Heights, MA: Allyn & Bacon.

McGoldrick, M. (1999c). Becoming a couple. In B. Carter & M. McGoldrick (Eds.), *The expanded family life cycle: Individual, family, and social perspectives* (3rd ed.) (pp. 231–248). Needham Heights, MA: Allyn & Bacon.

McGoldrick, M. (2002). *Re-visioning family therapy: Race, culture, and gender in clinical practice.* New York: Guilford.

McGoldrick, M., & Carter, B. (1999). Remarried families. In B. Carter and M. McGoldrick (Eds.), *The expanded family life cycle: Individual, family, and social perspectives* (3rd ed.) (pp. 417–435). Needham Heights, MA: Allyn & Bacon.

McGoldrick, M., & Gerson, R. (1985). *Genograms in family assessment.* New York: Norton.

McGoldrick, M., & Giordano, J. (1996). Overview: Ethnicity and family therapy. In M. McGoldrick, J. Giordano, & J. Pearce (Eds.). *Ethnicity and family therapy.* (pp. 1–30). New York: Guilford Press.

McGoldrick, M., Giordano, J., & Pearce, J. (Eds.). (1996). *Ethnicity and family therapy.* New York: Guilford Press.

McGoldrick, M., & Walsh, F. (1999). Death and the family life cycle. In B. Carter & M. McGoldrick (Eds.), *The expanded family life cycle: Individual, family, and social perspectives* (3rd ed.) (pp. 346–361). Needham Heights, MA: Allyn & Bacon.

McGoldrick, M., Watson, M., & Benton, W. (1999). Siblings through the life cycle. In B. Carter & M. McGoldrick (Eds.), *The expanded family life cycle: Individual, family, and social perspectives* (3rd ed.) (pp. 141–152). Needham Heights, MA: Allyn & Bacon.

McIver, J., & Carmines, E. (1981). *Unidimensional scaling.* Sage Paper Series on Quantitative Applications in the Social Sciences, 07-024. Beverly Hills: Sage.

McPherson, T. (1997). *Unpublished MSW case study.* Calgary, Alberta: The University of Calgary, Faculty of Social Work.

Miller, B., & Pylpa, J. (1995). The dilemma of mental health paraprofessionals at home. *American Indian and Alaska Native Mental Health Research, 6*(2), 13–33.

Miller, L., & McLeod, E. (2001). Children as participants in family therapy: Practice, research, and theoretical concerns. *Family Journal: Counseling and Therapy for Couples and Families, 9*(4), 375–383.

Miller, R. (2001). Do children make a marriage unhappy? *Journal of Marriage and the Family, 49.* http://marriageandfamilies.byu.edu/issues/2001/April.children.htm.

Miller, S., Hubble, S., & Duncan, B. (1995). No more bells and whistles. *Networker,* 53–63.

Miller, T., Veltkamp, L., Lane, T., Bilyeu, J., & Elzie, N. (2002). Care pathway guidelines for assessment and counseling for domestic violence. *Family Journal: Counseling and Therapy for Couples and Families, 10*(1), 41–48.

Milner, J., & Wimberly, R. (1979). An inventory for the identification of child abusers. *Journal of Clinical Psychology, 35*(1), 95–110.

Mindel, C. (1985). Instrument design. In R. Grinnell (Ed.), *Social work research and evaluation,* (pp. 206–230). Itasca, IL: F.E. Peacock.

Minuchin, P., Colapinto, J., & Minuchin, S. (1998). *Working with families of the poor.* New York: Guilford Press.

Minuchin, S. (1974). *Families and family therapy.* Cambridge, MA: Harvard University Press.

Minuchin, S., & Montalvo, B. (1971). Techniques for working with disorganized low socioeconomic families. In J. Haley (Ed.), *Changing families: A family therapy reader* (pp. 202–211). New York: Grune & Straton.

Miranda, A., Estrada, D., & Firpo-Jimenez, M. (2000). Differences in family cohesion, adaptability, and environment among Latino families in dissimilar stages of acculturation. *Family Journal: Counseling and Therapy for Couples and Families, 8*(4), 341–350.

Model Curriculum. http://www.nicwa.org/catalog/catalogu.htm.

Molina, B., Estrada, D., & Burnett, J. (2004). Cultural communities: Challenges and opportunities in the creation of "Happily Ever After" stories of intercultural couplehood. *Family Journal: Counseling and Therapy for Couples and Families, 12*(2), 139–147.

Moore Hines, P., Preto, N., McGoldrick, M., Almeida, R., & Weltman, S. (1999). Culture and the family life cycle. In B. Carter, & M. McGoldrick (Eds.), *The expanded family life cycle: Individual, family, and social perspectives* (3rd ed.) (pp. 69–87). Needham Heights, MA: Allyn & Bacon.

Morrissette, V., McKenzie, B., & Morrissette, L. (1993). Towards an Aboriginal model of social work practice. *Canadian Social Work Review, 10*(1), 91–107.

Munns, A. (2004). Helping families at home. *Australian Nursing Journal, 12*(2), 37.

Munson, C. (1993). *Clinical social work supervision.* New York: Haworth Press.

Murray, K. (2002). Religion and divorce: Implications and strategies for counseling. *Family Journal: Counseling and Therapy for Couples and Families, 10*(2), 190–194.

Myers, J. (2003). Coping with caregiving stress: A wellness-oriented, strengths-based approach for family counselors. *Family Journal: Counseling and Therapy for Couples and Families, 11*(2), 153–161.

Neckoway, R., Brownlee, K., Jourdain, L., & Miller, L. (2003). Rethinking the role of attachment theory in child welfare practice with Aboriginal people. *Canadian Social Work Review, 20*(1), 105–119.

Nelson, S. (1987). *Incest: Act and myth.* London, England: Redwood Burn.

Ng, K. (2005). The development of family therapy around the world. *Family Journal: Counseling and Therapy for Couples and Families, 13*(1), 35–42.

Nichols, M., & Schwartz, R. (2004). *Family therapy: Concepts and methods.* Boston: Allyn & Bacon.

Norusis, M. (1990). *SPSS/PC+ Statistics 4.0.* Chicago: SPSS Inc.

Nunnally, J. (1978). *Psychometric theory.* Toronto: McGraw-Hill.

Okun, B. (1996). *Understanding diverse families.* New York: Guilford Press.

Olson, D. (1983). *Families: What makes them work.* Beverly Hills, CA: Sage.

Olson, D. (1986). Circumplex model VII: Validation studies and FACES III. *Family Process, 26,* 337–351.

Olson, D., Russell, C., & Sprenkle, D. (1989). *Circumplex model: Systematic assessment and treatment of families.* New York: Haworth.

Osterlind, S. (1983). *Test item bias.* Sage University Paper Series on Quantitative Applications in the Social Sciences, 07-030, Beverly Hills, CA: Sage.

Patterson, C. (1995). Lesbian mothers, gay fathers, and their children. In A. D'Augelli & C. Patterson (Eds.), *Lesbian, gay and bisexual identities over the lifespan* (pp. 262–290). New York: Oxford.

Patterson, G. (1974). Interventions for boys with conduct problems: Multiple settings, treatments and criteria. *Journal of Consulting and Clinical Psychology, 42*(4), 471–481.

Patterson, G. (1982). *Coercive family process: A social learning approach.* Eugene, OR: Castalina.

Patterson, G., Capaldi, D., & Bank, L. (1991). An early starter model for predicting delinquency. In D. Pepler & K. Rubin (Eds.), *The development and treatment of childhood aggression.* Hillsdale, NJ: Lawrence Erlbaum Associates.

Patterson, G., DeBaryshe, B., & Ramsey, E. (1989). A developmental perspective on antisocial behavior. *American Psychologist, 44,* 329–325.

Patterson, G., & Fleischman, M. (1979). Maintenance of treatment effects: Some considerations concerning family systems and follow–up data. *Behavior Therapy, 10,* 168–185.

Pedhazur, E., & Pedhazur, L. (1991). *Measurement, design and analysis.* Hillsdale, NJ: Lawrence Erlbaum Associates.

Peluso, P. (2002). Counseling families affected by suicide. *Family Journal: Counseling and Therapy for Couples and Families, 10*(3), 351–357.

Peluso, P. (2003). The ethical genogram: A tool for helping therapists understand their ethical decision-making styles. *Family Journal: Counseling and Therapy for Couples and Families, 11*(3), 286–291.

Peterson, A., & Jenni, C. (2003). Men's experience of making the decision to have their first child: A phenomenological analysis. *Family Journal: Counseling and Therapy for Couples and Families, 11*(4), 353–363.

Peterson, L. (1989). Latchkey children's preparation for self-care: Overestimated, underrehearsed, and unsafe. *Journal of Clinical Child Psychology, 18,* 2–7.

Petro, N. (1999). Transformation of the family system during adolescence. In B. Carter & M. McGoldrick (Eds.), *The expanded family life cycle: Individual, family, and social perspectives* (3rd ed.) (pp. 274–286). Needham Heights, MA: Allyn & Bacon.

Petro, N., & Travis, N. (1985). The adolescent phase of the family life cycle. In M. Mirkin & S. Koman (Eds.), *Handbook of adolescent and family therapy.* New York: Gardner Press.

Pett, M. (1982). Predictors of satisfactory social adjustment of divorced parents. *Journal of Divorce, 5*(4), 25–39.

Piercy, F., & Sprenkle, D. (1986). *Family therapy sourcebook.* New York: Guilford Press.

Pimento, B. (1985). *Native families in jeopardy—The child welfare system in Canada.* Toronto: Centre for Women's Studies in Education, Occasional Papers, No. 11.

Pinderhughes, H. (2002). African American marriage in the 20th century. *Family Process, 41*(2), 269–282.

Pinsof, W. (2002). The death of "Till death us do part": The transformation of pair-bonding in the 20th century. *Family Process, 41*(2), 135–157.

Pleck, E. (1987). *Domestic tyranny: The making of social policy against family, violence from colonial times to the present.* New York: Oxford University Press.

Pogrebin, L. (1980). *Growing up free.* NY: McGraw-Hill.

Pollack, W. (2000). *Real boys' voices.* New York: Random House.

Powers, G. (1990). Design and procedures for evaluating crisis. In A. Roberts (Ed.), *Crisis intervention handbook: Assessment, treatment, and research* (pp. 303–325). Belmont, CA: Wadsworth.

Prochaska, J. & DiClemente, C. (2002). Transtheoretical therapy. In J. Lebow (Ed.), *Comprehensive handbook of psychotherapy: Integrative-eclectic, Vol. 4.* (pp. 165–184). New York: Wiley.

Prochaska, J., & Norcross, J. (2003). *Systems of psychotherapy.* Toronto: Nelson Thomson Learning.

Proctor, E. (2001). Editorial: Social work and vulnerable families: Economic hardship and service success. *Social Work Research, 25*(3), 131–132.

Proctor, E. (2004). Editorial: Social work's important work: Keeping families safe. *Social Work Research, 28*(3), 131–132.

Pulleyblank Coffey, E. (2004). The heart of the matter 2: Integration of ecosystemic family therapy practices with systems of care mental health services for children and families. *Family Process, 43*(2), 161–173

Rampage, C. (2002). Marriage in the 20th century: A feminist perspective. *Family Process, 41*(2), 261–268.

Rappaport, R. (1971). Ritual sanctity and cybernetics. *American Anthropologist, 73*(1), 59–76.

Razack, N., & Jeffery, D. (2002). Critical race discourse and tenets for social work practice. *Canadian Social Work Review, 19*(2), 257–271.

Red Horse, J. (1980). American Indian elders: Unifiers of Indian families. *Social Casework,* 490–493.

Red Horse, J., Lewis, R., Feit, M., & Decker, J. (1978). Family behavior of urban American Indians. *Social Casework, 59*(2), 67–72.

Reid, W., Davis Kenaley, B., & Colvin, J. (2004). Do some interventions work better than others? A review of comparative social work experiments. *Social Work Research, 28*(2), 71–81.

Ribner, D., & Knei-Paz, C. (2002). Client's view of a successful helping relationship. *Social Work, 47*(4), 379–387.

Richardson, C. (1996) *Family life: Patterns and perspectives.* New York: McGraw Hill Ryerson Limited.

Richmond, M. (1917, reprinted 1964). *Social diagnosis.* Philadelphia: Russell Sage Foundation.

Roberts, J. (2005). Transparency and self-disclosure in family therapy: Dangers and possibilities. *Family Process, 44*(1), 45–63.

Rojano, R. (2004). The practice of community family therapy. *Family Process, 43*(1), 59–78.

Rostosky, S., Korfhage, B., Duhigg, J., Stern, A., Bennett, L., & Riggle, E. (2004). Same-sex couple perceptions of family support: A consensual qualitative study. *Family Process, 43*(1), 43–58.

Rothbaum, F., Rosen, K., Ujiie, T., & Uchida, N. (2002). Family systems theory, attachment, and culture. *Family Process, 41*(3), 328–350.

Rothery, M. (1993). The ecological perspective and work with vulnerable families. In M. Rodway & B. Trute (Eds.), *Ecological family practice: One family, many resources* (pp. 21–50). Queenston, Ontario: Edwin Mellen.

Rotter, J. (2000). Family grief and mourning. *Family Journal: Counseling and Therapy for Couples and Families, 8*(3), 275–277.

Rovers, M., DesRoches, L., Hunter, P., & Taylor, B. (2000). A family of origin workshop: Process and evaluation. *Family Journal: Counseling and Therapy for Couples and Families, 8*(4), 368–375.

Safonte-Strumolo, N., & Balaguer Dunn, A. (2000). Consideration of cultural and relational issues in bereavement: The case of an Italian American family. *Family Journal: Counseling and Therapy for Couples and Families, 8*(4), 334–340.

Saleebey, D. (1996). The strengths perspective in social work practice: Extensions and cautions. *Social Work, 41*(3), 296–305.

Sanders, G., & Kroll, I. (2000). Generating stories of resilience: Helping gay and lesbian youth and their families. *Journal of Marital and Family Therapy, 26,* 433–442.

Sanders, J., & James, J. (1983). The modification of parent behavior: A review of generalization and maintenance. *Behavior Modification, 7*(1), 3–27.

Sandler, J., VanDercar, C., & Milhoan, M. (1978). Training child abusers in the use of positive reinforcement practices. *Behavior Research and Therapy, 16,* 169–175.

Satir, V. (1967). *Conjoint family therapy.* Palo Alto, CA: Science and Behavior Books.

Satir, V. (1971). The family as a treatment unit. In J. Haley (Ed.), *Changing families: A family therapy reader* (pp. 127–132). New York: Grune & Straton.

Satir, V. (1972). *Peoplemaking.* Palo Alto, CA: Science and Behavior Books.

Satir, V., & Baldwin, M. (1983). *Satir step by step: A guide to creating change in families.* Palo Alto, CA: Science and Behavior Books.

Schact, A., Tafoya, N., & Mirabala, K. (1989). Home-based therapy with American Indian families. *American Indian and Alaska Native Mental Health Research, 3*(2), 27–42.

Sheafor, B., Horejsi, C., & Horejsi, G. (1997). *Techniques and guidelines for social work practice* (4th ed.). Toronto: Allyn & Bacon.

Sheidow, A., & Woodford, M. (2003). Multisystemic therapy: An empirically supported, home-based family therapy approach. *Family Journal: Counseling and Therapy for Couples and Families, 11*(3), 257–263.

Sheperis, C., & Sheperis, S. (2002). The matrix as a bridge to systems thinking. *Family Journal: Counseling and Therapy for Couples and Families, 10*(3), 308–314.

Shulman, L. (1992). *The skills of helping individuals, families, and groups* (3rd ed.). Itasca, IL: F. E. Peacock.

Sims, M. (2002). *Designing family support programs.* Australia: Common Ground Publishing.

Sluzki, C., & Againi, F. (2003). Small steps and big leaps in an era of cultural transition: A crisis in a traditional Kosovar Albanian family. *Family Process, 42*(4), 479–484.

Smith, S. (1984). Significant research findings in the etiology of child abuse. *Social Casework, 65*(6), 337–345.

Snyder, W., & McCollum, E. (1999). Their home is their castle: Learning to do in-home family therapy. *Family Process, 38*(2), 229–244.

Softas-Nall, B., Baldo, T., & Tiedman, T. (1999). A gender-based, solution-focused genogram case: He and she across the generations. *Family Journal: Counseling and Therapy for Couples and Families, 7(2),* 177–180.

Spanier, G., Lewis, R., & Cole, E. (1975). Marital adjustment over the family life cycle: The issue of curvilinearity. *Journal of Marriage and the Family, 37,* 263–275.

Stanley, S., Markman, H., & Whitton, S. (2002). Communication, conflict, and commitment: Insights on the foundations of relationship success from a national survey. *Family Process, 41*(4), 659–675.

Staveteig, S., & Wigton, A. (2000). Racial and ethnic disparities: Key findings from the National Survey of America's Families. *New Federalism: National Survey of America's Families,* The Urban Institute, Series B, No. B-5, 1–6.

Steffen, J., & Karoly, P. (1980). Toward a psychology of therapeutic persistence. In P. Karoly & J. Steffen (Eds.), *Improving the long-term effects of psychotherapy: Models of durable outcome* (pp. 3–24). New York: Gardner Press.

Steinhauer, P. (1991). Assessing for parenting capacity. In J. Veevers (Ed.), *Continuity and change in marriage and family* (pp. 283–294). Toronto: Holt, Rinehart & Winston.

Stokes, T., & Baer, D. (1977). An implicit technology of generalization. *Journal of Applied Behavior Analysis, 10*(2), 349–367.

Straus, M., & Gelles, M. (1988). How violent are American families? Estimates from the National Family Violence Resurvey and other studies. In G. Hotaling, D. Finkelhor, J. Kirkpatrick, & M. Strauss (Eds.), *Family abuse and its consequences* (pp. 14–37). Newbury Park, CA: Sage Publications.

Straus, M., Gelles, R., & Steinmetz, S. (1980). *Behind closed doors: Violence in the American family.* Garden City, NY: Anchor Press.

Suarez-Orozco, C., Todorova, I., & Louie, J. (2002). Making up for lost time: The experience of separation and reunification among immigrant families. *Family Process, 41*(4), 625–643.

Sue, D., & Sue, D. (1990). *Counseling the culturally different: Theory and practice.* New York: Wiley.

Sue, S., & Zane, N. (1987). The role of cultural techniques in psychotherapy. *American Psychologist, 42*(1), 37–45.

Sutton, C., & Broken Nose, M. A. (1996). American Indian families: An overview. In M. McGoldrick, J. Giordano, & J. Pearce (Eds.), *Ethnicity and family therapy* (pp. 31–44). New York: Guilford Press.

Taanila, A., Laitinen, E., Moilanen, I., & Jarvelin, M. (2002). Effects of family interaction on the child's behavior in single-parent or reconstructed families. *Family Process, 41*(4), 693–708.

Tafoya, T. (1989). Circles and cedar: Native Americans and family therapy. *Journal of Psychotherapy, 6*(1/2), 71–98.

Thomason, T. (1991). Counseling Native Americans: An introduction for Non-native American counselors. *Journal of Counseling and Development, 69,* 321–327.

Thomlison, R., & Foote, C. (1987). Child welfare in Canada. *Child and Adolescent Social Work, 4*(2), 123–142.

Thompson, C., and L. Rudolph. (1992). *Counseling Children* (3rd ed.). Pacific Grove, CA: Brooks/Cole.

Thompson, C., Rudolph, L., & Henderson, D. (2003). *Counseling children* (6th ed.). Pacific Grove, CA: Wadsworth.

Tomm, K. (1987a). Interventive interviewing: Part I: Strategizing as a fourth guideline for the therapist. *Family Process, 26,* 3–13.

Tomm, K. (1987b). Interventive interviewing: II. Reflexive questioning as a means to enable self-healing. *Family Process, 26,* 167–183.

Tomm, K. (1988). Interventive interviewing: III. Intending to ask lineal, circular, strategic, or reflexive questions? *Family Process, 27,* 1–15.

Tomm, K., & Wright, L. (1984). Training in family therapy: Perceptual, conceptual, and executive skills. *Family Process, 18,* 227–250.

Toseland, R., & Rivas, R. (1984). *An introduction to group work practice.* New York: Macmillan Publishing.

Trepper, T., & Barrett, M. (Eds.). (1986). *Treating incest: A multiple systems perspective.* New York: Haworth Press.

Truax, C., & Carkhoff, R. (1967). *Toward effective counseling and psychotherapy: Training and practice.* New York: Haworth Press.

Tubbs, C., Roy, K., & Burton, L. (2005). Family ties: Constructing family time in low-income families. *Family Process, 44*(1), 77–91.

Tuzlak, A., & Hillock, D. (1991). Single mothers and their children after divorce: A study of those "who make it." In J. Veevers (Ed.), *Continuity and change in marriage and the family* (pp. 303–313). Toronto: Holt Rinehart & Winston of Canada.

Ungar, M. (2002). Alliances and power: Understanding social worker-community relationships. *Canadian Social Work Review, 19*(2), 227–243.

Ungar, M. (2003). The professional social ecologist. *Canadian Social Work Review, 20*(1), 5–23.

Ungar, M. (2004). The importance of parents and other caregivers to the resilience of high-risk adolescents. *Family Process, 43*(1), 23–40.

Unrau, Y. (1995a). Predicting child abuse and service outcomes in an intensive family preservation services program. Unpublished doctoral dissertation. Salt Lake City: University of Utah.

Unrau, Y. (1995b). Defining the black box of family preservation services: A conceptual framework for service delivery. *Community Alternatives, 7*(2), 49–60.

Viere, G. (2001). Examining family rituals. *Family Journal: Counseling and Therapy for Couples and Families, 9*(3), 285–288.

Visher, W., & Visher, J. (1982). Stepfamilies in the 1980's. In J. Hansen & L. Messinger (Eds.), *Therapy with remarriage families* (pp. 105–119). Rockville, MD: Aspen Systems Corporation.

Wahler, R. (1980). The insular mother: Her problems in parent-child treatment. *Journal of Applied Behavior Analysis, 13,* 207–219.

Walker, S. (2003). Family support and family therapy—same difference? *International Journal of Social Welfare, 12,* 307–313.

Wallerstein, J. (1983). Children of divorce: The psychological tasks of the child. *American Journal of Orthopsychiatry, 53,* 230–243.

Wallerstein, J. & Kelly, J. (1980). *Surviving the breakup: How children and parents cope with divorce.* New York: Basic Books.

Walsh, F. (1998). *Strengthening family resilience.* New York: Guilford Press.

Walsh, F. (Ed.). (1999). *Spiritual resources in family therapy.* New York: Guilford Press.

Walsh, F. (2003). Family resilience: A framework for clinical practice. *Family Process, 42*(1), 1–18.

Wares, D., Wedel, K., Rosenthal, J., & Dobrec, A. (1994). Indian Child Welfare: A multicultural challenge. *Journal of Multicultural Social Work, 3*(3), 1–15.

Watts-Jones, D. (2002). Healing internalized racism: The role of a within-group sanctuary among people of African descent. *Family Process, 41*(4), 591–601.

Watts-Jones, D. (2004). The evidence of things seen and not seen: The legacy of race and racism. *Family Process, 43*(4), 503–508.

Watzlawick, P., Beavin, J., & Jackson, D. (1967). *Pragmatics of human communication.* New York: W. W. Norton.

Watzlawick, P., Weakland, J., & Fisch, R. (1974). *Change: Principles of problem formation and problem resolution.* New York: W. W. Norton.

Weakland, J., & Fry, W. (1974). Letters of mothers of schizophrenics. In D. Jackson (Ed.), *Communication, family, and marriage* (pp. 122–150). Palo Alto, CA: Science and Behavior Books.

Weaver, H. (1996). Social work with American Indian youth using the orthogonal model of cultural identification. *Families in Society, 77*(2), 98–107.

Weaver, H. (1997a). The challenges of research in Native American communities: Incorporating principles of cultural competence. *Journal of Social Service Research, 23*(2), 1–15.

Weaver, H. (1997b). Training culturally competent social workers: What students should know about Native people. *Journal of Teaching in Social Work, 15*(1/2), 97–111.

Weaver, H. (1999). Indigenous people and the social work profession: Defining culturally competent services. *Social Work, 44*(3), 217–225.

Weaver, H., & White, B. (1997). The Native American family circle: Roots of resiliency. *Journal of Family Social Work, 2*(1), 67–79.

Weaver, H., & Wodarski, J. (1995). Cultural issues in crisis intervention: Guidelines for culturally competent practice. *Family Therapy, 22*(3), 215–223.

Weaver, H., & Yellow Horse Brave Heart, M. (1999). Examining two facets of American Indian identity: Exposure to other cultures and the influence of historical trauma. *Journal of Human Behavior in the Social Environment, 2*(1/2), 19–33.

Weber, M. (1996). Family preservation can be an appropriate strategy if realistic expectations are maintained. *NRCCSA News.* http://www.casanet.org/library/familypreservation/famprev.htm (1999, February 1).

Webster-Stratton, C., & Hammond, M. (1990). Predictors of outcome in parent training for families with conduct problem children. *Behavior Therapy, 21,* 319–337.

Webster-Stratton, C., & Reid, M. J. (2003). Treating conduct problems and strengthening social and emotional competence in young children. *Journal of Emotional and Behavioral Disorders, 11*(3), 130–143.

Weine, S., Muzurovic, N., Kulauzovic, Y., Besic, S., Lezic, A., Mujagic, A., Muzurovic, J., Spahovic, D., Ware, N., Knafl, K., & Pavkovic, I. (2004). Family consequences of refugee trauma. *Family Process, 43*(2), 147–160.

Wells, K., & Whittington, D. (1993). Child and family functioning after intensive family preservation services. *Social Service Review, 9*(6), 505–523.

Wendel, R. (2003). Lived religion and family therapy: What does spirituality have to do with it? *Family Process, 42*(1), 165–179.

Whiffen, V., Kerr, M., & Kallos, Lilly, V. (2005). Maternal depression, adult attachment, and children's emotional distress. *Family Process, 44*(1), 93–103.

White, M. (1986). Negative explanation, restraint and double description: A template for family therapy. *Family Process, 25*(2), 169–183.

White, M. (1989). *The externalizing of the problem and the reauthoring of the lives and relationships.* Adelaide, Australia: Dulwich Centre Publishers.

White, M., & Epston, D. (1990). *Narrative means to therapeutic ends.* New York: W. W. Norton & Company.

Wiggins Frame, M. (2000). Spiritual and religious issues in counseling: Ethical considerations. *Family Journal: Counseling and Therapy for Couples and Families, 8*(1), 72–74.

Wiggins Frame, M. (2001). The spiritual genogram in training and supervision. *Family Journal: Counseling and Therapy for Couples and Families, 9*(2), 109–115.

Wilcoxon, A. (1991). Grandparents and grandchildren: An often-neglected relationship between significant others. In J. Veevers (Ed.), *Continuity and change in marriage and the family* (pp. 342–345). Toronto: Holt, Rinehart & Winston of Canada.

Williams, E., & Ellison, F. (1996). Culturally sensitive social work practice with American Indian Clients: Guidelines for non-Indian social workers. *Social Work, 41*(2), 147–151.

Williams, M., Grinnell, R., & Unrau, Y. (2005). Case-level designs. In R. Grinnell & Y. Unrau (Eds.), *Social work research and evaluation: Quantitative and qualitative approaches* (7th ed.) (pp. 171–184). New York: Oxford.

Williamson, J., Softas-Nall, B., & Miller, J. (2003). Grandmothers raising grandchildren: An exploration of their experiences and emotions. *Family Journal: Counseling and Therapy for Couples and Families, 11*(1), 23–32.

Wolfe, D., Sandler, J., & Kaufman, K. (1981). A competency-based parent-training program for child abusers. *Journal of Consulting and Clinical Psychology, 49*(5), 633–640.

Wolfe, L. (2001). Children, depression, and divorce. Unpublished doctoral dissertation. Faculty of Social Work, University of Calgary, Calgary, Alberta, Canada.

Wolin, S. (1993). *The resilient self: How survivors of troubled families rise above adversity.* New York: Villard Books.

Wong, Y., Cheng, S., Choi, S., Ky, K., LeBa, S., Tsang, K., & Yoo, L. (2003). Deconstructing culture in cultural competence. *Canadian Social Work Review, 20*(2), 149–167.

Wood, K., & Geismar, L. (1986). *Families at risk: Treating the multiproblem family.* New York: Human Sciences Press.

Woodford, M. (1999). Home-based family therapy: Theory and process from "friendly visitors" to multisystemic therapy. *Family Journal: Counseling and Therapy for Couples and Families, 7*(3), 265–269.

Worden, M. (1994). *Family therapy basics.* Pacific Grove, CA: Brooks/Cole.

Wright, L., & Leahey, M. (1994). *Nurses and families: A guide to family assessment and intervention.* Philadelphia, PA: F. A. Davis.

Wycoff, S., Bacod-Gebhardt, M., Cameron, S., Brandt, M., & Armes, B. (2002). Have families fared well from welfare reform? Educating clinicians about policy, paradox, and change. *Family Journal: Counseling and Therapy for Couples and Families, 10*(3), 269–280.

Young, M. (2004). Healthy relationships: Where's the research? *Family Journal: Counseling and Therapy for Couples and Families, 12*(2), 159–162.

Yuan, Y., & Rivest, M. (Eds). (1990). *Preserving families.* Newbury Park, CA: Sage.

Zurvain, S., & Grief, G. (1989). Normative and child-maltreating AFDC mothers. *Social Casework, 7*(2), 76–84.

Name Index

SUBJECT INDEX